Maida Heatter's
Cakes

Maida Heatter's Cakes

Foreword by Nancy Silverton

Andrews McMeel
Publishing, LLC

Kansas City • Sydney • London

Maida Heatter's Cakes copyright © 1982, 1985, 1997, and 2011 by Maida Heatter. All rights reserved. Printed in China. No part of this book may be used or reproduced in any manner whatsoever without written permission except in the case of reprints in the context of reviews.

Andrews McMeel Publishing, LLC
an Andrews McMeel Universal company
1130 Walnut Street, Kansas City, Missouri 64106

www.andrewsmcmeel.com

11 12 13 14 15 TEN 10 9 8 7 6 5 4 3 2 1

ISBN: 978-1-4494-0114-6

Library of Congress Cataloging-in-Publication data is on file.

ATTENTION: SCHOOLS AND BUSINESSES
Andrews McMeel books are available at quantity discounts with bulk purchase for educational, business, or sales promotional use. For information, please e-mail the Andrews McMeel Publishing Special Sales Department: specialsales@amuniversal.com

Contents

Foreword

viii

How I Started to Write Cookbooks

xi

Foreword

The first time I heard Maida Heatter's name was when I was apprenticing at a restaurant in Northern California in 1976. There was a discussion going on among a group of chefs in the kitchen about Maida's Palm Beach Brownies. And I was standing there on the fringes, nodding my head, pretending that I knew who they were talking about. I didn't want anyone to know I was out of the loop. *Maida Heatter's Book of Great Desserts* had been out only two years but she generated such respect in the food community that her last name had already become superfluous. Immediately afterward, I rushed to a bookstore and my Maida library began.

It wasn't until the mid-eighties that Maida and I actually met. At the time, I had been at Spago for two years when my employers, Wolfgang Puck and Barbara Lazaroff, asked me to help out at a benefit for the ballet in Miami Beach.

Our first stop after we landed at Miami International Airport was for lunch at her oceanfront home in South Beach. She was a relatively new friend of Wolfgang and Barbara's—they'd bonded at an economic summit conference that Maida and Wolfgang were invited to cook at and the three immediately hit it off. What I remember mostly was walking in and being led straight to the kitchen where every counter was filled with jars and platters, each holding different cookies and crackers. Before we sat down to eat, Maida gave us a guided tour, pointing to each container, explaining what inspired her to make *this*, assuring Barbara and Wolf that there was a fresh batch of that, and letting us know that she was still working on *these*.

The lunch was memorable. First of all, the platter of stone crab, with spicy mayonnaise on the side, was the largest I've ever seen. Then there was the matter of the tuna sandwiches she served, seasoned with a little bit of curry and stuffed into pita bread, just the way I know Wolf liked them. What I could tell immediately was that here was someone whose idea of a flawless meal had nothing to do with dazzling her colleagues with her culinary genius; what made Maida seem like a soul mate is that she was genuinely obsessed with making food that pleased the company she was serving. I remember the sun being a little too warm. And how I cooled myself off with a few too many glasses of Grgich chardonnay. And how I found myself out on a deck chair on her back lawn, thinking woozily, "I love this woman."

The afternoon taught me everything I needed to know about Maida—how thoughtful she is, and generous, and infinitely curious about food. As soon as she hears anyone talk about some kind of confection that she's never heard of before, she has to not only make it, but make it taste better and in astonishing quantities. Like anyone at the top of her field, nobody is more excited about what she is doing than she is. Just casually mention a craving you've had for her chocolate ginger sandwich cookies and you can be sure that sometime in the next few days a brown paper package will arrive in the mail, filled with the sweet biscuits, each wrapped in cellophane with crisply folded hospital corners.

HER PASSION RUNS IN PHASES, USUALLY INSPIRED BY A DESSERT THAT SHE FALLS IN LOVE WITH, . . .

Her passion runs in phases, usually inspired by a dessert that she falls in love with, then lives and breathes and prepares in endless variations until she has baked it out of her system. And her tastes always seem to be on the cusp of the next craze. I'll never forget when she began to sing the praises of sour cherries. Or biscotti. (If I recall that long-ago first lunch correctly, that was the year that Maida was obsessed with lavosh.) Whenever a new Maida Heatter book comes out, the first page I turn to is the introduction because that's where I'll discover what her latest fixation is. "For almost 40 years, I tried (I often gave up and quit, but mostly I kept trying) to duplicate a certain chocolate cake recipe from a bakery in New York City" is how *Maida Heatter's New Book of Great Desserts* opens.

I love cooking from Maida's books because she does such an amazing job of re-creating the feeling I've had when she's helped me with a recipe. I feel as if I am standing alongside her as she chats and dissects the problems, as I observe how closely she follows her own techniques. I often find myself laughing out loud as I read her anecdotes about her successes and her failures and the visible euphoria she experiences about the little discoveries she makes along the way. (No one can string together so many superlatives about an ingredient she's taken a liking to. For Maida, apple cider jelly is not just delicious, it's "gorgeous," it's "elegant," it's "seductive," and on and on and on.)

But what beginners can expect from Maida's book is an extremely high success rate. What the layman might not know is that when a recipe bombs, it's not always their fault. Often, I've been aghast by the gap between how a cookbook author instructs the reader and what it's like to watch them prepare a dish. What always impressed me about Maida is how true she remains to her word.

If she specifies that it takes ten turns with the spatula to incorporate the egg whites, you can be sure that that's how many strokes she'll use.

Not only is her language concise but by the time her recipes are in print you can be sure that they've been tested and retested and tested again until her recipes are absolutely foolproof. First, they have to meet her approval. Then she'll begin trying them out on non-foodies—the gardener, the mailman, her personal trainer, and, according to one of her books, the seagulls. Then comes the more critical audience—Craig Claiborne, Jacques Pepin, the food editor of the *Miami Herald*. Along the way, she spends most of her waking moments refining and revising. And more often than not, she'll take what seems like a miniscule problem to bed with her, only to rise in the middle of the night with a brainstorm.

Each time one of Maida's books comes out, she threatens that it will be her last. If any other of our national treasures made this declaration, there would be cause for genuine alarm. In Maida's case, though, you wait until she becomes passionate again. "This is what I do—I write dessert books, and I can't stop," Maida once told a reporter who asked her why she'd written another dessert book. "Don't you run out of ideas?" the reporter then asked. "On the contrary," Maida informed him. "I run out of time, or butter, and eggs—even chocolate. But not ideas."

NANCY SILVERTON

The recipes in this book were originally published in

Maida Heatter's New Book of Great Desserts (1982) and

Maida Heatter's Book of Great American Desserts (1985).

How I Started to Write Cookbooks

*P*eople often ask me how I started to write cookbooks.

My husband owned a restaurant in Miami Beach. I made all of the desserts for the restaurant. I made them at home and my husband took them to the restaurant (often by boat). The year was 1967, and the Republican party held a convention here to nominate a president. I had an idea. I said, "The symbol of the Republican party is an elephant. If you serve an elephant meat omelet in the restaurant you will get a lot of publicity." It turned out to be more than I had imagined. And it was more than just publicity for the restaurant. It completely changed my life.

The elephant meat omelet was front-page news in major newspapers and on national television. Among the many calls we received was one from Craig Claiborne, the food editor of *The New York Times*. He said that the only news coming out of the convention was the elephant meat omelet, and he said that he would like to come to interview me. I was thrilled. I had never met Craig, but I had read his columns and his recipes and his cookbooks for many years.

When Craig came here, I had a large table in our home covered with all the desserts I wanted to show off. Craig was wonderful, I fell in love with him, and during the interview he said, "You ought to write a cookbook."

I would never have done it if Craig had not told me that I should. So I did, I wrote seven. So far.

P.S. *Incidentally, we bought the elephant meat in cans from Bloomingdale's. It was canned by Reese. And it was delicious. It was like Boeuf Bourguignonne.*

What was the omelet like? The three-egg omelet was rolled around the elephant meat and placed on a plate. On two sides of the omelet were lengthwise halves of sautéed banana. And the top was sprinkled with salted peanuts. I didn't design this without professional help. I had called two chefs. One was at Treehouse, a restaurant that William Holden owned in Kenya, Africa. Another was at a club called the Explorers Club, which at that time was somewhere near Washington, D.C. (I had been told that the members were animal hunters). Both gentlemen were helpful and interested and did not sound surprised.

MAIDA HEATTER

Cake-Making Basics

Ingredients

M uch of the following material entitled Ingredients, Equipment, and Techniques is repeated here from my other books because it still holds true.

FLOUR

Many of these recipes call for sifted flour. That means that even if the package is labeled "pre-sifted," you should sift it before measuring. If not, since flour packs down while standing, 1 cup of unsifted flour is liable to be a few spoonfuls more than 1 cup of just-sifted flour.

Sift the flour onto a large piece of wax paper. Make sure that there is no flour left in the sifter. Then transfer the sifter to another piece of wax paper. Use a metal measuring cup and lightly spoon the sifted flour into the cup or lift it on a dough scraper and transfer it to the cup—do not pack or press the flour down—and scrape the excess off the top with any flat-sided implement. Place the flour in the sifter, add any ingredients to be sifted with it, and sift onto the second piece of wax paper. Again, make sure there is nothing left in the sifter.

It is not necessary ever to wash a flour sifter; just shake it out firmly and store it in a plastic bag.

SUGARS

All sugars should be measured in the graded measuring cups that are made for measuring dry ingredients.

Brown Sugars

Most brown sugars are made of white granulated sugar to which a dark syrup has been added. Dark brown sugar has a mild molasses, and light brown sugar has a milder, lighter syrup (which may also be molasses). Dark brown has a slightly stronger flavor, but they may be used interchangeably. The label on Grandma's Molasses says, "You can easily make your own brown sugar as you need it by blending together ½ cup of granulated sugar with 2 tablespoons of unsulphured molasses. The yield is equivalent to ½ cup of brown sugar."

Brown sugar is moist; if it dries out it will harden. It should be stored airtight at room temperature. If it has small lumps in it, they should be strained out. With your fingertips press the sugar through a large strainer set over a large bowl. The Savannah Sugar Refinery is now printing the following directions on their boxes of brown sugar: "If your brown sugar has been left open and becomes hard, place a dampened (not wet) paper towel inside the resealable poly bag and close the package tightly for 12 hours or more. A slice of apple can be used in place of the dampened towel or you can process it in a food processor."

Confectioners' Sugar

Confectioners' sugar and powdered sugar are exactly the same. They are both granulated sugar that has been pulverized very fine and has had about 3% cornstarch added to keep it in a powdery condition. Of these, 4-x is the least fine and 10-x is the finest. They may be used interchangeably. Confectioners' sugar should be strained; you can do several pounds at a time if you wish. (It does not have to be done immediately before using as flour does.) Store it airtight.

If directions say to sprinkle with confectioners' sugar, place the sugar in a fine strainer and shake over the top of the cake.

Vanilla Confectioners' Sugar

This is a flavored confectioners' sugar that is used to sprinkle over cakes and cookies. It adds a nice mild flavor and delicious aroma. To make it, fill a jar that has a tight cover with confectioners' sugar. Split one or two vanilla beans lengthwise and bury them in the sugar. Cover tightly and let stand for at least a few days before using. As the sugar is used it may be replaced; the vanilla bean will continue to flavor the sugar for a month or two.

When you make vanilla confectioners' sugar, don't bother to strain the sugar beforehand. The vanilla beans give off a certain amount of moisture which the sugar absorbs, causing the sugar to become lumpy and making it necessary to strain it just before using.

Crystal Sugar

Crystal sugar, also called pearl sugar, or hagelsucker in German, is generally used to sprinkle over certain European cookies and pastries before baking. It is coarser than granulated sugar.

It can be bought from Sweet Celebrations (formerly Maid of Scandinavia) in Minneapolis, MN, (800) 480-2505. It comes in 1-pound bags and is labeled "Medium Grain."

WHIPPING CREAM

Plain old-fashioned whipping cream is almost impossible to find nowadays unless you have your own cow. Too bad, because the new super- or ultra-pasteurized (known as UHT—ultra-high-temperature pasteurized) is not as good, at least I don't think so. The reason dairies make it is that is has a 6- to 8-week shelf life. (They call it a "pull date"; the store has to pull it off their shelves if it is not sold by the date stamped on the container.) This product is called either Heavy Whipping Cream or Heavy Cream, depending on the manufacturer. Either type can be used in recipes calling for Heavy Cream.

The process of making ultra-pasteurized cream involves heating the cream to 250° for 1 second. It gives the cream a slight caramel flavor (so mild you might not notice it), and makes it more difficult to whip (it will take longer). It is advisable to chill the bowl and the beaters in the freezer for about half an hour before using. And keep the cream in the refrigerator until you are ready to whip; do not let it stand around in the kitchen—it should be as cold as possible.

It seems to me that baked custards take longer to set if they are made with ultra-pasteurized cream, and ice cream takes longer to churn.

How to Whip Cream

The best way to whip either plain old-fashioned or UHT cream is to place it in a large bowl, set the bowl in a larger bowl of ice and water, and whip with a large, thin-wired, balloon-type whisk. You get more volume that way, and it tastes better.

If that seems like more than you want to fuss with, use an electric mixer or an eggbeater, and chill the bowl and beaters before using them. If the bowl does not revolve, then move the beaters around the bowl to whip all the cream evenly at the same time.

When I whip cream with an electric mixer, I always (and I recommend this to everyone) finish the whipping by hand with a wire whisk; there is less chance of overwhipping. At this stage you can use a smaller whisk than if you do it all by hand.

Whipped cream, which can be heavenly, is not quite so delicious if it is whipped until it is really stiff—softer is better.

Eggs

Size

Use eggs graded "large."

To Open Eggs

If directions call for adding whole eggs one at a time, they may all be opened ahead of time into one container and then poured into the other ingredients approximately one at a time. Do not open eggs directly into the other ingredients—you would not know if a piece of shell had been included.

To Separate Eggs

Eggs separate more safely—there is less chance of the yolk breaking—when they are cold. Therefore, if a recipe calls for separated eggs, it is usually the first thing I do when organizing the ingredients so they are cold from the refrigerator.

The safest way to separate eggs is as follows: Place three small cups or bowls in front of you (or use shallow drinking glasses; glasses generally have a sharper edge and therefore crack the shell more cleanly). One container is for the whites and one for the yolks. The third might not be needed, but if you should break the yolk when opening an egg, just drop the whole thing in the third bowl and save it for some other use.

Tap the side of the egg firmly (but not too hard or you might break the yolk) on the edge of the bowl or glass to crack the shell, with luck, in a rather straight, even line. Then, holding the egg in both hands (so that the halves each make a cup), separate the halves of the shell, letting some of the white run out into the bowl or glass. Pour the yolk back and forth from one half of the shell to the other, letting all of the white run out. Drop the yolk into the second bowl or glass.

Many professional cooks simply open the egg into the palm of one hand, then hold their fingers, slightly separated, over a bowl. They let the white run through their open fingers and then slide the left-behind yolk into the second bowl.

As each egg is separated, the white should be transferred to another container (that is, in addition to the three—it could be another bowl or glass or it might be the mixing bowl you will beat them in), because if you place all of the whites in one container there is a chance that the last egg white might have some yolk in it, which could spoil all of the whites. Generally, a tiny bit of yolk or shell can be removed from the whites with an empty half shell. Or try a piece of paper towel dipped in cold water.

To Beat Egg Whites

The success of many recipes depends on properly beaten whites. After you have learned how, it becomes second nature.

First, the bowl and beaters must be absolutely clean. A little bit of fat (like egg yolks) will prevent the whites from incorporating air as they should and from rising properly.

Second, do not overbeat or the whites will become dry and you will not be able to fold them into other ingredients without losing the air you have beaten in.

Third, do not beat them ahead of time. They must be folded in immediately after they are beaten; if they have to wait, they separate. Incidentally, if the whites are being folded into a cake batter, the cake must then be placed in the oven right away.

You can use an electric mixer, a rotary beater, or a wire whisk (although a wire whisk and a copper bowl are said to give the most volume and therefore the best results).

If you use an electric mixer or a rotary beater, be careful not to use a bowl that is too large or the whites will be too shallow to get the full benefit of the beater's action. If the bowl or beaters do not revolve by themselves (as they do in electric mixers on a stand), move the mixer or beater around the bowl to beat all the whites evenly. If you use a mixer on a stand, use a rubber spatula frequently to push the whites from the side of the bowl into the center.

If you use a wire whisk, it should be a large, thin-wired balloon-type, at least 4 inches wide at the top. The bowl should be very large, the larger the better, to give you plenty of room for making large circular motions with the whisk. An unlined copper bowl is the best, or you may use glass, china, or stainless steel—but do not beat egg whites in aluminum, which might discolor the whites, or plastic, which is frequently porous and might be greasy from some other use.

A copper bowl should be treated each time before using as follows: Put 1 or 2 teaspoons of salt in the bowl and rub thoroughly with half a lemon, squeezing a bit of the juice and mixing it with the salt. Then rinse with hot water (no soap) and dry. After using a copper bowl, wash it as you would any other, but be sure to treat it before beating egg whites again.

When I beat whites with an electric mixer, if they do not have sugar added (sugar makes them more creamy and slightly lessens the chance of overbeating), I always—and I recommend this to everyone—finish the beating with a wire whisk. There is less chance of overbeating, and the whisk seems to give the whites a slightly creamy consistency. At this stage you can use a smaller whisk than the one mentioned above; use one that seems to fit the bowl the whites are in.

People always ask me if I bring whites to room temperature before beating them. If I do, it is a rare occasion and was not planned. They are usually cold when I beat them (because I do not plan ahead and do not have the patience to wait, and because I have had equally good results whether cold or at room temperature).

To Freeze Egg Whites or Yolks

Some of these recipes call for yolks and no whites, and some call for only whites. If you have just a few extra of either left over and do not want to save them for something else, add them to scrambled eggs.

Leftover egg whites may be kept covered in the refrigerator for a few days or they may be frozen. I freeze them individually (or occasionally 2 or 4 together) in ovenproof glass custard cups. When they are frozen, hold one cup upside down under running hot water until the frozen egg white can be removed (but not until it melts). Quickly wrap each frozen egg white individually in plastic wrap and return to the freezer. To use, remove the number you want, unwrap, place them in a cup or bowl, and let stand at room temperature to thaw. Or place them in a cup or bowl in a slightly warm oven or in a larger bowl of warm water.

To freeze egg yolks, stir them lightly just to mix, and for every yolk, stir in ⅓ teaspoon of granulated sugar or ½ teaspoon of honey. Freeze them in a covered jar, labeling so you will know how many yolks and how much sugar or honey. When thawed, stir to mix well—they will not look exactly the same as before they were frozen (not as smooth), but they will work in recipes.

Nuts

Nuts can turn rancid rather quickly—walnuts and pecans more so than almonds. Always store all nuts airtight in the freezer or refrigerator. In the refrigerator nuts will last well for 9 months; in the freezer at 0° they will last for 2 years. Bring them to room temperature before using; smell and taste them before you use them (preferably as soon as you buy them)—you will know quickly if they are rancid. If you even suspect that they might be, do not use them; they would ruin a recipe.

To Toast Pecans

Pecans occasionally become limp after they are frozen, so I toast them. Toasted pecans are so great that now I toast all pecans (those that have been frozen and those that have not) before using them, as follows. Place them in a shallow pan in the middle of a preheated 350° oven for 12 to 15 minutes, stirring them occasionally, until they are very hot but not until they become darker in color.

To Blanch Almonds

(Blanched almonds are skinned almonds.)

Cover the almonds with boiling water—the skin will loosen almost immediately. Spoon out a few nuts at a time and one by one, hold them under cold running water, squeezing the nuts between your thumb and forefinger. The nuts will pop out and the skin will remain between your fingers. Place the peeled almonds on a towel to dry, then spread them in a single layer in a shallow baking pan and bake in a 200° oven for half an hour or so until they are completely dry. Do not let them brown.

If the almonds are to be split, sliced, or slivered, they should remain in the hot water longer to soften; let them stand in the water until the water cools enough for you to touch it. Then, one at a time, remove the skin from each nut and immediately, while the nut is still soft, place it on a cutting board and cut with a small, sharp paring knife. Bake to dry as above. Sliced almonds are those that have been cut into very thin slices; slivered almonds are the fatter, oblong, "julienne"-

shaped pieces. Don't expect sliced or slivered almonds that you have cut yourself to be as even as the bought ones.

To Blanch Hazelnuts

Spread the hazelnuts on a baking sheet and bake at 350° for about 15 minutes or until the skins parch and begin to flake off. Then, working with a few at a time, place them on a large, coarse towel (I use a large terry-cloth bath towel). Fold part of the towel over to enclose the nuts. Rub firmly against the towel, or hold that part of the towel between both hands and rub back and forth. The rubbing and the texture of the towel will cause most of the skins to flake off. Pick out the nuts and discard the skins. Don't worry about the few little pieces of skin that may remain.

This is not as quick and easy as it sounds.

Pistachio Nuts

A light sprinkling of chopped green pistachio nuts is an elegant and classy touch. But don't overdo it; less is better than more. Fine pastries in swanky patisseries might have only about a teaspoonful of them in the center of a 9-inch cake, sprinkled on the center of chocolate icing or whipped-cream topping.

Chop them coarsely or fine on a board using a long, heavy knife. Don't worry about the little pieces of skin that flake off; you can use them with the nuts (or pick out the large pieces of skin if you wish).

DRIED AND/OR CANDIED FRUIT

In most recipes that call for candied fruit of one kind or another, or several kinds, it is perfectly all right to substitute a different kind. For instance,

if you wish, dates, raisins, figs, prunes, or apricots may be substituted for candied pineapple or citron, etc.

COFFEE AS A FLAVORING

Often people ask about the instruction "use powdered, not granular, coffee." If a recipe specifies powdered, it is because the granular would stay in granules and would not dissolve. Spice Islands brand, generally available in specialty food stores, makes powdered instant espresso and also a powdered instant coffee. And Medaglia D'Oro instant espresso, which is powdered, is generally available in Italian grocery stores.

When a recipe calls for dissolving instant coffee in water, if you leave out the coffee, do not leave out the water.

FRESH GINGER

Do not buy any that is soft and wrinkled—it should be firm and hard (like potatoes). To store: For a few days—or even weeks, if it is firm and fresh—it can just stand at room temperature (like potatoes). For a longer time, it can be stored in the vegetable crisper in the refrigerator—wrapped or unwrapped does not seem to make any difference. Or it can be frozen, wrapped airtight in plastic or foil.

(A chef at a famous San Francisco restaurant told me that he keeps fresh ginger for weeks at room temperature, lying on its side in a shallow dish with about ½ inch of water in the dish, and he adds water occasionally as it evaporates. About a month ago, when I had just bought some nice, fresh ginger, I put one piece in water, and another alongside it but not in water. Now, a month later, the piece which is not in water looks healthier. The piece that is in water looks barely wrinkled—or is it my imagination? This experiment proves that if it is in good condition when you buy it, ginger is strong and hardy and lasts well almost in spite of what you do to it.)

It is not necessary to peel ginger. It may be grated on a standing metal grater on the side that has small round openings (rather than diamond-shaped openings). It may be grated if it is at room temperature, or refrigerated, or frozen. Either way, it is slow work to grate much. But it is quick and easy—it is a breeze—to grate it in a food processor. First slice it crossways into very thin slices, or about ⅛ inch thick. (Although the processor will grate the ginger very well, it will leave fibers in the mixture; slicing it thin before processing reduces the length of fibers. Incidentally, older ginger is more fibrous than young ginger; it is also more gingerly and flavorful. But either is wonderful.) Fit the processor with the metal chopping blade. With the motor going, add the slices of ginger one or two at a time through the feed tube, pausing briefly between additions. Stop the machine once or twice to scrape the sides of the bowl with a rubber spatula and then process again for a few seconds.

If you plan to freeze the ginger and then grate it, frozen, in a food processor, it is best to slice it thin before you freeze it. But it is possible, if necessary, to cut up (slice) frozen ginger with a heavy Chinese cleaver, a strong arm, and patience.

It is also possible to grate the ginger (easiest in a processor) and wrap it in measured amounts and freeze it; thaw before using. Or coarsely chop the block of frozen, grated ginger with a heavy cleaver, and drop the pieces through the feed tube of a processor (fitted with the metal chopping blade) with the motor going, and process until it returns to the grated texture. It will be wetter than ginger that has been grated but not frozen, but that does not noticeably affect its use in baking (although sometimes I think that ginger that has been frozen is not as sharp and gingerly as it was before it was frozen, but that is hard to judge).

Incidentally, fresh produce people tell me that Hawaiian ginger is the best.

Equipment

ELECTRIC MIXERS

I use an electric mixer on a stand that comes with two different-size bowls and a pair of beaters (rather than one). Mine is a Sunbeam, and I am so dependent on it that when I do cooking demonstrations, I bring my own with me.

I think it is important, or at least extremely helpful, for many dessert recipes to use a mixer that:

    a. is on a stand;

    b. comes with both a small and a large bowl; and

    c. has space to scrape around the bowl with a rubber spatula while the mixer is going.

I especially recommend that you buy an extra set of bowls and beaters—they are generally available wherever mixers are sold.

Incidentally, although I have a handheld mixer, I could live without it. (But if I did not have any other I am sure I would learn to love it.) If you are using a handheld mixer (or an eggbeater), when I say "small bowl of electric mixer" that means one with about a 7-cup capacity, and "large bowl of electric mixer" means about a 16-cup capacity.

THERMOMETERS

One of the most important and often most overlooked requirements for good results in baking is correct oven temperature. The wrong temperature can cause a cake to fall, to burn, to be underdone, to refuse to rise; it can ruin a soufflé; it can turn cookies that should be wonderfully crisp into pale, limp, soggy messes; and it could be the cause of almost any other baking disaster that you might have experienced or heard about.

No matter how new or how good your oven is, *please* double-check the temperature every time you bake. Use a small, portable oven thermometer from the hardware store or kitchen shop. Buy the mercury kind—it is best. Turn on your oven at least 20 minutes ahead of time and place the thermometer in the middle of the oven. Give the oven plenty of time to heat and cycle and reheat before you read the thermometer; read it (and all thermometers) at eye level. If it does not register the heat you want, adjust the thermostat up or down until the mercury thermometer registers the correct heat, no matter what the oven setting says.

When you put unbaked cakes or cookies in the oven they reduce the oven temperature more than you would expect. If you check the temperature on a portable oven thermometer during about the first 10 minutes of baking don't think that your oven suddenly got sick; give it time to reheat.

Other Thermometers

A friend told me she did not know that her refrigerator was too warm until she served a large chocolate icebox cake at a dinner party and found that the middle was thin and runny instead of firm as it should have been. And once I didn't know that my freezer was misbehaving until the very last minute, when a photographer was here to take pictures of a chocolate dessert; I had waited until he was ready to shoot before I took the big, gorgeous chocolate curls that I had made so carefully out of the freezer and found they had flattened and were no longer curls.

Keep a freezer thermometer in your freezer and a refrigerator thermometer in your refrigerator—and look at them often.

And for some of the recipes in this book you will need a thermometer labeled a "candy-jelly-frosting thermometer." This thermometer clips on to the side of a saucepan; bend down and read it at eye level in order to get a correct reading. And make sure the stem is deep enough in the liquid being cooked to give an accurate reading.

And a frying thermometer is essential for making doughnuts.

CAKE PANS

When I first started writing cookbooks, it was often hard to find all kinds of pans and baking equipment in many cities. Nowadays, with all manner of excellent local cooking supply stores, national chains, and mail-order catalogs, buying the right equipment has become a lot easier.

Bundt Pan

Bundt pan is a trade name for a one-piece tube pan that has a specific fancy design. There are many other similar pans with different designs; in each case the name of the pan is descriptive of the design. Turk's head, turban, and kugelhopf are the most common. When a recipe calls for a Bundt pan, any of these other pans may be substituted.

Swirl Tube Pan
(a.k.a. Turk's Head Mold)

Another tube pan that I use very often for many of these recipes is 10 inches in diameter, 4 inches high, has a 1¾-inch-wide tube at the top, a 12-cup capacity, is made in France of heavy tin, and has a beautiful swirl pattern that makes gorgeous cakes.

My Favorite So-Called 9-Inch Loaf Pan

The most popular 8-cup loaf pan measures 9 x 5 x 3 inches. But my favorite shape, available in many kitchen shops, makes a longer and narrower loaf. The pan measures 10¼ x 3¾ (width at the top) x 3⅜ (depth) inches and is made of heavy aluminum (but is not a dark metal).

Dull/Dark Pans

Bright, shiny surfaces reflect the heat away from the item being baked, preventing the item from browning. Dark, dull metal (black, blue, blue/black, dark brown) and nonstick finishes absorb and hold the heat, encouraging a dark crust on the item being baked. This is especially noticeable when what is being baked is a yeast dough, or a pastry in a quiche or tart pan. These dark pans are available more than they used to be. But if you are baking a chocolate cake it is best to use a shiny pan or the crust will become too dark.

Tube Pan

In all of the recipes that call for a tube pan, use a one-piece pan unless the recipe specifies a two-piece pan.

Cheesecake Pan

A professional cheesecake pan, the kind that is generally used by bakers and pastry chefs, is a one-piece pan, because cheesecakes are frequently baked in a pan of water. And they are deeper than layer cake pans. They come in a variety of sizes. Many of these recipes call for an 8 x 3-inch cheesecake pan. They are available at almost all well-equipped kitchen shops.

DOUBLE BOILERS

Many of these recipes call for a double boiler. You can buy them in hardware stores or kitchen shops. The thing to look for is one in which the upper section is not too deep (shallow is better) and is smooth (no ridges).

If necessary, you can create your own by placing a heatproof bowl over a saucepan of shallow hot water. The bowl should be wide enough at the top so its rim rests on the rim of the saucepan, keeping the bowl suspended over the water.

ROLLING PINS

If you have many occasions to use a rolling pin (and I hope that you will—with the yeast cakes and doughnuts in this book), you really should have different sizes and different shapes. Sometimes a very long, thick, and heavy one will be best; for other doughs you will want a smaller, lighter one. The French style, which is extra long, narrow, and tapered at both ends is especially good for rolling dough into a round shape as for a pie crust, while the straight-sided pin is better for an oblong shape.

However, in the absence of any rolling pin at all, other things will do a fair job. Try a straight-sided bottle, tall jar, or a drinking glass.

CAKE-DECORATING TURNTABLE

If you ice many cakes, this is a most important piece of equipment. Not that you can't ice a cake without it, but it will not look the same. You will love the smooth, professional-looking results, and the ease of using a turntable. It works on the same principle as a lazy Susan and although a lazy Susan can be used in place of a turntable, it usually does not turn quite so easily.

I put the cake on a cake plate and then put the plate on the turntable.

First put the icing on freely just to cover the cake. Then hold a long, narrow metal spatula in your right hand, with the blade at about a 30° angle against the side or top of the cake. With your left hand slowly rotate the turntable. Hold your right hand still as the cake turns and in a few seconds you will have a smooth, sleek, neat-looking cake. It is fun. And exciting.

I also use the turntable when trimming and then fluting the edge of pie crust (you will love using it for this).

Turntables are available at specialty kitchen equipment shops and at wholesale restaurant and baker suppliers. They do not have to be expensive. The thing to look for is one that turns very easily. There is no reason why a turntable, if it is not abused, should not last a lifetime or two.

PASTRY BAGS

The best pastry bags for many years have been those that are made of canvas and are coated on one side only with plastic. Use them with the plastic coating inside. The small opening generally has to be cut a bit larger to allow the metal tubes to fit.

Either kind should be washed in hot soapy water, then just hung up to dry.

When filling a pastry bag, unless there is someone else to hold it for you, it is generally easiest if you support the bag by placing it in a tall and wide glass or jar.

SMALL, NARROW METAL SPATULA

Many of my recipes call for this tool for smoothing icing around the sides of a cake. Mine is 8 inches long; it has a 4-inch blade and a 4-inch wooden handle. The blade is ⅜ inch wide and has a rounded tip. Although it can bend, it is more firm than flexible. Metal spatulas are generally available in a variety of sizes and shapes in specialty kitchen supply stores. A table knife can be used in place of this small spatula.

Techniques

TO GRIND NUTS IN A FOOD PROCESSOR

Add about ¼ cup (or more) of the sugar or flour called for in the recipe; that will prevent the nuts from becoming oily. And process for 50 to 60 seconds even though you will think it is done sooner—the finer the nuts are, the better.

ABOUT MEASURING

Meticulously precise measurements are essential for good results in baking.

Glass or plastic measuring cups with the measurements marked on the side and the 1-cup line below the top are only for measuring liquids. Do not use them for flour or sugar. With the cup at eye level fill carefully to exactly the line indicated.

Measuring cups that come in graded sets of four (¼ cup, ⅓ cup, ½ cup, and 1 cup) are for measuring flour, sugar, and other dry ingredients—and for thick sour cream. Fill the cup to overflowing and then scrape off the excess with a dough scraper, a metal spatula, or the flat side of a knife.

Standard measuring spoons must be used for correct measurements. They come in sets of four: ¼ teaspoon, ½ teaspoon, 1 teaspoon, and 1 tablespoon. For dry ingredients, fill the spoon to overflowing and then scrape off the excess with a small metal spatula or the flat side of a knife.

TO ADD DRY INGREDIENTS ALTERNATELY WITH LIQUID

Begin and end with dry. The procedure is generally to add about one-third of the dry, then half of the liquid, a second third of the dry, the rest of the liquid, and then the rest of the dry.

Use the lowest speed on an electric mixer for this (or it may be done by hand using a rubber or wooden spatula—some few people do it with a bare hand). After each addition mix only until smooth. If your mixer is the type that allows you to use a rubber spatula while it is in motion, help the mixing along by scraping the sides of the bowl with the spatula. If the mixer does not allow room, or if it is a handheld mixer, stop it frequently and scrape the bowl with the spatula; do not beat any more than necessary.

ABOUT FOLDING INGREDIENTS TOGETHER

Many of these recipes call for folding beaten egg whites and/or cream into another mixture. The whites and/or cream have air beaten into them, and folding rather than mixing is done in order to retain the air.

This is an important step and should be done with care. The knack of doing it well comes with practice and concentration. Remember that you want to incorporate the mixtures without losing any air. That means handle as little as possible.

It is important not to beat the whites or whip the cream until they are actually stiff; if you do you will have to stir and mix rather than fold, thereby losing the air.

Do not let beaten egg whites stand around or they will become dry and deflate the cream. Generally it is best to fold the lighter mixture into the heavier one, and to actually stir a bit of the lighter mixture into the heavier (to lighten it a bit) before you start to fold. Then, as a rule, it is best not to add all of the remaining light mixture at once; do the folding in a few additions. The first additions should not be folded thoroughly.

Although many professional chefs use their bare hands for folding, most home cooks are more comfortable using a rubber spatula. Rubber is better than plastic because it is more flexible. Spatulas come in three sizes. The smallest is called a bottle scraper. For most folding, the medium size is the one to use. But for folding large amounts in a large bowl, the largest rubber spatula can be very helpful. The one I mean might measure about 13 to 16 inches from the end of the blade to the end of the handle; the blade will be about 2¾ inches wide and about 4½ inches long. This large size is difficult to locate; try specialty kitchen equipment shops or wholesale restaurant suppliers.

To fold ingredients together it is best to use a bowl with a rounded bottom, and it is better if the bowl is too large rather than too small. Following the recipe, place part (occasionally all, depending on the recipe) of the light mixture on top of the heavier mixture. Hold the rubber spatula, rounded side toward the bottom and over the middle of the bowl, and cut through to the bottom of the bowl. Bring the spatula toward you against the bottom, then up the side and out, over the top, turning your wrist and the blade as you do this so the blade is upside down when it comes out over the top. Return the spatula to its original position, then cut through the middle of the mixture again. After each fold, rotate the bowl slightly in order to incorporate the ingredients as much as possible. Continue only until both mixtures are combined.

Occasionally a bit of beaten egg white will rise to the top. If it is just one or two small pieces, instead of folding more, simply smooth over the top gently with the spatula.

If the base mixture has gelatin in it, it should be chilled until it starts to thicken.

When folding, it is ideal to have the gelatin mixture, the whipped cream, and/or the egg whites all the same consistency (although in some cases that is not possible).

To Measure the Capacity of a Cake Pan

Fill a large measuring cup with water and pour it into the pan to overflowing. If it is a two-piece pan, and the water would run out, fill it with sugar or rice or beans instead of water.

About Preparing Cake Pans

In many recipes, after buttering the pan (always with unsalted butter), I dust it with bread crumbs, because in many recipes, but not all, there is less chance of sticking if you use crumbs rather than flour. The crumbs should be fine and dry. They may be homemade (see following page), but I always have purchased ones on hand. If you use purchased ones, be sure to buy the ones marked "plain" or "unseasoned," not "seasoned." Some brands are okay just as they are, some are a bit coarse; they may be ground a little finer in a food processor or blender—but don't overdo it; they should be crumbs, not powder. You can grind a whole boxful and store them ready to use.

To prepare a tube pan: When directions call for buttering the pan and then coating it with flour or crumbs, the only way to get the flour or crumbs on the tube itself is by lifting them with your fingers and sprinkling them around the tube with your fingers.

In all of these recipes, the butter and flour or bread crumbs used to prepare the pans are in addition to those called for in the ingredients.

HOMEMADE DRY BREAD CRUMBS

Remove and discard the crusts from sliced white bread. Place the slices in a single layer on cookie sheets in a 225° oven and bake until the bread is completely dry and crisp (although if it is so stale that it is completely dry, it is not necessary to bake it). Break up the slices coarsely and grind them in a processor or a blender until the crumbs are rather fine, but not as fine as powder.

TO BUTTER A FANCY-SHAPED TUBE PAN

If you spread the butter with a piece of wax paper it feels clumsy and seems inefficient. If you melt the butter and brush it on, it seems as though most of the butter runs down to the bottom of the pan. It is best to let some butter stand at room temperature to soften. Then use a pastry brush to brush it carefully all over the pan.

HOW TO PREPARE ORANGES AND LEMONS

I use the juice of fresh lemons or oranges in all recipes calling for their juice. If possible, I recommend that you do the same for the best flavor.

In recipes that call for the grated rind of lemons or oranges, the grated rind of fresh fruit has a better flavor than bought dried grated rind.

To Grate the Rind

It is best to use firm, deep-colored, thick-skinned fruit. And it is best if the fruit is cold; the rind is firmer and grates better. Use a standing metal grater—usually they have four sides, or some are round. Hold the grater up to the light and look at the shapes of the holes from the inside. You should use the small holes that are round, not diamond-shaped. Place the grater on a piece of wax paper on the work surface. Wash and dry the fruit. Hold the grater firmly in place with your left hand. With your right hand, hold the fruit cupped in your palm at the top of the grater. Now, press the fruit firmly against the grater as you push the fruit down toward the bottom of the grater. Press firmly, but do not overdo it—all you want is the zest (the thin, colored outer part), so do not work over the same spot on the fruit or you will be grating the white underneath; rotate the fruit in your hand as you press it against the grater. Remove the gratings from the inside of the grater with a rubber spatula.

To Pare the Rind

Use a vegetable peeler with a swivel blade to remove the thin, colored outer rind.

ABOUT DECORATING CAKES

Cake decorating can be just as much a creative art as painting or sculpting. But to me, the pure untouched simplicity of a smooth, shiny chocolate glaze, or a topping of barely firm whipped cream, is perfection and adding anything to it would detract from an already perfect work of art. The same goes for an uniced pound cake or loaf cake. Of course there are times when I would like to wield a pastry bag and don't ever want to quit. But please don't feel that every cake needs decoration; simplicity is often decoration enough. Anything else might be gilding the lily.

Very often, a few small, fresh, beautiful flowers are a wonderful decoration. Either place them on the plate alongside the cake, or cut the stems short and place a few (or sometimes only one) directly on top of the cake, either resting on the cake, or inserted into it.

HOW TO PREPARE THE SERVING PLATE

This is done to keep any icing off the plate. It will result in a clean, neat, professional-looking finished product.

Begin by tearing off a 10-inch piece of wax paper. Fold it crossways into four equal strips (fold it in half and then in half again), then cut through the folds with a sharp knife, making four 10 x 3-inch strips.

Lay the strips in a square pattern around the rim of the plate, put the cake on the plate over the strips, and check to be sure that they touch the cake all around.

After the cake is iced (and before the icing hardens) remove the wax papers by pulling each one out toward a narrow end.

IF YOU PLAN TO TRANSPORT A CAKE

If you plan to transport a cake that is iced, here's a trick I learned during the years when I baked des-

serts at home and my husband carried them in a station wagon or boat to his restaurant.

Melt about ½ ounce of semisweet chocolate and place it in the center of the cake plate. Place the cake directly on the chocolate, which will act as a paste to keep the cake from sliding.

HOW TO WASH A PASTRY BRUSH

If you have used the brush for a sugar glaze, just rinse it under warm running water, separating the bristles a bit with your fingers so the water reaches all of them. If you have used it to butter a pan, it is important to remove every bit of butter or it will become rancid on the brush, and I don't know any way to ever get rid of that. First rinse the brush briefly under running hot water. Then rub it well on a cake of soap, first rubbing one side of the bristles and then the other. Rinse well under hot running water, then repeat the soaping and rinsing one or two more times to be sure. Just let it stand bristle side up in a dish drainer or in a glass to dry.

ABOUT FREEZING CAKES

I don't think that any baked dessert tastes as good after freezing as when it is fresh. However, if it is frozen for only a short time (a few days or weeks) the difference might be infinitesimal. I have indicated in many of these recipes that the dessert can be frozen. If it is a big help to you to prepare it ahead, do it. But if you have your choice, fresh is best.

If you want to ice a cake first and then freeze it, it may be frozen directly on the cake plate and left on the plate, or, to keep the cake from sticking to the plate, it may be placed on wax paper or baking-pan liner paper (cut to fit the bottom of the cake) on the plate, and then removed from the plate and wrapped when it is frozen. Freeze until the icing is firm, then wrap it airtight with plastic wrap and, if you wish, rewrap it in foil or a freezer bag.

Everything should be thawed completely before it is unwrapped. (Foods sweat while thawing. If they thaw while they are still wrapped, the moisture will form on the outside of the wrapping; if they thaw after they are unwrapped, the moisture will form on the food itself—that could spoil the looks of a beautiful smooth glaze or icing.) However, if you have a cake in the freezer and you want some right away, unwrap it, cut it, and serve it. Many cakes are delicious frozen. Just don't let the rest of the cake stand around uncovered—rewrap it immediately.

Label packages—if not, you might wind up with a freezer full of UFOs (Unidentified Frozen Objects).

About Cutting Cakes

I can do a better job if I stand rather than sit.

Cakes should be cut carefully and neatly with a very sharp knife that is long enough. You may not use the whole blade, but it gives leverage. Some cakes cut best with a sawing motion—try it. Some cut best with a serrated knife—try that also.

If it is a round cake, always start cutting each pie-shaped wedge from the exact center. Mark the center with the tip of the knife. Or, to find the center, lightly score the cake in half first in one direction and then in the opposite direction. Then, if you don't trust yourself to cut freehand, mark each quarter lightly with the tip of the knife, marking the outside edge into 2 to 6 portions. But always keep your eye on the center so that the slices all radiate out from there.

Talking about size of portions, unless it is for a restaurant—and sometimes even if it is—small portions are better than large. If it is a loaf cake or a square cake, it may be a big help to use a ruler and toothpick to mark the portions.

Fruitcakes cut best when they are very cold.

So do pound cakes.

Sponge cakes, angel-food cakes, chiffon cakes—all light and airy cakes—should be cut with a serrated bread knife. Use a sawing motion and do not press down on the cake or you will squash it.

Occasionally, for certain cakes (for many cheesecakes, for some layer cakes with sticky icing, and for some others) it is best if the knife blade is hot and wet. In the kitchen, work next to the sink. Or, in the dining room, have a tall jar or pitcher of hot water handy. And have a towel to wipe the blade after cutting each slice.

Mainly, take your time. And if it isn't going too well, remember all the options—try a different knife, or a wet blade, or simply wipe the blade.

A Final Word

I once put a cake in the oven and then realized that I had forgotten to use the baking powder that the recipe called for. (The cake had beaten egg whites in it and there was no way I could still add the baking powder.) I learned the hard way that it is necessary to organize all the ingredients listed in a recipe—line them up in the order they are called for—before you actually start mixing. As you use an ingredient, set it aside. That way, nothing should be left on the work surface when you are through. A quick look during and after mixing will let you know if something was left out.

Plain
Cakes

EAST 62ND STREET LEMON CAKE

10 PORTIONS

My daughter created this cake. When the recipe was reprinted in The New York Times *we heard from many people who said it was their favorite cake. The list of hosts and hostesses who now have this on hand at all times reads like a Who's Who.*

3 cups sifted
all-purpose flour

2 teaspoons
baking powder

½ teaspoon salt

8 ounces (2 sticks)
unsalted butter

2 cups granulated sugar

4 eggs

1 cup milk

Finely grated rind of
2 large and firm lemons

Adjust an oven rack one-third up from the bottom of the oven and preheat to 350°. You need a 9 x 4½-inch tube pan. It should have a 12-cup capacity. Butter the pan and then dust it all lightly with fine, dry bread crumbs. Set aside.

Sift together the flour, baking powder, and salt, and set aside. In the large bowl of an electric mixer, beat the butter until soft. Add the sugar and beat until incorporated. Beat in the eggs one at a time, scraping the bowl as necessary with a rubber spatula. (The mixture might look curdled—it's okay.) On lowest speed add the dry ingredients alternately in three additions with the milk in two additions, beating only until incorporated after each addition. Remove the bowl from the mixer and stir in the lemon rind. Turn the batter into the prepared pan. Level the top of the batter by rotating the pan briskly from left to right and from right to left. Bake for 1 hour and 5 to 10 minutes until a cake tester comes out clean. Let the cake stand in the pan for 5 minutes and then cover with a rack and invert. Remove the pan, leaving the cake upside down. Place over a large piece of foil or wax paper and prepare the glaze.

GLAZE

⅓ cup lemon juice

⅔ cup sugar

The glaze should be used immediately after it is mixed.

Mix the lemon juice and sugar and brush it all over the hot cake. The cake will absorb it.

Let cool completely and then transfer to a cake plate.

It is best to wait a few hours before cutting the cake.

P.S. I have a key lime tree. I have made this cake with ½ cup key lime juice instead of ⅓ cup lemon juice (in the glaze) and it is wonderful. I think any kind of lime juice would be equally wonderful. But even if you use lime juice instead of lemon juice, don't change the grated rind in the cake itself (lemon is better there).

THE BEST DAMN LEMON CAKE

8 TO 10 PORTIONS

I once served this to friends who have eaten their way through all of my books. The first thing they said became the name. And then they added, "This is my favorite of all. . . . If someone went into business making and selling this they would get very rich." You will need lemon extract as well as fresh lemons. The surprise in the recipe is that it contains ground almonds. This is better when it is not too fresh—it is still wonderful after several days.

½ cup blanched almonds

1½ cups sifted all-purpose flour

1 teaspoon baking powder

¾ teaspoon salt

¼ pound (1 stick) unsalted butter

1 cup granulated sugar

2 eggs

½ cup milk

one 1-ounce bottle lemon extract

Finely grated rind of 2 extra-large or 3 medium-size lemons (juice will be used for the Glaze)

Adjust a rack one-third up from the bottom of the oven and preheat the oven to 350°. Butter an 8½ x 4½ x 2¾-inch loaf pan with a 6-cup capacity (see Note). Dust it all with fine, dry bread crumbs, invert over a piece of paper, and tap firmly to shake out excess. Set the pan aside.

The almonds must be ground very fine. It can be done in a food processor (see To Grind Nuts in a Food Processor, page 13) or a nut grinder. Then set them aside.

Sift together the flour, baking powder, and salt, and set aside.

In a small, heavy saucepan over low heat, melt the butter.

Transfer it to the large bowl of an electric mixer. Add the sugar and beat a bit to mix. On low speed, beat in the eggs one at a time, beating only to mix well. Then, still on low speed, add the sifted dry ingredients in three additions alternating with the milk in two additions, scraping the bowl with a rubber spatula and beating until mixed after each addition. Mix in the lemon extract.

Remove from the mixer. Stir in the grated rind and then the ground almonds.

It will be a rather thin mixture. Turn it into the prepared pan.

Bake for 65 to 75 minutes, until a cake tester carefully inserted into the center of the cake, all the way to the bottom, comes out just barely clean and dry. (If the pan is long and narrow, the cake will bake in less time than if it is short and wide. During baking, the cake will form a large crack or two on the top; the crack, or cracks, will remain light in color—it is okay.)

Two or 3 minutes before the cake is done, prepare the glaze.

GLAZE

⅓ cup plus 2 tablespoons granulated sugar

⅓ cup fresh lemon juice

NOTE: For this cake, do not use a nonstick pan, a black metal pan, or a glass pan; it should be aluminum, preferably heavy weight. And do not double the recipe and bake it in one larger pan, it is not as good—it is better to make two or more cakes in the specified 6-cup loaf pan.

Stir the sugar and juice in a small, heavy saucepan over moderate heat only until the sugar is dissolved; do not boil the mixture.

When the cake is removed from the oven, let it stand for 2 to 3 minutes. Then, with a brush, brush the hot glaze very gradually over the hot cake; the glaze should not be applied quickly—it should take about 5 minutes to apply it all.

Let stand until tepid, not quite completely cool. Then, gently invert the cake onto a rack. (If the cake sticks in the pan, cover it loosely with foil or wax paper, turn it upside down onto your right hand, tap the bottom of the pan with your left hand, and the cake will slide out.) Turn the cake right side up.

When the cake is completely cool, wrap it in plastic wrap or foil and let stand for 12 to 24 hours before serving. Or place it in the freezer for about 2 hours, or in the refrigerator for about 4 hours, before serving.

LEMON BUTTERMILK CAKE #2

12 TO 15 PORTIONS

Shortly after my first dessert book was published, I received several calls and letters from people who said there was something wrong with the Lemon Buttermilk Cake.

I said it couldn't be. I had made the cake many times. I had taught it. My daughter made it often.

I compared the recipe in the book with my original copy and they looked the same (with a minor change in wording). Then I made the cake from the book and there was indeed something wrong. The cake sank and was like a wet pudding. I tried everything I could think of, but I simply could not correct it. In desperation I had to delete the recipe from later editions of the book. (I wanted to ask my publisher to recall all of the books. I wanted to say, "General Motors does it, why can't we?")

We live about two miles from where Isaac Bashevis Singer lived. When Mr. Singer won the Nobel Prize for literature I heard him speak on television. He explained that his biggest problems in writing were caused by demons, who, he said, frequented the Singer home and created disasters.

Then I knew what had happened to the Lemon Cake. Demons! Anyone who has spent much time baking knows that demons are never far away.

Recently I rewrote the recipe completely. It is #2. This works.

Finely grated rind of 2 or 3 large lemons (juice will be used below and for the Glaze)

3 tablespoons lemon juice

3 cups sifted all-purpose flour

½ teaspoon baking soda

½ teaspoon salt

½ pound (2 sticks) unsalted butter

2 cups granulated sugar

3 eggs

1 cup buttermilk

Adjust a rack one-third up from the bottom of the oven and preheat the oven to 350°. You will need a tube pan with a 10-cup capacity (that is generally 9 inches in diameter); it can be a pan with a design or a 9 x 3½-inch tube pan without a design. If you use a pan with a design, butter it (even if it is nonstick) and then dust it all over with fine, dry bread crumbs. If you use the plain 9 x 3½-inch tube pan, butter it, line the bottom with parchment or wax paper cut to fit, butter the paper, and dust all over with crumbs. With either pan, tap to shake out excess crumbs over a piece of paper. Set aside.

Place the lemon rind and juice in a small cup and set aside.

Sift together the flour, baking soda, and salt, and set aside.

In the large bowl of an electric mixer, beat the butter until it is slightly soft. Add the sugar and beat until well mixed. Add the eggs one at a time, beating well after each addition. On low speed add the sifted dry ingredients, alternating with the buttermilk in two additions, scraping the bowl with a rubber spatula, and beating only until smooth after each addition.

Remove from the mixer and stir in the lemon rind and juice.

Turn into the prepared pan and smooth the top.

Bake for 1 hour to 1 hour and 15 minutes, or until a cake tester gently inserted into the middle comes out clean and dry.

As soon as the cake is put in the oven, mix the glaze.

GLAZE

½ cup fresh lemon juice

⅓ cup granulated sugar

Mix the juice and sugar and let stand, stirring occasionally, while the cake is baking.

Remove the cake from the oven and let it stand in the pan for 5 minutes. Then cover it with a rack and very carefully turn over the pan and the rack and place it over a large piece of foil. Remove the pan. If you have used a paper lining, peel it off now.

With a pastry brush, brush the glaze all over the top, sides, and tube of the hot cake.

Let stand until completely cool.

BUTTERMILK LOAF CAKE
ONE 10-INCH LOAF

This is perfectly plain/beautiful/delicious, and is easy to make.

3 cups sifted
all-purpose flour

½ teaspoon
baking powder

½ teaspoon baking soda

¾ teaspoon salt

8 ounces (2 sticks)
unsalted butter

1½ teaspoons
vanilla extract

2 cups granulated sugar

4 eggs

1 cup buttermilk

Finely grated rind
of 2 or 3 lemons

Adjust a rack one-third up from the bottom of the oven and preheat the oven to 325°. Butter a 10 x 5 x 3-inch loaf pan, or any other loaf pan with a 10-cup capacity (or two smaller pans), dust all over with fine, dry bread crumbs, and tap to shake out excess crumbs over a piece of paper.

Sift together the flour, baking powder, baking soda, and salt, and set aside.

In the large bowl of an electric mixer, cream the butter. Beat in the vanilla. Add the sugar and beat only until well mixed, scraping the bowl as necessary with a rubber spatula. Add the eggs one at a time, beating only until incorporated after each addition. Beat for about 1 minute after the last addition. On low speed, alternately add the sifted dry ingredients in three additions with the buttermilk in two additions, scraping the bowl as necessary and beating only until incorporated after each addition.

Remove from the mixer and stir in the grated rind.

Turn the batter into the prepared pan and shake the pan a bit to level it.

Bake for 1 hour and 30 to 35 minutes (less time in smaller pans), until a cake tester gently inserted into the middle of the cake comes out clean. The top will be richly browned and only slightly mounded.

Let cool in the pan for 10 to 15 minutes. Cover with a rack and turn the pan and the rack over, remove the pan, cover with another rack and turn over again, leaving the cake right side up to cool.

This can be served either side up.

If you can wait, wrap and refrigerate the cooled cake at least overnight, or freeze it for about an hour before serving.

POPPY SEED CAKE

12 PORTIONS

"I left my heart in San Francisco . . ." When my husband and I were there on a tour for my chocolate book, the divine French pastry and chocolate specialty shop Chocolat baked an array of chocolate goodies for us that were magnifique! Sheila Linderman was the chef in charge of the affair. And to top it off, she gave me this nonchocolate recipe that she says is "my absolute favorite cake—number one on my list and everyone else's." It is a delicious plain cake that is like a cross between a sponge cake and a pound cake. It is baked in a tube pan and has no icing. The poppy seeds give an interesting appearance and a mild, nutty flavor and slightly crunchy texture. The cake lasts remarkably well.

2 cups *unsifted* all-purpose flour

1 teaspoon baking soda

½ teaspoon baking powder

8 ounces (2 sticks) unsalted butter

1½ cups granulated sugar

5 eggs, separated, plus 1 additional white

1 cup sour cream

¼ cup poppy seeds

1½ teaspoons vanilla extract

Pinch of salt

¼ teaspoon cream of tartar

Adjust a rack one-third up from the bottom of the oven and preheat the oven to 350°. You will need a plain (no design), loose-bottomed (bottom and tube in one piece, sides in a separate piece) tube pan (angel-food pan) with a 12-cup capacity that will be 10 inches in diameter and 4 inches in depth; it should be an aluminum pan—it must not have a nonstick finish. Do not butter or line the pan.

Sift together the flour, baking soda, and baking powder, and set aside.

In the large bowl of an electric mixer, cream the butter. Add 1¼ cups sugar to the butter, reserving the remaining ¼ cup of sugar, and beat well for several minutes until light and creamy. Add the yolks all at once and beat for 2 or 3 minutes, scraping the bowl as necessary with a rubber spatula.

In a small bowl stir the sour cream, poppy seeds, and vanilla together to mix.

On low speed beat about one-third of the dry ingredients into the butter mixture. Then add the sour-cream mixture, scraping the bowl as necessary with a rubber spatula and beating only until incorporated. Add the remaining dry ingredients and beat only until smooth. Remove from the mixer and set aside.

Place the egg whites in the small bowl of an electric mixer, add the salt, and, with clean beaters, beat until foamy. Add the cream of tartar and beat until the whites hold soft peaks when the beaters are raised. Gradually add the reserved ¼ cup of sugar and beat until the whites hold definite peaks but are not stiff or dry.

Fold one-quarter of the whites into the batter; do not be completely thorough at this stage. Fold in another quarter and then add the remaining whites and fold together only until blended.

Turn into the pan and rotate the pan briskly first in one direction, then the other, to level the batter.

Bake for 50 to 55 minutes, until a cake tester gently inserted into the cake comes out clean and dry. There will be a crack in the top of the cake—this is okay. The cake will not come to the top of the pan—also okay.

Remove from the oven and immediately turn the pan over and let the cake stand upside down in the pan until it is completely cool. To freeze the cake: It is best to freeze the cake before cutting it out of the pan. Wrap it all with aluminum foil and freeze.

To remove the cake from the pan: You will need a sharp knife with a firm blade (it must be firm) about 6 inches long. Insert the blade at one side of the pan between the cake and the pan, inserting the blade until its tip touches the bottom of the pan. Press the blade firmly against the pan in order not to cut into the sides of the cake. With short up-and-down motions saw all around the cake, continuing to press the blade against the pan. Then saw around the tube—if you have a knife with a narrow blade (such as a boning knife) use it to cut around the tube.

Remove the sides of the pan. Then carefully, again pressing the blade against the pan, cut the bottom of the cake away from the pan. Cover the cake with a flat cake plate and turn the cake and the plate over. Remove the bottom of the pan, leaving the cake upside down.

P.S. Johan Mathiesen, editor of Word of Mouth, *the fascinating food news letter, recently reprinted this recipe. And he said that it is "such an extraordinarily good basic cake that I like to think of it as just that: a basic cake of which poppy seed is a sterling variation."*

ORANGE CHIFFON CAKE
16 PORTIONS OR MORE

In 1927, Henry Baker, a 64-year-old California insurance salesman who liked to bake, invented a cake. It was as light as angel food and as rich as a butter cake. The recipe was a closely guarded secret for 20 years. Baker often made the cake for famous Hollywood restaurants and for celebrities, and both he and his cake became famous.

Eventually, Mr. Baker sold his secret to Betty Crocker. The details of the deal were kept as secret as the recipe had been, but Betty Crocker and General Mills wound up with the recipe and in 1948, when they introduced it to America as Chiffon Cake, it was hailed as "the cake discovery of the century." The mystery ingredient, new to cake-making, was vegetable oil.

It is a large cake that will make many portions. It keeps well. It may be baked a day before serving, or it may be served as soon as it is cool, or it may be frozen. It is easy to make.

2 cups sifted
all-purpose flour

1½ cups granulated sugar

3 teaspoons
baking powder

1 teaspoon salt

½ cup tasteless vegetable
oil (e.g., Mazola,
Wesson, or safflower)

7 eggs, separated

Finely grated rind
of 2 lemons

Finely grated rind of 3
deep-colored oranges

¾ cup orange juice
(see Notes)

½ teaspoon cream
of tartar

Optional:
Confectioners' sugar

Adjust a rack one-third up from the bottom of the oven and preheat the oven to 325°. You will need a 10 x 4-inch tube pan (angel-food cake pan). It must not be a nonstick pan. And it must be the kind that is made in two pieces, the bottom and tube in one piece and the sides in a separate piece. Do not butter the pan.

Into a large mixing bowl, sift together the flour, sugar, baking powder, and salt.

Make a wide well in the middle of the dry ingredients. Add in the following order, without mixing, the oil, egg yolks (reserve the whites), the lemon and orange rinds, and the orange juice. With a large or medium-size strong wire whisk, beat until smooth. Set aside.

In the large bowl of an electric mixer, beat the egg whites with the cream of tartar until they hold a stiff peak when the beaters are raised. For this recipe they must be stiffer than usual; when they hold a stiff (or firm) peak, beat for 1 minute more. That should make them just right; they should not be beaten until they are dry.

In three additions, fold about three-quarters of the yolk mixture into the whites. Then fold the whites into the remaining yolk mixture. Do not handle any more than necessary. (The yolk mixture is heavier; it will sink in the whites. To incorporate the two mixtures without additional folding, it may be necessary to gently pour the mixture from one bowl to another once or twice.)

Gently pour the batter into the cake pan.

NOTES: *Do not decide to use lemon juice in place of the orange juice. When I tried it several times, some kind of a chemical reaction took place and the cakes fell.*

Many angel-food cake pans have little feet to raise the inverted pan, but often they do not raise the cake enough and it is necessary to hang the cake on a funnel or the neck of a bottle. But there are some new pans now that have a raised extension on the center tube, and that usually does raise the cake enough, so it is not necessary to use the funnel or bottle. The cake should be at least 1 inch above the counter.

Bake for 55 minutes at 325°. Then increase the temperature to 350° and bake for an additional 10 or 15 minutes, until the top springs back when it is lightly pressed with a fingertip.

Immediately hang the pan upside down over the point of a funnel or over the neck of a narrow bottle (see Notes). Let the cake hang in the pan until it is completely cool. To freeze the cake: It is best to freeze it before cutting it out of the pan. Wrap in aluminum foil and freeze.

To remove the cake from the pan: You will need a sharp knife with a firm blade (it must be firm) about 6 inches long. Insert the blade at one side of the pan between the cake and the pan, inserting the blade all the way down to the bottom of the pan and pressing it firmly against the side of the pan in order not to cut into the cake. With short up-and-down motions, saw all around the cake, continuing to press the blade against the pan. Then cut around the tube (I use a knife with a very narrow blade for cutting around the tube; a wider blade will cut into the cake slightly).

Remove the sides of the pan. Then carefully, again pressing the blade against the pan, cut the bottom of the cake away from the pan.

Cover the cake with a flat cake plate and turn the cake and the plate over. Remove the bottom of the pan and leave the cake upside down.

Sprinkle with the optional confectioners' sugar, sprinkling it through a strainer; make it a generous coating.

CHOCOLATE WHIPPED CREAM

This cream is frequently served with the Orange Chiffon Cake; however, it is optional.

2 cups heavy cream

1 cup strained confectioners' sugar

½ cup unsweetened cocoa powder (preferably Dutch process)

Pinch of salt

½ teaspoon vanilla extract

In a chilled bowl with chilled beaters, whip all the ingredients together until the cream is stiff enough to hold a shape. Spread it all over the cake shortly before serving. Or serve it separately as a sauce, and spoon it over each portion.

A beautiful presentation is made by covering the cake with the chocolate whipped cream and surrounding it all with a generous ring of huge fresh strawberries, unhulled. It is a picture!

Sand Torte

12 PORTIONS

Don't let the name scare you. This is a plain, firm, fine-grained, dense, and compact pound cake. The texture is a little sandy, but deliciously so.

Sand Torte is an old classic cake that is extremely popular in many European countries. I was told about an enterprising young taxi driver in Denmark who displayed the sign "Sandkage" in the rear of his cab—his wife baked them and he sold as many as she could produce to the people who rode in his cab.

Serve this with coffee, tea, or wine; or with ice cream, fruit, or custard.

You will need a tube pan with an 8- to 10-cup capacity. It really should be one with a fancy design (although this can be made in a pan without a design). I have been making it lately in a black iron Bundt pan available at many kitchen shops.

It is best to make this a day before serving; it should stand for 24 hours, preferably in the refrigerator, before it is sliced.

Finely grated rind
of 1 large lemon

2 tablespoons lemon juice

1 cup sifted
all-purpose flour

1 cup unsifted cornstarch

1¾ teaspoons
baking powder

8 ounces (2 sticks)
unsalted butter

1 cup granulated sugar

6 eggs, separated

¼ teaspoon salt

Optional: Confectioners'
sugar (to be sprinkled
over the cake)

Adjust a rack one-third up in the oven. Preheat the oven to 350°. Butter an 8- to 10-cup-capacity tube pan with a fancy design. The best way is to use soft (but not melted) butter and a pastry brush, brushing in all directions to be sure the pan is thoroughly coated. Then dust with fine, dry bread crumbs. Tap over paper to shake out excess.

Mix the lemon rind and juice and set aside.

Sift together the flour, cornstarch, and baking powder, and set aside.

In the large bowl of an electric mixer, beat the butter until it is soft. Add ¾ cup of the sugar, reserving the remaining ¼ cup, and beat for at least 2 or 3 minutes. Then add the egg yolks (all at once is okay) and beat at high speed for at least 5 minutes, scraping the bowl as necessary with a rubber spatula. The mixture should be beaten until it is very pale, silky smooth, and almost liquid.

On low speed add about half of the sifted dry ingredients and beat only to mix. Remove from the mixer.

Add the rind and juice mixture and stir until incorporated. Then add the remaining sifted dry ingredients and stir with a rubber spatula until the mixture is perfectly smooth.

You will need the large mixer bowl again now for beating the whites. If you do not have an additional large bowl for your mixer, transfer the egg-yolk mixture to any other large mixing bowl.

The bowl and beaters must be absolutely clean and grease-free. Add the salt to the egg whites and beat until they hold a soft shape. Reduce the speed to moderate and gradually add the reserved ¼ cup of sugar. Then increase the speed again and beat only until the whites hold a definite shape but are not stiff and dry.

Add about one-quarter of the beaten whites to the yolk mixture and stir it in. Then add another quarter and fold it in—do not fold completely until the end. Then fold in another quarter. Finally, fold in the remainder, handling lightly and as little as possible to blend the mixtures.

Turn the batter into the prepared pan and smooth the top.

Bake for 45 to 55 minutes (the timing will vary with different pans), until the top is richly colored and springs back when lightly pressed with a fingertip and a cake tester gently inserted into the middle of the cake comes out clean and dry. Do not overbake or the cake will become dry and crumbly.

Remove the pan from the oven but do not remove the cake from the pan until it has cooled to room temperature. Then cover the pan with a plate, turn the pan and the plate over, remove the pan, and leave the cake upside down.

Refrigerate the cake until it is firm enough to handle. Then wrap it in plastic or in a plastic bag and refrigerate overnight. Before serving, the top may be covered with confectioners' sugar sprinkled through a fine strainer held over the cake.

Cut into thin slices, two or three to a portion.

ENGLISH MADEIRA CAKE
1 SMALL LOAF

This is an old English recipe for a cake that does not contain Madeira; it has this name because it was for many years, and still is, served with Madeira—or with sherry. It is a plain, plain loaf, with an especially fine texture and an extra-light, tender, delicate, marvelous pound cake. It keeps well. It slices beautifully. It makes a very nice gift and/or it is great to have on hand as a coffee or tea cake. And it is easy to make.

2 cups sifted
all-purpose flour

2 teaspoons
baking powder

¼ teaspoon salt

6 ounces (1½ sticks)
unsalted butter

1 teaspoon vanilla extract

¾ cup granulated sugar

3 eggs

½ cup milk

Finely grated rind of 1
large or 2 small lemons

Adjust a rack to the center of the oven (if you bake this lower, the top will be too pale). Preheat the oven to 350°. You will need a loaf pan with at least a 4-cup capacity; that could be 8 x 4 x 2½ inches. It is possible to bake this in a larger pan, but if you do, the cake will not be as high and as beautiful. Butter the pan and dust it all over with fine, dry bread crumbs. (I use bought bread crumbs and because this is such a fine-grained cake, I grind the crumbs a bit more in the processor—just enough to make them slightly finer but not long enough to grind them to a powder.) Then turn the pan upside down over a piece of paper and tap lightly to shake out excess.

Sift together the flour, baking powder, and salt, and set aside.

In the small bowl of an electric mixer (it must be the small bowl; in a large bowl the beaters will not reach enough of the mixture) beat the butter briefly until it is soft. Add the vanilla and granulated sugar and beat at high speed for 5 minutes until the mixture is pale and soft. Scrape the sides occasionally with a rubber spatula. Add the eggs one at a time, beating until each addition is incorporated. Then beat again at high speed for 5 minutes more until the mixture is a very pale cream color and almost liquid.

Transfer to the large bowl of the electric mixer. On low speed, add the sifted dry ingredients in three additions alternately with the milk in two additions. Remove from the mixer, stir in the grated rind, and turn into the prepared pan. Smooth the top. The batter will be only about half an inch below the top—it's okay.

Bake for 1 hour and 10 minutes, or until a cake tester gently inserted into the middle of the cake comes out clean and dry. If you have baked it in a larger pan, the cake will be shallower and will therefore bake in less time. (In a 10-inch loaf pan it bakes in 45 minutes.)

NOTE: *This will rise in the
middle and form a crack in the
center; the crack will be paler
than the rest of the cake. That
is as it should be.*

Let the cake cool in the pan on a rack for 20 to 25 minutes. Then gently
turn it out onto a rack. And, with your hands, gently turn it right side up.
Let stand to cool. It is best to wrap the cooled cake and refrigerate it for a
few hours or overnight before serving.

MIAMI BEACH SOUR CREAM CAKE

12 TO 16 PORTIONS

*This is an outstanding "plain" cake, one of the very best I've ever eaten. It has a gorgeous golden, honey-colored almond
crust, a mild almond and lemon buttery flavor, and a fine-grained sensational texture that is truly magical.*

About ⅔ cup
blanched almonds (to
prepare the pan)

3 cups twice-sifted cake
flour (see Notes)

¼ teaspoon baking soda

¼ teaspoon salt

3½ ounces (⅓ cup) almond
paste or marzipan

8 ounces (2 sticks)
unsalted butter

½ teaspoon almond extract

2⅓ cups granulated sugar

6 eggs, separated

1 cup sour cream

Finely grated rind of
1 large lemon

Adjust a rack one-third up from the bottom of the oven and preheat the
oven to 300°. Butter a 10 x 4 or 4½-inch tube pan (that is, a straight-sided
pan, like an angel-food pan, with a 16-cup capacity); butter the pan even
if it has a nonstick finish. Grind the almonds in a food processor by turning the machine on/off quickly a few times, and then letting it run for
about 30 seconds until most of the nuts are rather fine, with a few still in
small pieces. Or grind the nuts in any nut grinder. They do not have to be
completely powdered.

Turn the ground nuts into the buttered pan. Hold the pan over paper and
rotate the pan so that the nuts coat the entire buttered surface. To make
the nuts stick to the center tube you must pick them up with your fingers
and sprinkle them onto the tube. Loose nuts that do not stick to the pan
may just be sprinkled onto the bottom of the pan. Set the pan aside.

Sift the flour twice more with the baking soda and salt (see Notes) and
set aside.

In the large bowl of an electric mixer, beat the almond paste or marzipan
with the butter until soft and smooth. Beat in the almond extract. Then
add the sugar and beat until thoroughly mixed. Add the yolks and beat,
scraping the bowl with a rubber spatula, until thoroughly mixed.

On low speed beat in ½ cup of the sour cream, then half of the sifted dry
ingredients, the remaining ½ cup of sour cream, and the remaining dry
ingredients, scraping the bowl and beating only until mixed.

Remove the bowl from the mixer and stir in the grated lemon rind.

In a small bowl (with clean beaters), beat the egg whites until they hold a definite shape when the beaters are raised, but not until the whites are stiff or dry. (Since these whites are not beaten with any sugar added to them—which would help to keep them creamy [see Notes]—it is especially important not to overbeat them or they will be too dry to fold in properly.)

With a large rubber spatula, stir in a few tablespoons of the whites into the batter and then, in about three additions, fold in the remaining whites, without being thorough about the folding until the end.

Turn the mixture into the prepared pan.

To level the top, briskly rotate the pan a bit first in one direction, then the other. The pan will be only half filled—it is okay.

Bake for 1½ hours. During baking the cake will rise to ½ inch or 1 inch below the top of the pan. When the cake is done, a cake tester inserted gently into the cake will come out clean and the top will spring back if it is pressed gently with a fingertip. (There will be a shallow crack around the circumference—it is all right.)

Remove from the oven and let stand for 20 minutes, during which time the cake will sink down about an inch—that's okay, too.

Cover with a rack, turn the pan and rack over, remove the pan, cover with another rack, and turn over again, leaving the cake right side up to cool completely.

Transfer the cooled cake to a cake plate. You could sprinkle confectioners' sugar on the top, but I think that this is too good to need or want anything at all.

VARIATION: *The wife of the mayor of Miami Beach asked me if I would create a cake specifically for Miami Beach. That was a great challenge, because people who live here in Miami Beach know a good cake when they taste one, and they expect the best.*

I had just been working on the recipe for Miami Beach Sour Cream Cake. I thought of all the people I know here, and I came to the conclusion that they would approve. But to make it especially appropriate, I changed it slightly to an orange cake.

Miami Beach Orange Cake

Follow the recipe on page 32 with these additions.

Grate the rind of 1 large or 2 medium-size deep-colored oranges finely. Stir the rind into the cake mixture along with the grated lemon rind; that is, just before you beat the egg whites.

While the cake is baking, prepare this Orange Glaze.

Orange Glaze

¾ cup orange juice

¼ cup granulated sugar

In a small saucepan, mix about ¼ cup of the juice with the sugar and stir over moderate heat until the sugar is dissolved. Add the warm mixture to the remaining ½ cup of juice.

When you remove the cake from the oven, let it stand for about 5 minutes. Then slowly spoon the glaze over the cake. After the glaze is all applied, let the cake stand for 15 to 20 minutes. Then cover with a large flat cake pan and carefully turn the plate and the pan over. Remove the pan, leaving the cake upside down. Do not try to move the cake; it is too moist.

OLD-FASHIONED COCONUT CAKE

12 PORTIONS

This is a pretty little black and white coconut cake; the shallow top part of the cake is dark chocolate, and you will wish for more of it.

You will need a fancy tube pan with a 10- to 12-cup capacity; the cake looks lovely in the 12-cup swirl tube pan (see page 10).

1¼ cups sifted all-purpose flour

1¼ cups sifted cake flour

1 teaspoon baking powder

¼ teaspoon salt

8 ounces (2 sticks) unsalted butter

1 tablespoon vanilla extract

1 teaspoon coconut extract

¼ teaspoon almond extract

one 1-pound box (3¼ cups, packed) confectioners' sugar (it can be unsifted)

4 eggs

1 cup whipping cream

2 tablespoons unsweetened cocoa powder (preferably Dutch-process)

3½ ounces (1 cup, firmly packed) shredded coconut (it can be sweetened or unsweetened)

Adjust a rack one-third up from the bottom of the oven and preheat the oven to 350°. Butter a 10- to 12-cup fancy tube pan (even if it has a nonstick finish), dust the pan all over with fine, dry bread crumbs (use your fingers to crumb the tube), tilt the pan from side to side over paper, and then invert it and tap out excess crumbs. Set aside.

Sift together both of the flours with the baking powder and salt, and set aside.

In the large bowl of an electric mixer, beat the butter to soften. Add the vanilla, coconut, and almond extracts and the sugar and beat to mix, scraping the bowl as necessary with a rubber spatula. Add the eggs one at a time, beating well after each addition. On low speed add the sifted dry ingredients in three additions alternately with the whipping cream in two additions.

Remove the bowl from the mixer. Transfer 1 cup of the batter to a small bowl. Add the cocoa to the small bowl and stir well to mix. Add the coconut to the remaining batter and stir to mix.

Place tablespoons of the chocolate mixture just touching one another in the bottom of the pan. Do not spread to smooth. Then pour in the coconut mixture. Smooth the top. The cake wants to rise high in the middle, around the tube, and will be served upside down; therefore use the bottom of a large spoon to spread the dough out toward the rim of the pan, making it higher around the rim and lower around the tube. (This will not make the top flat as you might like, but it will help a bit.)

Bake for 1 hour and about 25 minutes. Then cover the pan with a rack, turn the pan and the rack over, and remove the pan—unless the pan does not want to be removed, in which case simply bang the pan and the rack together against a hard surface until the cake drops out.

Let the cake stand until it is completely cool and then for several hours more before serving.

Key West Rum Cake

10 to 12 portions

This is from the southern tip of Florida, where it is called Pirate's Cake. It is similar to a pound cake, but the top is dark, semisweet, candylike chocolate and the bottom, which is light colored, is flavored with almond and loaded with pecans. The entire cake is drenched with a powerful rum syrup. The combination of flavors is sensational, and when you cut into the cake you will be surprised and delighted to see what the chocolate mixture did. Also, it keeps well. (We took one of these, just wrapped in plastic, on a car trip from Florida to New York during a heat wave. Four days after we left home we brought it to a luncheon at a friend's house. It was divine.) This is an old recipe that many old-time local cooks treasure as a secret.

You will need a tube pan with a 13- or 14-cup capacity; it is gorgeous.

2 cups sifted
all-purpose flour

2 teaspoons baking powder

¼ teaspoon salt

2 ounces semisweet
chocolate

1 ounce unsweetened
chocolate

8 ounces (2 sticks)
unsalted butter

1 teaspoon vanilla extract

½ teaspoon almond extract

1½ cups granulated sugar

4 eggs

¼ teaspoon baking soda

7 ounces (2 cups) toasted
pecans (see To Toast
Pecans, page 6   ), broken
into medium-size pieces

Adjust a rack one-third up from the bottom of the oven and preheat the oven to 325°. Butter a tube pan with a 13- to 14-cup capacity and dust all over with fine, dry bread crumbs (use your fingers to crumb the tube); invert the pan over paper and tap lightly to shake out excess crumbs. Set aside.

Sift together the flour, baking powder, and salt, and set aside.

Place both of the chocolates in the top of a small double boiler over warm water on moderate heat. Cover the pot with a folded paper towel (to absorb the steam) and with the pot cover. Let stand over the heat until the chocolate is almost all melted, then stir until completely melted. Remove the top of the double boiler and set aside.

In the large bowl of an electric mixer, beat the butter until soft. Beat in the vanilla and almond extracts and then the sugar. Add the eggs one at a time, beating until thoroughly incorporated after each addition. Then, on low speed, gradually add the sifted dry ingredients, scraping the bowl as necessary with a rubber spatula and beating only until incorporated.

With your finger, scrape the beaters and then replace them, unwashed, in the mixer. Remove the bowl from the mixer. Remove 1 cup of the batter and place it in the small bowl of the mixer. Add the baking soda and the melted chocolate and beat until mixed.

Use a teaspoon (a regular teaspoon—not a measuring spoon) to place the chocolate batter in the bottom of the pan. With the bottom of the spoon, spread it to make a rather smooth layer.

Now mix the pecans into the remaining cake batter and place it, with a teaspoon or a tablespoon, evenly over the chocolate layer. Smooth the top.

Bake for 1 hour, until a cake tester inserted gently into the middle of the cake comes out clean.

While the cake is baking, prepare the syrup.

Rum Syrup

½ cup water

⅔ cup granulated sugar

⅔ cup light rum (I use Bacardi Silver Label)

1 tablespoon lime juice

Stir the water and sugar in a small saucepan over moderate heat until the mixture comes to a boil. Let boil without stirring for 5 minutes. Remove from the heat and let stand until almost completely cool. Then stir in the rum and lime juice.

When the cake is done, do not remove it from the pan. Spoon or brush the syrup over the hot cake until it all is absorbed.

Then, while the cake is still hot, place a flat cake plate over the pan and, holding the plate and pan firmly together, turn them over. Now, remove the pan and let the cake cool.

Do not try to cut the slices too thin—they will crumble.

Jelly Roll
6 to 8 portions

This little fat-bellied jelly roll is quick, easy, simple, plain, homey, old-fashioned, and very, very good. Serve a slice with tea or coffee. Or the jelly roll can be the beginning of many fancy desserts, e.g., serve a slice on each plate with a generous pile of fresh strawberries or raspberries mounded on top with soft whipped cream over it all. Or jelly roll, ice cream, and chocolate sauce. Et cetera.

The cake itself is soft enough to roll easily without cracking, and yet it is firm enough to hold up and be delicious.

Adjust a rack to the center of the oven and preheat the oven to 400°. Prepare a 15½ x 10½ x 1-inch jelly-roll pan as follows. Invert the pan, cover it with a piece of foil shiny side down several inches longer than the pan, fold down the sides and the corners of the foil to shape it, then remove the foil, turn the pan right side up, and place the shaped foil in

4 eggs, at room
temperature

¾ teaspoon baking
powder

½ teaspoon salt

¾ cup granulated sugar

1 teaspoon vanilla extract

¾ cup sifted cake flour
(do not substitute
all-purpose flour)

Generous ¾ cup firm, tart
jelly (currant is good)

Additional granulated
sugar for sprinkling
on the cake

the pan. Press it into place. Place some butter in the pan (for buttering the foil), place it in the oven just until the butter is melted, and then brush or spread the butter all over the foil. Set aside.

Place the eggs, baking powder, and salt in the small bowl of an electric mixer. Beat at high speed for about 3 minutes until very fluffy. Reduce the speed slightly and gradually add the ¾ cup granulated sugar. Increase the speed to high again and beat for 10 to 12 minutes more (total beating time is 13 to 15 minutes), until the mixture is quite thick and falls in a wide and heavy ribbon when the beaters are raised.

Transfer to the large bowl of the mixer. Beat in the vanilla. Then sift the flour over the batter (sift it even though you sifted it before measuring it) and beat on low speed, scraping the bowl with a rubber spatula only until incorporated—do not overbeat.

Instead of dumping the whole mixture into the middle of the prepared pan, it is better to pour it in a thick ribbon down the length of one side of the pan and then the other side. Then with a rubber spatula spread the mixture to make it even—do not handle any more than necessary.

Bake for 13 minutes, until the top springs back when pressed lightly with a fingertip and the foil begins to come away from the sides of the pan.

While the cake is baking, place the jelly in a small bowl and stir it well with a fork or a wire whisk just to soften it. Have ready a few spoonfuls of granulated sugar, a smooth cotton towel, and a flat cookie sheet.

As soon as the cake is done, sprinkle the top with granulated sugar, cover the cake with a smooth cotton towel (a tea towel), and cover the towel with a flat cookie sheet. Invert the cake pan and the cookie sheet. Remove the cake pan. Peel off the foil (it will come off beautifully without sticking). Pour the jelly over the cake and spread it with a rubber spatula to make a thin layer; cover all but about half an inch at one narrow end.

Roll the cake from the narrow end opposite the one where the jelly stops short. Use the towel to help start the roll. Roll tightly but gently.

Transfer the cake, seam down, to a flat platter or a board.

Serve at room temperature or refrigerated. Serve two or three thin slices, overlapping, for each portion.

WALNUT CAKE

12 PORTIONS

This fabulous "plain" cake has a luxurious flavor and an irresistible, crunchy, and nutty crust. The pan is coated with butter and ground nuts which, with long, slow baking, become deliciously crusty. The cake is loaded with ground nuts, which keep it moist and rich. It is wonderful for any occasion, or make it as a delicious gift for someone very special.

It is easiest to prepare the nuts in a food processor.

9 ounces (2½ cups) walnuts

2 cups sifted all-purpose flour

1 teaspoon baking powder

½ teaspoon salt

½ teaspoon mace or nutmeg

8 ounces (2 sticks) unsalted butter

1 teaspoon vanilla extract

¼ teaspoon almond extract

1 tablespoon plus 2 teaspoons brandy

2 cups granulated sugar

5 eggs

Adjust a rack one-third up from the bottom of the oven and preheat the oven to 325°. You will need a tube pan that has at least a 9-cup capacity—I have used one with a swirl pattern (see page 10) and also a Bundt pan (this can be made in a slightly larger pan and still look nice). Butter the pan well, even if it has a nonstick finish; it must be heavily buttered (best done with soft butter—not cold and firm, and not melted). Set aside for a moment.

Place 1 cup of the nuts (reserve the remaining 1½ cups of nuts) in the bowl of a food processor fitted with the metal chopping blade. Process on/off quickly 8 to 10 times, or for 8 to 10 seconds. Some of the nuts will be ground, some will remain in small pieces—that is okay.

Turn the nuts into the buttered pan (do not wash the processor now). Over a piece of paper, tilt the pan in all directions to coat it generously with the nuts. The only way to get the nuts onto the center tube is to sprinkle them on, with your fingertips. Then, over the paper, invert the pan for a moment—do not tap the pan—to allow a spoonful or two of the loose nuts to fall onto the paper. If more than that should fall out of the pan pick up the excess with your fingertips and sprinkle them back over the bottom of the pan. Set the pan aside. (Reserve the spoonful or 2 of ground nuts to sprinkle over the top of the cake when it is in the pan.)

Place the remaining 1½ cups of the nuts in the processor bowl and process on/off 5 or 6 times (5 or 6 seconds). The nuts should have a few slightly larger pieces than those that were used for coating the pan. Set the nuts aside.

Sift together the flour, baking powder, salt, and mace or nutmeg. Set aside.

In the large bowl of an electric mixer, beat the butter until soft. Beat in the vanilla and almond extracts and the brandy.

Add the sugar and beat for about a minute. (Occasionally, when someone has trouble with a recipe like this, which is similar to a classic pound cake, we have found that the trouble was caused by overbeating. Do not beat until the sugar liquefies.)

Then add the eggs one at a time, scraping the bowl with a rubber spatula as necessary and beating until incorporated after each addition. Beat for about a minute after the last addition. On low speed, gradually add the sifted dry ingredients and beat only until smoothly incorporated.

Remove the bowl from the mixer and stir in the reserved 10 cups of ground nuts.

Turn the batter into the prepared pan and smooth the top. With your fingertips sprinkle the reserved 1 or 2 spoonfuls of ground nuts over the top of the cake.

Bake for about 1 hour and 45 minutes, until a cake tester inserted gently in the middle of the cake comes out clean. The top of the cake forms a crack during baking—it is okay.

Let the cake stand in the pan for 20 to 30 minutes. Then cover it with a cake plate. Hold the pan and plate firmly together and turn them over, then lift off the pan; if it does not slip right off, bang both the pan and the plate together against the countertop—but be gentle.

Let the cake stand until cool. Then chill it in the freezer or refrigerator before slicing. After the cake has been chilled it can wait at room temperature, can be stored in the refrigerator, or can be frozen.

When this is cold, it slices beautifully with any really sharp knife, but if it is to be sliced at room temperature, use a serrated bread knife.

WALNUT RUM-RAISIN CAKE

12 PORTIONS

The early New England sailors were given a ration of rum every day, a custom carried over to the New World from England. Rum was a popular drink as well as a popular ingredient in baking and dessert making.

This pretty cake, made in a tube pan, is loaded with rum-soaked raisins, and then generously basted with a tropical rum sauce. It is moist, keeps well, is easy to make, and is especially delicious. Soak the raisins at least overnight before making the cake.

5 ounces (1 cup) light
or dark raisins or a
mixture of both

⅓ cup dark rum
(I use Myers's, from
Kingston, Jamaica)

8½ ounces (2¼ cups)
walnuts (see Note)

2½ cups sifted
all-purpose flour

2 teaspoons
baking powder

1 teaspoon baking soda

¼ teaspoon salt

¼ teaspoon nutmeg

8 ounces (2 sticks)
unsalted butter

1 teaspoon vanilla extract

1 cup granulated sugar

2 eggs

1 cup buttermilk

Finely grated rind
of 2 lemons

Finely grated rind
of 2 oranges

Optional:
Confectioners' sugar

Soak the raisins with the rum in a covered jar overnight, turning the jar occasionally (if the jar might leak, place it in a small bowl). Adjust a rack one-third up from the bottom of the oven and preheat the oven to 350°. Butter a fancy tube pan (even if it is a nonstick pan) that has at least a 9-cup capacity.

Place ¾ cup of the walnuts (reserving the remaining 1½ cups of walnuts) in the bowl of the food processor fitted with the metal chopping blade and process on/off 10 to 12 times (10 to 12 seconds) until the nuts are chopped medium-fine. Or chop them any other way. To coat the pan, place the chopped nuts into the buttered pan and turn the pan from side to side to cover it all with the nuts. Sprinkle the nuts with your fingers onto the tube of the pan. Excess or loose nuts may remain in the bottom of the pan. Set aside.

Place the remaining 1½ cups of walnuts in the food processor bowl and process on/off 6 to 8 times (6 to 8 seconds) until the nuts are chopped into medium-size pieces. Or chop them any other way. Set aside.

Sift together the flour, baking powder, baking soda, salt, and nutmeg. Set aside.

In the large bowl of an electric mixer beat the butter until it is soft. Add the vanilla and sugar and beat to mix. Then beat in the eggs. On low speed add the sifted dry ingredients in three additions alternately with the buttermilk in two additions.

Remove the bowl from the mixer and stir in the lemon rind, orange rind, and the rum-soaked raisins, along with any rum that has not been absorbed. Stir the reserved nuts into the batter.

Turn into the prepared pan and smooth the top.

Bake for 55 to 60 minutes, until a cake tester inserted gently in the middle comes out clean. Let the cake stand in the pan for about 10 minutes. Meanwhile, prepare the Rum Sauce.

RUM SAUCE

½ cup granulated sugar

¼ cup water

¼ cup orange juice

3 tablespoons lemon or lime juice

¼ cup dark rum

NOTE: *After this recipe was printed in* The New York Times *I received a lovely letter from a lady whose husband is allergic to walnuts. She substituted almonds and said, "I can't believe it would taste better with the walnuts! It's a wonderful cake—and perfect for the holidays."*

In a small saucepan over moderate heat, stir the sugar and water until the mixture comes to a boil. Let boil without stirring for 2 minutes. Remove from the heat. Cool for a few minutes. Stir in the orange and lemon or lime juices, and then the rum.

Now, to remove the cake from the pan, cover it with a cake plate. Holding the cake plate and the pan firmly together, turn them over and remove the cake pan.

With a wide pastry brush, brush the warm sauce all over the warm cake; the cake will easily absorb all the sauce. Let cool.

If you wish, sprinkle confectioners' sugar through a fine strainer over the top before serving.

MARBLEIZED SPICE CAKE

12 TO 16 PORTIONS

Marble cakes intrigue me, visually as well as otherwise. This is one of the most visually stunning—and delicious. It is a spice cake. You will make two batters: a dark one with molasses, yogurt, cocoa, and spices, and a light one with vanilla and almond.

DARK BATTER

This recipe is adapted from one in Just Desserts *by Helen McCully (Ivan Obolensky, Inc., 1961).*

2 cups sifted cake flour

1 teaspoon baking soda

1 teaspoon cinnamon

½ teaspoon nutmeg

½ teaspoon
ground ginger

¼ teaspoon salt

1 tablespoon
unsweetened cocoa
powder (preferably
Dutch-process)

1 teaspoon powdered
(not granular) instant
coffee or espresso

4 ounces (1 stick)
unsalted butter

1 cup dark brown
sugar, firmly packed

4 egg yolks (you will
use the whites in
the light batter)

½ cup dark molasses

1 cup unflavored yogurt
(I use Dannon)

Adjust a rack one-third up from the bottom of the oven and preheat the oven to 350°. You need a tube pan with a 14 cup capacity; the new cake pan that I mention measures 9½ inches in diameter and 3¾ inches in depth and has a wider tube in the middle than most tube pans. Butter the pan and then dust it all over with fine, dry bread crumbs; to coat the center tube with crumbs, it is necessary to sprinkle them on with your fingertips. Invert the pan over paper and tap to shake out excess. Set the pan aside.

Sift together the flour, baking soda, cinnamon, nutmeg, ginger, salt, cocoa, and coffee or espresso, and set aside. In the large bowl of an electric mixer, beat the butter until soft, add the sugar, and beat to mix; then add the yolks all at once with the molasses. Beat until smooth and slightly lighter in color. On low speed add the sifted dry ingredients in three additions alternately with the yogurt in two additions. Beat, scraping the bowl with a rubber spatula as necessary, until the ingredients are smooth. Set aside, or if you do not have another large bowl for the mixer and another set of beaters, transfer the mixture to any other bowl and then set aside.

LIGHT BATTER

2½ cups sifted cake flour

2 teaspoons
baking powder

¼ teaspoon salt

4 ounces (1 stick)
unsalted butter

1 teaspoon vanilla extract

¼ teaspoon
almond extract

1 cup granulated sugar

¾ cup milk

4 egg whites (left
from using the yolks
in the dark batter)

NOTE: *We love this plain, as is, with nothing. But we also love it with ice cream and chocolate sauce; a sensational party dessert.*

Sift together the flour, baking powder, and salt, and set aside. In the large bowl of an electric mixer, beat the butter until soft. Add both extracts and ¾ cup of the sugar (reserve the remaining ¼ cup), and beat until thoroughly mixed. On low speed add the sifted dry ingredients in three additions alternately with the milk in two additions. Beat, scraping the bowl with a rubber spatula as necessary, until the ingredients are smooth. Set aside.

In the small bowl of an electric mixer (with clean beaters), beat the egg whites until they hold a soft shape. Reduce the speed to moderate and gradually add the remaining ¼ cup of sugar. Increase the speed again and beat briefly only until the whites hold a definite shape.

With a rubber spatula, fold the egg whites in three additions into the batter (do not fold thoroughly until the end).

Now comes the fun—putting the two batters into the pan in a pattern. Here's how: Use two large serving spoons, one for each batter. Start with the dark batter. Place 4 or 5 spoonfuls in the bottom of the pan, leaving a space between each of the dark mounds (for some of the light cake). Then place a spoonful of the light batter in each space and place a spoonful of the light over each mound of dark. Continue alternating the batters.

Rotate the pan briefly and briskly, first in one direction, then the other, to smooth the top.

Bake for about 1 hour, until a cake tester inserted gently to the bottom comes out clean. Cool the cake in the pan for 10 minutes. Then cover with a rack, turn the pan and the rack over, remove the pan—gorgeous!—and let stand until cool.

Mocha Chip Chiffon Cake

12 PORTIONS

The original chiffon cake was flavored with orange juice and orange rind. I have heard of chiffon cakes in a variety of flavors. But this one is brand new, inspired by the success of mocha chip ice cream.

This is not too sweet, with a fascinating coffee flavor and bits of semisweet chocolate all through it.

It is lovely with tea or coffee, or along with ice cream and/or fruit for a fancy dessert.

3 ounces semisweet chocolate (see Note)

1 cup sifted all-purpose flour

1¾ cups granulated sugar

1 tablespoon powdered (not granular) instant coffee or espresso

1 tablespoon baking powder

½ teaspoon salt

½ cup vegetable oil

7 eggs, separated

½ cup Kahlúa or Tia Maria or any coffee-flavored liqueur

¼ cup cold tap water

2 teaspoons vanilla extract

½ teaspoon cream of tartar

Optional: Confectioners' sugar

Adjust a rack one-third up from the bottom of the oven and preheat the oven to 325°. You will need a 10 x 4-inch tube pan (angel-food cake pan); it must not be a nonstick pan, and it must be the kind that is made in two pieces—the bottom and tube in one piece and the sides in a separate piece. Do not butter the pan.

On a board, with a heavy knife, cut the chocolate into small pieces. Aim for pieces about ¼ inch in diameter, although some pieces will be larger and some will be smaller and some will be crumbs; do not leave any pieces larger than ¼ inch, because this is a very light cake and larger pieces might sink to the bottom. Set aside.

In a large mixing bowl sift together the flour, 1¼ cups of the sugar, the powdered instant coffee or espresso, the baking powder, and the salt.

With a rubber spatula, make a wide well in the middle of the dry ingredients. Add, in the following order, without mixing, the oil, egg yolks (reserve the egg whites), coffee liqueur, water, and vanilla. With a large or medium-size strong wire whisk, beat the ingredients until smooth. Remove the whisk and with a rubber spatula stir/fold in the chopped chocolate. Set aside.

In the large bowl of an electric mixer, beat the egg whites until foamy, add the cream of tartar, and beat at high speed until the whites hold a soft shape. Reduce the speed to moderate and gradually add the remaining ½ cup of sugar. Then, on high speed again, beat until the whites hold a straight and stiff peak when the beaters are withdrawn. For this recipe the whites should be stiffer than for most; when the whites are firm, beat for 1 minute more to be sure. That should make them just right; more beating than that might make them too dry.

NOTE: *Use any good choco-late, preferably semisweet or bittersweet, and preferably a chocolate that is a thin bar rather than a thick one; it will be easier to cut it up.*

If you have a large-size rubber spatula, use it now; if not, the regular size is the best thing. In three additions, fold about three-quarters of the yolk mixture into the whites, without being too thorough (without being even a bit thorough). Then fold the whites into the remaining yolk mixture, this time being thorough enough to just barely incorporate the mixtures.

Gently pour the batter into the cake pan and gently smooth the top if necessary.

Bake for 1 hour and 10 to 15 minutes, until the top springs back when pressed gently with a fingertip. The top will crack during baking—it is okay.

Immediately turn the pan over and hang it upside down over the neck of a narrow bottle. (Even if your pan has a raised tube in the middle or three little feet on the sides, they probably will not raise the cake enough to keep it off the countertop.)

When the cake is completely cool, remove it from the pan as follows: You will need a sharp knife with a firm blade about 6 inches long. Insert the knife between the cake and the rim of the pan, all the way to the bottom, pressing the blade firmly against the rim in order not to cut into the cake. With short up and down motions, saw all around the cake, continuing to press the blade against the side of the pan. Then cut around the tube (if possible, use a knife with a narrower blade here).

Remove the sides of the pan by pushing up on the bottom of the pan. Then, carefully cut the bottom of the cake away from the pan, still press-ing against the pan.

Cover the cake with a wide, flat cake plate, turn the cake and the plate over, and lift off the bottom of the pan, leaving the cake upside down.

Sprinkle the optional confectioners' sugar over the cake through a fine strainer, although the dramatic height of this cake (almost 5½ inches) is beauty enough.

Use a serrated bread knife and a sawing motion to slice the cake without squashing it.

THE FARMER'S DAUGHTER'S CAKE

9 SQUARES

An 8-inch square, single-layer white cake—light and tender, but with body—covered with an old-fashioned chocolate icing. Since this is made with whipping cream (and no butter), my guess is that the recipe was perfected on a dairy farm where they had plenty of real heavy cream. But it works with the kind of cream available for sale in stores today.

This is so easy it is hard to believe.

2 cups sifted
all-purpose flour

2 teaspoons
baking powder

¼ teaspoon salt

2 eggs

1 teaspoon vanilla extract

¼ teaspoon
almond extract

1 cup granulated sugar

1 cup whipping cream
(not whipped)

Adjust a rack to the middle of the oven and preheat the oven to 350°. Butter an 8 x 8 x 2-inch square cake pan, dust all over lightly with fine, dry bread crumbs, invert it over paper, and tap lightly to shake out excess crumbs. Set aside.

Sift together the flour, baking powder, and salt, and set aside.

In the small bowl of an electric mixer beat the eggs, beat in the vanilla and almond extracts, and the sugar. Then beat in the cream and finally, on low speed, add the sifted dry ingredients and beat only until smooth.

Pour into the prepared pan and if necessary smooth the top.

Bake for 35 to 40 minutes, until the cake just begins to come away from the sides of the pan and until a toothpick inserted gently in the middle comes out clean. (The cake will rise with a domed top but will flatten as it cools; the top might or might not form a crack during baking—if it does it is okay.)

Remove from the oven and let stand for 5 minutes, then cut carefully around the sides to release, and let stand for 5 minutes more.

Cover with a rack, turn the pan and rack over, remove the pan, and let the cake stand upside down to cool. When cool, transfer the cake bottom side up to a cake plate or a cutting board. There is a chance that more icing might run down on the sides than you want; therefore, protect the plate by sliding a 12 x 2- to 3-inch piece of parchment or wax paper under each side of the cake.

The icing can be made up to the beating stage while the cake is baking, or while it is cooling.

OLD-FASHIONED CHOCOLATE ICING

Gorgeous—dark and delicious and very easy.

4 ounces unsweetened chocolate

½ cup cold milk

1⅓ cups granulated sugar

2 egg yolks

1 tablespoon plus 1 teaspoon unsalted butter

1 teaspoon vanilla extract

Place the chocolate, milk, and sugar in a heavy, small saucepan over moderate heat. Stir until the chocolate is melted and the sugar is dissolved (this does not have to boil). Remove from the heat and let stand for a minute.

In a small bowl stir the yolks lightly with a small wire whisk just to mix. Very gradually stir in about half of the warm chocolate mixture, and then add the yolks to the remaining warm chocolate mixture.

Cook over low heat, stirring, for 1 minute. (The mixture might not look smooth now, but if you did not add the warm chocolate mixture to the yolks too quickly, it will be okay.)

Transfer to the small bowl of an electric mixer and stir in the butter and vanilla. Let stand until cool. (The icing can be made up to this point while the cake is baking or cooling if you wish.)

Then beat the icing at high speed for 10 to 15 minutes (reduce the speed as necessary if the icing splashes), until the mixture is smooth/shiny/very slightly paler in color and as thick as a heavy syrup.

If you pour the icing all at once now onto the cake, too much of it will run down the sides. Pour about half of it onto the cake. Let stand for a minute or so, then pour a bit of the icing onto the middle and toward the corners of the cake. Wait another minute or so. Now you can probably pour the remaining icing over the top, and probably only very little will run down the sides (which is the way it should be), but if it still seems too runny, pour more gradually. It is not necessary to smooth the top.

Let the cake stand for a few hours for the icing to set. The icing will become dry to the touch but it will remain deliciously soft.

Slowly pull each piece of parchment or wax paper out toward a narrow end.

WHITE PEPPER AND GINGER LEMON CAKE

8 TO 10 PORTIONS

This is a brand-new version of an early American buttermilk cake (white pepper and fresh ginger are "hot" now) similar to a pound cake, but so rich and moist it is almost a pudding with a fascinating combination of dynamite flavors. Beautiful, delicious, unusual, and so easy—it is a piece of cake.

Finely grated rind of
2 large lemons

2 tablespoons lemon juice

½ ounce (a piece about
½ inch long x 1 inch
wide) fresh ginger (see
Fresh Ginger, page 7)

3 cups sifted
all-purpose flour

¾ teaspoon baking soda

¾ teaspoon
baking powder

½ teaspoon salt

2 teaspoons moderately
packed, finely ground
white pepper (preferably
fresh ground)

8 ounces (2 sticks)
unsalted butter

1¾ cups granulated sugar

3 eggs

1 cup buttermilk

Adjust a rack one-third up from the bottom of the oven and preheat the oven to 325°. Butter a 10- to 12-cup tube pan with a design (butter the pan even if it has a nonstick finish), dust it with fine, dry bread crumbs (be sure to butter and crumb the center tube—sprinkle the crumbs on the tube with your fingers), then invert it over paper, tap to shake out excess crumbs, and set aside.

In a small cup, mix the rind and juice. Grate the fresh ginger and add it to the lemon juice mixture.

Sift together the flour, baking soda, baking powder, salt, and white pepper, and set aside.

In the large bowl of an electric mixer beat the butter until soft. Add the sugar and beat for about a minute. Then add the eggs one at a time, beating until incorporated after each addition.

On low speed, add the sifted dry ingredients in three additions alternately with the buttermilk in two additions. Remove from the mixer and stir in the lemon and ginger mixture.

Turn into the prepared pan. Smooth the top by briskly rotating the pan first in one direction, then the other (the batter will be rather heavy).

Bake for 1 hour and 15 to 20 minutes, until a cake tester inserted gently in the middle comes out clean and dry. (If you have used a 12-cup pan the cake will not rise to the top of the pan—it is okay.)

Let the cake stand in the pan for 5 to 10 minutes. Cover with a rack, turn the pan and rack over, remove the pan, and place the cake on the rack over a large piece of aluminum foil (to catch drippings of the glaze).

LEMON GLAZE

This should be mixed as soon as the cake is put in the oven.

⅓ cup lemon juice

½ cup granulated sugar

NOTE: *From 1 to 10, my husband Ralph rated this a 4 for hotness; I give it a 7. It can be made more or less hot with more or less pepper and ginger.*

Stir the juice and sugar together and let stand while the cake is baking.

When the cake is removed from the pan, stir the glaze and, with a pastry brush, brush it all over the cake (including the hole in the middle). The cake will easily absorb it all. If some of the glaze drips onto the foil, transfer the rack and pour the glaze that dripped back over the cake.

Let stand until cool.

With two wide metal spatulas, or using a flat-sided cookie sheet as a spatula, transfer to a serving plate. This is even better if it ages for a day or two—the spicy hotness cools a bit as it ages—covered with plastic wrap.

Serve in thin slices.

GINGER GINGER CAKE

16 TO 24 SLICES

This is not even remotely like "gingerbread." It is a moist sour cream cake made gingery with generous amounts of both fresh and candied ginger. The texture is somewhat like a pound cake but more moist than most. During baking, part of the candied ginger will settle to the bottom of the cake, which will become the top when it is turned out of the pan, and it will have a deliciously chewy and candylike texture. I made this for a friend who is crazy about candied ginger; he said the longer he kept it the better it got. (This has no salt; it doesn't need it.)

3 cups sifted all-purpose flour

¼ teaspoon baking soda

6 ounces (about ¾ cup) candied ginger

Adjust a rack one-third up from the bottom of the oven and preheat the oven to 350°. Butter a 10 x 4¼-inch angel-food tube pan (it may be a one-piece nonstick pan) with an 18-cup capacity; butter the pan even if it has a nonstick finish. Dust it all over with fine, dry bread crumbs, invert it over paper and shake out excess crumbs, and set the pan aside.

Sift together the flour and baking soda and set aside.

Cut the candied ginger into ¼- to ⅓-inch pieces and set aside.

Grate the fresh ginger and set aside.

In the large bowl of an electric mixer, beat the butter until it is soft. Gradually beat in the grated fresh ginger and 2¼ cups of the sugar (reserve the remaining ½ cup). Then beat in the egg yolks.

3 to 4 ounces (a piece
3 to 4 inches long and
about 1 inch thick)
fresh ginger (see Fresh
Ginger, page 7)

8 ounces (2 sticks)
unsalted butter

2¾ cups granulated sugar

6 eggs, separated

1 cup sour cream

On low speed, gradually add the sifted dry ingredients in two additions alternately with the sour cream in one addition. Remove the bowl from the mixer.

Stir in half of the diced, candied ginger (reserve the remaining diced, candied ginger). Set aside.

In the small bowl of the electric mixer (with clean beaters), beat the egg whites until they hold a soft shape. Reduce the speed to moderate and gradually add the remaining ½ cup of sugar. Then increase the speed again and beat only until the whites hold a peak when the beaters are withdrawn.

In three additions, fold the whites into the batter; with the first two additions fold only partially—do not be too thorough—and with the last addition do not fold more than necessary to incorporate the whites.

Turn into the prepared pan and smooth the top. Sprinkle with the reserved candied ginger. Bake for about 1½ hours, until a cake tester inserted gently into the cake comes out clean. (The cake will not rise to the top of the pan.)

Let the cake cool in the pan for 10 to 15 minutes. (The cake will sink about an inch as it cools.) Then cover the pan with a cake plate and, holding the pan and the plate firmly together, turn them over; remove the pan and let the cake cool.

Chocolate Cakes

QUEEN MOTHER'S CAKE

12 PORTIONS

This was in my first book. It is one of the most popular recipes in all of my books and is the one cake I make more often than any other. I originally got the recipe in 1962 from a food column by Clementine Paddleford in The New York Herald Tribune.

The story is that Jan Smeterlin, the eminent Polish pianist, loved to cook. And he collected recipes. This is one that was given to him on a concert tour in Austria.

When the Queen Mother was invited to tea at the home of some friends of the Smeterlins, the hostess baked the cake according to Smeterlin's recipe. The Queen Mother loved it and asked for the recipe. Then—as the story goes— she served it often at her royal parties. Including the time she invited the Smeterlins to her home.

It is a flourless chocolate cake that is nothing like the flourless chocolate cakes that are so popular today. It is not as heavy or dense. This has ground almonds and the texture is almost light, although it is rich and moist. It is divine.

6 ounces (scant 1½ cups) blanched or unblanched almonds

6 ounces semisweet chocolate, cut into small pieces

¾ cup granulated sugar

6 ounces (1½ sticks) unsalted butter

6 eggs, separated

⅛ teaspoon salt

1 teaspoon lemon juice

First toast the almonds in a single layer in a shallow pan in a 350° oven for 12 to 15 minutes, shaking the pan a few times, until the almonds are lightly colored and have a delicious smell of toasted almonds when you open the oven door. Set aside to cool.

Adjust a rack one-third up in the oven and preheat the oven to 375°. Butter the bottom and sides of a 9 x 3-inch springform pan and line the bottom with a round of baking-pan liner paper cut to fit. Butter the paper. Dust the pan all over with fine, dry bread crumbs, invert over paper, and tap lightly to shake out excess. Set the prepared pan aside.

Place the chocolate in the top of a small double boiler over warm water on moderate heat. Cover until partially melted, then uncover and stir until just melted and smooth. Remove the top of the double boiler and set it aside until tepid or room temperature. Place the almonds and ¼ cup of the sugar (reserve remaining ½ cup sugar) in a food processor fitted with a metal chopping blade. Process very well until the nuts are fine and powdery. Stop the machine once or twice, scrape down the sides, and continue to process. Process for at least a full minute. I have recently realized that the finer the nuts are, the better the cake will be. Set aside the ground nuts.

In the large bowl of an electric mixer beat the butter until soft. Add ¼ cup of the sugar (reserve the remaining ¼ cup sugar) and beat to mix. Add the egg yolks one at a time, beating and scraping the sides of the bowl as necessary until smooth. On low speed add the chocolate and beat until mixed. Then add the processed almonds and beat, scraping the bowl, until incorporated.

Now the whites should be beaten in the large bowl of the mixer. If you don't have an additional large bowl for the mixer, transfer the chocolate mixture to any other large bowl. Wash the bowl and beaters.

In the large bowl of the mixer, with clean beaters, beat the egg whites with the salt and lemon juice, starting on low speed and increasing it gradually. When the whites barely hold a soft shape, reduce the speed a bit and gradually add the remaining ¼ cup sugar. Then, on high speed, continue to beat until the whites hold a straight point when the beaters are slowly raised. Do not overbeat.

Stir a large spoonful of the whites into the chocolate mixture to soften it a bit.

Then, in three additions, fold in the remaining whites. Do not fold thoroughly until the last addition and do not handle any more than necessary.

Turn the mixture into the prepared pan. Rotate the pan a bit briskly from left to right in order to level the batter.

Bake for 20 minutes at 375° and then reduce the temperature to 350° and continue to bake for an additional 50 minutes (total baking time is 1 hour and 10 minutes). Do not overbake; the cake should remain soft and moist in the center. (The top might crack a bit—it's okay.)

The following direction was in the original recipe, and although I do not understand why, I always do it. Wet and slightly wring out a folded towel and place it on a smooth surface. Remove the cake pan from the oven and place it on the wet towel. Let stand until tepid, 50 to 60 minutes.

Release and remove the sides of the pan (do not cut around the sides with a knife—it will make the rim of the cake messy). Now let the cake stand until it is completely cool, or longer if you wish.

The cake will sink a little in the middle; the sides will be a little higher. Use a long, thin, sharp knife and cut the top level. Brush away loose crumbs.

Place a rack or a small board over the cake and carefully invert. Remove the bottom of the pan and the paper lining. The cake is now upside down; this is the way it will be iced. Place four strips of baking-pan liner paper (each about 3 x 12 inches) around the edges of a cake plate. With a large, wide spatula, carefully transfer the cake to the plate; check to be sure that the cake is touching the papers all around (in order to keep the icing off the plate when you ice the cake).

If you have a cake-decorating turntable or a lazy Susan, place the cake plate on it.

ICING

½ cup whipping cream

2 teaspoons powdered (not granular) instant espresso or coffee (see Note)

8 ounces semisweet chocolate, cut into small pieces

NOTE: *I use Medaglia D'Oro instant espresso.*

Scald the cream in a 5- to 6-cup saucepan over moderate heat until it begins to form small bubbles around the edges or a thin skip on top. Add the dry espresso or coffee and whisk to dissolve. Add the chocolate and stir occasionally over heat for 1 minute. Then remove the pan from the heat and whisk or stir until the chocolate is all melted and the mixture is smooth.

Let the icing stand at room temperature, stirring occasionally, for about 15 minutes or a little longer, until the icing barely begins to thicken.

Then, stir it to mix, and pour it slowly over the top of the cake, pouring it onto the middle. Use a long, narrow metal spatula to smooth the top and spread the icing so that a little of it runs down the sides (not too much—the icing on the sides should be a much thinner layer than on the top). With a small, narrow metal spatula, smooth the sides.

Remove the strips of paper by pulling each one out toward a narrow end.

OPTIONAL: *Chocolate Cigarettes (see right), whipped cream, and fresh raspberries.*

Decorate the cake or individual portions with the optional chocolate cigarettes. Place a mound of optional whipped cream (lightly sweetened with confectioners' sugar and lightly flavored with vanilla extract) on one side of each portion on individual dessert plates, and a few optional raspberries on the other side of each portion.

CHOCOLATE CIGARETTES

These are long thin curls of chocolate that are used as a decoration. They are very professional.

NOTE: If the room is too cold or the chocolate stands too long it might not curl or it could crack when you form the cigarettes.

Use compound chocolate, also known as coating chocolate. To make a very generous amount (you can make much less) coarsely chop about 8 ounces of a compound chocolate. Melt the chocolate slowly in the top of a double boiler over warm water on moderate heat. When partially melted, remove from the water and stir until completely melted. Pour onto a work surface, forming a ribbon 3 to 4 inches wide and 10 inches long. The chocolate will be ¼ to ⅜ inch thick. Let cool at room temperature until it is no longer soft or sticky.

To make the curls use a long, heavy knife—I use a Sabatier cook's knife with a 12-inch blade. Hold it at a 45° angle across the width and right near the end of the chocolate. Cut down slowly and firmly. The chocolate will roll around itself as it is cut. Repeat, each time placing the blade very close to the cut end—the curls should be paper thin. Transfer them with a wide metal spatula to a shallow tray. Cover with plastic wrap and store either at room temperature if it is not too warm, or in the refrigerator or freezer.

CHOCOLATE SOUFFLÉ CAKE

10 PORTIONS

At one time, one of the most talked-about chocolate cakes in New York City was the Chocolate Soufflé Cake from Fay and Allen's Foodworks (a former restaurant and fancy food store). I had heard raves about it. It was described as a soft, moist, rich, dark chocolate mixture with a crisp, brownie-like crust!

In September 1980, my husband and I were on a tour to promote my chocolate book, and were in New York for only a few hectic days. As we were checking out of our hotel I suddenly remembered the Chocolate Soufflé Cake. With the taxi waiting, I rushed to the phone to call Fay and Allen's, and to my surprise and joy, within a few minutes I had the recipe. I spoke to Mr. Mark Allen, the man who baked the cakes, and the son of the owner. He could not have been nicer or more agreeable. He told me that he got the recipe when he attended the Culinary Institute of America.

It is a flourless mixture similar to a rich chocolate mousse, baked in a large Bundt pan. During baking, a crisp crust forms on the outside; the inside stays quite wet.

The recipe calls for long, slow baking. It is best to serve it hot, right out of the oven.

8 ounces semisweet
chocolate

8 ounces (2 sticks)
unsalted butter

2 tablespoons
vegetable oil

8 eggs, separated

1 cup granulated sugar

1 teaspoon vanilla extract

¼ teaspoon salt

Optional:
Confectioners' sugar

Adjust a rack one-third up from the bottom of the oven and preheat the oven to 300°. You will need a 10-inch Bundt pan or any other fancy-shaped tube pan with a 12-cup capacity. (Mine is labeled Bundt; it is made by Northland Aluminum Products; it has a nonstick lining.) Butter the pan (even if it has a nonstick lining); the best way is to use room-temperature melted butter, and brush it on with a pastry brush. Then sprinkle granulated sugar all over the pan; in order to get the sugar on the tube, sprinkle it on with your fingertips. Shake the pan to coat it thoroughly with sugar, and invert it over a piece of paper and tap to shake out excess. Then sprinkle 1 to 2 teaspoons of sugar evenly in the bottom of the pan. Set the pan aside.

Break up or coarsely chop the chocolate and place it in the top of a large double boiler over hot water on moderate heat. Cut up the butter, and add it and the oil to the chocolate. Cover and let cook until almost completely melted. Then stir, or whisk with a wire whisk, until completely melted and smooth. Remove from the hot water.

In a mixing bowl, stir the yolks a bit with a wire whisk just to mix. Then gradually, in a few additions, whisk about half of the hot chocolate mixture into the yolks, and then, off the heat, add the yolks to the remaining hot chocolate mixture and mix together (the mixture will thicken a bit as the heat of the chocolate cooks the eggs). Add the sugar and vanilla and stir to mix. Set aside.

In the large bowl of an electric mixer, add the salt to the egg whites and beat until the whites hold a point but are not stiff or dry.

Fold a few large spoonfuls of the whites into the chocolate mixture. Then add the chocolate mixture to the whites and fold together gently only until incorporated.

Gently turn the mixture into the prepared pan.

Bake for 2¼ hours. During baking the cake will rise and then sink; it will sink more in the middle than on the edges. That is as it should be. It is okay.

Remove from the oven and, without waiting, cover the cake with an inverted serving plate. Hold the pan and the plate firmly together, and turn them over. The sugar coating in the pan forms a crust and the cake will slide out of the pan easily.

Serve while still hot. If you wish, cover the top of the cake generously with confectioners' sugar, sprinkling it on through a fine strainer held over the cake. Brush excess sugar off the plate.

(A few years later, while in New York I went to Fay and Allen's to eat this cake there. I was thrilled to see that it was precisely the same as the ones I had made. They served it quite warm, just out of the oven, with a generous topping of icy cold whipped cream.)

WHIPPED CREAM

2 cups heavy cream

¼ cup confectioners' sugar

1½ teaspoons vanilla extract

NOTE: *When cutting this cake it will crumble a bit as you cut through the bottom (previously the top) crisp crust. (It did at Fay and Allen's, too.) Don't try to cut thin slices. Do try to cut with a serrated knife.*

In a chilled bowl with chilled beaters, whip the ingredients only until the cream holds a shape; it is more delicious if it is not really stiff. (If you whip the cream ahead of time and refrigerate it, it will separate slightly as it stands; just whisk it a bit with a wire whisk before serving.) Serve the cream separately, spooning a generous amount over and alongside each portion.

This is even better if you serve a few fresh raspberries and/or strawberries with each portion.

THE ROBERT REDFORD CAKE

16 PORTIONS

Chocolate News once printed a photo of Robert Redford along with a recipe for a chocolate honey cake which, they said, he had enjoyed at the Hisae restaurant in New York City.

I broke the 4-minute mile getting to the kitchen to try the recipe, and it was a delicious cake.

Soon after that, my husband and I were in New York and went to Hisae. With the first bite, I knew the cake was different from the one I had made. This one had less of a honey taste, but it was a sweeter cake. The management was extremely generous about sharing the recipe. (The fact that it is very different from the one in Chocolate News is a mystery I am not trying to solve.)

This is the recipe from the restaurant. It is closely related—about like a big sister—to Queen Mother's Cake (see Note), which is in both my first dessert book and my chocolate book. This has honey instead of sugar, it has fewer nuts, and it is a larger cake and makes more portions. It is super dense—compact, moist and rich, not too sweet, and it really should be served with whipped cream and, if possible, berries.

If it hadn't been for Redford's picture, I probably would not have noticed the recipe to begin with. So thank you, Robert Redford—you are a gentleman and a scholar and a man of good taste indeed.

6½ ounces (1¼ cups) blanched hazelnuts or blanched almonds (see page 6 for blanching directions)

12 ounces semisweet chocolate

6 ounces (1½ sticks) unsalted butter

½ cup honey

10 eggs, separated

¼ teaspoon salt

Adjust a rack one-third up from the bottom of the oven and preheat the oven to 375°. Butter a 10 x 3-inch round or springform cake pan. Line the bottom with a round of wax paper or baking-pan liner paper cut to fit, butter the paper, and dust all over with fine, dry bread crumbs. Tap to shake out excess crumbs over a piece of paper; set the pan aside.

The blanched hazelnuts or almonds must be ground to a fine powder; it can be done in a food processor (see To Grind Nuts in a Food Processor, page 13) or a nut grinder. Set the ground nuts aside. Break up or coarsely chop the chocolate and place it in the top of a large double boiler over shallow, warm water on moderate heat. Cover with a folded paper napkin or paper towel (to absorb condensation) and with the pot cover. Let stand until partly melted, then uncover and stir until completely melted. Remove the top of the double boiler, carefully dry the bottom (a drop of moisture in the chocolate would make it "tighten"), and transfer the chocolate to a bowl (to stop the cooking). Stir occasionally until tepid or cooled to room temperature.

Meanwhile, in the large bowl of an electric mixer, beat the butter until it is soft. Gradually add the honey and beat until smooth. Then add the egg yolks, two or three at a time, beating until smooth after each addition. (The mixture will look curdled now, it is okay.) Beat only until mixed.

Add the chocolate and beat, scraping the bowl with a rubber spatula, only until mixed. (The curdled look will go away now.)

Add the ground nuts and beat only to mix.

Now, to beat the egg whites, you will either need the same bowl and beaters you used for the chocolate mixture (in which case, transfer the chocolate mixture to another large bowl, and thoroughly wash the bowl and beaters), or if you have an additional large bowl for your mixer and an extra set of beaters, use those, or a large copper bowl and a large, balloon-shaped wire whisk. Whichever you use, add the salt to the whites and beat only until the whites just barely stand up straight when the beater or whisk is raised, or when some of the whites cling to a rubber spatula.

With a large rubber spatula, fold about one-quarter of the whites into the chocolate mixture. Then fold in another quarter.

Now, if you have a larger mixing bowl (I use an 8-quart one), transfer the folded mixture to the larger bowl, add the remaining whites, and fold together gently only until the mixtures are blended. If you do not have a larger bowl to finish the folding, it can be done in the large mixer bowl, but not quite as easily—it is a large amount of batter.

Turn the mixture into the prepared pan. Bake at 375° for 20 minutes, then reduce the temperature to 350° and bake for 50 minutes more (total baking time is 70 minutes), until a cake tester comes out clean. Turn off the oven, open the oven door, and let the cake cool in the oven for about 15 minutes. Then remove it from the oven and let it stand at room temperature until completely cool. During the cooling, the cake will sink more in the center than along the rim; that is what it should do.

When the cake is completely cool, cover it with a rack and turn over the pan and rack. Remove the pan and the paper lining. Cover the cake with another rack and invert again, leaving the cake right side up.

Now the top of the cake must be cut with a long, thin, sharp knife to make it level. (It is easiest to do this if you place the cake on a cake-decorating turntable.)

The cake may be iced either side up; if the sides taper in toward the top (which happens sometimes), it is best to ice it right side up, but if the sides are straight it is best to ice it upside down. Place the cake carefully on a large cake platter or a serving board. If you have a cake-decorating turntable, place the cake platter or serving board on it.

To protect the plate while you ice the cake, you will need four 10 x 3-inch strips of wax paper. Use a wide metal spatula to gently raise one side of the cake and slide a strip of the paper partly under the cake. Repeat with the remaining papers, and check to be sure that the papers touch the cake all around.

Prepare the icing.

ICING

¾ cup heavy cream

12 ounces semisweet chocolate (it may be the same as the chocolate in the cake, or it may be a different one)

In a heavy saucepan over moderate heat, cook the cream until it forms a wrinkled skin on the top. Meanwhile, break up or coarsely chop the chocolate. When the cream is ready, add the chocolate, reduce the heat to low, and stir with a small wire whisk until the mixture is perfectly smooth. Transfer it to a bowl to stop the cooking. Stir occasionally until cool and very slightly thickened.

Pour the cooled icing over the top of the cake. Carefully spread it to allow only a small amount of it to run down the sides of the cake. With a long, narrow metal spatula, spread the top very smoothly (easy, if you are working on a cake-decorating turntable) and then with a small, narrow metal spatula, smooth the sides. (The icing on the sides might run down a bit onto the wax papers on the plate; if so, it might be necessary to use a rubber spatula to scoop it up and replace it on the sides, and then to smooth it again.)

Remove the wax-paper strips by pulling each one out toward a narrow end, pulling them slowly and gently.

This may be served soon while the icing is soft, or it may wait overnight at room temperature. (If you make the cake ahead of time it may be frozen. Thaw and ice it the day it is to be served, or a day ahead.)

This cake really is just not complete without whipped cream. Fresh raspberries or strawberries are also part of the recipe. (If the berries aren't fresh, do not serve any.)

WHIPPED CREAM

NOTE: *Many people have written to thank me for Queen Mother's Cake, Hungarian Rhapsody, The Orient Express Chocolate Torte (all three are in my chocolate book), and other flourless chocolate cakes—especially because they are so good for Passover. They tell me that they make them with kosher chocolate, matzo meal instead of bread crumbs, and pareve margarine. And they say, "It was the hit of the Seder."*

The amount of whipped cream to prepare depends on the number of portions you will serve. Plan on 1 cup of heavy cream for each 4 or 5 portions. For each cup of cream, add 2 tablespoons of confectioners' or granulated sugar, or 1 tablespoon of honey, and ½ teaspoon of vanilla extract. In a chilled bowl with chilled beaters, whip all the ingredients only until the cream holds a soft shape; it should not be stiff. If you whip the cream early in the day for that evening, refrigerate it; it will separate a bit—just whip it a bit with a small wire whisk before serving.

Serve the cream and the berries separately; spoon a generous amount of each alongside each portion, cream on one side of the cake and berries on the other side.

FRENCH CHOCOLATE LOAF CAKE

In my chocolate book I told the story of my lifelong search for the recipe for a particular chocolate cake sold at a French pastry shop in New York City. I confessed that I still could not make it but would keep on trying. And I did.

Eureka!

These ingredients and these directions might not be the same as those used in the elusive Le Trianon—I probably will never know—but the result is mighty close to, if not the same as, the cake I fell in love with almost forty years ago.

The cake as it is sold today does not taste the same to me as it did years ago. I can still remember the sensation, and my descriptive adjectives: moist, smooth, rich, dense, dark, and delicious—a cross between fudge candy, chocolate pudding, and chocolate cheesecake.

That is what this recipe will make.

For the first dozen or so years that I tried to make this, I concentrated on recipes with only 1 or 2 spoonfuls of flour and only about 15 minutes of baking. The results were too much like an icing. Years later, when I used cornstarch instead of flour, more of it, and a longer baking time, I felt that I was getting close, but the cakes always cracked badly and were unattractive, and they had a too-dry outside and a too-wet inside.

One day, out of the blue, my husband suggested baking it in a pan of water. I did not think that would make a bit of difference, but I had run out of other things to try. I could not believe my eyes! Without the water, the recipe rose in a high mound with a deep crack down the middle and hollows on the sides. With the water, it rose only slightly—very flat, very beautiful, no cracks and no hollows.

This cake may be made ahead of time and may be frozen for a month or so. It is possible to serve it directly from the freezer—it will not be too hard to slice—but it is more tender and more delicate at room temperature.

It is a very plain-looking loaf, which may be covered with optional chocolate curls (easily made with milk chocolate), and may be served alone or with whipped cream and berries.

¾ cup sifted cornstarch (sift before measuring and do not pack down when measuring)

8 ounces semisweet chocolate (see Notes)

1 teaspoon instant coffee

¼ cup boiling water

3 ounces (¾ stick) unsalted butter

½ cup granulated sugar

4 eggs, separated

⅛ teaspoon salt

Adjust a rack one-third up from the bottom of the oven and preheat the oven to 350°. You will need a loaf pan with a 6-cup capacity; mine measures 8½ x 4½ x 2¾ inches.

To line the pan with foil: Place the pan upside down on the work surface. Measure the bottom of the pan—the bottom of my pan measures 7⅜ x 3⅜ inches (yours may vary). Cut two strips off oil; one to fit the length (bottom and sides) and one to fit the width (bottom and sides) of the pan. For the measurements of my pan, one piece is cut a scant 7⅜ x about 10 inches, and one piece is cut a scant 3⅜ x about 14½ inches (both measurements allow a little excess to extend over the rim of the pan when the foil is in place). If the foil is not measured carefully and is too wide, it will wrinkle when it is placed in the pan. (I mark the foil with a pencil and tear it against a straight-edge table or countertop.) Now, to shape the foil to fit the pan without wrinkling the foil, carefully place one piece over the upside-down pan, center it, and fold it down on the sides of the pan. Remove the foil and set it aside. Repeat the procedure with the second piece of foil, folding it down on the remaining two sides of the pan. Remove the second piece of foil. Turn the pan upright. Carefully place one piece of the foil in the pan, press it into place, and then place the other piece in the pan and press it into place. There will be two thicknesses on the bottom. The sides of the foil may extend about ½ inch or so above the pan, and may be folded down over the rim. (Since the pan flares at the top, the upper corners of the pan will remain unlined—it is okay.)

During the preparation of the pan, handle the foil carefully and do not wrinkle it—the wrinkles would show up in the finished cake. (Incidentally, I could line several pans in less time than it took me to describe it.)

Now, there are two ways of treating the foil. One is to brush it carefully with melted butter. The other is to set the pan aside until just before you are ready to pour the batter in, and then spray it generously with Pam or any other vegetable cooking spray. The Pam does a slightly better job than butter; with butter the cake might stick, but it will only be a very little bit.

After sifting and measuring the cornstarch, resift it 3 more times and set it aside.

Break up or coarsely chop the chocolate and place it in a heavy saucepan that has about a 4-cup capacity. Dissolve the coffee in the water and pour it over the chocolate. Cover, place over low heat, and let stand for a few minutes until the chocolate starts to melt. Do not overcook. Stir (preferably with a small wire whisk) until smooth and then transfer to a small bowl to stop the cooking and set aside to cool slightly. Meanwhile, in the large bowl of an electric mixer, beat the butter until soft. Gradually add the sugar and beat for 2 to 3 minutes, scraping the bowl occasionally with a rubber spatula. Add the yolks one at a time, scraping the bowl and beating after each addition until incorporated. Then continue to beat for a few minutes until the mixture is pale and creamy.

On low speed add the chocolate, which may still be slightly warm or at room temperature. Scrape the bowl and beat only until smooth. Then add the cornstarch, scrape the bowl, and beat only until smooth. Remove from the mixer and set aside.

In the small bowl of the electric mixer, with clean beaters (or if you prefer, in any small bowl with an eggbeater), beat the whites and the salt only until the whites just stand up straight when the beaters are raised—do not overbeat.

Add 1 rounded tablespoonful of the whites (just guess the amount—don't measure) to the chocolate mixture and stir to mix. Repeat with a second spoonful, and then with a third. Fold in about half of the remaining whites without being too thorough, and then fold in the balance of the whites, folding gently but completely.

If you are using Pam, spray the pan now, rather generously. Pour the batter into the pan. Lift the pan with both hands and move it gently from left to right and front to back in order to smooth the top of the batter.

Place the cake pan in a larger pan, which must be no deeper than the cake pan. (Incidentally, if the larger pan is made of aluminum, sprinkle about ½ teaspoon of cream of tartar in the pan to keep it from discoloring.) Pour boiling water into the large pan until it is about an inch deep.

Bake for 50 to 55 minutes until a cake tester gently inserted into the middle, all the way to the bottom, comes out just barely clean and dry. Test very carefully several times to be sure. There will be a thin crust on the top; the middle of the cake will be soft. Do not overbake.

Turn off the heat and open the oven door a few inches; let cool that way for 20 minutes. Then open the oven door all the way and let the cake stand for about an hour until cooled to room temperature. (If you need the oven, let the cake cool in the oven for only half the time, and then let it finish cooling in the kitchen.)

Remove the cake pan from the water and dry the pan. Cover the cake with a flat serving plate or a board. Turn over the plate or board and the cake pan, remove the pan and the foil. Serve the cake upside down. (The cake may now be frozen.)

Before serving, the cake may be covered with chocolate curls (see below), and then sprinkled generously with confectioners' sugar sifted through a strainer held over the top.

This may be served as it is, but it is better with a spoonful of softly whipped cream (sweetened only slightly with confectioners' or granulated sugar, and flavored with vanilla extract). And with a spoonful of fresh raspberries or strawberries, or with just barely thawed and partially drained frozen raspberries.

Make the portions small.

Milk Chocolate Curls

These are the easiest chocolate curls, and they're adorable. They are made with a swivel-bladed vegetable peeler and with milk chocolate, which will give you what you want with the least amount of trouble. You will use only about an ounce or so of the ½-pound bar, but you will have better results with a thick piece of chocolate than with a smaller bar.

Work over wax paper. If you are right-handed, hold a piece of the chocolate in your left hand, making the curls either from the side of the piece of chocolate or from the bottom; try both. Move the vegetable peeler along the chocolate, moving it toward yourself, pressing it very firmly against the chocolate.

Spoon the curls onto the cake, piling on as many as will stay.

PENNI'S MOCHA NUT LOAF
ONE 9½-INCH LOAF

This is the cake that my friend Penni Linck made for Christmas gifts when she was the food and wine editor of House & Garden. It is one of the darkest of all chocolate cakes, and is a terrifically good, not-too-sweet, coffee-flavored, sour-cream loaf that you will love to give away or keep for yourself any time of the year.

1½ cups sifted
all-purpose flour

1 teaspoon salt

1½ teaspoons
baking soda

½ cup unsweetened
cocoa powder (preferably
Dutch-process)

¼ cup powdered (not
granular) instant
espresso or coffee

1 egg

1¼ cups sour cream

1 cup granulated sugar

2⅔ ounces (5⅓
tablespoons) unsalted
butter, melted

5 ounces (1¼ cups)
pecans, cut or broken
into medium-size pieces

Adjust an oven rack one-third up from the bottom of the oven and pre-heat the oven to 350°. You will need a loaf pan with a 7-cup capacity; mine measures 9½ x 4½ x 3 inches. If necessary, use a larger pan, but not smaller. (It is best to check by capacity, rather than dimensions.) Butter the pan and dust well with fine, dry bread crumbs, then, over a piece of paper, tap firmly to shake out excess crumbs. Set the pan aside.

Sift together the flour, salt, baking soda, cocoa, and powdered instant espresso. Set aside.

In the large bowl of an electric mixer, on low speed, beat the egg, sour cream, and sugar just to mix. Beat in the melted butter.

On low speed add the sifted dry ingredients—they may be added all at once—scraping the bowl with a rubber spatula and beating only until the mixture is smooth. Remove from the mixer and stir in the nuts.

Turn the mixture into the prepared pan and smooth the top.

Bake for 1 hour until a cake tester gently inserted into the middle comes out clean and dry.

Cool the cake in the pan for 10 to 15 minutes. Then cover it with a rack, turn over the pan and the rack, remove the pan, cover with another rack, and turn over again, leaving the cake right side up. Let stand until com-pletely cool.

When the cake is cool, wrap it in plastic wrap and refrigerate or freeze it until it is thoroughly chilled, or refrigerate it for a day or two. It is best to slice the cake when it is cold. Cut it into 18- to 20½-inch slices. The cake may be served cold or at room temperature.

Chocolate Festival Cake

24 portions

I made this up when the Hershey company held their First Annual Chocolate Festival in Hershey, Pennsylvania, in 1982. I wanted a cake that was as American as a Hershey bar. I demonstrated it before a large audience and then served it to everyone there. Although it is a very large cake, that day I cut it into extra-thin slices and was able to serve many more than 24 portions. I don't know for sure if the audience was impressed by my dexterity in being able to serve so many people from one cake or if the applause was for the cake itself; however, the cake and I got a standing ovation.

It is dark-dark chocolate, a cross between a pound cake and a fudge cake, made with peanut butter, bananas, and both chocolate and cocoa. It is firm but moist, rich and dense, not too sweet, and easy to make. It is thickly covered with a swirly chocolate and peanut butter icing.

4 ounces semisweet
chocolate

3 cups sifted
all-purpose flour

1 tablespoon
baking powder

2 teaspoons baking soda

1 teaspoon salt

8 ounces (2 sticks)
unsalted butter

1 cup smooth
peanut butter

1 tablespoon
vanilla extract

1 pound (2¼ cups,
packed) dark brown sugar

1 cup (about 2) finely
mashed fully ripened
bananas (see Note)

6 eggs

Adjust a rack one-third up from the bottom of the oven and preheat the oven to 350°. You will need a 10 x 4-inch tube pan with an 18-cup capacity; it can be nonstick or not and it can be a one-piece pan or one with detachable sides. Butter the pan (even if it is nonstick), line the bottom with a round of parchment or wax paper cut to fit, then butter the paper, dust all over with fine, dry bread crumbs, invert the pan over paper and tap out excess crumbs. Set aside.

Place the chocolate in the top of a small double boiler over warm water on moderately low heat and cover the pot with a folded paper towel (to absorb steam) and with the pot cover. Let cook until the chocolate is almost melted, then uncover and stir until completely melted. Remove the top of the double boiler and set aside to cool.

Sift together the flour, baking powder, baking soda, and salt, and set aside.

In the large bowl of an electric mixer, beat the butter until soft. Beat in the peanut butter and vanilla, then the sugar, scraping the bowl as necessary with a rubber spatula. Next, mix in the melted chocolate, then the mashed bananas, and then the eggs, one at a time, beating until incorporated after each addition. On lowest speed, add the cocoa, still scraping the bowl as necessary, and beat until smooth.

On low speed, gradually add half of the milk, then half of the sifted dry ingredients, then the remaining milk, and finally the remaining dry ingredients, beating until smooth after each addition.

Turn the mixture into the prepared pan. Briskly rotate the pan a bit, first in one direction, then the other, to smooth the top.

Bake for 1 hour, then cover the top loosely with foil to prevent over-browning, and continue to bake for an additional 25 to 30 minutes until

1 cup strained unsweetened cocoa powder (preferably Dutch-process)

1¼ cups milk

NOTE: The bananas must be fully ripened, with brown/black spots on the skin, to have the best flavor for baking. Mash them on a large, flat plate with a fork. (In a processor they become too liquid.)

a cake tester gently inserted into the cake—in several places, all the way to the bottom—comes out clean (total baking time is 1 hour and 25 to 30 minutes). The top of the cake will crack during baking—it is okay.

Cool in the pan for 20 minutes. Then cover with a rack, turn the pan and the rack over, remove the pan and the paper lining, and let the cake cool upside down on the rack.

When the cake is completely cool, place four 10 x 3-inch strips of parchment or wax paper in a square pattern on a large flat cake plate. Transfer the cake to the plate and check to be sure that the papers are touching the cake all around.

If you have a cake-decorating turntable, place the cake plate on it.

CHOCOLATE-PEANUT BUTTER ICING

16 ounces milk chocolate, broken up

2 ounces unsweetened chocolate, chopped coarsely

4 ounces (1 stick) unsalted butter, cut into ½-inch pieces

1 egg

12 ounces (1½ cups) smooth peanut butter

Place both chocolates in the top of a large double boiler over warm water on rather low heat. Cover for a few minutes, then uncover and stir frequently until melted and smooth.

Remove the top of the double boiler. Add the butter a few pieces at a time, stirring with a wooden spoon until smooth.

In the large bowl of an electric mixer, beat the egg just to mix, then add the peanut butter and the chocolate mixture (which can be warm or cool) and beat until very smooth. As this mixture cools it will thicken; you might want to chill it quickly by putting it in the freezer or by placing the bowl in a larger bowl of ice and water. Or just let it stand awhile. When it is thick enough to hold its shape, beat it again for a moment.

This is a lot of icing and it makes a thick layer. Spread it first on the sides and then on the top of the cake. With a long, narrow metal spatula, smooth the sides first and then the top. Then, form peaks and swirls all over the sides and top as follows. Dip a teaspoon into water (hot or cold), shake it off, and with the back of the wet spoon form little curls and swirls in the icing. Continue to wet the spoon every time you move it to form another swirl (the wet spoon gives the icing a smooth finish).

Remove the paper strips by pulling each one out slowly toward a narrow end.

Big Daddy's Cake

12 PORTIONS

A big, gorgeous cake baked in a large Bundt pan, topped with a dark, thick chocolate glaze that runs down the sides unevenly. When you cut into the cake, you will find a moist, tender white cake, studded with pecans, and containing a tunnel of soft and gooey chocolate sauce. Most delicious. And a total mystery, to me at least. The white batter is poured into the pan, then topped with a chocolate sauce. During baking they change places; the chocolate sauce goes down to the bottom of the white batter, without leaving a trace of chocolate on the white. Ah, sweet mystery . . .

If you can serve this before the icing and the surprise chocolate tunnel inside become firm, it is best. I have made this cake late in the morning and after dinner the icing and the chocolate tunnel were still properly soft and moist. Longer than that and they became firm.

7 ounces (2 cups) toasted pecans (see page 6)

4 cups sifted all-purpose flour

2 teaspoons baking powder

1 teaspoon salt

6 ounces semisweet chocolate

3 tablespoons hot water or strong coffee (2 to 3 teaspoons instant coffee in 3 tablespoons water)

3 tablespoons whipping cream

12 ounces (3 sticks) unsalted butter

1½ teaspoons vanilla extract

¼ teaspoon almond extract

Adjust a rack one-third up from the bottom of the oven and preheat the oven to 350°. Generously butter a 10-inch Bundt pan or any other fancy tube pan with a 12- to 14-cup capacity (butter it even if it has a nonstick finish).

Coarsely break up half the pecans and set them aside to sprinkle on the batter just before baking. Chop the remaining cup of pecans finely. (I do it on a large board with a long, heavy chef's knife—the pieces will be uneven, but aim for pieces about the size of rice.)

Place the finely chopped pecans in the buttered pan, turn the pan and shake it from side to side to coat it completely with the nuts. Invert the pan over paper and allow loose nuts to fall out. Then, with your fingers, sprinkle those loose nuts into the bottom of the pan and set aside.

Sift together the flour, baking powder, and salt, and set aside.

Break up or chop the chocolate coarsely and place it in the top of a small double boiler over hot water on moderate heat. Add the water or coffee. Cover the pan and cook until the chocolate is melted. Remove the top of the double boiler from the heat, stir briskly with a small wire whisk until smooth, add the whipping cream, and whisk again until smooth. Set aside.

Beat the butter in the large bowl of an electric mixer until soft and smooth, then beat in the vanilla and almond extracts and the sugar and continue to beat for about 2 minutes. Then add the eggs one at a time, scraping the bowl as necessary, and beating until thoroughly incorporated after each addition. On low speed, gradually add the sifted dry ingredients. (After adding the milk, and even after adding the dry ingredients, the mixture will appear curdled—it is okay.)

2¼ cups granulated sugar

6 eggs

1¼ cups milk

Turn the batter into the prepared pan and smooth the top. With the bottom of a large spoon form a trench around the middle of the top of the cake (about ½ inch deep and 1½ inches wide).

Stir the prepared chocolate mixture and spoon it into the trench, keeping away from the sides of the pan.

With your fingertips, sprinkle the reserved coarsely broken pecans all over the top of the batter (they should touch the sides of the pan).

Bake for 50 to 55 minutes, then cover the top of the pan loosely with foil to prevent overbrowning. Continue to bake for 15 to 20 minutes (total baking time is 1 hour and 5 to 15 minutes), until a cake tester inserted gently in the middle of the cake comes out clean. (During baking the top will form a deep crack—it is all right.)

Let the cake cool in the pan for 20 minutes. Then cover it with a wide, flat cake plate and, holding the pan and the plate firmly together, turn them both over. Be careful while doing this—the cake is very heavy. Get a good secure grip on the cake pan with a pot holder; the other hand should be over the middle of the plate with your fingers spread apart for support. Remove the pan.

Let the cake stand until cool, and then make the glaze.

BIG DADDY'S GLAZE

6 ounces semisweet chocolate

2 teaspoons solid vegetable shortening (e.g., Crisco)

Break up or coarsely chop the chocolate and place it with the shortening in the top of a small double boiler, uncovered, over hot water on moderate heat. Stir occasionally, until melted and smooth.

Pour the glaze over the top of the cake. Then smooth the top a bit, allowing a small amount of the glaze to run down into the grooves of the cake. Let stand at room temperature and serve at room temperature.

CHOCOLATE SPONGE CAKE
10 TO 12 PORTIONS

A lady told me that the best sponge cake she ever made is the one in Craig Claiborne's New York Times Cook Book (Harper & Brothers, 1961). But, she said, she wished it was chocolate and asked me how she could change it to a chocolate cake. I took a guess, without knowing the recipe, and suggested that she try to substitute cocoa for ¼ cup of the flour. Then I decided to try it myself. This is it.

As the lady said, "You just put everything in the mixer and that is all there is to it (well, almost) and it is so light it feels as though it might fly away."

You need an electric mixer on a stand for all the beating.

¾ cup sifted cake flour

½ teaspoon salt

1 teaspoon cinnamon

2 teaspoons powdered (not granular) instant coffee or espresso

¼ cup unsweetened cocoa powder (preferably Dutch-process)

6 eggs

2 teaspoons vanilla extract

1 cup granulated sugar

Adjust a rack one-third up from the bottom of the oven and preheat the oven to 325°. You will need a 10 x 4-inch angel-food tube pan with a loose rim—the bottom and tube being in one piece. It must not be a nonstick pan. Do not butter or line the pan. Place it in the sink (which is where you will need it) until you are ready for it.

Sift together the flour, salt, cinnamon, powdered instant coffee, and cocoa. Then resift together six more times. Set aside.

Place the eggs and vanilla in the small bowl of an electric mixer and beat at high speed for a few minutes, until the eggs rise to the top of the bowl. Transfer the eggs to the large bowl of the mixer and continue to beat at high speed for about 15 minutes, until the eggs have thickened to the consistency of soft whipped cream.

Then, while still beating at high speed, very slowly add the sugar, 1 tablespoon at a time. It should take 3 minutes to add the sugar.

Now, on the lowest speed, add the dry ingredients 1 heaping tablespoon at a time. While adding the dry ingredients, it is helpful to scrape the bowl gently a few times with a rubber spatula. Do not beat any longer than necessary now, or you will deflate the eggs.

Quickly run cold water into the cake pan in the sink, then pour it out, leaving the pan wet and cold. Gently pour the cake batter into the pan, pouring first on one side of the tube and then on the other. (The batter will reach only halfway to the top of the pan.)

Bake for 50 to 55 minutes until the top just barely springs back when it is pressed gently with a fingertip. (This cake is so extraordinarily light that you might not see it spring back.) The top of the cake will be flat and it will have risen to about 1 inch below the top of the pan.

Remove the cake from the oven and immediately, gently, turn the pan over and let stand upside down until the cake is completely cool.

(When I know I want to freeze this whole, I freeze it in the pan, before cutting it loose.)

Use a sharp knife that has a firm 6- or 7-inch blade; slide the blade in around the edge of the cake, pressing it against the pan (away from the cake). Slowly and carefully cut all around the cake, using a short up-and-down sawing motion and always pressing against the pan.

Then raise the pan from the counter and push the bottom up to release the sides; then lift out the tube. Next, with the pan upright, cut the bottom of the cake away from the bottom of the pan, still pressing the blade against the pan. Finally, cut around the center tube.

Cover the cake with a serving plate, turn the cake and the plate over, remove the bottom of the pan, and leave the cake as it is, upside down.

I like the simplicity of this just plain, but it is also very nice with a bit of confectioners' sugar sprinkled through a fine strainer over the top, then surrounded with a ring of large fresh strawberries with the stems and the hulls left on.

Use a serrated bread knife and a sawing motion to cut this; do not press down on it or it will squash.

KANSAS CITY CHOCOLATE DREAM

8 OR 9 PORTIONS

Variations of this recipe pop up in many areas of the country under many different names: Chocolate Upside-Down Cake, Chocolate Sauce Pudding, Chocolate Pudding Cake, Hot Fudge Sauce Cake, to name a few. In most cases, whatever the name, you will have a square pan of chocolate cake floating in a rather thin, dark chocolate syrup; both the cake and the syrup are spooned out together and served like a pudding with a sauce.

This Missouri recipe is similar, but is something else. It is a small, shallow square upside-down cake which, when it is turned onto a cake plate, covers itself with a thick layer of dark chocolate topping that resembles nothing I can think of. The topping is as dark and shiny as black patent leather, as tender and semi-firm as a pot de crème, and as mocha-chocolate flavored as you might weave dreams about.

The topping and the cake are baked together. Sensationally quick/easy/foolproof. This is wonderful just as soon as it has barely cooled, or it can wait hours, or it can be frozen.

Cake

1 cup sifted
all-purpose flour

2 teaspoons
baking powder

¼ teaspoon salt

2 tablespoons
unsweetened cocoa
powder (preferably
Dutch-process)

⅔ cup granulated sugar

¾ cup milk

1 teaspoon vanilla extract

1 ounce (¼ stick)
unsalted butter, melted

½ cup walnuts, broken
into medium-size pieces

Adjust a rack one-third up from the bottom of the oven and preheat the oven to 350°. Butter a shallow 8-inch square cake pan and set aside.

Sift together into the small bowl of an electric mixer the flour, baking powder, salt, cocoa, and sugar. Add the milk, vanilla, and melted butter, and beat until smooth and slightly pale in color. Remove the bowl from the mixer. Stir in the nuts. Turn into the buttered pan and smooth the top. Let stand.

Topping

⅓ cup granulated sugar

6 tablespoons
unsweetened cocoa
powder (preferably
Dutch-process)

½ cup dark brown
sugar, firmly packed

2 teaspoons granular
instant coffee

1 cup water

In a small, heavy saucepan combine all the ingredients. Stir over rather high heat until the sugars melt and the mixture comes to a full boil.

Gently ladle the boiling hot mixture all over the cake batter.

Bake for 40 minutes until a toothpick inserted gently into the cake comes out clean. (During baking the topping will sink to the bottom.) Set aside to cool in the pan.

When the cake has cooled, cover with a square or oblong serving plate or a cutting board. Holding them firmly together, turn the pan and the plate over. If the cake does not slide out of the pan easily (and it probably will not), hold the plate and the pan firmly together upside down and tap them on the work surface. Now the cake will come out, and it will be covered with the topping, some of which will still be in the pan; use a rubber spatula to remove it all and put it on the cake. Smooth the top gently or pull the topping up into uneven peaks.

Serve immediately or let stand all day or freeze. (If you freeze this do not cover with plastic wrap; the topping never does freeze hard and plastic wrap will stick to it. Just cover the whole thing with an inverted box deep enough so it doesn't touch the cake.) Freezing diminishes the flavor of all foods, especially this. Although this can be served frozen, it has more flavor if it is brought to room temperature.

This cake does not need a thing but a plate and fork. However, if you are serving it for a birthday party or some other festivity, ice cream is wonderful with it.

DIONE'S CHOCOLATE ROLL

10 PORTIONS

The first cooking programs I remember on American television were done by Dione Lucas. She was a sensational cook, entertainer, and teacher. When she opened an omelet restaurant in New York City called The Egg Basket, I think I was one of the first customers. The restaurant had a counter, where you could watch while Dione Lucas prepared omelets for everyone. I had the first stool, and I had the time of my life. She was a magician with omelets.

The restaurant served only one dessert, Dione Lucas' famous Chocolate Roll.

Some time later I considered myself extremely lucky to be able to attend cooking classes at Ms. Lucas' cooking school in the basement of a brownstone in New York City. There were about seven people in each class, and everyone cooked—all at once. We were allowed to choose whatever we wanted to cook. I chose this at my first class.

You will need a 12 x 18-inch (across the top) jelly-roll pan. That is larger than the usual size. It is available at kitchen shops.

Adjust a rack to the middle of the oven and preheat the oven to 350°. Now you must line a 12 x 18 x 1-inch jelly-roll pan with aluminum foil. Heavy-duty foil, which is wide enough for this, is too stiff. Regular lighter-weight foil is not wide enough; therefore you have to use two lengths. Tear off two 21-inch lengths of regular foil. Turn the pan upside down. Place one length of foil over the pan, shiny side against the pan, placing it off to one side so that when it is pressed into place there will be about ½ inch of foil extending above the rim of one long side, and the two short sides, of the pan. Place the second length of foil so that it partly covers the first and

8 ounces semisweet chocolate

⅓ cup boiling water

8 eggs, separated

1 cup granulated sugar

Pinch of salt

¼ cup unsweetened cocoa powder (preferably Dutch-process, to be used after the cake is baked)

Additional cocoa powder, if necessary

will extend above the other long side of the pan. With your hands, fold down the sides and corners of the foil, shaping it to fit the pan. Remove the foil. Turn the pan right side up. Place the shaped foil in the pan, and press it into place.

To butter the foil, place a piece of butter in the pan and set the pan in the oven to melt the butter, then spread it with a pastry brush or with a piece of crumpled wax paper over the bottom and sides. Set aside.

Break up the chocolate and place it and the boiling water in the top of a double boiler over warm water on moderate heat and cover until the chocolate is almost melted. Then stir until completely melted and smooth. Remove the top of the double boiler. If the mixture is not completely smooth, beat it with a beater or an electric mixer, and then let stand to cool until tepid or room temperature.

Place the egg yolks in the small bowl of an electric mixer and add ¾ cup of the sugar (reserving the remaining ¼ cup of sugar). Beat at high speed for 5 minutes until almost white. In a larger bowl, fold together the cooled chocolate and the yolk mixture until smoothly colored. Set aside.

Place the egg whites and the salt in the clean large bowl of the electric mixer. With clean beaters, beat until the whites hold a soft shape. Reduce the speed to moderate and gradually add the remaining ¼ cup of sugar. Increase the speed to high again and continue to beat only until the whites just barely hold a straight point when the beaters are raised—not so long that they become stiff or dry.

With a large rubber spatula, fold about one-third of the whites into the chocolate mixture without being thorough. Fold in another third just briefly. Then add all the remaining whites and carefully fold together until no whites show. (It was at this point that Ms. Lucas took the spatula from my hand and said, "When there are just one or two areas of white, and they rise to the top of the chocolate, smooth over them gently with the spatula, like this—instead of folding too much.")

Turn into the prepared pan. In order not to handle this any more than necessary, it is better to place it in large mounds all over the pan—instead of in one mound. Gently smooth it into the corners and level the top.

Bake for 17 minutes.

Meanwhile, wet a large linen or smooth cotton towel with cold water and wring it out.

When the cake is removed from the oven it should remain in the pan for 20 minutes, covered with the damp towel. And, to keep the steam and moisture in the cake, the damp towel should be covered with one or two layers of dry linen or cotton towel, or with foil or plastic wrap.

After 20 minutes, remove the towels from the top of the cake.

Through a fine strainer held over the top, dust the ¼ cup of cocoa all over the cake, including the edges.

Cover the cake with two overlapping lengths of wax paper and cover the wax paper with a large cookie sheet (or a tray or board or what have you). Holding the pan and the cookie sheet together firmly, turn them over. Remove the pan. Slowly remove the foil (it will come off easily).

Cover the cake with plastic wrap or wax paper to prevent drying out and let the cake cool completely while you prepare the whipped cream.

WHIPPED CREAM FILLING

Whipped cream for filling a cake roll should be just as stiff as is possible without curdling. Chilling the bowl and the beaters helps it to whip stiffly with less chance of trouble.

(Dione Lucas had her own way of doing it. She placed the cream in a large bowl, and that into a larger bowl partly filled with ice and water. And she beat with a large balloon whisk. Sometime in my youth I must have whipped too long, making butter instead of whipped cream. That must be why I have always been gun-shy of overwhipping. During that first class with Dione Lucas, I whipped the cream in a bowl set over ice and I whipped with the balloon whisk as I was told. Every time my whisking slowed down, because I thought the cream was stiff enough, no matter where she was in the room and no matter what she was doing [fluting mushrooms or decorating a ballotine she called out, "More—it's not stiff enough." I did what she said. It became the stiffest whipped cream I had ever made and it was not butter. The ice-cold bowl was the secret.)

1½ cups whipping cream

3 tablespoons confectioners' sugar

1 teaspoon vanilla extract

In a chilled bowl, with chilled beaters or a large whisk, whip the cream with the sugar and vanilla until the cream is firm.

Uncover the cake and place the cream by large spoonfuls all over it. With a long, narrow metal spatula spread the cream evenly up to the edge on three sides of the cake; stop the cream about 1 inch short of one long side.

Using the wax paper to help, roll the cake the long way toward the long side that has the 1-inch border.

As you finish rolling the cake, the final turn should deposit the cake seam down onto a chocolate roll board or any long, narrow serving platter.

There will be a few cracks on the surface of the cake—it is to be expected. If you wish, you can sift additional cocoa over the cracks to hide them a bit.

Refrigerate, and serve cold.

WILLIAMS-SONOMA CHOCOLATE CAKE

8 PORTIONS

Offhand, I can't think of any great chocolate recipes that include wine in the ingredients. Cognac, rum, bourbon, even Scotch whisky, and most liqueurs, but not wine. Some foods scream out "Where's the wine?" but chocolate does not.

Once when I was in San Francisco, Wes Halbruner (the book buyer for Williams-Sonoma) gave me this wonderful chocolate recipe that uses port wine (I was told to use Ficklin brand). It is an extraordinary cake, a taste thrill, a rare treat.

Wes said I should use Callebaut chocolate (which surely is divine), but I have made this with other delicious semi-sweet chocolates as well and the cake was always wonderful.

The recipe, as I received it, said that the cake must be served hot, right from the oven. Hot is fantastic, but I love it at any temperature—even frozen.

Serve it plain. Or with whipped cream and fresh raspberries or strawberries. And/or chocolate sauce.

4 ounces (1 stick) unsalted butter

½ cup port wine

4 ounces semisweet chocolate

1 cup granulated sugar

3 eggs, separated

¾ cup sifted all-purpose flour

⅛ teaspoon salt

Adjust a rack to the center of the oven and preheat the oven to 325°. Butter a 10-inch springform pan (which may be 2 to 3 inches deep), line the bottom with parchment or wax paper cut to fit, butter the paper, dust all over with flour, and then invert the pan and tap out excess. Set aside.

Place the butter, port, and chocolate in a small, heavy pan over rather low heat and stir occasionally until the butter and chocolate are melted.

Meanwhile, remove and reserve 2 tablespoons of the sugar. Add the remaining sugar to the egg yolks in the small bowl of an electric mixer and beat at high speed for a few minutes until very pale. On low speed, gradually add the warm melted chocolate mixture (I suggest that you pour your mixture into a pitcher first to make it easier to add), and beat until smooth. Then beat in the flour. Remove the bowl from the mixer.

This may be prepared hours ahead to this point; if so, cover this bowl and the bowl of whites and let stand at room temperature.

In a clean small bowl with clean beaters, beat the egg whites and the salt until the whites hold a soft shape. Gradually, add the reserved 2 tablespoons of sugar and beat until the whites hold a definite shape but are not stiff or dry.

Fold about one-third of the beaten whites into the chocolate mixture. Then transfer both the remaining chocolate mixture and the egg-white mixture to a larger bowl and fold them together only until just incorporated. Do not handle any more than necessary.

Pour the mixture into the prepared pan.

Bake for 30 minutes, until a toothpick inserted near the middle comes out clean but not dry.

Remove from the oven and let stand for 5 minutes. Then, gently cut around the sides of the cake with a table knife to release it from the pan, and then remove the sides of the pan.

Cover the cake with a plate and turn the plate and cake over. Remove the bottom of the pan and the paper lining. Serve upside down. The cake will be only 1 inch high.

Serve as soon as possible (or later). Be prepared for a custard-like quality if you serve the cake right away.

Cowtown Chocolate Cake

12 PORTIONS

Many Texans call Fort Worth "Cowtown," a name that came about when Fort Worth was the center of the cattle industry. This cake was famous years ago at a Fort Worth coffee shop. It is an extremely chocolaty two-layer cake with an equally chocolaty semisoft icing that stays semisoft.

Adjust a rack to the middle of the oven and preheat the oven to 350°. Butter two 9-inch round layer-cake pans, line them with rounds of parchment or wax paper cut to fit, then butter the paper, and dust the pans all over with fine, dry bread crumbs. Invert the pans over paper and tap lightly to shake out excess. Set the pans aside.

1½ cups sifted
all-purpose flour

¼ cup unsweetened
cocoa powder (preferably
Dutch-process)

1 teaspoon baking soda

½ teaspoon salt

1 teaspoon powdered
(not granular) instant
coffee or espresso

5 ounces unsweetened
chocolate

4 ounces (1 stick)
unsalted butter

1 teaspoon vanilla extract

1 cup light brown
sugar, firmly packed

1 cup granulated sugar

3 eggs, separated

1¼ cups buttermilk

Sift together the flour, cocoa, baking soda, salt, and powdered coffee or espresso. Resift the ingredients one more time and set aside.

Place the chocolate in the top of a small double boiler over warm water on moderate heat. Cover the pan with a folded paper towel (to absorb steam) and then the pot cover. Let cook until the chocolate is almost completely melted and smooth. Remove the top of the double boiler and set aside.

In the large bowl of an electric mixer, beat the butter until it is soft. Beat in the vanilla and brown sugar.

Remove and reserve 3 tablespoons of the granulated sugar; beat the remaining granulated sugar into the butter mixture. Add the yolks and beat well. Then add the melted chocolate (which may be slightly warm or cool) and beat until smooth.

On low speed, add the sifted dry ingredients in three additions alternately with the buttermilk in two additions, scraping the bowl as necessary with a rubber spatula and beating only until smooth after each addition. Remove the bowl from the mixer and set aside.

In the small bowl of the electric mixer (with clean beaters), beat the egg whites until they hold a soft shape. Reduce the speed to moderate and gradually add the reserved 3 tablespoons of granulated sugar. Increase the speed again and continue to beat only until the whites hold a point when the beaters are raised. They should not be stiff or dry.

The chocolate mixture will be thick; add about one-quarter of the whites and fold the two together, or stir a bit to incorporate if necessary. Then add the remaining beaten whites and fold until completely incorporated.

Place half of the batter in each of the cake pans and smooth the tops.

Bake for about 35 minutes, until the tops of the cakes barely spring back when pressed gently with a fingertip and the cakes just begin to come away from the sides of the pans.

Remove from the oven and cut gently around the sides of the cakes with a small, sharp knife to release. Let stand for 5 minutes.

Cover each cake with a rack, turn the cake pan and rack over, remove the cake pan and paper lining, cover with another rack, and turn over again, leaving the cakes right side up to cool.

When you are ready to ice the cake, place four 10 x 3-inch strips of parchment or wax paper in a square pattern on a large flat cake plate. Place one layer on the plate upside down, checking to be sure that the papers touch the cake all around. If you have a cake-decorating turntable, place the cake plate on it.

ICING

1 cup whipping cream

1 cup granulated sugar

4½ ounces unsweetened chocolate

Pinch of salt

4 ounces (1 stick) unsalted butter, cut into slices

1 teaspoon vanilla extract

Stir the cream and sugar in a 2½- to 3-quart heavy saucepan over moderate heat until the mixture comes to a boil. Reduce the heat and let the mixture simmer for 6 minutes, stirring occasionally. Remove the pan from the heat, add the chocolate, and stir until it is melted; then add the salt, butter, and vanilla, and stir until the butter is melted and the mixture is smooth.

Place the pan in a large bowl of ice and water and scrape the bottom continuously for a few minutes with a rubber spatula, until the mixture is cool and slightly thickened. Transfer the mixture to the small bowl of an electric mixer and beat at high speed for a few minutes until the color becomes slightly lighter and the icing is thick enough to hold its shape.

Spread a layer of the icing about ¼ inch thick over the layer on the plate. Place the other layer on it, right side up (bottoms together). Spread the remaining icing thinly on the sides of the cake, and more thickly on the top. With a small, narrow metal spatula smooth the sides, and then with a long, narrow metal spatula smooth the top.

Now, to form a pattern on the top, with the tip of the metal spatula make a straight row of little peaks just touching each other down the middle of the cake. Then repeat, making rows of peaks, just touching each other (and the rows just touching) to cover the top of the cake completely.

Remove the paper strips by pulling each one out toward a narrow end.

OREO COOKIE CAKE

16 PORTIONS

A Washington-based reporter from USA Today called me to say she was doing a story on bought chocolate cookies and asked if I ever buy any. (Yes, I do. Especially Afrikas from specialty food stores, and chocolate-covered graham crackers.) During our conversation she told me that Oreo cookies are the most popular commercial cookies in the world: More Oreo cookies are sold than any other. (I would have guessed chocolate chip cookies.)

The conversation inspired me to add Oreo cookies to a white sour cream cake I had been making just before the phone rang. As a matter of fact, as you will see, part of the batter was in the pan already when the phone rang. And when I baked it, it was so good, I wrote the recipe that way.

See if anyone can guess before you tell them what this cake is. No one could when I served it. It is similar to a pound cake but more moist; it has a divine flavor, a delicious crust—and Oreo cookies.

14 to 15 Oreo
sandwich cookies

2¾ cups sifted
all-purpose flour

½ teaspoon salt

1 teaspoon baking soda

8 ounces (2 sticks)
unsalted butter

1 teaspoon vanilla extract

¼ teaspoon
almond extract

1½ cups granulated sugar

3 eggs

1 cup sour cream

Optional:
Confectioners' sugar

Adjust a rack one-third up from the bottom of the oven and preheat the oven to 350°. You need a tube pan with a 10- to 12-cup capacity, preferably one with a rounded bottom and a fancy design (this is especially beautiful made in the swirl-patterned pan with a 12-cup capacity, see page 10). Butter the pan well (even if it has a nonstick finish) and dust all over with fine, dry bread crumbs, invert it over paper, and tap out excess crumbs. Set the pan aside.

Place the cookies on a cutting board. With a sharp, heavy knife cut them one at a time into quarters; at least, that should be what you have in mind—actually, they will crumble and only a few will remain in quarters. Set aside.

Sift together the flour, salt, and baking soda, and set aside.

In the large bowl of an electric mixer, beat the butter until soft. Add the vanilla and almond extract and the granulated sugar, and beat to mix well. Then add the eggs one at a time, beating until thoroughly incorporated after each addition. On low speed add the dry ingredients in three additions alternately with the sour cream in two additions, scraping the bowl as necessary with a rubber spatula and beating only until incorporated after each addition.

Place about 1½ cups of the mixture by heaping teaspoonfuls in the bottom of the pan. Smooth with the bottom of a teaspoon and then, with the bottom of the spoon, form a rather shallow trench in the mixture.

Now add the cut-up Oreo cookies to the remaining batter and fold them in very gently, folding as little as possible just to mix them with the batter.

With a teaspoon, place the mixture by heaping spoonfuls into the pan over the plain batter. And, with the bottom of the spoon, smooth the top. This is going to be the bottom of the cake, but the cake doesn't know that and it rises in a round dome shape. To prevent that a bit, spread the batter slightly up on the sides of the pan, leaving a depression in the middle. It will not fix it completely, but it will help.

Bake for 1 hour, until a cake tester inserted gently into the cake comes out clean and dry. When done, the top will feel slightly springy to the touch. During baking the cake will form a crack around its surface and the crack will remain pale—that is as it should be.

Cool in the pan for 15 minutes. Then cover the pan with a rack and turn the pan and rack over. Remove the pan. Let the cake cool.

The cake can be served as it is, plain (plain, but moist and wonderful) or with confectioners' sugar sprinkled through a fine strainer over the top, or with the following gorgeous, thick, dark chocolate, candylike glaze just poured unevenly over the top. To glaze, place the cake on a rack over a large piece of wax paper or aluminum foil.

GLAZE

6 ounces semisweet chocolate

2 ounces (½ stick) unsalted butter

About 1 tablespoon whipping cream

Break up the chocolate and place it in the top of a small double boiler over warm water on low heat. Cover with a folded paper towel (to absorb steam) and with the top cover and let cook until barely melted. Then remove the top of the double boiler and stir the chocolate until completely smooth.

Cut the butter into small pieces and add it to the chocolate, stirring until melted and smooth. Then stir in the cream very gradually (different chocolates use different amounts of cream); the mixture should be thick, just barely thin enough to flow slowly and heavily.

Pour the glaze around and around over the top of the cake, letting it run down unevenly in places.

Let the cake stand until the glaze has set and then transfer to a cake plate.

Layer
Cakes

American Chocolate Layer Cake

20 or more portions

I remember a heart-wrenching disappointment when I was very young. I had been told that I was going to have a piece of chocolate layer cake; my anticipation was overwhelming. But when it came I was thrown into despair. It was a white cake—a white cake with chocolate icing.

I learned that that's what Americans call a chocolate layer cake.

This is it, the most stupendous of all chocolate layer cakes (over 5 inches high). It is enough for a very large party, or a small army.

It has four layers of rich butter cake, two of which have optional chunky walnut pieces throughout. The icing is a dark chocolate sour cream concoction that is miraculous; it is thick/smooth/shiny, it doesn't care if you use it right away or after lunch, and it doesn't care if you work over it again and again.

What's more, both the cake and the icing are easy and foolproof.

(You need five cake racks for removing four layers from the pans.)

4 cups sifted all-purpose flour	Adjust two racks to divide the oven into thirds and preheat the oven to 350°. Butter four 9-inch round layer-cake pans, line them with parchment or wax paper cut to fit, butter the paper, dust the pans all over with fine, dry bread crumbs, tilt the pans from side to side to coat them evenly, and then turn them upside down over paper and tap them to shake out loose crumbs. Set the pans aside.
4 teaspoons baking powder	
¼ teaspoon baking soda	
½ teaspoon salt	Sift together the flour, baking powder, baking soda, and salt, and set aside.
1 pound (4 sticks) unsalted butter	In the large bowl of an electric mixer, beat the butter until soft. Add the vanilla and almond extracts and then the sugar, and beat to mix. Add the eggs one or two at a time, and beat until incorporated after each addition. On low speed, add the sifted dry ingredients in three additions alternating with the milk in two additions.
1½ teaspoons vanilla extract	
½ teaspoon almond extract	Remove the bowl from the mixer. You will have a generous 8 cups of batter. Place a generous 2 cups in two of the prepared pans. Stir the optional nuts into the remaining batter and place half of it (a generous 2 cups) in each of the two remaining pans.
2 cups granulated sugar	
6 eggs	With the back of a large spoon, spread the batter to the sides of the pans. To encourage the cakes to rise with flat tops (without domes) spread the batter more thickly around the edges and slightly thinner in the middle of the pans.
¾ cup milk	
Optional: 6 ounces (1½ cups) walnuts, cut or broken into medium-size pieces	Place two of the pans on each oven rack, staggering them so that the pans on the lower rack are not directly below those above.

Bake for 25 to 28 minutes. (I have made this cake many times and have never found it necessary to change the positions of the pans during baking; somehow they always bake evenly, even though that is unusual for my oven.) Bake until the tops just barely spring back when they are gently pressed with a fingertip and the sides of the cakes just barely begin to come away from the sides of the pans. Do not overbake or the cake will be dry.

As soon as the cakes are done, remove them from the oven; cover each one with a rack and turn the pan and rack over. Remove the pan—if the paper lining does not come off by itself leave it on—cover with another rack, and invert again, leaving the cakes right side up to cool.

When they have cooled, cover each one with a rack and turn over briefly to remove the paper linings. Then turn right side up again. Brush each cake with a pastry brush to remove loose crumbs on the sides.

Prepare a large flat cake plate by lining it with four strips of wax paper. Place one cake on the plate, checking to be sure that it touches the papers all around. If you have a cake-decorating turntable, place the cake plate on it.

Let stand, and make the icing. Or if you wish, the icing may be made while the cakes are baking.

CHOCOLATE SOUR CREAM ICING

This doesn't run and it doesn't harden; you can apply it smoothly or in swirls—it works like a charm with a pastry bag.

16 ounces milk chocolate

12 ounces semisweet chocolate

Pinch of salt

1 teaspoon vanilla extract

1 pint (2 cups) sour cream, at room temperature

Break up the chocolates and place them in the top of a large double boiler over shallow warm water on low heat. Cover the pot with a folded paper towel (to absorb the steam) and with the pot cover. Let cook until almost completely melted, then uncover and stir with a wooden spatula until completely melted.

Transfer to the large bowl of an electric mixer. Add the salt, vanilla, and sour cream, and beat on low speed until as smooth as satin (this is spectacular looking).

If the icing is too thin, let stand at room temperature for about an hour or so until slightly thickened.

If you have a cake-decorating turntable and are experienced at using it, you will probably want to smooth the icing on the top and sides; without a turntable, you will probably want to form the icing into swirls. If you plan to smooth it, you will probably also want to form a circle of rosettes around the top rim. If so, remove and reserve about ⅔ cup of the icing.

Whether you plan to smooth the icing or swirl it, do not use too much between the layers or you will not have enough to go around (in spite of the fact that this looks like enough icing for a dozen cakes).

With a long, narrow metal spatula, spread a scant ¼-inch layer of icing over the cake, making it a bit thicker at the rim to fill in the space. Place the next layer on (if you have used nuts, alternate the nut layers with the plain ones) right side up, and ice it the same as you did the first. Place the third layer on, right side up (align the layers carefully), ice, and then place the fourth layer on, right side up (all four layers are right side up).

Cover the sides of the cake with the icing, and then the top. Make sure it is all straight and even. Then smooth or swirl. Carefully remove the paper strips by slowly pulling each one out toward a narrow end.

If you have smoothed the icing and if you would like to decorate the rim (I do), fit a 12-inch pastry bag with a #7 star-shaped tube. Fold down the sides of the bag toward the outside to make a 2- to 3-inch hem, and twist the top of the bag closed.

If you are working on a countertop, transfer the cake and the turntable to a table; it is easier to decorate the top of a cake if you are working above it rather than alongside it—especially a cake this high. Form a row of rather large rosettes (about the size of Hershey's Kisses) just touching one another on top of the cake around the rim.

Now, how about that? I salute you.

Serve this on wide plates.

PRUNE AND WALNUT LAYER CAKE

24 PORTIONS

This beauty consists of three layers of moist and rich, prune and nut, buttermilk and sour cream cake, mildly spiced, and generously filled and covered with a fantastic and extravagant chocolate-cream cheese-buttercream mousse. Prune cakes of all kinds were made on the farms and in the cities many years ago; this one is an old favorite—it is wonderful.

Generous 1½ cups stewed pitted prunes, tightly packed (see Notes)

3 cups minus 2 tablespoons sifted all-purpose flour

1 teaspoon baking soda

½ teaspoon baking powder

½ teaspoon salt

1 teaspoon cinnamon

1 teaspoon nutmeg

1 teaspoon ground cloves

2 tablespoons unsweetened cocoa powder (preferably Dutch-process)

8 ounces (2 sticks) unsalted butter

1 teaspoon vanilla extract

1¾ cups granulated sugar

3 eggs, separated

½ cup buttermilk

½ cup sour cream

Ingredients continued on next page.

Adjust two racks to divide the oven into thirds and preheat the oven to 350°. Butter three 9-inch round layer-cake pans, line them with rounds of parchment or wax paper cut to fit, then butter the paper, dust all over with fine, dry bread crumbs, and invert over paper and tap out excess crumbs. Set aside.

Coarsely chop the prunes (I chop them on a board with a large chef's knife—or you can cut them with scissors) and place them in a wide strainer or a colander over a bowl to drain, but not to dry completely (they add moisture to the cake). Sift together the flour, baking soda, baking powder, salt, cinnamon, nutmeg, cloves, and cocoa, and set aside.

In the large bowl of an electric mixer, beat the butter until soft. Add the vanilla and 1½ cups of the sugar (reserving the remaining ¼ cup of sugar) and beat to mix. Add the egg yolks and beat until incorporated. On low speed, add the sifted dry ingredients in three additions, alternating with the buttermilk and then the sour cream, scraping the bowl with a rubber spatula and beating until smooth after each addition. Remove the bowl from the mixer and stir in the prunes and nuts. Set aside.

In the small bowl of an electric mixer (with clean beaters), beat the egg whites until they hold a soft point. Reduce the speed slightly and gradually add the remaining ¼ cup of sugar. Then beat again briefly, at high speed, only until the whites just barely hold a straight point when the beaters are raised.

In two additions, fold the whites into the batter. Divide the batter among the pans and smooth the tops.

Bake for 35 to 40 minutes, until the cakes just begin to come away from the sides of the pans and the tops spring back when they are pressed lightly with a fingertip in the middle. Do not overbake. Toward the end of the baking, if the cakes are not browning evenly, change the positions of the pans.

8 ounces (generous
2 cups) walnuts,
cut or broken into
medium-size pieces

Let stand for 2 to 3 minutes and then cover each pan with a rack, turn the pan and rack over, remove the pan and paper lining, cover the cake with another rack, and turn it over again, leaving the cakes right side up to cool on the racks.

Before icing the cake, prepare a wide, flat cake plate by placing four 12 x 4-inch strips of parchment or wax paper in a square around the sides of the plate. Place one cake layer on the plate upside down (all three layers will be upside down). Check to see that it touches the papers all around. If you have a cake-decorating turntable, place the cake plate on it.

CHOCOLATE CREAM CHEESE MOUSSE ICING

14 to 16 ounces
semisweet chocolate
(see Notes)

8 ounces cream
cheese, preferably at
room temperature

8 ounces (2 sticks)
unsalted butter

1 teaspoon vanilla extract

½ cup plus 2 tablespoons
granulated sugar

2 eggs, separated

1 cup whipping cream

Pinch of salt

Break up the chocolate and place it in the top of a large double boiler over warm water on low heat. Cover with a folded paper towel (to absorb steam) and the pot cover and heat until almost completely melted. Then uncover and stir until completely melted. Remove the top of the double boiler and set aside briefly.

In the large bowl of an electric mixer, beat the cream cheese and butter with the vanilla and ½ cup of the sugar (reserve the remaining 2 tablespoons of sugar) until well mixed. Add the melted chocolate (which should still be warm to help dissolve the granules of sugar), and beat well until the sugar is dissolved. Beat in the 2 egg yolks (reserve the whites), beating at high speed until the mixture is as smooth as honey and has lightened slightly in color. Set aside.

In a small bowl, with chilled beaters, whip the cream until it is very firm or as firm as you can make it without taking any chance that it might turn to butter. (The safest way to do this is to use the mixer only until the cream holds a soft shape. Then finish the whipping with a whisk. That way you have better control of what is happening and there is less chance of overbeating.) Set aside.

In a clean small bowl, with clean beaters, beat the egg whites with the salt until the whites hold a soft shape. Reduce the speed to moderate and gradually add the remaining 2 tablespoons of sugar. Increase the speed again and continue to beat briefly until the whites hold a straight shape when the beaters are raised, but are not stiff or dry. Set aside.

NOTES: *If you want to stew the prunes yourself, you will need a 12-ounce box of dried pitted prunes or 1 pound of prunes with pits. If you buy them already stewed, you will need a 1-pound 9-ounce jar.*

I have made this with 14 ounces of Poulain chocolate and also with 16 ounces of Callebaut chocolate, and it was wonderful both ways.

Without being too thorough, fold the whipped cream in two additions into the chocolate mixture, then add the beaten whites and continue to fold gently only until the mixtures are blended—do not handle any more than necessary.

With a long, narrow metal spatula spread a layer of the icing a generous ½ inch thick over the bottom layer of cake. Place the second layer of cake upside down over the icing. Spread that with another generous ½-inch-thick layer of icing. Cover with the top layer of cake (also upside down).

Spread a rather thick layer of the icing all around the sides, and then over the top. If you wish, reserve about ¾ cup of the icing for decorating the cake. (To do this, place the icing in a small pastry bag fitted with a #4 or medium-size star-shaped tube. Form a row of small rosettes just touching one another around the top rim of the cake.)

CAUTION: *Do not tilt the cake plate until the icing has been refrigerated or the layers will slide out of place. Take my word for it and hold the plate very carefully.*

Remove the strips of parchment or wax paper by pulling each one out slowly toward a narrow end.

Refrigerate for at least several hours before serving. The cake should be very cold when it is served. Serve small portions.

DECORATION

2 to 3 ounces milk chocolate

Unsweetened cocoa powder (preferably Dutch-process)

Confectioners' sugar

With a vegetable parer, form small curls of milk chocolate, allowing them to fall onto a piece of wax paper. With a large spoon or wide spatula gently transfer the curls to the top of the cake, placing them within the ring of rosettes, or, if you have not made rosettes, cover the top of the cake all the way to the edges. Make it a generous layer of chocolate curls.

Then sprinkle the top of the cake with unsweetened cocoa powder through a fine strainer held over the cake. And then, using a clean, fine strainer, cover with a layer of confectioners' sugar.

STAR-SPANGLED BANNER CAKE

20 PORTIONS

I made three of these for a big New Year's Eve party at Craig Claiborne's home on Long Island. After icing each cake, I wrapped a shiny yellow ribbon around its middle, made big fluffy bows, inserted tiny yellow and white silk flowers in each bow, and taped a little "Happy New Year" sign onto one of the streamers of each bow. (I inserted a long bamboo skewer deep into the cake right under each bow to support its weight.)

The secret is to make the whole thing, ribbon, bow, and bouquet, ahead of time, using a cake pan as a dummy. Cut the ribbon at the side of the pan opposite the bow, then just "dress" the cake by taping the ribbon together at the back of the cake.

The cakes were beautiful, but they are equally delicious and equally attractive without these decorations.

This is a big, bold, beautiful four-layered Southern banana-nut cake, 6 inches high, with a mountain of fluffy white icing and a shower of coconut. This is for occasions: birthdays, New Year's Eve, or for the cover of a magazine. It is not difficult to make, there is nothing tricky, but stacking the four layers with the abundance of icing takes courage.

3 cups sifted
all-purpose flour

2 teaspoons
baking powder

½ teaspoon salt

6 ounces (1½ sticks)
unsalted butter

1 teaspoon vanilla extract

¼ teaspoon
almond extract

2 cups granulated sugar

3 eggs

About 5 large fully
ripened bananas (to
make 2½ cups, mashed)

1 teaspoon baking soda

6 ounces (1½ cups)
pecans, chopped
finely (not ground)

½ cup buttermilk

Adjust two racks to divide the oven into thirds and preheat the oven to 350°. Prepare four 9-inch round layer cake pans as follows. Butter the bottoms and sides, line the bottoms with rounds of parchment or wax paper cut to fit, then butter the paper, dust with fine, dry bread crumbs, then invert over paper and lightly tap out excess crumbs. Set the pans aside.

Sift together the flour, baking powder, and salt, and set aside.

In the large bowl of an electric mixer, beat the butter until it is soft. Beat in the vanilla and almond extracts and the sugar, beating only to combine well. Add the eggs one at a time, beating thoroughly after each addition. (The mixture might appear curdled—it is okay.)

Coarsely mash the bananas on a wide plate with a fork (they should not be liquefied or puréed). Place them in a bowl and mix in the baking soda. Beat the bananas and then the nuts into the creamed butter mixture.

On low speed add half of the sifted dry ingredients, then the buttermilk, and finally the remaining dry ingredients, beating only until mixed after each addition.

Divide the batter among the pans. Smooth the tops. The layers will be very thin. Place two pans on each rack; do not place pans directly over or under other pans.

Bake for 28 to 30 minutes, until the tops spring back when pressed gently with a fingertip and the layers barely begin to come away from the sides of the pans.

Covering each layer with a rack, invert the pan and rack, remove the pan and paper lining, cover with another rack, and turn the layers over again, leaving them right side up to cool.

With a dry pastry brush, brush the sides of the cooled layers to remove loose crumbs.

Before icing the cake, place four 12 x 4-inch strips of parchment or wax paper in a square pattern around the sides of a large cake platter. Place one layer on the platter right side up and check to be sure that the papers touch the cake all around. (See Variation.)

If you have a cake-decorating turntable, place the platter on it.

SOUTHERN FLUFFY WHITE ICING

You will need an electric mixer with a 4-quart bowl.

3 cups granulated sugar

⅓ cup light corn syrup (e.g., Karo)

¾ cup boiling water

¾ cup egg whites (from about 6 eggs; they may be whites that were frozen and then thawed)

Pinch of salt

1 teaspoon vanilla extract

¼ teaspoon almond extract

14 ounces (5⅓ cups, loosely packed) moist shredded coconut

Place the sugar, corn syrup, and boiling water in a 2⅓- to 3-quart saucepan over moderate heat. Stir frequently with a wooden spoon until the sugar is dissolved. When the mixture comes to a full boil, remove it from the heat and set it aside briefly.

In the large bowl of an electric mixer, beat the egg whites with the salt until the whites stand up straight when the beaters are raised.

Transfer the hot syrup to a pitcher that is easy to pour from and, beating at high speed, pour the hot syrup in a thin threadlike stream into the whites, holding the pitcher about 12 inches above the mixer bowl. Pour slowly and scrape the sides of the bowl occasionally with a rubber spatula to keep the entire mass well mixed. It will look as though the bowl will not hold all of the icing; it will, but you must watch it carefully and reduce the speed if necessary to prevent the icing from overflowing.

After all the syrup has been beaten in, add the vanilla and almond extracts and continue to beat (at high speed, if possible) for about 15 more minutes until the icing is very stiff and holds a straight peak when the beaters are raised. Remove the bowl from the mixer.

Spread a generous layer of the icing about 1 inch thick over the first layer of cake. Then place the second cake layer over the icing, also right side up. Cover it with another inch-thick layer of icing. Continue layering the cakes and the icing.

Spread a thick layer of the icing around the sides and then spread all the remaining icing (it will be a thick layer) over the top.

With a long, narrow metal spatula smooth the sides and then the top (be sure the sides are straight and the top is flat).

Place the coconut on a large piece of paper right up against the cake platter. Take a handful of the coconut in the palm of your hand, then turn your hand to place the coconut on the side of the cake. Some of the coconut will stick to the cake and some will fall to the platter; with your fingers, transfer the fallen coconut to the pile of coconut on the paper. Pick up another handful and continue to coat the sides with the coconut. If there are spots on the sides near the bottom where there is not coconut, just fold the paper strips up against the cake and the coconut that has fallen onto the strips will stick to the sides of the cake. Then sprinkle all the remaining coconut over the top of the cake.

Remove the paper strips gently by pulling each one out toward a narrow end.

Let the cake stand at room temperature.

To serve, have dinner plates ready—cake plates are too small for this. Use a long, sharp knife and have a deep pitcher of very hot water to dip the knife into before each cut, so you can cut with a hot, wet blade. Or if you prefer to serve on smaller plates, serve the two top layers first (making 10 two-layer portions) and then the two bottom layers (10 more portions).

VARIATION: *Sprinkle a generous amount of light rum onto each layer when it is in place on the plate, just before icing it. If you do use the rum, use enough so that you really taste it.*

PECAN SWEET POTATO CAKE

10 TO 12 PORTIONS

Hallelujah! An old-fashioned Southern spectacular production, a majestic, regal, three-layer sweetheart, 6 inches high, light/moist/spicy/chunky/nutty, with a generous amount of marshmallow filling and icing and a coating of shredded coconut over all. It is made with shredded raw (uncooked) sweet potatoes—most unusual and most delicious.

The cake can be made ahead of time and frozen, if you wish, but wait until the day of the party to ice it.

2¼ cups sifted all-purpose flour

1 tablespoon baking powder

¼ teaspoon salt

1 teaspoon ground ginger

1 teaspoon nutmeg

2 cups granulated sugar

1½ cups vegetable oil

4 eggs, separated

¼ cup boiling water

1 teaspoon vanilla extract

1 pound (about 1½ large) raw sweet potatoes or yams (to make 2 cups, tightly packed, when shredded)

6 ounces (1½ cups) toasted pecans (see page 6), broken into large pieces

Ingredients continued on next page.

Adjust a rack to the middle of the oven and preheat the oven to 350°. Butter three 8-inch round layer-cake pans, line them with parchment or wax paper cut to fit, then butter the paper, dust all over with fine, dry bread crumbs, invert the pans over paper and tap gently to shake out excess, and set aside.

Sift together the flour, baking powder, salt, ginger, and nutmeg, and set aside. In the large bowl of an electric mixer, beat the sugar and oil just to mix; add the egg yolks and beat to mix. On low speed, add the sifted dry ingredients in three additions alternating with the boiling water and vanilla in two additions. Remove the bowl from the mixer and set aside.

To prepare the sweet potatoes, peel them with a vegetable parer and then grate them on the fine grater of a food processor or with a hand-held grater set over a piece of aluminum foil. Use the side of the grater that has small, round—not diamond-shaped—openings (to see the shape of the openings hold the grater up and look at the holes through the back). Measure 2 cups, tightly packed.

Stir the potatoes and then the pecans into the batter.

In the small bowl of an electric mixer (with clean beaters), beat the whites until they hold a straight shape when the beaters are raised, but are not stiff or dry.

Without being too thorough, fold about one-third of the whites into the batter, then fold in the remaining whites, handling as little as necessary until just incorporated.

Divide the batter among the prepared pans and smooth the tops.

Bake the three pans on the same oven rack for 30 to 35 minutes, until the cakes barely begin to come away from the sides of the pans. (These layers might not spring back when pressed with a fingertip, even though they will be done.)

⅓ cup apricot preserves (to be used when icing the cake)

7 ounces (2⅔ cups, loosely packed) shredded coconut (to be used when icing the cake)

Cool in the pans for 2 to 3 minutes. Then cover each pan with a rack, turn the pan and rack over, remove the pan and paper lining, cover with another rack, and turn over again, leaving the layers right side up to cool.

When you are ready to ice the cake, place four 12 x 4-inch strips of parchment or wax paper in a square pattern around the sides of a large cake plate. There will be such a thick layer of icing that it does not matter if the layers are placed right side up or upside down (I place them all right side up). Place one layer on the plate, checking to see that it touches the papers all around. If you have a cake-decorating turntable, place the cake plate on it.

Stir the apricot preserves in a small saucepan over moderate heat to melt. Then press them through a strainer. With a teaspoon or a pastry brush, spread the first cake layer with one-third of the preserves. Reserve the remaining preserves.

MARSHMALLOW ICING

You will need a candy thermometer.

1½ cups granulated sugar

⅔ teaspoon cream of tartar

⅔ cup water

⅛ teaspoon salt

⅔ cup egg whites (from 4 to 5 eggs; they may be whites that were frozen and then thawed)

1 teaspoon vanilla extract

¼ teaspoon almond extract

Place the sugar, cream of tartar, and water in a 6-cup saucepan (preferably one that is tall and narrow—in a wide one the mixture will be too shallow to reach the bulb of a candy thermometer). With a wooden spoon stir over moderate heat until the mixture begins to boil. Cover airtight and let boil for 3 minutes. (This keeps the steam in a pot and dissolves any sugar crystals that cling to the sides. However, if you still see any granules when you remove the cover, dip a pastry brush in cold water and use it to wipe the sides.)

Uncover and insert a candy thermometer. Raise the heat to high and let boil, without stirring, until the thermometer registers 242°.

Shortly before the sugar syrup is done (or when the thermometer registers about 236°—soft-ball stage), add the salt to the egg whites in the large bowl of an electric mixer and beat until the whites are stiff. (If the sugar syrup is not ready, turn the beater to the lowest speed and let it beat slowly until the syrup is ready. Or you can let the whites stand, but no longer then necessary.)

When the syrup reaches 242° (medium-ball stage), turn the mixer to high speed and gradually add the syrup in a thin stream (it may be easiest if you pour the syrup into a pitcher and add it from the pitcher). Then continue to beat at high speed, scraping the bowl occasionally with a rubber spatula, for about 5 minutes, or until the icing is quite thick and stiff. Add the vanilla and almond extracts a minute or two before the icing is stiff enough. If necessary, beat some more. The icing may still be warm when it is used.

Spread the first cake layer with icing about ½ inch thick. Place the second layer over it and spread with one-third of the melted apricot preserves, and then cover it with a layer of the icing, again ½ inch thick. Cover with the third cake layer and the remaining preserves.

Now, it is best to ice the sides first. Use a long, narrow metal spatula to ice the sides, thinly at first, and then build it up until it is about ½ inch thick, or thicker. Smooth the sides. Use the remaining icing on the top. Spread it smooth. After the sides and the top are smooth and even, then, with the back of a teaspoon or with the spatula, form swirls and peaks evenly on the top of the cake.

To coat the sides with the coconut, first spread out the coconut on a length of foil or wax paper next to the cake plate. Take a handful of the coconut in the palm of your hand and turn your hand to place the coconut on the sides of the cake, starting at the top and working your way down. When much of the coconuts falls onto the plate, remove it with your fingers and replace it either on the cake or on the pile of coconut on the paper. Then use a long, narrow metal spatula to pick up coconut that has fallen to the plate and turn it onto the sides of the cake. Finally, fold the paper strips around the bottom up against the cake, and the coconut that has fallen to the strip will stick to the base of the cake. Last, sprinkle all the remaining coconut over the top.

Remove the paper strips by pulling each one slowly and gently toward a narrow end.

Since this cake is so high, use a long-bladed knife to cut it and dinner plates to serve it on; it will fall off the edges of smaller plates.

BOSTON CREAM PIE

8 PORTIONS

Long ago there was a famous American dessert called "pudding-cake pie." When the great Parker House Hotel opened in Boston, in 1855, they added a chocolate icing to the dessert and renamed it Boston Cream Pie. It immediately became, and has remained, one of America's most loved desserts. It is a plain white two-layer sponge cake (moist and tender) with a vanilla pastry-cream filling (like a vanilla pudding, creamy and delicate) and a thin layer of dark semisweet chocolate glaze on top: an addictive combination.

It is so very simple and easy looking that you might think it should be easy to make, but simple-looking and plain things are often more difficult than elaborate things. Making this cake involves great care with folding in beaten whites and yolks and sifted dry ingredients and melted butter. And the filling calls for patience in making the custard carefully and slowly so you don't wind up with scrambled eggs.

But then—joy! It is a great accomplishment. My congratulations to you.

There are many recipes for Boston Cream Pie. This is the best I've ever had. We originally ate it in Boston; the recipe is adapted from one in the revised edition of the Boston Globe Cookbook *(Boston Pequot Press, 1981).*

I don't know why this cake is called a pie.

VANILLA PASTRY CREAM

Unless you want to make the cake ahead of time and freeze it, make this first in order to chill it well before using.

2 eggs

¼ cup plus 1 tablespoon sifted all-purpose flour

¼ teaspoon salt

⅔ cup granulated sugar

2 cups milk

1 teaspoon vanilla extract

¼ teaspoon almond extract

1 ounce (¼ stick) unsalted butter, cut into small pieces

In a small bowl beat the eggs lightly just to mix; set aside. Mix the flour, salt, and sugar in a heavy 2-quart saucepan. Gradually stir in the milk, then cook, stirring constantly, over medium-low heat until the mixture comes to a boil and starts to thicken. Continue to stir and boil gently for a minute or two. The mixture should become as thick as a medium white sauce—or about like vichyssoise.

Remove the pan from the heat. With a ladle add about ½ cup of the hot mixture to the eggs and stir well to mix. Repeat, adding ½ cup at a time, until you have added about half of the hot mixture to the eggs. Then, very slowly, stirring constantly, stir the egg mixture into the remaining hot milk mixture.

Place the pan over low heat and cook, still stirring constantly, for 2 minutes. Remove from the heat. Mix in the vanilla and almond extracts and the butter.

Immediately (to stop the cooking) pour the mixture into a bowl. Cut a round of wax paper to fit on top of the pastry cream (touching it), and place the paper directly on the cream. This will prevent a skin from forming.

Now, either let this stand until cool and then refrigerate for at least an hour, or save time by placing the bowl in a larger bowl of ice and water to cool quickly, and then refrigerate for at least an hour.

Boston Sponge Cake

1 cup sifted
all-purpose flour

1 teaspoon baking
powder

3 eggs, separated

¼ teaspoon salt

⅔ cup granulated sugar

1 teaspoon vanilla extract

1 tablespoon lemon juice

2 tablespoons
cold tap water

3 tablespoons unsalted
butter, melted

Adjust a rack to the middle of the oven and preheat the oven to 350°. Butter a 9 x 1½-inch round cake pan, line the bottom with a round of parchment or wax paper cut to fit, then butter the paper, and dust all over with fine, dry bread crumbs. Invert the pan over paper and tap lightly to shake out excess crumbs. Set the pan aside.

Sift together the flour and baking powder and set aside.

Beat the egg whites and the salt in the small bowl of an electric mixer until the whites hold a soft shape. Reduce the speed to moderate and gradually add ⅓ cup of the sugar (reserve the remaining ⅓ cup of sugar). Then increase the speed again and continue to beat very briefly, only until the whites just hold a point when the beaters are raised. Do not let the whites become stiff or dry.

Transfer the beaten whites to the large bowl of the mixer. Scrape the beaters with your finger to remove most of the whites and scrape the bowl with a rubber spatula. (It is not necessary to wash the bowl or beaters.) Set aside.

Place the yolks in the small bowl of the mixer. Beat briefly, then gradually add the remaining ⅓ cup of sugar and continue to beat at high speed until the mixture is very light—almost white. Beat in the vanilla and lemon juice; then on low speed add the cold tap water, scraping the bowl as necessary and beating only until the mixture is smooth.

In about four additions, fold the yolks into the whites (do not handle any more than necessary and do not be too thorough, especially with the first few additions).

Place the dry ingredients in a sifter and hold the sifter over the bowl, sifting with one hand and folding with the other. The dry ingredients should be added in four or five additions. (Do not handle any more than necessary.)

The melted butter may be slightly warm or it may have cooled to room temperature, but it must still be liquid. Add it all at once to the batter and fold gently only until barely (but not absolutely) incorporated.

Turn the batter into the prepared pan and smooth the top.

Bake for about 30 minutes, until the top springs back when pressed gently with a fingertip.

Remove from the oven. With a small, sharp knife cut around the rim of the cake to release it. Let stand in the pan for 5 minutes. Then cover the pan with a rack, turn the pan and the rack over, remove the cake pan—do not remove the paper lining, which should be clinging to the cake—cover the cake with another rack and turn over again, leaving the cake right side up to cool.

The next step is to cut the cake into two thin layers. I think it is easiest and safest if you first chill the cake in the freezer for about 30 minutes or longer. Place the cold cake upside down on a flat cake plate. Remove the paper lining from the cake. If you have a cake-decorating turntable, place the cake plate on it. Use a long, thin, sharp knife (I use a ham slicer—or you might like to use a serrated knife) and carefully cut the cake into two thin layers.

Carefully remove and set aside the top layer.

Turn the chilled pastry cream onto the bottom layer of the cake. With a long, narrow metal spatula spread the pastry cream to ½ inch from the edges of the cake. (If it goes any closer to the edges, the weight of the top layer might spread it out too far.)

Cover with the top layer. Now refrigerate the cake while you make the glaze.

CHOCOLATE GLAZE

¼ cup whipping cream

4 ounces semisweet chocolate, chopped coarse

Place the cream in a small, heavy saucepan over moderate heat until it begins to bubble. Add the chocolate, stir briefly until partly melted, then remove the pan from the heat and continue to stir until completely melted. Transfer the glaze to a small bowl and let stand for about 10 minutes, stirring occasionally.

Pour the glaze onto the cake; then, with a long, narrow metal spatula, smooth it just to the edge of the cake. Try to avoid having the glaze run down the sides of the cake, but if a bit does, leave it. Refrigerate and serve cold.

Kentucky Cake
10 to 12 portions

This was a famous Southern cake more than 100 years ago. Versions of it were also called Union Cake. It is a large two-layer cake, each layer mixed and baked separately; one layer dark and spicy, the other white and lemony. It is filled and iced with a thick coating of marshmallowlike 7-minute icing. Fancy and gorgeous, it makes a scrumptious birthday cake or Christmas cake. The layers can be made way ahead of time and frozen, if you wish; the cake should be iced the day it is served.

Dark Layer

⅓ cup dark raisins

1 cup sifted
all-purpose flour

¼ teaspoon salt

⅓ teaspoon baking soda

½ teaspoon cinnamon

⅛ teaspoon ground cloves

¼ teaspoon nutmeg

¼ teaspoon mace

¼ teaspoon allspice

¼ teaspoon dry mustard

3 ounces (¾ stick)
unsalted butter

⅓ cup dark brown
sugar, firmly packed

2 eggs, separated
(reserve the whites
for the white layer)

⅓ cup buttermilk

⅓ cup dark or
light molasses

Adjust a rack one-third up from the bottom of the oven and preheat the oven to 375°. Since you will eventually make two layers of cake, why not prepare both pans now? Butter two 9-inch round layer cake pans, line the bottoms with rounds of parchment or wax paper cut to fit, then butter the paper, dust with fine, dry bread crumbs, and invert over paper and shake out excess crumbs. Set the pans aside.

Cut the raisins coarsely by placing them on a board and cutting down on them with a long, heavy chef's knife. Put them in a small bowl, add about 1 tablespoon of the flour, and toss to separate and coat the pieces thoroughly.

Sift the remaining flour with the salt, baking soda, cinnamon, cloves, nutmeg, mace, allspice, and mustard, and set aside. In the small bowl of an electric mixer beat the butter until soft, then beat in the sugar. Add the yolks and beat until incorporated. On low speed gradually add the buttermilk and molasses, and then the sifted dry ingredients (the mixture will appear slightly curdled—it is okay). Remove the bowl from the mixer. Stir in the floured raisins (along with any loose flour in the bowl).

Turn into the prepared pan, smooth the top, and bake for 25 to 30 minutes, until the top of the cake springs back when it is pressed gently with a fingertip and the cake begins to come away from the sides of the pan.

Let stand for a minute or two, cover with a rack, turn the pan and the rack over, remove the pan and the paper lining, cover the cake with another rack, and turn over again, leaving the cake right side up on the rack to cool.

With a dry pastry brush, brush away any loose crumbs from the sides of the cool cake.

WHITE LAYER

1 cup sifted
all-purpose flour

⅛ teaspoon salt

1 teaspoon baking
powder

3 ounces (¾ stick)
unsalted butter

½ teaspoon vanilla extract

1 teaspoon lemon extract

⅔ cup granulated sugar

⅓ cup milk

Finely grated rind
of 1 large lemon

2 egg whites (reserved
from making the
dark layer)

Optional: 1 tablespoon
bourbon (to be used
when icing the cake)

Adjust a rack one-third up from the bottom of the oven and preheat the oven to 375°.

Sift the flour with the salt and baking powder and set aside.

In the small bowl of an electric mixer beat the butter until soft; beat in the vanilla and lemon extracts and the sugar. On low speed add about one-third of the sifted dry ingredients and then gradually add all of the milk (the mixture will probably appear curdled after adding the milk—it is okay). Still on low speed add the remaining dry ingredients and beat only until smooth.

Remove the bowl from the mixer and stir in the grated lemon rind.

In a clean small bowl, with clean beaters, beat the whites only until they hold a straight shape when the beaters are raised but are not stiff or dry. Then, in several additions, small at first, fold the whites into the batter, handling as little as possible (the first few additions should not be thorough).

Turn into the prepared pan and smooth the top.

Bake for 25 minutes, until the top of the cake springs back when pressed lightly with a fingertip and the sides of the cake begin to come away from the pan.

Let stand for a minute or two, cover with a rack, turn the pan and rack over, remove the pan and the paper lining, cover with another rack, and turn over again, leaving the cake right side up to cool on the rack.

With a dry pastry brush, brush away loose crumbs from the sides of the cool cake.

To ice the cake, place four 12 x 4-inch strips of parchment or wax paper in a square pattern around the sides of a large cake platter and place the dark layer upside down on the plate, making sure it is touching the paper all around. If you have a cake-decorating turntable, place the cake platter on that.

Pour the optional bourbon into a small cup and, with a pastry brush, brush it over the layer. (Or hold your thumb over the top of the bottle, turn the bottle upside down, and allow the bourbon out very slowly; just drizzle it onto the cake.)

7-MINUTE ICING

½ cup egg whites (from about 4 eggs; they may be whites that were frozen and then thawed)

1½ cups granulated sugar

¼ cup plus 1 tablespoon cold water

1 teaspoon cream of tartar

⅛ teaspoon salt

1 teaspoon vanilla extract

½ teaspoon lemon extract

To make this amount of icing it is best to use a double boiler that has at least a 10-cup capacity. If yours has less, create your own large one. Use a metal or heavy pottery bowl with a slightly rounded bottom and place the water in a saucepan only slightly narrower than the bowl. The bowl should rest on the rim of the saucepan. The water in the saucepan should not be deep enough to touch the bowl.

Place all of the ingredients, except the extracts, in the bowl over water on moderate heat.

With a portable electric mixer start to beat at high speed immediately; cook and beat for about 5 minutes (it used to take 7 minutes before electric mixers), or until the mixture stands in straight peaks when the beaters are raised.

Instantly transfer the mixture to the large bowl of an electric mixer (unless that is what you cooked it in, in which case replace it on the mixer stand) and continue to beat, scraping down the sides occasionally with a rubber spatula. Add the vanilla and lemon extracts and beat for a few minutes until the icing is quite stiff. Use immediately.

Spread a smooth layer of the icing, about ¾ inch thick, over the dark layer.

Place the white layer over the icing right side up (bottoms together), brush or sprinkle on the optional bourbon, and spread a thick layer of the icing around the sides of the cake. Then place all of the remaining icing on the top. With a long, narrow metal spatula smooth the sides and top. Then, with the back of a teaspoon, form even rows of peaks right next to one another on the top and then on the sides.

Remove the paper strips by pulling each one out slowly toward a narrow end.

When serving the cake it will be a help to dip the knife in a deep pitcher of hot water before each cut and, if necessary, to wipe the blade after each cut.

Fancy
Cakes

WALNUT TART FROM SAINT-PAUL-DE-VENCE

16 PORTIONS

This is called a tart and is made with pastry, but it is really a very fancy cake.

I once taught cooking classes at Ma Cuisine, a cooking school connected to Ma Maison, a wonderful restaurant in Los Angeles. One day we wound up a beautiful lunch in the restaurant with a divine chocolate-walnut-honey pastry that was brand new to me and so good I couldn't stand it. A gentleman who was one of the students in my classes there heard me rave about it and gave me what he said was the recipe. And then one of the food magazines printed the recipe. Then a big French cookbook printed it. All three recipes were similar, and none of the three worked for me.

I recently came across an old pamphlet published by the Cuisinart people. And there was the recipe again. But this time it came from Gino Cofacci, one of the best pastry chefs in New York. Gino got it from Le Mas des Serres, a restaurant in a picturesque little medieval walled village on the French Riviera. Gino's recipe was different from the other three and hallelujah—it worked!

It is a French pastry dough formed in a quiche pan, surrounding a rich walnut-and-honey mixture. After it is baked and cooled it is inverted, iced with chocolate, and decorated with walnuts. It is a large dessert that makes 16 portions, and Mr. Cofacci says that it will keep in the refrigerator for a week or two. Or you can freeze it, even with the icing. And I have kept it at room temperature for a few days. Heaven!

This is not quick and easy, and is not a recipe for a beginning baker. When you make this, you will be so pleased that my congratulations will be lost in the excitement; however, I do congratulate you.

Just a note to give an idea of how special I consider this dessert: When I was invited to dinner at Julia and Paul Child's, this is the dessert I brought.

The following is my own adaptation of the recipe.

You will need an 11 x 1-inch loose-bottomed quiche pan. The pan must be made of blue or black steel (in a shiny pan the bottom will not brown). Mine is made in France by Matfer, and is available in many kitchen shops.

The filling should be made first.

FILLING

1½ cups granulated sugar

½ cup water

7 ounces (1¾ sticks) unsalted butter, cut into pieces, at room temperature

In a 2½- to 3-quart saucepan, cook the sugar and water over moderate heat, stirring with a wooden spoon, until the sugar is dissolved and the mixture comes to a boil. Wash down any sugar crystals clinging to the sides of the pan with a pastry brush dipped in cold water. Increase the heat to high and let boil without stirring. When the mixture starts to color, swirl the pan occasionally, until the syrup caramelizes to a rich butterscotch color. It will take 7 or 8 minutes of hard boiling.

1 cup less 2 tablespoons milk

⅓ cup honey

12 ounces (3½ cups) walnuts, cut into small pieces (the nuts must be in small pieces but they must not be ground, see Notes)

Remove the pan from the heat and, with a long-handled wooden spoon or spatula, slowly stir in the butter. Then, very gradually, stir in the milk. Adjust the heat so the mixture just simmers for 15 minutes; stir it occasionally. If the mixture appears to be curdled, beat it briskly with a medium-size wire whisk; it might not smooth out completely—that's okay (the curdled look will disappear when the tart is baked). After the 15 minutes are up, stir in the honey and then the nuts.

Pour the mixture into a large bowl and stir occasionally until cooled to room temperature. (If this is made a day ahead, it may be refrigerated. If so, let it stand at room temperature for at least an hour and stir it to soften before using.)

PASTRY

3 egg yolks

⅓ cup ice water

4 cups sifted all-purpose flour (as with all the recipes in this book that call for sifted flour, sift it before measuring even if the package says presifted)

¼ cup granulated sugar

¼ teaspoon salt

9 ounces (2¼ sticks) unsalted butter, cold and firm, cut into small pieces (the pieces should be no larger than ¼- to ½-inch square; cut the butter ahead of time and refrigerate it)

The pastry can be mixed in an electric mixer, or by hand, or in a food processor. Whichever method you use, first stir the yolks and water with a fork in a small bowl just to mix, and then refrigerate.

In a mixer: Place the flour, sugar, salt, and butter in the large bowl of an electric mixer. Beat on the lowest speed. If you are using a wide, flat-bottomed bowl, continually push the ingredients in toward the beaters with a rubber spatula (a cone-shaped bowl does it by itself). When the mixer has cut the butter into such small pieces that the mixture resembles coarse oatmeal (which takes about 5 minutes), add the egg-yolk-and-water mixture and beat for only a few seconds, scraping the bowl with the spatula, until well mixed but not until the mixture holds together.

By hand: Place the dry ingredients in a large bowl and use a pastry blender to cut in the butter until the particles are fine. Then use a large fork to stir in the egg-yolk mixture. It will be dry and crumbly.

In a food processor: This quantity is too much for the original-size processor. If you have one of the larger models, it can be used, following the same procedure as for a mixer.

To use the regular-size food processor, not the extra-large one, I have used the following procedure with excellent results. Place half of the flour, sugar, salt, and butter in the processor bowl. Process with 12 to 15 quick

Notes: *The nuts must be chopped but not ground. If the pieces are not small enough, it is difficult to serve the tart, and more difficult to eat it. I cut the nuts one at a time with a small paring knife. But I'm a nut; you could do them all at once on a board with a long, heavy chef's knife. Try for pieces or slices about ⅛ inch thick. Prepare the nuts before you start the recipe—even days before, if you wish.*

At Ma Maison this was served with a small mountain of whipped cream and a mound of fresh raspberries. Both of which make this even more divine. (Try flavoring the whipped cream with kirsch or framboise. For each cup of cream use 2 tablespoons of granulated or confectioners' sugar and 1 tablespoon of kirsch or framboise.)

If you have any leftover scraps of pastry, use them to make sugar cookies. Press the scraps together, roll them out to about ⅛-inch thickness, cut with a cookie cutter, place on an unbuttered cookie sheet, brush the tops with milk, and sprinkle them generously with granulated sugar. Bake them high in the oven at 425°, until the cookies are lightly browned on the bottoms and around the

on-and-off pulses (12 to 15 seconds) until the butter particles are fine. Transfer to a large bowl. Repeat with the remaining ingredients. Stir the two processed mixtures together. Then use a large fork to stir in the egg-yolk mixture.

Turn the dough out onto a work surface, squeeze it between your hands and knead it only until the dough holds together. (Do not handle so much that the butter melts.) Form the dough into a fat sausage shape about 6 inches long with flat ends. Score it lightly into thirds. Then cut it into two pieces—the one piece, for the bottom crust, should be a scant two-thirds (about 3½ inches long), and the other, for the top, should be a generous one-third (about 2½ inches long).

Form both pieces into smooth round balls, flour them lightly, and flatten them a bit into rounds with smooth edges. Wrap each piece in plastic wrap and let stand at room temperature for 20 to 30 minutes, or if the room is very warm refrigerate the dough for 20 to 30 minutes, but no longer, or it will crack when it is rolled.

Adjust a rack one-third up from the bottom of the oven. Preheat the oven to 475°. Have ready an 11 x 1-inch loose-bottomed blue or black steel quiche pan; do not butter it, and do not place it on a cookie sheet. If you have a cake-decorating turntable, place the quiche pan on it.

On a floured pastry cloth with a floured rolling pin, roll the larger piece of dough into a 14-inch circle (when it is in place in the pan it must extend a generous ½ inch above the sides of the pan). Loosely drape the pastry over the rolling pin and unroll it over the pan, centering it carefully. Press it into place in the pan. Trim the edges with scissors, leaving a generous ½ inch of pastry standing up above the sides of the pan.

On the floured pastry cloth with the floured rolling pin, roll the remaining piece of dough into a circle a little wider than the quiche pan. Let it stand.

Spoon the filling over the bottom crust and gently smooth it—it must not be mounded in the middle.

Flour your fingers lightly and thin out the raised rim of dough that extends above the pan (I use my thumb and the side of my folded-under index finger). That section will be a double thickness when the top is in place; if it is too thick, it will not bake through.

rims. Then place them briefly under the broiler to melt the sugar; broil until the sugar is bubbly and slightly colored.

The big difference between Mr. Cofacci's recipe and the other three is the egg yolks in the pastry; the others didn't have any. And the others used less flour and less butter.

Now, carefully fold down the pressed-thin rim, folding it in to cover the outside edge of the filling all the way around. With a brush, brush that folded-down section with water.

Drape the rolled-out top crust over the rolling pin and unroll it over the filling, centering it carefully. With your fingers press down on the rim to cut off excess pastry; then, with the back of the fork tines (floured if necessary), press all around carefully to ensure that the crusts are pasted together. It is best to hold the fork so the handle is over the center of the tart and the end of the prongs touch the inside of the rim of the pan. With a small, sharp knife, pierce the top in two or three places near the center.

Bake for 20 minutes, until the top is golden brown. Watch it carefully and constantly; if it bubbles up anywhere, make a small slit with a sharp paring knife to release trapped air, and, if necessary, press down on the bubble with a metal spatula to flatten it. Remove from the oven. If the top is uneven, place a lightweight board or baking sheet on it for a few minutes to flatten it a bit as it cools.

Let stand in the pan until completely cool. Then cover the tart with a large, flat serving platter or board and very carefully turn over the platter and the tart. Remove the sides and bottom of the quiche pan.

Cut six strips of wax paper about 8 x 3 inches. Carefully lift the edges of the tart (with a wide metal spatula, or with your fingers) just enough to allow you to slide the edges of the wax papers under the tart to protect the platter while you ice the tart.

If you have a cake-decorating turntable or a lazy Susan, place the platter on it.

ICING

9 ounces semisweet
chocolate

3½ ounces (1 stick
minus 1 tablespoon)
unsalted butter, cut
into small pieces, at
room temperature

16 perfectly shaped
walnut halves (for
decoration)

Break up or chop the chocolate into small pieces and place it and the butter in the top of a large double boiler over hot water on moderate heat. Cover for a few minutes until partly melted. Then uncover and stir until completely melted and smooth. If it is not perfectly smooth, whisk it with a small wire whisk. Remove from the hot water and let stand for about 10 minutes.

Pour all of the icing over the top of the tart.

With a long, narrow metal spatula, smooth the icing over the top, spreading it so that the top is very smooth and a bit runs down on the sides. With a small, narrow metal spatula, smooth the icing over the sides to cover them completely and smoothly. Or better yet, instead of spreading the icing on the sides, when you spread the icing on the top, do it so that enough of it runs down on the sides to completely cover the sides.

Place the walnut halves in a rim around the top.

Do not allow the icing to dry before the paper strips are removed. Carefully remove the wax-paper strips by pulling each one out toward a narrow end.

This may be refrigerated for a week or two when it is firm (refrigerate and then cover it with plastic wrap). But bring it to room temperature before unwrapping, or it may be frozen (wrap after the icing is frozen firm, and thaw before unwrapping). Just remember to bring it to room temperature before serving.

PARIS-BREST

8 PORTIONS

This is extra special! It is dramatically beautiful and wonderfully delicious—you will love it. This is for a party, and although it is not difficult, it is not one I recommend for a beginner. It is a monster eclair shaped like a doughnut for the Jolly Green Giant, with a luscious pastry cream (the best!) and with a layer of whipped cream. And although that should be enough to make the cover of a magazine, you can, if you wish, fill the center with a mound of fresh strawberries. I did, when I made this as a birthday cake, and placed a ring of candles all around the top. Wow!

This is a classic French dessert. In the late nineteenth century there was a famous bicycle race from Paris to Brest and back to Paris; this was created to commemorate the race—it had to do with the shape of the racetrack—or was it the shape of the bicycle wheels?

I have made the whole thing from start to finish in about 1½ hours, a record time. But, if you wish, both the cream puff and the pastry cream can be made a day ahead. Or the empty cream puff can be frozen. It takes only a few minutes to whip the cream and put it all together. Plan to put it together as close to serving time as is possible and comfortable; it will be okay refrigerated for a few hours if necessary.

There are many ways of shaping the pastry into a large ring. I have the best results with a pastry bag and a plain round giant-size tube, 1¼ inches in diameter. But that size tube is too hard to find, so you can simply use the bag itself without any tube. The pastry bag should be about 16 inches long and must be made of plastic-coated canvas (mine is made by Ateco) because you will cut the opening to make it larger and that type bag does not have to be hemmed. With scissors, cut the small opening in the bag to make it 2 inches in diameter. Later on, you will also need a smaller bag with a star-shaped tube for applying the whipped cream.

CREAM PUFF PASTRY (PÂTE À CHOUX)

3 ounces (¾ stick)
unsalted butter, cut
into small pieces, at
room temperature

1 cup boiling water

1 teaspoon
granulated sugar

Pinch of salt

1 cup sifted
all-purpose flour

4 eggs

Adjust an oven rack one-third up from the bottom of the oven and preheat the oven to 425°. Butter a cookie sheet and dust it all over with flour; invert and tap to shake off excess flour. With the tip of a knife, lightly trace around a 9-inch cake pan or plate on the center of the cookie sheet, and set it aside.

Off the heat; place the butter, boiling water, sugar, and salt in a heavy saucepan with a 2- to 3-quart capacity. Stir until the butter melts. Then place it on high heat and let stand only until the mixture comes to a full boil. (Do not boil unnecessarily or too much water will evaporate.)

Remove from the heat and immediately add the flour all at once and beat vigorously with a wooden spatula or wooden spoon until the mixture forms a ball and comes away from the sides of the pan. Then return to low heat and cook, stirring, for 30 seconds.

Turn the mixture into the large bowl of an electric mixer. On medium-low speed add the eggs one at a time and beat only until completely mixed after each addition. That's it.

Fold down a deep cuff on the outside of the prepared large pastry bag and transfer the warm mixture to the bag. Be careful not to let the mixture drip out of the bottom opening. Unfold the cuff and gently twist the top of the bag closed. (See Note.)

Place the prepared cookie sheet on a table. (It is easier to work with a pastry bag at table height than at counter height.) Hold the pastry bag at a right angle to the sheet with the opening very close to the sheet, and centered over the guideline. Press from the top of the bag so the pastry comes out slowly and thickly, forming a wide band of pastry. The ends should overlap slightly. Any pastry remaining in the bag may be pressed out in a thinner band on top of the heavy one, or it may be used to build up a low spot if there is one. Then, with the back of a spoon, smooth over any uneven areas. The band of pastry should be a generous 1½ inches wide and a scant 1 inch high. (If the shape is slightly uneven don't worry, but if it is terrible, scrape it all back into the pastry bag, wash/butter/flour the sheet, and try again.)

TOPPING

1 egg yolk

1 teaspoon water

¼ cup slivered (julienne) blanched almonds

Combine the egg yolk and water. With a soft pastry brush, brush the mixture over the top only of the pastry. (Do not let it run down on the sides or it may keep the pastry from rising.) Sprinkle the almonds on top.

Bake for 20 minutes. Then reduce the temperature to 350° and bake for 40 minutes more (total baking time is 1 hour). The ring will rise to gargantuan proportions and it will become beautifully browned; don't worry if the almonds seem too dark—they are okay. About 10 minutes before the baking is finished, reach into the oven and, with a small, sharp, paring knife, cut about a dozen small slits all over the ring to allow steam to escape.

Transfer the baked pastry to a cake-decorating turntable or to a countertop or cutting board.

(In order to be able to replace the top in the correct spot over the bottom, place two toothpicks in the side, one above the line where you will cut, and one below it.)

Then, without waiting, while the pastry is very hot, cut it as follows: Use a serrated knife (preferably the small one called a tomato knife). Do not cut in the middle, but cut about one-third down from the top, in order to make the bottom deep enough to hold the filling. Carefully remove the top. Either with your fingers or with a fork, remove most of the excess moist dough from both the bottom and the top.

Let the ring stand at room temperature until you are ready to fill it. If it is going to wait overnight, cover it just loosely with plastic wrap; if you wrap it airtight it might soften. Or wrap and freeze it; to thaw, place the frozen halves cut sides up on two cookie sheets, on two racks, in a 425° oven for about 5 minutes (that should both thaw and recrisp them).

Pastry Cream (Crème Pâtissière)

2 cups milk

4 egg yolks

⅔ cup sugar

⅛ teaspoon salt

¼ cup cornstarch

2 tablespoons unsalted butter, cold and firm, cut into 6 or 8 pieces

1¼ teaspoons vanilla extract

Place 1½ cups (reserve ½ cup) of the milk in a saucepan over moderate heat and cook, uncovered, until it is scalded.

Meanwhile, place the egg yolks in a mixing bowl, stir to mix with a small wire whisk, then gradually add the sugar, whisking constantly and briskly. (If you add the sugar all at once, it might granulate the yolks.) Add the salt and continue to whisk for about a minute.

Place the remaining ½ cup milk and the cornstarch in a small bowl and stir to dissolve the cornstarch.

When the milk in the saucepan forms tiny bubbles on the edge or a thin skin on the top, add it, very gradually at first, to the yolks, whisking constantly.

Slowly add the cornstarch mixture to the warm milk mixture, stirring constantly.

Transfer the mixture to a heavy 2- to 2½-quart saucepan. (If you do not have a large enough pan that is heavy, use any large pan placed over shallow hot water in a larger pan, thereby making a double boiler.)

Cook over moderate heat, scraping the bottom constantly with a rubber spatula. As you do, add the butter, one piece at a time. Continue to cook, continuing to scrape the bottom of the pan, until the mixture thickens. It will thicken faster on the bottom of the pan, so keep it all moving. As it starts to thicken on the bottom, reduce the heat slightly.

The pastry cream should cook until it thickens to the consistency of a heavy mayonnaise. (It might take about 8 minutes.) It should just barely start to bubble but not actually boil. Reduce the heat to very low and continue to stir gently for about 2 minutes more.

Remove from the heat and transfer to a wide mixing bowl. Stir in the vanilla. If the cream is lumpy, whisk it very briefly for only a few seconds (beating it hard now could actually thin it).

Stir gently occasionally as it cools to prevent a skin from forming and to release steam. (You can speed up the cooling by placing the bowl of pastry cream in a larger bowl of ice and water.)

The pastry cream can be used now or it can be refrigerated overnight. (If you refrigerate it, cover the top of the bowl or container with a paper towel—above but not touching the pastry cream—to absorb the moisture and then cover with foil, plastic wrap, or the top of the container.)

WHIPPED CREAM

1½ cups heavy cream

2 tablespoons confectioners' sugar

¾ teaspoon vanilla extract

NOTE: Whenever you use a pastry bag, after filling it, unfold the cuff, twist the top closed, and, holding the bag with the point upright, twist the wide part of the bag to force out air and to force the mixture right up to, but not out of, the opening.

In a chilled bowl with chilled beaters, whip all of the ingredients until the cream holds a firm shape. Fit a 12- to 14-inch pastry bag with a #7 star-shaped tube. Fold down a deep cuff on the outside of the bag. Transfer the cream to the bag and unfold the cuff.

To assemble the Paris-Brest, place the bottom half of the puff on a large, flat serving plate. Spoon the pastry cream into the shell and smooth it.

Now, the thing to remember about putting the whipped cream over the pastry cream is that the outside edge of it will show and should look pretty. I make reversed "C" shapes, each one about 1½ inches long (or half-moon shapes with the horns facing in). Use any remaining whipped cream to form rosettes over the middle of the filling; they will help to keep the top slightly raised.

Replace the top of the cream puff, allowing the whipped cream to show slightly around the edge.

Refrigerate.

Before serving, sprinkle the top generously with confectioners' sugar, sprinkled through a fine strainer held over the top.

When you cut this into portions be careful not to squash it; use a serrated knife (preferably the small one called a tomato knife).

VARIATION: Make the cream puff as in Paris-Brest, cool, and split. Fill it with small scoops of ice cream in a variety of flavors and colors, put the top on, wrap in plastic wrap, and freeze. This wonderful dessert can be made any time and kept in the freezer—no last-minute work.

This may be served with any kind of fruit—fresh, canned, frozen and thawed, raw or stewed, plain or brandied. Or with the following World's Best Hot Fudge Sauce from my chocolate book.

THE WORLD'S BEST HOT FUDGE SAUCE

1 CUP

This is very thick, coal black, as shiny as wet tar, and not too sweet. It will turn chewy and even thicker when it is served over cold ice cream—great! It may be served hot or warm, but at room temperature or chilled it will be too thick. It may be refrigerated for a week or two before serving.

½ cup heavy cream

3 tablespoons unsalted butter, cut into small pieces

⅓ cup granulated sugar

⅓ cup dark brown sugar, firmly packed

Pinch of salt

½ cup strained Dutch-process cocoa powder (it must be Dutch-process to have the right color and flavor)

Place the cream and butter in a heavy 1-quart saucepan over moderate heat. Stir with a small wooden spoon until the butter is melted and the cream just comes to a low boil. Add both sugars and stir for a few minutes until they are dissolved. (The surest test is to taste; cook and taste carefully without getting burned until you do not feel any undissolved granules in your mouth.)

Reduce the heat. Add the salt and cocoa and stir briskly with a small wire whisk until smooth. (If the sauce is not smooth—if there are any small lumps of undissolved cocoa—press against them, and stir well, with a rubber spatula. Or blend it briefly in a blender.)

Serve immediately, or cool and reheat slowly in the top of a double boiler over hot water, or in a heavy saucepan over the lowest heat.

This should be thick, but when it is released it may be too thick. If so, stir in a bit of hot water, adding very little at a time.

NOTE: *If you plan to store the sauce in the refrigerator, use a straight-sided jar or a container that flares out at the top. The sauce will become too firm when it is chilled to be spooned out of a jar. It is best to place the jar or container in hot water until the block of sauce melts on the outside and can be poured out of the container. Pour it into the top of a small double boiler over hot water, or into a small, heavy saucepan over the lowest heat. Stir and cut into pieces with a wooden spatula until completely melted.*

ZUGER KIRSCHTORTE

12 TO 16 PORTIONS

Kirsch is German for cherries. Kirschwasser (also known as kirsch) is a brandy made from cherries. A Kirschtorte can be almost any cake that contains kirsch or cherries. But a Zuger Kirschtorte, from the town of Zug in Switzerland, is something special. It is a world-famous, old-world, gorgeous, and elegant dessert cake that is probably Switzerland's best-known cake. It is a big production to make. And worthy of every minute it takes. Once you make this you can be mighty proud. This is seldom mentioned in cookbooks for nonprofessionals, and is seldom found in bakeries or restaurants.

To describe it, from the bottom up: There is a layer of crisp almond meringue; a layer of kirsch buttercream; a 2-inch-thick, divine, light, buttery sponge cake soaked in a generous amount of kirsch syrup; then more of the buttercream; another layer of the meringue; and still more of the buttercream. The sides are covered with buttercream and toasted slivered almonds and the top has a simple crosshatch design in the buttercream. Classy and beautiful!

If you wish, the layer of cake and the two layers of meringue can be made a day before completing the cake (store the meringue in the turned-off oven). The finished cake may be refrigerated for a day or two before it is served.

CAKE LAYER

½ cup sifted
all-purpose flour

6 tablespoons
sifted cornstarch

2½ ounces
(5 tablespoons)
unsalted butter

4 eggs plus 3 egg yolks
(the whites will be used
for the meringue)

¾ cup granulated sugar

Adjust a rack one-third up from the bottom of the oven and preheat the oven to 350°. Butter a 9 x 2- or 3-inch springform pan. Line the bottom with a round of wax paper or baking-pan liner paper cut to fit. Butter the paper and dust all over with flour. Tap lightly over a piece of paper to shake out excess flour. Set the pan aside.

Sift together the flour and cornstarch and set aside.

Cut the butter into small pieces and place it in a small pan over low heat to melt slowly. Then set it aside to cool to tepid or room temperature, but not long enough for it to harden.

Meanwhile, place the eggs and yolks in the small bowl of an electric mixer, or, if you don't have that kind of electric mixer, use a 7-cup capacity bowl. Add the sugar and beat at high speed for about 5 minutes, until the mixture increases in volume and reaches the top of the bowl. Transfer it to the large bowl of the mixer and continue to beat for 3 to 5 minutes more (8 to 10 minutes of beating altogether), until the mixture is very pale and thick and has tripled in volume.

Remove the bowl from the mixer.

Place the flour and cornstarch mixture in the sifter (over a piece of paper). Sift about one-third of the mixture over the egg mixture and, with a large rubber spatula, fold it in. Repeat, sifting about one-third at a time over the eggs and folding gently and carefully to incorporate.

Now, in about four or five additions, add the melted and cooled butter, gently folding it in. Do not fold or handle a bit more than necessary. (With the first few additions, do not fold in the butter completely.)

Turn into the prepared pan. Bake for about 35 minutes. Then, with a small, sharp knife, gently and carefully cut around the sides to release. Remove the sides of the pan. Cover the cake with a rack. Invert the cake and the rack. Remove the bottom of the pan; do not remove the paper lining. Leave the cake upside down to cool.

Meringue Japonaise

A meringue Japonaise has ground nuts folded into the egg-white mixture.

⅓ cup blanched almonds

1 cup granulated sugar

½ tablespoon all-purpose flour

4 egg whites (you will have 2 whites left over from the cake layer and 4 from the buttercream; use any of those, or you can use whites that were left over from another recipe, frozen, and then thawed)

Adjust two racks to divide the oven into thirds and preheat the oven to 275°. Line two cookie sheets with baking-pan liner paper or aluminum foil. With a pencil, trace a 9-inch circle on each piece of paper or foil. Spread butter within the circle and about ¼ inch beyond. (It is not necessary to flour the buttered section. Curiously, in my experience the meringue sticks to buttered and floured wax paper.)

The nuts must be finely ground. They can be ground in a processor, blender, or nut grinder (if you grind them in a processor or blender, add a bit of the sugar to keep them from lumping)—they must be fine, dry, and powdery. In a small bowl, stir the ground nuts with ⅓ cup (reserve the remaining ⅔ cup) of the sugar and the flour. Set aside.

In the small bowl of an electric mixer, beat the whites until they hold a soft shape. Reduce the speed to moderate and gradually, 2 tablespoons at a time, add the reserved ⅔ cup of sugar, beating for 10 to 15 seconds between additions. Then increase the speed to high and continue to beat until the sugar is dissolved (rub a bit between your fingers to be sure) and the meringue is very stiff—do not underbeat. Remove from the mixer.

In two additions, carefully fold the almond mixture into the meringue. Do not handle any more than necessary, but be sure that the almond mixture is evenly incorporated.

To keep the baking-pan liner or foil in place while you work on it, use a bit of the meringue as a paste on each corner of the cookie sheet under the paper or foil.

To shape the meringue with a pastry bag, fold down a deep cuff on the outside of a large (about 15-inch) pastry bag. Fit it with a #6 (½-inch) plain round tube. To make it easy to fill the bag, stand it upright in a tall, narrow glass or jar. Transfer the meringue to the bag. Unfold and close the top of the bag.

Pressing on the top of the bag, press the mixture out, starting with a spot directly in the middle of the circle, and then pressing the meringue out into a long, continuous spiral like a coiled rope until the traced circle is filled in (the lines of meringue should just barely touch each other); however, the meringue will spread slightly in baking, and the meringue layers and the cake layer should have the same diameter—therefore, stop the meringue a scant ¼ inch inside the traced circle. (But if the layers become too wide it can be corrected later.)

After shaping both meringue layers, use a long, narrow metal spatula to smooth the tops and fill in any empty spots.

If you prefer, you can shape the meringue without the pastry bag by just spreading it. But it is much easier to form even layers if you use the bag.

Bake the layers for about 30 minutes. Then reverse them top to bottom and back to front and continue to bake for 30 minutes more (total baking time is 1 hour) until the meringues are crisp and dry and slightly browned. Turn off the oven heat and allow the meringues to remain in the oven until completely cool.

BUTTERCREAM

1 cup granulated sugar

¾ cup water

4 egg yolks

1 cup sifted confectioners' sugar

8 ounces (2 sticks) unsalted butter

1 tablespoon kirsch

Place the sugar and water in a small, narrow saucepan over moderate heat. Stir with a small wooden spoon until the sugar is dissolved and the mixture comes to a boil. Insert a candy thermometer, raise the heat to high, and continue to boil without stirring until the thermometer registers 234° (soft-ball stage). Meanwhile, place the egg yolks and the confectioners' sugar in the small bowl of an electric mixer. Stir slightly just to mix.

When the syrup is ready, start the mixer at high speed, hold the saucepan of syrup 10 to 12 inches above the mixing bowl, and very gradually, in a thin stream, add the hot syrup to the yolks. When it is all added, continue to beat until cool.

In another bowl (if you do not have another small bowl for the mixer, you can do this in a large bowl) beat the butter (you can use the same beaters without washing) until it is soft. Add the kirsch and beat to mix. Then gradually add the softened butter to the egg-yolk mixture, beating until smooth. Set aside at room temperature.

KIRSCH SYRUP

⅓ cup water

3 tablespoons granulated sugar

⅓ cup kirsch

Place the water and sugar in a small saucepan over moderate heat. Stir with a small wooden spoon until the sugar is dissolved and the mixture comes to a boil. Set aside to cool to room temperature. Stir the kirsch into the cooled syrup.

To assemble the cake, place four strips of wax paper around the outer edges of a flat serving plate. If you have a cake-decorating turntable or a lazy Susan, place the plate on it.

Place a generous teaspoonful of the buttercream right in the middle of the plate to keep the cake from sliding while you ice it and also while you serve it.

Place one of the meringue layers, right side up, on the plate. Cover with a thin layer (about ¼ inch thick) of the buttercream.

Remove the round of wax paper or baking-pan liner paper from the bottom of the cake layer. Place the cake upside down on top of the buttercream.

With a pastry brush, brush the kirsch syrup, a little at a time, slowly over the cake until it is all absorbed. The cake will absorb it all.

Cover with another thin layer (¼ inch thick) of the buttercream.

On top of that, place the remaining meringue layer upside down (flat side up). If the meringue layers extend out beyond the cake layer, it is easy to trim them with scissors (especially if the meringues are as crisp and dry as they should be).

Now, cover the sides and then the top with the remaining buttercream, spreading the buttercream as smoothly as you can.

DECORATION

3½ ounces (1 cup) blanched almonds, thinly sliced

Confectioners' sugar

The almonds can and should be toasted ahead of time (they should not be warm when you use them). To toast, place them on a jelly-roll pan in the center of a 350° oven, stirring occasionally, for about 15 minutes, until they are lightly colored.

With your fingers, pick up some of the cooled toasted almonds and place them on the buttercream around the sides of the cake, placing the almonds more heavily along the top of the sides than the bottom. Continue until you have used all of the almonds and the top of the sides is well covered. As you do this, quite a few of the almonds will fall onto the wax-paper strips on the plate. With a long, narrow metal spatula, lift some of the fallen almonds and turn the spatula blade sideways to put the almonds on the buttercream around the bottom of the sides, so that the sides are covered evenly.

Strain a few spoonfuls of confectioners' sugar through a fine strainer over the top of the cake—there should be a rather generous coating of the sugar.

Remove the wax-paper strips by slowly pulling each one out toward a narrow end.

Refrigerate the cake for about half an hour.

Then, score a design of diamonds on the top as follows: Use a long, sharp knife and press the length of the blade gently into the buttercream to make a line. Repeat, placing the lines ⅓ or ¼ inch apart, parallel with one another, all over the top. Whenever some of the buttercream sticks to the blade, wipe the blade clean to keep the lines neat. Then repeat, this time making the lines at an angle to the first ones, so you have a pattern of small diamonds all over the cake.

Refrigerate for a day or two. Serve cold.

JALOUSIES

6 PORTIONS

This is one of my favorite recipes. It is the Counterfeit Puff Pastry from my first dessert book shaped into a chic, classy classic French pastry, like the ones you see only in the most elegant French bakeries.

This should be served while it is very fresh—the fresher the better—but the pastry must be made ahead of time, and it really does not take long to put the Jalousie together.

This recipe can be doubled.

COUNTERFEIT PUFF PASTRY

8 ounces (2 sticks) unsalted butter

1½ cups *unsifted* all-purpose flour

½ cup sour cream

The butter should be cold and firm, and cut into very small squares; cut each stick into lengthwise quarters and then slice each strip into pieces about ½ inch wide. It is best to cut it ahead of time and refrigerate it for a while before you use it.

The first step may be done either by hand or in a food processor.

By hand: Place the flour in a wide mixing bowl. With a pastry blender cut the butter into the flour until the mixture resembles coarse crumbs; some of the pieces of butter may remain the size of small dried peas. Do not work it anymore; it should not be a smooth mixture.

In a food processor: Fit the processor with the metal blade. Place the flour and butter in the bowl of the processor. Process on and off (quick "pulses") for only about 10 seconds. Be careful not to overprocess; the mixture should not be homogeneous—you should see little pieces of butter in it. Then transfer the mixture to a large mixing bowl.

After cutting in the butter, either by hand or by machine, add the sour cream and stir briefly. Do not handle too much. Turn the mixture out onto a work surface and knead only until it holds together. Flour your hands, form the mixture into an oblong about 3 x 5 inches, flour it lightly, wrap it in plastic wrap and refrigerate for at least 2 hours, overnight or longer, or freeze it. (Thaw in the refrigerator overnight.)

You will need a 10½ x 15½-inch (or larger) jelly-roll pan. (This must be baked in a pan with sides, because so much butter runs out during baking.) Do not butter the pan.

With a strong and sharp knife, cut the dough lengthwise into two different-size oblongs—one piece should be one-third of the dough and the other should be two-thirds. Replace the larger piece in the refrigerator.

Flour a pastry board or work surface, and a heavy rolling pin. Place the smaller piece of dough on the floured surface. If it is too hard to be rolled, pound it firmly with the rolling pin, but do not pound it out of shape. Then carefully roll the dough into an oblong 15 inches long, 5 inches wide, and ⅛ inch thick. While rolling, keep the shape as even as you can, although the edges will be trimmed later.

If the kitchen is warm, work quickly.

While you are rolling the dough you will see that the pieces of butter form a marbleized effect. That is how it should be, and how it will be if you did not handle the dough too much while mixing it.

Fold the dough over so that the short ends meet, but be careful not to press down on the fold. With your hands, carefully transfer the folded dough to the unbuttered jelly-roll pan, placing the folded edge in the middle of the pan. Then unfold the dough. The short ends should just reach the short ends of the pan.

Filling

⅓ cup apricot, currant, or other thick preserves

Stir the preserves lightly to soften.

Wet a pastry brush with cold water and then shake it out well (the brush should not be dripping); with the brush (re-wet it as necessary), wet a 1-inch border around the dough.

Then spread the preserves on the dough, excluding the wet border.

If the kitchen is warm, place the pan in the refrigerator.

Now roll the larger piece of dough into the same shape and size as the other; this piece will be thicker than the first piece.

Quickly fold this piece, but not the way the other was folded—fold this one in half the long way. Now, to cut slits that will give a jalousie effect, use a small, sharp knife and cut through the folded edge (at a right angle to the fold), making cuts 1 inch long (when you unfold this, each cut will be 2 inches long).

Unfold, and then in order to make it easier to transfer, fold the strip in the opposite direction (both short ends meeting) and center it over the bottom layer. Unfold. Then, with the sides of your hands or with your fingertips, press gently to seal the edges, but keep away from the very outside edge (if you press directly on the edge it will prevent the cake from rising properly on the edge); press but do not squash the 1-inch border. Do this carefully and thoroughly or the filling will run out.

Now the four sides must be cut even. I find it easiest to do this with a pizza cutter. Or use a small, sharp knife. (The pastry will rise better if the edges are cut neat and sharp—again, be careful not to squash them together.) You can cut as much as ¼ inch off each side if it is necessary to straighten the edges.

GLAZE

1 egg (see Note)

NOTE: *If you use a glaze of only egg yolk mixed with ½ teaspoon of water instead of the whole egg, it will make a darker and shinier crust. I like it better. But I am writing it this way in order to warn you; do not let it fool you—you must bake the crust the full time in spite of the dark color.*

Prepare the icing a few minutes before the baking is finished.

Beat the egg lightly just to mix. The glaze will be brushed over the top to give the Jalousie a beautiful golden color. However, if it drips down on the cut sides, it will prevent the dough from rising properly. If you have a small, soft artist's watercolor brush, that is the best. But whatever brush you use, it should not be so wet that the egg runs and drips. With a brush that is only slightly wet, brush the top. Brush it again if you wish.

Place the Jalousie in the refrigerator for about half an hour or more (it should be very cold when it goes into the oven).

Adjust a rack one-quarter or one-third down from the top of the oven. (If this is baked any lower the bottom will burn.) Preheat the oven to 400°.

Place the cold Jalousie in the oven and immediately reduce the temperature to 350°. Bake for 40 minutes until well colored. You must be very careful not to take this out of the oven too soon. If it is not baked enough it will have wet dough inside.

ICING

¾ cup sifted confectioners' sugar

Boiling water

NOTE: *Any leftover scraps of the dough may be used for making delicious sugar cookies.*

Press them together, wrap, and chill. Then roll the dough in granulated sugar instead of flour, sugaring both sides generously. Roll the dough to ⅛- or ¼-inch thickness. Cut into strips, long or short, wide or thin; 3 x 1½ inches is a happy medium.

Place the sugar in a small bowl and add only about 1 tablespoon of the water. Stir to mix. The mixture should be thick but fluid. If necessary, add more water, but only a few drops at a time. If it gets too thin, add more sugar.

As soon as the cake comes out of the oven, immediately, with a pastry brush, brush the icing over the hot cake, including the openings where the jelly shows. It does not have to be a solid coating—it can be drizzled. The heat of the cake will melt the icing and make a shiny and almost transparent coating.

Let stand for about 10 minutes. Then, carefully, run a firm wide metal spatula under the cake to make sure it is not stuck anywhere. And then use a flat-sided cookie sheet or two wide spatulas to transfer the Jalousie to a rack to cool.

Turn one end of the strip to twist it in the middle (like a corkscrew) and place on an unbuttered jelly-roll pan. Sprinkle with a bit more sugar. Chill. Bake one-third of the way down in a 350° oven until thoroughly dry, crisp, and golden brown. Do not underbake; they are better if the sugar caramelizes a little.

When it is completely cool, if you have a chocolate-roll board, slide the cake onto it. Or transfer it to a long and narrow platter. This is extremely light/flaky/fragile/delicate, so handle with care.

Cut the cake with a very sharp knife into slices 1 inch wide, and serve 2 to a portion.

HALEAKALA CAKE

12 GENEROUS PORTIONS

In Hawaii, Haleakala means "house of the sun." Here, it means a two-layer cake originally from the Royal Hawaiian Hotel in Waikiki Beach. The layers, which are so easy you will think there is a mistake, are moist and delicious. The thick pineapple filling goes both between the layers and also on top, under the icing. It is the best high, white, fluffy 7-minute or marshmallow-type icing I know. And the cake is covered all over with a thick layer of shredded coconut.

This is a big, dramatic cake to make for a special occasion. For a lot of people. For a happy celebration. For a birthday—or any party.

(And to top all this joy is the fact that both the cake and the icing call for only egg whites—no yolks. If you did not know what you were saving those whites for in the freezer, this could be it.)

If you wish, the layers can be frozen, and the filling can be refrigerated for a few days. But the icing should be made and the cake should be assembled the day it is to be served.

PINEAPPLE FILLING

This can be made a day or two ahead and refrigerated until you are ready for it.

Two 1-pound, 4-ounce cans (each 2½ cups) crushed pineapple (packed in its own juice)

Ingredients continued on next page.

Pour the pineapple into a large strainer set over a large bowl. Press firmly on the pineapple with a large spoon or spatula to press out all the juice. Set the pineapple aside and measure the juice—you should have 2 cups of juice. Add the lemon juice.

In a heavy 6- to 8-cup saucepan stir together the cornstarch, sugar, and salt. Mix thoroughly. Then, very gradually at first, stir in the pineapple juice. The mixture should be smooth.

2 tablespoons fresh
lemon juice

2 tablespoons plus 1½
teaspoons cornstarch,
firmly pressed into the
measuring spoon

2 tablespoons
granulated sugar

⅛ teaspoon salt

Yellow food coloring
(optional)

1 teaspoon vanilla extract

Place over moderate heat and cook, stirring and scraping the bottom and sides with a rubber spatula, until the mixture thickens and comes to a boil. Reduce the heat and simmer, stirring gently, for 1½ minutes.

Remove from the heat. Stir in 6 or 7 drops of yellow food coloring (coloring optional) and the vanilla. Then stir in the drained pineapple. Cool, stirring occasionally, and then refrigerate for at least a few hours or up to a few days.

Hawaiian Cake

2 cups sifted
all-purpose flour

3½ teaspoons
baking powder

1 teaspoon salt

4 ounces (1 stick)
unsalted butter

1 teaspoon vanilla extract

1½ cups granulated sugar

1 cup milk

4 egg whites (about ½
cup; they may be whites
that were left over from
another recipe, frozen,
and then thawed)

Adjust a rack one-third up from the bottom of the oven and preheat the oven to 350°. Cut baking-pan liner paper or wax paper to fit the bottoms of two 9 x 1½-inch layer-cake pans. Butter the sides of the pans and one side of the papers. Place the papers in the pans, buttered sides up. Then dust the pans with flour and tap the pans lightly over a piece of paper to shake out excess flour. Set aside.

Sift together the flour, baking powder, and salt, and set aside.

In the large bowl of an electric mixer, beat the butter until it is soft and smooth. Add the vanilla and then gradually add the sugar and beat well, scraping the sides occasionally and beating until thoroughly mixed. On low speed alternately add the sifted dry ingredients in three additions with the milk in two additions, scraping the bowl and beating after each addition until it is incorporated. Beat on high speed for 10 to 15 seconds. Then add the unbeaten egg whites (yes, unbeaten) and beat on high speed for 2 more minutes. The mixture will look slightly curdled—that is okay.

Pour half of the batter (a somewhat generous 2 cupfuls) into each pan. Tilt the pans slightly to level the batter. Then, to make them more level, hold a pan with both hands 6 or 8 inches above the work surface and drop it onto the work surface two or three times. That levels it about as level as it can get.

Bake for 30 to 35 minutes, until the tops are nicely browned, the layers have come away from the sides of the pans, and the tops barely spring back when they are lightly and gently pressed with a fingertip.

As soon as you remove the cakes from the oven, cut around them with a table knife. Then let them stand for 5 minutes. Cover each pan with a rack, turn it over, remove the pan and carefully and slowly peel off the paper lining, removing a small part at a time; cover with another rack and turn over again, leaving the cakes right side up to cool.

Before you start the icing, prepare a large, flat cake plate or a serving board by placing four strips of wax paper around the outer edge. Place one cooled cake layer on the plate, placing the cake upside down. Check to be sure that the wax paper touches the cake all around. Then, if you have a cake-decorating turntable, place the cake plate on it.

MARSHMALLOW ICING

This should be used as soon as it is made. Cakes with this icing should not be frozen. You will need a candy thermometer.

1½ cups granulated sugar

⅔ teaspoon cream of tartar (see Note)

⅔ cup water

⅛ teaspoon salt

⅔ cup egg whites (from 4 to 5 eggs; they may be whites that were left over from another recipe, frozen, and then thawed)

1¼ teaspoons vanilla extract

Place the sugar, cream of tartar, and water in a 6-cup saucepan (preferably one that is tall and narrow—in a wide one the mixture will be too low to reach the bulb of the candy thermometer). With a wooden spoon, stir over moderate heat until the sugar is dissolved and the mixture begins to boil. Cover the saucepan so that it is airtight (if the pan has a spout, cover it securely with foil or a pot holder) and let boil for 3 minutes. (This keeps the steam in the pot and dissolves any sugar granules that stick to the sides.)

Uncover and insert a candy thermometer. Raise the heat to high and let boil without stirring until the thermometer registers 242°.

Shortly before the sugar syrup is done (or when the thermometer registers about 236°, soft-ball stage), add the salt to the egg whites in the large bowl of an electric mixer and beat on high speed until the whites are stiff. (If the sugar syrup is not ready when the whites are, turn the beater to the lowest speed and let beat slowly until the syrup is ready. Or you can let the whites stand but no longer than necessary. If it looks as though the syrup might be done before the whites are ready, lower the heat to slow the cooking slightly.)

When the syrup is ready (242°, medium-ball stage), with the mixer on high speed very gradually add the syrup in a thin, threadlike steam, holding the pan about 12 inches above the top of the bowl of whites. Then beat at high speed for about 5 minutes more until the icing is like a thick marshmallow mixture. Mix in the vanilla. The icing may still be—probably will be—warm when it is used.

Spread half of the pineapple filling on the bottom cake layer. Place the other cake layer over the filling, right side up (both bottoms meet in the middle).

Spread the reserved filling on top.

Now you have a mountain of gorgeous icing to cover it all. First, with a small metal spatula, spread a thin layer of the icing on the sides of the cake to seal any loose crumbs. Then build up more and more icing on the sides until it is ½ to ¾ inch thick. Smooth the sides. Then gradually, carefully, place the remaining icing all over the top and smooth it. With the back of a spoon, form swirls and peaks on the sides only.

COCONUT TOPPING

NOTE: To measure ⅔ teaspoon: Measure 1 teaspoon and, with a small metal spatula or with a table knife, mark it into thirds. Then cut away ⅓ and return it to the box.

Use about ½ cup of shredded coconut and sprinkle it generously in a thick layer all over the top.

Then carefully remove the wax-paper strips by pulling each one out slowly toward a narrow end.

Let the cake stand uncovered at room temperature.

BLACK-AND-WHITE LAYER CAKE

10 TO 12 PORTIONS

This is a high, six-layer, loaf-shaped cake composed of alternate chocolate and white sponge layers (made from two separate recipes) with chocolate buttercream between the layers and as an icing. It is elaborate, fancy, special, dramatic, gorgeous, and delicious. Make it for a party, and make it ahead of time if you wish; it freezes perfectly.

This is not quick and easy—but it is not difficult; it is exciting to make and a thrill to serve.

WHITE SPONGE SHEET

5 eggs, separated

⅓ cup granulated sugar

1 teaspoon vanilla extract

¼ cup sifted
all-purpose flour

Pinch of salt

Pinch of cream of tartar

Adjust a rack to the middle of the oven. Preheat the oven to 350°. You will need a 10½ x 15½ x 1-inch jelly-roll pan. To line the pan with foil, turn the pan over, cover it with a piece of foil a few inches longer than the pan, press down the sides and the corners to shape the foil, remove the foil, turn the pan right side up, place the foil in the pan, and carefully press it into place. To butter the foil, place a piece of butter in the pan and place the pan in the oven to melt the butter, then brush it all over the foil. Set the pan aside. (Incidentally, I have found that buttered foil is the most successful method of preparing a pan for a sponge sheet—that goes for this recipe or any other sponge sheet.)

Place the yolks in the small bowl of an electric mixer. Add 3 tablespoons of the sugar (reserve the remaining sugar) and the vanilla, and beat at high speed for a few minutes until pale (almost white) and thick. On low speed add the sifted flour, scraping the bowl with a rubber spatula, and beating only until smooth.

Transfer the mixture to a larger mixing bowl. (It is easier to combine ingredients in a large bowl.)

Use the small bowl of the electric mixer, or any other small bowl and an eggbeater, or use a large bowl and a wire whisk (the bowl and beaters must be clean) to beat the egg whites with the salt and cream of tartar until they hold a soft shape. Gradually add the reserved sugar and beat until the whites hold a definite shape but not so long that they are stiff or dry.

Fold about a third of the whites into the yolks—do not be too thorough—and then fold the remaining whites into the yolks, folding carefully only until blended.

Transfer the mixture to the prepared pan. Spread it smooth (it will stay where you put it and will not run during baking).

Bake for 20 to 23 minutes, until the top springs back when it is lightly pressed with a fingertip and the cake begins to come away from the sides of the pan.

Place a long piece of wax paper over the baked cake. Cover with a flat cookie sheet. Holding them firmly together, invert the cake pan and the cookie sheet. Remove the cake pan and carefully peel off the foil. Do not allow the cake to remain upside down any longer than necessary or the top (which is now on the bottom) will stick to the paper. Quickly cover the cake with another cookie sheet and turn over again, remove the wax paper, and leave the cake right side up to cool.

CHOCOLATE SPONGE SHEET

6 ounces semisweet chocolate (see Note)

1 teaspoon instant coffee (powdered or granular)

¼ cup boiling water

4 eggs, separated

⅓ cup granulated sugar

1 teaspoon vanilla extract

⅓ cup sifted all-purpose flour

Pinch of salt

Pinch of cream of tartar

Prepare the oven and the jelly-roll pan as in the above directions for the White Sponge Sheet.

Break up or coarsely chop the chocolate and place it in the top of a small double boiler over hot water on moderate heat. Dissolve the coffee in the water and add to the chocolate. Stir occasionally until the chocolate is melted. Remove the top of the double boiler and set it aside to cool slightly.

In the small bowl of an electric mixer, beat the yolks with 3 tablespoons of the sugar (reserve the remaining sugar) and the vanilla. Beat for a few minutes until the mixture is thick and pale.

On low speed add the tepid chocolate scraping the bowl with a rubber spatula and beating only until mixed. Then mix in the flour. Remove from the mixer and transfer to a larger bowl.

Use the small bowl of the electric mixer, or any other small bowl and an eggbeater, or use a large bowl and a wire whisk (the bowl and beaters must be clean) to beat the egg whites with the salt and cream of tartar until they hold a soft shape. Gradually add the reserved sugar and continue to beat until the whites hold a definite shape but not so long that they become stiff or dry.

Fold about one-third of the whites into the chocolate mixture—do not be too thorough—and then fold in the remaining whites, folding carefully only until blended; do not handle any more than necessary.

Turn the batter into the prepared jelly-roll pan and spread it smooth.

Bake at 350° for 15 minutes, or until it feels set and firm when lightly pressed with a fingertip.

Cover the cake with a long piece of wax paper, cover the paper with a flat cookie sheet, and invert the pan and the sheet. Remove the pan and gently peel off the foil; quickly cover with another cookie sheet and turn over again, remove the wax paper, and leave the cake right side up to cool.

CHOCOLATE BUTTERCREAM

6 ounces semisweet chocolate (see Note)

2 tablespoons heavy cream

8 ounces (2 sticks) plus 1 tablespoon unsalted butter

7 egg yolks

1 cup strained confectioners' sugar

Pinch of salt

1 teaspoon vanilla extract

NOTE: *Use sweet, semisweet, or bittersweet, but use the best quality chocolate you can get.*

Break up or coarsely chop the chocolate and place it in the top of a small double boiler over hot water on low heat. Add the heavy cream and 1 tablespoon of the butter (reserve the remaining 2 sticks at room temperature). Stir until smooth.

Meanwhile, in the small bowl of an electric mixer, beat the egg yolks at high speed for a few minutes until pale and thick. On low speed gradually add the warm chocolate mixture, scraping the bowl constantly with a rubber spatula.

Transfer the mixture to the top of the double boiler (the one the chocolate was melted in) over hot water on low heat and cook for 5 minutes, scraping the bottom and sides constantly with a rubber spatula. The mixture must never get really hot.

Now transfer the chocolate mixture to a mixing bowl. Place some ice and water in a larger mixing bowl. Then place the bowl of chocolate in the bowl of ice water and stir gently until the chocolate cools to tepid.

Meanwhile, in the large bowl of an electric mixer, beat the reserved 2 sticks of butter with the confectioners' sugar, salt, and vanilla until soft and smooth. Then add the chocolate mixture and continue to beat for just a minute or two until smooth, creamy, and gorgeous.

You will need a long, narrow, flat serving tray—a chocolate-roll board (measuring about 5 x 18 inches) is perfect.

Use a ruler and toothpicks to mark the cakes, the long way, into thirds (you will have three 15½ x 3½-inch strips). It is important to mark and cut them carefully—they must all be the same width. Use a long, thin, sharp knife to cut the cakes.

Carefully place a strip of white cake on the serving tray or board. Spread a thin layer of buttercream over the cake; the buttercream should completely cover the cake, but keep it thin or you will not have enough.

Now place a chocolate layer on top. (The chocolate cake is fragile and if it does not want to cooperate, here's how to do it: Cut the chocolate strip crosswise into two or three even pieces, and transfer each piece separately, using a metal pancake turner to transfer with. You should not have any trouble this way and it will not show that the strips were patched.)

Spread more buttercream over the chocolate layer. Continue to alternate white and chocolate layers with buttercream between them.

Do not ice the top and sides yet. Reserve the remaining buttercream at room temperature.

Make room for the cake in the freezer or refrigerator. Cover the top of the cake with a piece of plastic wrap. To flatten the cake slightly—and to level the top—place a tray or a cookie sheet or another chocolate-roll board (or anything flat) on top of the cake. If you have used another chocolate-roll board on top it will be heavy enough to flatten the cake, but if you have used something lighter, place a few weights (small cans or whatever) evenly distributed over the top. But be careful that whatever is on top is not so heavy it squashes the cake. Place in the freezer for about half an hour or in the refrigerator for a little longer.

Just before you are ready to finish icing the cake, beat the reserved buttercream well with the mixer.

Then spread it to coat the top and sides completely. It may be smooth (that's how I do it) or it may be in peaks. If you make it smooth, try to reserve about ½ cup or so of the buttercream to use as decoration. Place the ½ cup of buttercream in a pastry bag fitted with a star-shaped tube (the tube should be #2 or #3, that is, a moderately small size) and form a row of small rosettes touching each other on each long edge of the top.

Wow—gorgeous!

Refrigerate the cake and serve it cold. Or freeze it (freeze until firm before wrapping); to thaw, place the wrapped cake in the refrigerator for a few hours, then unwrap and serve.

COFFEE CREAM SPONGE CAKE

8 PORTIONS

This is a light, delicate cake to make as dessert for a dinner or for a tea party. It is a two-layer, coffee-flavored sponge cake, filled and iced with coffee- and chocolate-flavored whipped cream. The layers may be made ahead of time and frozen if you wish; it is best if the whipped cream is made and put on the cake the day you serve it, but it may be done in the morning for that night.

1 cup sifted
all-purpose flour

1 teaspoon baking
powder

1 tablespoon
instant coffee

¼ cup boiling water

3 eggs, separated

1 cup granulated sugar

½ teaspoon vanilla extract

¼ teaspoon salt

Adjust a rack to the middle of the oven and preheat the oven to 350°. Butter two round 9-inch layer-cake pans, line the bottoms with baking-pan liner or wax paper cut to fit, butter the paper, dust with flour, then, over a piece of paper, tap to shake out excess.

Sift together the flour and baking powder and set aside. Dissolve the coffee in the water and set aside. In the small bowl of an electric mixer beat the yolks with ¾ cup of the sugar (reserve the remaining ¼ cup of sugar), beating for several minutes until the mixture is pale and thick. On low speed, mix in a few tablespoons of the sifted dry ingredients. Then add the vanilla and coffee, scraping the bowl with a rubber spatula and beating only until smooth. Add the remaining dry ingredients and beat, still on low speed, only until incorporated.

In a clean, small bowl with clean beaters, beat the egg whites and the salt until they hold a soft shape. Gradually add the reserved ¼ cup of sugar and continue to beat until the whites hold a definite shape but are not stiff or dry.

Fold a few spoonfuls of the whites into the yolks. Then, in a larger bowl, fold in the yolks and the remaining whites until they are blended. Do not handle any more than necessary.

Divide the mixture between the prepared pans and smooth the tops.

Bake for 20 to 25 minutes, until the tops spring back when lightly pressed with a fingertip.

Cool the layers in the pans for 2 or 3 minutes. Then, to release them, very carefully cut around the sides with a small, sharp knife—be careful not to tear or cut the cakes. Cover each layer with a rack, turn over the pan and the rack, remove the pan (do not remove the paper lining now), cover with another rack and turn over again, leaving the layers right side up. When the cakes have cooled, cover each one with a rack, invert, peel off the paper lining, cover with another rack, and turn over again, leaving the cakes right side up.

Prepare a flat cake plate by lining the sides with four strips of wax paper. Place a cake layer upside down on the plate and check to see that the cake touches the paper all around. If you have a cake-decorating turntable, place the cake plate on it.

COFFEE-CHOCOLATE WHIPPED CREAM

1 ounce semisweet chocolate

1 tablespoon instant coffee

1 tablespoon boiling water

2 cups heavy cream

1 teaspoon vanilla extract

1½ tablespoons granulated sugar

Chop the chocolate very fine and place it in the top of a small double boiler over hot water on moderate heat. Dissolve the coffee in the boiling water and pour it over the chocolate. Stir until smooth and then remove from over the hot water and set aside to cool.

When it is completely cool, gradually add 2 or 3 tablespoons of the cream to the chocolate mixture, stirring until smooth and liquid.

In a small, chilled bowl with chilled beaters, whip the remaining cream with the vanilla and sugar until it holds a soft shape. Then, while beating, add the chocolate mixture and continue to beat until the cream is stiff enough to hold its shape as an icing. It is nicer if it is not too stiff; you must watch it very carefully—it stiffens more quickly than plain whipped cream.

Cover the bottom layer with a ½-inch-thick layer of the cream. Then place the top layer on, right side up (both bottoms meet in the center), and use the remaining cream to cover the sides and the top of the cake. Spread it smoothly or swirl it into curlicues.

Refrigerate for a few hours or all day.

OPTIONAL DECORATION: *If you wish, decorate the top with a few chocolate shavings, a sprinkling of grated choco-late, or a circle of hulled fresh strawberries standing point up on the top rim of the cake (strawberries and cream with coffee and chocolate are a wonderful combination). But the cake is lovely with or without any decoration.*

SPICY SPONGE ROLL

8 PORTIONS

This is a light sponge roll made with a delicious blend of spices and filled with chocolate- and cognac-flavored whipped cream. The spices make it a wonderful winter dessert; consider it for Christmas or Thanksgiving. It may be made the day before it is served, or it may be frozen (even for a few weeks) and sliced and served directly from the freezer (it will not be too stiff).

1 cup sifted
confectioners' sugar

3 tablespoons sifted
all-purpose flour

¼ teaspoon salt

¼ teaspoon finely
ground black pepper

1½ tablespoons powdered
instant espresso or
other powdered (not
granular) instant coffee

1½ teaspoons ginger

1 teaspoon allspice

1 teaspoon cinnamon

1 teaspoon nutmeg

1 teaspoon cardamom

⅛ teaspoon ground cloves

1 tablespoon unsweetened
cocoa powder

5 eggs, separated

½ teaspoon cream
of tartar

Ingredients continued on next page.

Adjust a rack to the center of the oven and preheat the oven to 350°. Butter a 10½ x 15½ x 1-inch jelly-roll pan. Line the pan with aluminum foil as follows: Turn the pan upside down, cover it with a piece of foil shiny side down about 19 inches long, fold down the sides and the corners to shape the foil, remove the foil, turn the pan right side up, place the foil in the pan and press it into place. To butter the foil, place a piece of butter in the pan, place the pan in the oven to melt the butter, then spread it with a brush or with crumpled wax paper to coat the foil.

Remove and set aside ½ cup of the sugar.

Sift the remaining ½ cup of sugar with the flour, salt, pepper, coffee, ginger, allspice, cinnamon, nutmeg, cardamom, cloves, and cocoa. Resift twice more (even if it is a triple sifter) and set aside.

In the small bowl of an electric mixer, beat the egg yolks at high speed for several minutes until they are pale lemon-colored. On low speed add the sifted flour mixture, scraping the bowl as necessary with a rubber spatula and beating only until incorporated. Set aside.

In the large bowl of the electric mixer, with clean beaters, beat the egg whites with the cream of tartar until they hold a soft shape when the beaters are raised. Gradually add the reserved ½ cup of confectioners' sugar and continue to beat until the whites hold a firm shape, but don't let them become stiff or dry.

In about three additions, carefully fold three-quarters of the whites into the yolks, and then fold the yolks into the remaining whites. Do not handle any more than necessary.

Turn the mixture into the lined pan and spread it smooth.

Bake for 15 minutes, until the cake barely springs back when it is gently pressed with a fingertip.

Additional confectioners' sugar (for turning the cake out of the pan)

Additional cocoa (for sprinkling on top)

While the cake is baking, spread out a smooth cotton towel. Sprinkle the additional confectioners' sugar on the towel (enough to coat it and to keep the cake from sticking).

Immediately turn the cake out onto the towel and remove the pan and the foil. Starting at a narrow end, roll the hot cake and the towel together, making a firm roll but not squashing the cake any more than necessary.

Transfer the cake in the towel to a rack and let stand until cool.

Filling

1½ cups heavy cream

¼ cup sifted confectioners' sugar

1 tablespoon unsweetened cocoa powder

½ teaspoon unflavored gelatin

2 teaspoons cold water

2 tablespoons cognac or brandy

Note: *Although this is delicious as it is, it is also wonderful served with The World's Best Hot Fudge Sauce (page 115). The sauce should be tepid, at room temperature, not really hot or cold. Ladle or pour a generous ribbon of it over each portion. If you are serving eight people, double the amount of sauce called for in the recipe.*

In the small bowl of an electric mixer, mix the cream, sugar, and cocoa; do not beat, just mix. Refrigerate until you are ready to use it.

In a small heatproof cup, sprinkle the gelatin over the cold water and let stand for a few minutes.

Then place the cup in a small pan containing a little hot water over low heat. Let stand for a minute or so until the gelatin is dissolved. Set aside, but only briefly—do not let it cool completely.

Beat the cream-cocoa mixture until it holds a soft shape. Stir the cognac into the gelatin and quickly, while beating, add it to the softly whipped cream and continue to beat until the cream holds a firm shape.

Unroll the cooled sponge roll. Spread the cream over the cake, leaving about 1½ inches uncovered at one short end. Carefully roll the cake toward the end where the cream stops short. Place it, seam down, on a chocolate-roll board or on any long, narrow serving platter.

Refrigerate for at least 3 hours. Or cover well with plastic wrap and freeze.

Just before serving, sprinkle the top with unsweetened cocoa through a small strainer held over the cake.

Cheesecakes

Polka Dot Cheesecake

12 PORTIONS

This is new. The recipe is not in any of my other books. It is the latest variation (the ingredients are the same—the design is different) of Craig Claiborne's Cheesecake, which was in my first book. The design is quite unbelievable (you do it with a pastry bag). Part of the cheesecake mixture is dark chocolate and part is light. You make a pattern of large dark polka dots on the top of the cake. When you cut portions and cut through the polka dots, you will be thrilled to see that there is a perfect round ball about the size of a golf ball of the dark mixture under each polka dot. Stunning.

You need a one-piece, round cheesecake pan that measures 8 x 3 inches (see page 11).

If possible, make this a day ahead and refrigerate it overnight.

2 ounces unsweetened chocolate

2 pounds cream cheese (use Philadelphia brand—others do not all work the same)

1 teaspoon vanilla extract

¼ teaspoon almond extract

1¾ cups granulated sugar

4 eggs

About ⅓ cup graham cracker crumbs (to be used after the cake is baked and cooled)

Adjust a rack to the lowest position in the oven and preheat the oven to 350°. Butter an 8 x 3-inch one-piece cheesecake pan all the way up to the rim and including the inside of the rim itself. You will also need a larger pan (for hot water) to place the cake pan in while baking; the larger pan must not be deeper than the cheesecake pan. Set aside.

In the top of a small double boiler over hot water on low heat, melt the chocolate and set it aside.

In the large bowl of an electric mixer beat the cheese until it is completely smooth. During the beating frequently scrape the sides and bottom of the bowl with a rubber spatula. When the cheese is smooth beat in the vanilla and almond extracts and the sugar. Beat well and then add the eggs one at a time. After adding the eggs do not beat any more than necessary to mix.

Remove the bowl from the mixer. Place one-third of the batter (2 cups) in the small bowl of the electric mixer. Add the melted chocolate and beat until smooth.

Spray the buttered cake pan with Pam or some other nonstick spray, and then pour in the light-colored mixture. Rotate the pan briskly from side to side to level the batter.

Fit a large (about 16-inch) pastry bag with a plain #6 (½-inch) tube. Fold down a deep cuff on the outside of the bag and twist the tube end of the bag to prevent the mixture from running out.

Place the chocolate mixture in the bag.

Now, work at table height, not counter height (you will have better control at table height). Place the cake pan on the table. Unfold the cuff on the pastry bag. Untwist the tube end of the bag. Place the tip of the tube in the center of the top of the cake, inserting it only slightly into the cake. Squeeze out some of the chocolate mixture. It will form a ball (tennis ball- or golf ball-size, precise and perfectly round) in the cake and will leave a dark polka dot about 2 inches wide on top of the cake.

Then, using the same procedure, squeeze out six balls around the rim. In order to space the six balls evenly, place the first one at twelve o'clock (straight up). The next at six o'clock (straight down). Then two on each side. Doing it this way, the chances are that the spacing will be quite even. The balls around the rim should be smaller than the one in the center, and they should not touch each other or the center ball. If you have some chocolate mixture left over add it to the center ball; if you still have some left over add a bit to each of the other balls.

The top of the cake will not be smooth and level now, but it will level itself during baking. When baked, the polka dot in the center will be about 2½ inches wide, the dots around the rim will be about 1½ inches wide.

Place the cake pan into the larger pan. Place it in the oven and pour hot water into the larger pan about 1½ inches deep. (If the larger pan is aluminum, add about ½ teaspoon cream of tartar to prevent the water from discoloring the pan.)

Bake for 1½ hours. The top of the cake will become golden brown and it will feel dry to the touch but the cake will still be very soft inside (it will become firm when it has cooled and been refrigerated).

Lift the cake pan out of the water and place it on a cake rack. Cool the cake in the pan for 2½ hours. (Do not cool it in the refrigerator or the butter will harden and the cake will stick to the pan.)

Cover the pan with a piece of plastic wrap. Place a flat plate or small board upside down over the pan and turn the pan and the plate or board upside down. Carefully remove the pan.

Carefully and evenly sprinkle the graham cracker crumbs over the bottom of the cake. Gently place another flat plate or small board upside down over the cake and carefully turn it all upside down again (without squashing the cake), leaving the cake right side up. Remove the plastic wrap.

Refrigerate for several hours or overnight.

To serve, dip a sharp knife in very hot water or hold it under running hot water before making each cut, shake off the water but do not dry the blade. Make the first cut through the middle of one of the smaller dots and the second cut (the one that will release the first portion) between two of the smaller dots.

Everyone will ask, "How did you do that? How did you make that design? Do you have a special pan that does that?"

BULL'S-EYE CHEESECAKE

10 PORTIONS

"How did you do it?"—"I can't believe it."—"I never saw anything like it."

You will have two mixtures, one dark and one light. When you work your magic with them they will form a series of concentric circles (a bull's-eye) of dark and light cheesecake to produce this photogenic and delicious creation. When you cut into the cakes you will see gracefully curved, vertical stripes that are incredibly precise; they practically happen by themselves.

The recipe is foolproof and not difficult.

Although this tastes perfectly delicious any time at all, the design will be more clearly defined after the cake has been refrigerated for at least 8 hours overnight.

You need a one-piece 8 x 3-inch cheesecake pan (see page 11).

Measure the sour cream in a cup used for dry (not liquid) ingredients.

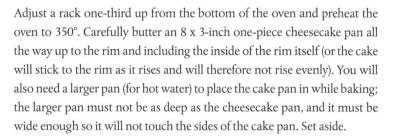

Adjust a rack one-third up from the bottom of the oven and preheat the oven to 350°. Carefully butter an 8 x 3-inch one-piece cheesecake pan all the way up to the rim and including the inside of the rim itself (or the cake will stick to the rim as it rises and will therefore not rise evenly). You will also need a larger pan (for hot water) to place the cake pan in while baking; the larger pan must not be as deep as the cheesecake pan, and it must be wide enough so it will not touch the sides of the cake pan. Set aside.

In the large bowl of an electric mixer, beat the cheese until it is soft and smooth, frequently scraping the sides of the bowl (with a rubber spatula) and the beaters themselves (with your finger) to be sure the cheese is uniformly smooth. Beat in the sour cream, then the vanilla and almond extracts, and the salt, and then the eggs one at a time, scraping the bowl occasionally and beating after each addition until it is incorporated.

32 ounces cream cheese (Use Philadelphia brand—others do not all work the same—preferably at room temperature)

¼ cup sour cream

1 teaspoon vanilla extract

¼ teaspoon almond extract

¼ teaspoon salt

4 eggs

⅔ cup granulated sugar

⅔ cup dark brown sugar, firmly packed

1 teaspoon powdered (not granular) instant coffee

2 teaspoons unsweetened cocoa powder

About ¼ cup graham cracker crumbs or crumbs made from Amaretti or any other crisp cookies (to be used after the cake is baked)

Remove the bowl from the mixer. You will have about 6 cups of the mixture. Place half of it (3 cups) in another bowl that is large enough to allow you to stir in it.

Add the granulated sugar to one bowl and the brown sugar to the other bowl. With a rubber spatula, for each bowl stir the ingredients for about a minute until the sugar has dissolved and the mixtures have thinned out.

To the dark mixture, add the instant coffee and, through a fine strainer, the cocoa. Stir. Stir some more until the coffee and cocoa have dissolved and there are not visible specks of either. If there are specks, strain the mixture through a fine strainer.

Spray the bottom of the buttered pan with Pam or some other nonstick baking spray.

Now, to form the design. You have a scant 4 cups of each mixture. The two mixtures will be placed alternately in the pan. Each segment will be one-quarter or a scant I cup of the mixture. I use two 1-cup glass measuring cups, one for the dark mixture and one for the light. (But you can do this any way you wish, even without measuring if that suits you better.)

If you are using the two 1-cup measuring cups, pour a scant cupful of one mixture into one cup and a scant cupful of the other into the other (use separate rubber spatulas to assist for each color).

It does not matter which color you use first. Pour the scant cupful of either directly into the middle of the prepared cake pan. (It will spread out by itself to cover the bottom of the pan.) Then pour the same amount of the other mixture directly into the middle of the first mixture. (That will spread out by itself also.) Then use the first color again, right in the middle. Do you see the bull's-eye forming?

Continue until you have used all of both mixtures (or four additions of each mixture).

Now, handle the pan very carefully in order not to disturb the design. Place the cake pan in the larger pan and pour hot water into the larger pan about 1½ inches deep. (If the larger pan is aluminum add about 1 teaspoon of cream of tartar to the hot water to keep the pan from discoloring.)

Carefully transfer to the oven and bake for 1½ hours.

Then remove the cake pan from the hot water and set aside to cool. (During baking the top of the cake will darken to a rich honey color and will rise up to, and sometimes above, the top of the pan; during cooling it will sink down to its original level.)

Let stand for 3 hours at room temperature before unmolding the cake.

Cover the cake pan with plastic wrap and then with a flat plate or board (clear, lightweight plastic cutting boards from the hardware store are wonderful for this), carefully hold the cake pan and the board firmly together, and turn them over.

Remove the pan. Sprinkle the crumbs over the cake (this will become the bottom and the crumbs will keep it from sticking to the plate), cover with a serving plate, a board, or another plastic cutting board, and very carefully (the cake is still soft and tender—do not press down on it) turn it all over again, leaving the cake right side up.

Refrigerate.

This will slice best if you dip the knife into a deep pitcher of very hot water before making each cut. Or, if you are serving from the kitchen, hold the knife under very hot running water—the hotter the better.

P.S. *In 1993, I received a letter from Brad Pool in Texas. He said, "Because of a divorce I no longer have access to your books." He asked where he could buy them all, or at least locate copies of his favorite recipes, which he listed. Bull's-Eye Cheesecake was at the top of the list.*

CURRANT CHEESECAKE
10 TO 12 PORTIONS

This is a large and impressive cream cheese pie in a graham cracker crumb crust made in a 10-inch glass pie plate. The cheese filling, which is studded with currants, is unbelievably smooth and mellow. The currants are unusual in a cheesecake, but so is the mixture of cream cheese and butter. Too good!

It can be made a day or two before serving or just a few hours before. Or, like most cheesecakes, this freezes well.

CRUMB CRUST

2 cups graham
cracker crumbs

3 tablespoons
granulated sugar

2 teaspoons cinnamon

4 ounces (1 stick)
unsalted butter, melted

Mix the crumbs, sugar, and cinnamon in the mixing bowl. Add the butter and stir/mix with a rubber spatula until the crumbs are evenly moistened. (The mixture will not hold together in the bowl.)

Turn the mixture into a 10-inch ovenproof glass pie plate. With your fingertips distribute the mixture evenly and loosely all over the plate. Then raise the mixture around the sides of the plate; it should still be loose—do not press firmly until the mixture is evenly distributed over the bottom and the sides. Before you start to press it firmly, try to have enough of the crumb mixture on the sides to form a slightly raised rim; there will be a generous amount of filling and the sides must be high enough to hold it all.

Press firmly on the sides first and then on the bottom. Refrigerate briefly.

FILLING

Boiling water

⅔ cup dried currants

24 ounces Philadelphia
brand cream cheese,
preferably at room
temperature

4 ounces (1 stick)
unsalted butter, at
room temperature

⅛ teaspoon salt

¾ cup granulated sugar

1½ teaspoons
vanilla extract

3 eggs

Adjust a rack to the center of the oven and preheat the oven to 350°.

Pour boiling water over the currants to cover them, let them stand for a minute, drain in a strainer, and then turn out onto a double thickness of paper towels. Fold the towels over the top and press lightly to absorb any remaining water. Set aside.

In the large bowl of an electric mixer beat the cream cheese and butter until they are soft and perfectly smooth. Add the salt, sugar, and vanilla, and beat well, scraping the bowl with a rubber spatula, until the mixture is as smooth as honey. Add the eggs one at a time, continuing to scrape the bowl as necessary and beating well after each addition. Remove from the mixer and stir in the currants.

Pour the filling into the crumb crust, watching the edges carefully—if there are any low spots in the crust do not use all of the filling. Smooth the top. Then rotate the pan briskly first in one direction, then the other, to level and smooth the top even more.

Bake for 35 minutes.

Now, to brown the top, turn the broiler on and place the cake 12 inches below the broiler—no closer. Broil, watching carefully, until the top turns a beautiful, rich golden brown. It will take only a minute—watch it every second.

Let the cake cool to room temperature.

It may be served at room temperature or refrigerated for a day or two. Or it may be frozen. However, wonderful as it is any way, it is most tender, delicate, creamy, and delicious at room temperature the day it is baked.

LONGCHAMPS' CHEESECAKE

10 TO 12 PORTIONS

In its heyday the Longchamps' chain of restaurants in New York City had two very popular desserts: baked apples the size of grapefruits and wonderful cheesecake. They usually sold out of both before the day was over. We lived near the branch on Fifth Avenue and 34th Street and ate there quite often. The manager gave my mother this recipe. Originally, it was prepared in a pastry crust, but I do not have that recipe and I have put in a crumb crust. It is lighter and less dense than many other cheesecakes and has a fresh-fruit topping. It can be baked a day or two before serving and is absolutely and perfectly marvelous.

CRUMB CRUST

1¾ cups graham cracker crumbs

⅓ cup granulated sugar

2 teaspoons cinnamon

7 tablespoons plus 1 teaspoon (1 stick minus 2 teaspoons) unsalted butter

Generously butter the sides only of a 9 x 2½- or 3-inch springform pan. (Leaving the bottom unbuttered makes it easier to transfer the baked cake to a serving plate.)

Combine the crumbs, sugar, and cinnamon in a mixing bowl. Melt the butter, add it, and stir until evenly distributed.

Remove and reserve 1½ cups of the mixture. Press the remainder onto the sides of the pan, but the crust should not be as deep as the pan—it should be 2 inches deep. (If the pan is 2½ inches deep, leave ½ inch uncovered at the top. If the pan is 3 inches deep, leave 1 inch uncovered.) Use your thumbnail to cut around the upper edge of the crust to make it straight. Then press the reserved mixture evenly onto the bottom. Press firmly all over. Place in the refrigerator or freezer until you are ready to use it.

FILLING

16 ounces Philadelphia brand cream cheese, preferably at room temperature

1 cup granulated sugar

¼ teaspoon salt

6 eggs

1 cup heavy cream

1 teaspoon vanilla extract

Finely grated rind of 2 large lemons

Adjust a rack one-third up from the bottom of the oven and preheat the oven to 350°.

In the large bowl of an electric mixer, beat the cheese until it is soft and very smooth. Add the sugar and beat very well, scraping the bowl as necessary with a rubber spatula—the mixture must be smooth. Add the salt and then the eggs, one or two at a time, beating well after each addition. Then beat in the cream and the vanilla. Remove from the mixer and stir in the rind.

Pour the mixture into the prepared crust.

Bake for 1 hour and 20 minutes.

Then, do not remove the cake from the oven, but turn the heat off, open the oven door 6 or 8 inches, and let the cake stand until cool.

With a small, narrow metal spatula or with a table knife, cut around the cake between the crust and the pan, pressing the blade against the pan. Carefully remove the sides of the pan.

Refrigerate for several hours or for a day or two.

The cake may be served on the bottom of the pan or it may easily be transferred to a flat cake plate. To transfer, use a strong and firm (not flexible), long, narrow metal spatula, or a strong knife with about a 6-inch blade. Insert the spatula or knife between the crust and the pan and gently ease it around to release the cake. It will be easy if the bottom of the pan has not been buttered and if the cake has been chilled enough. Then use either a flat-sided cookie sheet, the bottom of a loose-bottomed quiche pan, or two wide metal spatulas to transfer the cake.

TOPPING

This should be done a few hours before serving—at most, early in the day for that evening: the less time it stands, the better.

Use either about 2 cups of fresh blueberries or about 3 cups of fresh strawberries and ½ to ¾ cup of seedless red currant preserves.

If you use the blueberries, wash and drain them, then dry them thoroughly—they must be completely dry. Melt about ½ cup of preserves in a small saucepan, stirring over low heat. Let it just come to a boil. Mix it with the berries and spread the mixture over the top of the cake, leaving a 1-inch rim around the outside.

If you use strawberries, wash, hull, and drain them, then dry thoroughly—they must be completely dry. If the berries are small, place them point up all over the cake, leaving a 1-inch rim around the outside. If the berries are large, slice them in half and lay the halves, cut side down, overlapping one another in a ring pattern all over the top (again leaving a 1-inch rim). Large berries or small, it is easiest if you start placing them 1 inch from the edge rather than from the center. When the fruit is in place, put about ¾ cup of preserves in a small saucepan and stir over low heat until it is melted and comes to a boil. Spoon the preserves slowly and carefully over the berries to coat them completely.

WHIPPED CREAM

¾ cup heavy cream

2 tablespoons confectioners' sugar

½ teaspoon vanilla extract

Optional: additional confectioners' sugar

NOTE: *I believe that the Longchamps' chain has been sold many times and I don't suppose they still serve this cheesecake.*

In a chilled bowl with chilled beaters, whip the cream with the sugar and vanilla until the cream holds a definite shape, but don't let it get very stiff. Fit a large pastry bag with a large star-shaped nozzle, place the whipped cream in the bag, and form a border around the fruit on the uncovered 1-inch rim by pressing out rosettes of cream that touch one another. Refrigerate.

Just before serving, a tiny bit of confectioners' sugar may be sprinkled through a fine strainer over the center only of the fruit. This is a pleasure to serve. It looks gorgeous, cuts beautifully, and does not stick to the knife.

8-HOUR CHEESECAKE
10 TO 12 PORTIONS

The fun and excitement, the challenge, the satisfaction, the hoopla of cooking will never fade. On the contrary, for me it gets more so.

Surely I have had enough cheesecake to be satiated and to feel that I have had it with making cheesecakes. But recently a friend sent me a page from a New Jersey newspaper, and on the back was a story about cheesecakes written by Andrew Schloss, who writes regularly about food for the Philadelphia Inquirer. Mr. Schloss had a whole new theory about cheesecake. I did not need another cheesecake recipe or another theory, but when I read his story I couldn't wait to make the cake. And then with each bite I swooned.

Mr. Schloss points out that cheesecake is really just a custard: eggs, sugar, and cream cheese instead of milk or cream. He says that after years of trial and error he concluded that with a lower temperature "the ingredients simply melted together yielding a mousselike texture." When he says low he means low. The cake is baked at only 200° for 8 hours.

You will have a pure creamy-white cake that is stark in its simplicity, it will have an extremely creamy texture, the top will not crack or color or rise or fall, and when you serve the cake it will not cling to the knife. The "flayvah" (as Lauren Bacall says) is sensational.

I have adapted this recipe from the original. I make it in an 8 x 3-inch one-piece cheesecake pan (see page 11); Mr. Schloss uses a 2-quart soufflé dish.

2 pounds Philadelphia cream cheese, preferably at room temperature

1 cup granulated sugar

2 tablespoons (I repeat, 2 tablespoons) vanilla extract

2 tablespoons cognac

2 tablespoons Myers's Dark Rum (see Note)

5 eggs

Adjust a rack one-third up from the bottom of the oven and preheat the oven to 200°. Correct oven temperature is vital for this recipe (and most others) since you will not "bake until done," but you will bake for the specified time based on correct oven temperature (see Thermometers, page 9). Butter an 8 x 3-inch one-piece cheesecake pan or a 2-quart soufflé dish and set aside.

Have ready a large pan in which to place the cake pan or soufflé dish. It must not be deeper than the cake pan but it must be wider.

In the large bowl of an electric mixer beat the cheese until soft and perfectly smooth. To ensure the smoothness, scrape the bowl and the beaters a few times during mixing.

When the cheese is as smooth as possible, gradually beat in the sugar, vanilla, cognac, and rum. Then add the eggs one at a time, beating well after each addition. Spray the bottom of the buttered pan with Pam or some other nonstick baking spray. Pour the mixture into the pan or dish. Place the pan or dish into the larger pan. Pour hot water about 2 inches deep into the larger pan and place them in the oven.

NOTE: *I am not suggesting that you buy a bottle of Myers's rum for the 2 tablespoons you need. I mention the brand because it is the kind I use and because I have been told that no other dark rum tastes the same. But for such a small amount I think you can use any.*

Bake for 8 hours. Then remove from the hot water and let stand for several hours or overnight. Or if you bake the cake during the night let it cool for most of the day; it should stand for at least a few hours after it has reached room temperature.

To unmold, cover the cake pan with a flat cake plate or serving board, and turn the pan and plate over. If the cake does not slip out, gently bang the pan and plate on the work surface once or twice. Serve the cake upside down.

If you serve this before refrigerating or freezing (it freezes well), it will be especially delicate, creamy, tender, and custardy. If you do freeze or refrigerate the cake, bring it to room temperature before serving. (However, if it is cold when you serve it, it is still wonderful, only different—that's all.)

Serve this as it is, perfectly plain, or serve any type of fresh berries alongside.

EMILIO'S CHEESECAKE

16 TO 24 PORTIONS

The New Yorker *magazine, in their issue of March 27, 1971, published a recipe for a cheesecake made by Emilio Braseco which they said was the best cheesecake in New York.*

I tore the page out of the magazine and put it on my desk in the kitchen, planning to make it soon, but I didn't. Eventually I said to myself, "You haven't made it yet; what makes you think you ever will?" (I don't keep files of recipes.)

A few days after I threw it away, I received a letter from a friend in Mobile, Alabama, asking if I would like the world's best cheesecake recipe, and he mentioned, causally, that it was originally from an old issue of The New Yorker.

I wrote back immediately and said, "Yes, please." This time I did not wait; I made it minutes after the recipe arrived.

The story is that the cake was from a cafeteria for graduate students at the City University of New York. At the time the story was written, The New Yorker *said the cake was so popular that the cafeteria never had enough—and it soon became the talk of the town.*

Incidentally, this cake is not like Lindy's, or the so-called New York–style cheesecake. It is not as heavy or dense or cheesy; it is more creamy. It has no crust. It is quick and easy to make. It is wonderful for a large party. You will [heart] it. The following recipe has been adapted from the recipe for Emilio's; the adapting was done partly in Mobile, Alabama, and partly in my kitchen in Florida.

2 pounds Philadelphia cream cheese, preferably at room temperature

4 ounces (1 stick) unsalted butter, at room temperature

1 tablespoon vanilla extract

1½ cups granulated sugar

½ cup less 1 tablespoon cornstarch

7 eggs

2 cups whipping cream

¼ cup lemon juice

Adjust a rack one-third down from the top of the oven and preheat the oven to 350°. Butter a 13 x 9 x 2-inch pan and set aside.

In the large bowl of an electric mixer beat the cheese and butter until soft and smooth. Add the vanilla, sugar, and cornstarch, and beat, scraping the bowl with a rubber spatula as necessary, until smooth. Beat in the eggs one at a time and then on low speed gradually add the cream. Continue to scrape the bowl as necessary; the mixture will be thin, and it should be as smooth as honey. Add the lemon juice last and beat only to mix.

Spray the bottom of the buttered pan with Pam or some other nonstick baking spray. Pour the mixture into the prepared pan. Place the pan in a larger pan that must not be deeper than the cake pan. Place the pan in the oven and pour hot water almost 1 inch deep into the large pan.

Bake at 350° for 30 minutes; then, to ensure even browning, carefully turn both pans together front to back; raise the oven temperature to 375° and bake for 10 to 15 minutes more (total baking time is 40 to 45 minutes). Bake only until the top is a pale golden brown.

Carefully remove from the oven and remove the cake pan from the hot water. Let stand until the bottom of the pan is completely cool. (Do not refrigerate the cake until it has been removed from the pan.)

Cover the cake with a large serving board or tray. (I use a lightweight clear plastic board from a hardware store, or a wooden cutting board.) Center the board or tray very carefully over the cake. Hold the board or tray and the cake pan firmly together and turn them over. Remove the cake pan.

Refrigerate the cake as it is—upside down.

My friend in Alabama likes this best after it has been refrigerated for three days. I have served it after a few hours in the refrigerator, as well as the following day. We loved it both ways.

In Mobile, they serve this with strawberries and a mountain of whipped cream.

TRIPLE-THREAT CHEESECAKE

10 TO 12 PORTIONS

This is a variation of the cheesecake that I made every day for years for my husband's restaurants. There are three variations of it in my first book and one in my chocolate book. Now this. In this recipe, the cake is baked in a springform pan—it has a crumb crust on the bottom—and the cheese mixture is put into the pan alternately with ribbons and globs and lumps, large and small areas, of very thick, almost black, chewy, not-too-sweet chocolate sauce made with unsweetened chocolate, semisweet chocolate, and cocoa. Sensational!

The cake should be refrigerated for 5 to 6 hours or overnight before serving. (Nevertheless, I had this once at room temperature before it had been refrigerated. It was as custardy as crème brûlée and wonderful, the chocolate sauce was still a bit saucy, which made it run a little when served. It was so good my conscience tells me that I must let you know about it. But I think you should become familiar with it chilled first.)

CRUST

1 cup graham cracker crumbs

1 tablespoon granulated sugar

1 tablespoon unsweetened cocoa powder (preferably Dutch-process)

1 teaspoon cinnamon

½ teaspoon powdered (not granular) instant coffee or espresso

2 ounces (½ stick) unsalted butter, melted

You will need an 8 x 3-inch springform pan. With the sides and bottom in place, carefully butter only the sides up to and including the inside of the rim.

Place the crumbs in a mixing bowl and add the sugar, cocoa, cinnamon, and coffee. Stir with a rubber spatula to mix. Add the butter, stir, and press down with the spatula to mix thoroughly (the mixture will not hold together).

Turn the mixture into the pan. With your fingertips distribute the crumbs loosely but evenly over the bottom of the pan. Then with your fingertips and/or knuckles, press on the crumbs firmly to make a compact layer.

This will be baked in a large pan of shallow hot water. To make the springform pan watertight tear off a large square of wide heavy-duty aluminum foil. Place the pan in the center of the foil and, with your hands, bring up the sides of the foil and press them firmly against the sides of the pan. Then, with scissors, cut the foil even with the top of the pan or just below the top; or instead of cutting it you can fold it down to just below the top. Set aside.

CHEESECAKE MIXTURE

2 pounds Philadelphia
cream cheese, at
room temperature

Pinch of salt

1 teaspoon vanilla extract

1¾ cups granulated sugar

4 eggs

Adjust a rack one-third up from the bottom of the oven and preheat the oven to 350°.

In the large bowl of an electric mixer, beat the cheese until it is soft and perfectly smooth, scraping the bowl frequently with a rubber spatula. Do not underbeat at this stage. Beat in the salt, vanilla, and the sugar. Beat well again, scraping the bowl, for several minutes until thoroughly mixed. Then, on moderate speed, add the eggs one at a time, beating until thoroughly incorporated after each addition. (But do not overbeat after adding the eggs; the mixture should not become airy.) Set aside.

TRIPLE-THREAT CHOCOLATE SAUCE

½ cup whipping cream

2 ounces (½ stick)
unsalted butter

2 ounces unsweetened
chocolate

3 ounces semisweet
chocolate

⅓ cup granulated sugar

⅓ cup dark brown
sugar, firmly packed

2 teaspoons powdered
(not granular)
instant coffee

Pinch of salt

½ cup unsweetened
cocoa powder (preferably
Dutch-process)

In a 1½-quart heavy saucepan place the cream, butter, unsweetened chocolate, and semisweet chocolate. Whisk occasionally over rather low heat until the chocolate and butter are melted and the mixture is smooth. Add both sugars and stir over moderate heat until the granules are dissolved. Add the powdered coffee, salt, and cocoa. Stir with a wire whisk. Remove from the heat. Whisk or, if necessary, beat with a mixer until perfectly smooth.

This must be used right away while it is warm; as it cools it becomes too thick to pour. Here's how.

First, the cheese mixture should be divided into three parts, one part equal to half of the mixture and the other two parts each equal to one-quarter of the mixture. (You can just guess, or measure. To measure: There is a total of about 7 cups. Therefore, place half of it—3½ cups—in a bowl or a 1-quart measuring cup. And place the two smaller parts—1¾ cups each—in small bowls or 2-cup measuring cups.)

Pour the larger amount of the cheese mixture into the cake pan. Then, with a fork, slowly drizzle one of the parts of the chocolate sauce in a thin stream all over the cheese mixture, in a crisscross design or in circles or whatever pleases you; the only thing to concentrate on is that the mixture should not flop out in large globs. Cover the chocolate with one of the smaller parts of the cheese mixture, again pouring slowly, all over—not in large globs. Repeat drizzling the second half of the chocolate. And then repeat with the third and last part of the cheese mixture. When you pour this final layer of cheese mixture, remember that it will be the top of the cake, and it will look best if you do not allow any of the chocolate to show through. It is a help to pour very slowly (however, if a little bit of chocolate does show through it is okay).

Place the cake pan in a larger pan that must not be deeper than the cake pan (1½ inches is deep enough). Pour hot water about 1 inch deep into the larger pan. Carefully transfer to the oven.

Bake for 1½ hours. If, after about 1 hour of baking, the top seems to be browning too much, carefully lower the rack to the lowest position and continue baking. When done, the top of the cake will be a beautiful, smooth medium brown color.

Remove the pan from the oven. Carefully remove the cake pan from the water and transfer it to a rack. After about 20 minutes remove the foil. Let the pan stand on the rack until it is completely cool, or for at least 4 or 5 hours.

Carefully release and remove the sides of the pan.

Refrigerate for 5 to 6 hours or overnight.

The cake can be served from the bottom of the cake pan (which should be put on a folded napkin on a cake platter) or it can be transferred to a cake platter. To transfer it, first release the bottom of the cake as follows. Insert a heavy knife with about a 6½-inch blade and carefully work it around the cake to be sure the cake is not sticking. Then, with an extra-large wide metal spatula, or with two wide metal spatulas (one under each side), carefully lift and transfer the cake.

Chocolate Brownie Cheesecake

10 PORTIONS

This is a white cheesecake with chunks of extra-chocolate Brownies throughout. First you bake the Brownies. Then, mix the cheesecake and fold in small chunky pieces of the Brownies. When the cake is baked, the Brownies do not fall apart or sink to the bottom or lose their identity—they remain like black nuggets in the creamy cheesecake. It is fascinating to eat both cheesecake and Brownies in the same bite. And it is gorgeous.

People ask me, "Where do you get your ideas?" Usually I don't know where; they just happen. But this one came from my husband. When I told him I was making Chocolate Cheesecake Brownies, he came back with, "Why not Chocolate Brownie Cheesecake?" I think he was joking. But it is no joke; it is wonderful.

BROWNIES FOR CHEESECAKE

1 cup sifted
all-purpose flour

3 tablespoons
unsweetened cocoa
powder (preferably
Dutch-process)

4 ounces (1 stick)
unsalted butter

2 ounces unsweetened
chocolate

1 teaspoon powdered or
granular instant coffee

½ teaspoon vanilla extract

¼ teaspoon
almond extract

Pinch of salt

1 cup granulated sugar

2 eggs

3½ ounces (1 cup)
walnuts, broken into
rather large pieces

Adjust a rack one-third up from the bottom of the oven and preheat the oven to 350°. Prepare an 8-inch square cake pan as follows: Invert the pan on the work surface, center a 12-inch square of foil, shiny side down, over the pan. With your hands press down on the sides and corners to shape the foil to the pan. Remove the foil, turn the pan over, place the foil in the pan, and with a pot holder or a towel press the foil to fit smoothly into the pan. Place a piece of butter in the pan (additional to what is called for) and place the pan in the oven to melt the butter. Then, with a brush or with crumpled wax paper, spread the butter all over the foil. Set the pan aside.

Sift together the flour and cocoa and set aside.

Place the butter and the chocolate in a 2½- to 3-quart heavy saucepan. Stir occasionally, over rather low heat, until melted. Remove from the heat.

Stir in the coffee, vanilla, almond extract, and the salt. Then add the sugar, mix well, and add the eggs one at a time, mixing well after each addition. Then add the sifted ingredients and stir to mix. Finally, stir in the nuts.

Turn the mixture into the prepared pan, smooth the top, and bake for 23 to 25 minutes, until a toothpick inserted gently in the middle comes out clean and dry.

Remove from the oven and let stand until cool. Then place the pan in the freezer until the cake is very firm. Cover with a rack, turn the pan and rack over, remove the pan, peel off the foil, cover with another rack or cookie sheet, and turn over again, leaving the cake right side up.

The cake of brownies should be frozen or at least very cold when you cut it. Cut the cake into quarters. One-quarter will be left over for you to do something else with. The remaining three-quarters should be cut into ½-inch dice (they will be barely 1 inch deep). Return them to the freezer until you are ready for them. (If they are not very cold when they are folded into the cheesecake, they might crumble.)

153

CHEESECAKE

2 pounds Philadelphia cream cheese, at room temperature

1 teaspoon vanilla extract

Pinch of salt

1½ cups granulated sugar

4 eggs

⅓ cup graham cracker crumbs (to be used after the cake is baked)

NOTE: *For unmolding this cake, and other similar cheesecakes, I have the best results when I use two 8½-inch square lightweight clear plastic cutting boards (they have handles), which are available at most good kitchen supply stores.*

Adjust a rack one-third up from the bottom of the oven and preheat the oven to 350°. Generously butter an 8 x 3-inch one-piece round cheesecake pan (see page 11) up to and including the rim. The cake pan will be placed in a large pan of water during baking—the larger pan should not be deeper than the cake pan; 1½ to 2 inches is deep enough. (I use a 13 x 9 x 2-inch pan.)

In the large bowl of an electric mixer, beat the cheese until it is soft and smooth. Scrape the sides and the bottom of the bowl frequently with a rubber spatula during the mixing. Add the vanilla, salt, and sugar. Beat well until you are sure that it is thoroughly mixed, with no lumps of cheese remaining. Then, on moderately low speed, add the eggs one at a time, beating only until incorporated after each addition. (Do not beat any more than necessary after adding the eggs; this should not be an airy mixture.)

Remove the bowl from the mixer. Spray the bottom of the buttered pan with Pam or some other nonstick baking spray. Pour enough of the cheesecake mixture into the prepared pan to make a layer about ½ inch thick.

Add the cold, diced brownies to the remaining cheesecake mixture. Very gently, fold together, being careful not to break up or crumble the brownies, and turn into the pan. With the bottom of a spoon, smooth the top.

Place the cake pan in the larger pan and add hot water about 1½ inches deep to the larger pan.

Bake for 1½ hours. The top of the cake will rise about ¼ inch above the rim of the pan during baking, and it will become a lovely shade of brown. When the cake is done, remove the cake pan from the hot water and place it on a rack to cool. While cooling, the cake will sink back to its original level.

Let stand for 2 to 3 hours until the bottom of the pan is cool (see Note).

Cover the cake pan with plastic wrap. Place a flat cake plate or lightweight board over the plastic wrap. Hold the plate or board and cake pan together and turn them over. (The cake will fall out of the pan.) Quickly remove the cake pan, sprinkle the graham cracker crumbs over the bottom of the cake, cover with a cake plate or a serving board (I use my second lightweight plastic board), and quickly turn the cake and the plate or board over again, leaving the cake right side up. Do this without pressing on the cake or you will squash it. (In order to avoid the tricky business of inverting the cake the second time, some people serve it upside down without the graham cracker crumbs.)

This cake may be served at room temperature or refrigerated. Frankly, it is more deliciously creamy/custardy at room temperature. But it is firmer and therefore slices a little better when cold. My choice now is room temperature (although either way it's great).

BLACKBERRY WITH SCOTCH CHEESECAKE

12 PORTIONS

This was created by a friend of mine, Marcia Hamann, who owns the Springhill Bakery in Portland, Oregon. It is a small bakery that supplies delicious desserts for some of the best restaurants in the Portland area. She says, "This is a Northwesterly cake with a shortbread crust; the cheese mixture is flavored with cinnamon, Drambuie, and blackberries, and it is topped with sour cream."

Blackberries grow in the Portland area but Marcia uses the frozen ones because "they hold their shape better and do not discolor the whole of the cake the way the fresh berries do." Since fresh blackberries are available in Florida for about 45 minutes every year, I am delighted (and I am sure you will be) to use the frozen ones.

The blackberries that are embedded in the pale and creamy cheese mixture become an incredibly gorgeous shade of shocking pink. It slices like a dream; you will be thrilled to cut into it. And when you taste it you will probably just go limp as I did; the buttery and crunchy crust along with the smooth and mellow, sweet and tart cheesecake is pure cheesecake heaven.

You will need a springform pan 9 or 9½ inches in diameter and 2½ or 3 inches deep. (The completed cake is 2 inches high when it is made in a 9-inch pan.)

CRUST

1 cup sifted all-purpose flour

Adjust a rack one-third up from the bottom of the oven and preheat the oven to 375°.

¼ cup granulated sugar

4 ounces (1 stick) unsalted butter, cold and firm

Place the flour and sugar in a large bowl, or place them in the bowl of a food processor fitted with the metal chopping blade. Cut the butter into about ½-inch squares. Either cut the butter into the dry ingredients with a pastry blender or add it to the processor bowl and process with quick on/off pulses for 15 seconds until the mixture resembles coarse crumbs. If you have used a processor, now transfer the mixture to a wide bowl.

Gently rub the crumb mixture between your hands to form smaller crumbs. It should become an almost powdery mixture that does not hold together.

Turn the mixture into an unbuttered 9- or 9½-inch springform pan and distribute it evenly over the bottom of the pan. Then press down on the mixture firmly with your fingers to make a compact crust on the bottom only.

To prevent butter in the crust from leaking out of the pan during baking, place the pan on a 12-inch square of aluminum foil and fold the foil firmly up around the sides of the pan.

Bake for about 25 minutes, until the edges of the crust begin to brown and it is sandy or golden in the center. (The crust will not darken any more even though it will bake more after the filling is added.) Don't worry if the crust puffs up a bit during baking; it will settle down again.

Cheesecake Mixture

This can be prepared while the crust is baking, or the baked crust can wait.

Finely grated rind of
1 lemon or ½ orange

1 tablespoon lemon juice

19 ounces Philadelphia brand cream cheese (two 8-ounce packages plus one 3-ounce package), at room temperature

1 teaspoon vanilla extract

2½ tablespoons Drambuie

½ teaspoon cinnamon

¾ cup granulated sugar

3 eggs

8 ounces (2 cups) dry-packed frozen blackberries, not thawed

Place the rind and juice in a small cup and let stand.

In the large bowl of an electric mixer, beat the cheese until soft and smooth. Beat in the vanilla, Drambuie, cinnamon, and then the sugar. Add the eggs one at a time, beating until smooth after each addition. Remove from the mixer and stir in the rind-and-juice mixture. Set aside for a moment.

To butter the sides of the pan, melt a bit of butter and, with a pastry brush, brush it around the sides of the pan (which may be warm), carefully buttering all the way to, and touching, the crust.

Pour the cheese mixture over the crust. Now, carefully place the frozen blackberries one at a time evenly all over the cheese mixture with small spaces between them. Then, with your finger, press each berry down into the cheese; the berries should be just barely covered with the cheese mixture.

Bake at 375° for 35 to 40 minutes, until the sides have slightly risen and are lightly browned and the center—when pressed gently with a fingertip—feels as though it may be barely set (dry to the touch but soft inside).

The top of the cake might crack a bit; don't even look at it, it won't show.

Remove the cake from the oven and let stand for 20 minutes. Do not turn off the oven.

SOUR CREAM TOPPING

2 cups sour cream

1 tablespoon
granulated sugar

1 teaspoon vanilla extract

In a bowl, stir the sour cream with the sugar and vanilla. Pour over the cheesecake. With the back of a spoon spread and smooth the mixture.

Bake for 5 minutes. Remove from the oven. Remove the foil from the cheesecake pan. Let stand until cool.

When the cake is thoroughly cool, cut around the sides gently with a small, sharp knife to release the cake. Remove the sides of the pan. Place the cake, still on the bottom of the pan, in the refrigerator for several hours or overnight.

The cake may be served from the bottom of the pan. It should be placed on a folded napkin (to prevent slipping) on a cake plate or serving board. But I remove it from the bottom of the pan; it is not difficult to do and I think it is nicer. Use a heavy chef's knife with a blade about 6 inches long, ease the blade gently and carefully under the crust at one spot, and then gently and carefully work the blade all around under the crust. (The crust will not be stuck to the pan; it will be crisp and separate from the pan quite easily.) Then, without removing the knife completely (hold the tip of it under the crust), ease a wide metal pancake turner under half of the crust and then ease another wide metal pancake turner under the other half of the crust.

Holding one handle in each hand, raise the cake and transfer it to a flat plate or serving board.

Fruitcakes and Nut Cakes

Pearl's Southampton Fruitcake

16 to 18 pounds of cake in 4, 5, or 6 cakes

This recipe came about when I wanted to send a gift to my dear friend Pearl Borinstein. Pearl is the most generous and fabulous hostess I know—her parties are legendary. She was on a round-the-world cruise on the luxury liner Queen Elizabeth II. After several conversations with the post office, it was decided that there might be a better chance that she would receive it if I mailed it to Southampton, England, than to any of the other ports. And since I planned to send it weeks before she would arrive there, I decided on a fruitcake; it would surely last a long time.

Many people have said about this cake, "It's perfectly wonderful—I'm crazy about it, and I don't even like fruit-cake." Okay. But I was happier when an English gentleman who came to visit us said that it was as good as the one he makes and that one, he said, is the best there is.

This recipe makes 4 large cakes, each in a 9 or 10 x 1½- or 2-inch layer-cake pan, or 6 cakes if made in 8-inch pans. It is typically Olde English: dark, extravagant, luxurious, powerful, loaded with fruits and liquors. But I doubt that you will find this recipe in any book, English or otherwise; the recipe evolved because I had just received a large order of candied and dried fruits and I wanted to use some of each one.

The variety of fruits can be changed if certain ones are not available. Instead of buying the ones that are already cut into small pieces and packed in little plastic containers, I buy whole candied fruits by the pound and cut them up myself. I think it makes a world of difference. I also think the cake is better if the fruit is not cut too small.

Making this takes a lot of time. The fruit must marinate for a week or more, and the baking time is 5 hours. But it is worth every minute.

1 pound (generous 3 cups) raisins

1 pound (generous 3 cups) currants

1 pound (2 packed cups) pitted dates, each date cut into 2 or 3 pieces

½ pound (1½ firmly packed cups) dried apricots, each apricot half cut into 2 or 3 pieces

½ pound (1½ firmly packed cups) dried brown figs, cut into ½-inch pieces

In the absence of any of the following fruits, you may substitute others; just use about the same volume. The fruit can be prepared weeks ahead of time if you would like; I suggest a minimum of a week—it takes at least that long for the fruit to absorb all the liquor.

Place all of the fruit, the cognac, and the Grand Marnier in a large bowl. Stir to mix well. Then transfer to a large jar with a tight cover, or divide among two or three jars. Cover tightly. Let stand for a week or more, turning the jars from side to side and from top to bottom occasionally to marinate the fruit thoroughly. (It is best to do this on a tray of some kind in case a jar leaks.)

Adjust two racks to divide the oven into thirds and preheat the oven to 225° (check the temperature with a portable mercury thermometer; if it is any hotter the cakes will burn). Butter the sides only of four 9- or 10-inch layer-cake pans. (They may be 1½ or 2 inches deep. If they are only 1½ inches deep you might have enough batter for an additional small cake.) Cut baking-pan liner paper or aluminum foil to fit the bottoms of the pans, butter one side of the papers or foil, and place them buttered side up in the pans. Set aside.

6 ounces (1 cup)
candied ginger, cut
into ¼-inch pieces

½ pound (2 cups)
candied lemon rind,
cut into ½-inch pieces

½ pound (2 cups)
candied orange rind,
cut into ½-inch pieces

½ pound (1½ cups)
candied cherries,
cut into halves

½ pound (1½ cups)
candied pineapple, cut
into ½-inch pieces

½ pound (1½ cups)
candied citron, cut
into ½-inch pieces

1 cup cognac

½ cup Grand Marnier

2½ cups sifted
all-purpose flour

1 teaspoon baking
powder

3 tablespoons
unsweetened
cocoa powder

1 teaspoon ground cloves

1 teaspoon cinnamon

1 teaspoon mace

Ingredients continued on next page.

Sift together the flour, baking powder, cocoa, cloves, cinnamon, mace, and powdered instant coffee, and set aside.

In the large bowl of an electric mixer, cream the butter. Add the sugar and beat well until light in color. Add the eggs one at a time, beating well after each addition. (The mixture will appear curdled—it is okay.)

On low speed add the sifted dry ingredients in three additions alternating with the molasses in two additions. (It might still look curdled—that is okay.)

In the very large mixing bowl (or any very large container), mix the fruit into the batter—include any other liquor that has not been absorbed. Finally, mix in the nuts. Either use a large and heavy wooden spoon, or use your hands.

Divide the batter evenly among the prepared pans; it is all right if it fills the pans all the way to the tops. Pat the tops well to make them smooth and level and to make the batter compact, with no air spaces.

Bake for 5 hours, checking the temperature occasionally with a portable mercury thermometer. Once or twice during the baking reverse the positions of the pans, top to bottom and front to back, to ensure even baking.

Remove from the oven and cool for half an hour in the pan on racks. Carefully, with a small, sharp knife, cut around the sides to release. Then cover each pan with a rack, turn over the pan and rack, remove the pan and the paper lining, cover with another rack and turn over again, leaving the cakes right side up.

When the cakes have cooled—or while they are cooling—brush them with a conservative amount of additional cognac and/or Grand Marnier (I use a mixture of both). Then carefully wrap the cakes airtight in plastic wrap. (Until they are chilled handle them carefully—they are fragile.)

Store the cakes for at least a week in the refrigerator, brushing them once or twice again with more cognac and/or Grand Marnier. Then they may remain in the refrigerator or they may be frozen. They may be brushed occasionally with additional liquor; however, if they are frozen, let them stand at room temperature for about an hour before brushing them with more liquor—they absorb more when they are not frozen.

2 teaspoons powdered
(not granular) instant
coffee or instant espresso

1 pound (4 sticks)
unsalted butter

1 pound (2¼ firmly
packed cups) dark
brown sugar

9 eggs

1¼ cups dark molasses

1½ pounds (7 cups)
pecan halves

1½ pounds (7 cups)
walnut halves or
large pieces

Additional cognac
and/or Grand Marnier
(to be used after the
cakes are baked)

When I give this cake as a gift, I include the following note: "Refrigerate or freeze. Cake should be very cold when sliced. Use a very sharp, heavy knife. Cut small portions, this is RICH."

P.S. I was delighted when the wonderful food magazine Saveur printed this recipe in their December 1996 issue and said that it is their favorite classic fruitcake.

LIGHT FRUITCAKE

6½ POUNDS (1 TREMENDOUS CAKE)

Merry Christmas! This is a high, wide, and handsome cake especially appropriate for the holidays—it is marvelous for a very large party. It should be made weeks or even months ahead (although I once served it five days after making it and it was great) and wrapped in a cloth kept wet with cognac, or brushed with cognac while it ages.

This recipe calls for long, slow baking.

5 ounces (1 cup) light raisins

½ cup cognac or brandy

8 ounces (1½ cups) dried candied citron, cut into slices or small squares

5 ounces (1 cup) candied pineapple or candied ginger, cut into ¼-inch pieces

4 ounces (1 cup) candied red or green cherries, cut into halves

4 ounces (1 cup) candied orange rind, cut into slices or small squares

4 cups sifted all-purpose flour

8 ounces (2 cups) slivered (julienne) blanched almonds

4 ounces (generous 1 cup) pecan halves or large pieces

Ingredients continued on next page.

Mix the raisins and cognac or brandy in an airtight jar. Let stand, turning the jar occasionally, for at least an hour or overnight. Adjust a rack to the middle of the oven (even though it is a high cake, if you bake it lower in the oven, the top will remain too light because of the low temperature). Preheat the oven to 275°. You will need a 10 x 4-inch tube pan, which may be in one piece or it may be a two-piece pan (the sides separate from the bottom and tube); and it may be either nonstick or otherwise. Whichever you use, butter the pan even if it is a nonstick pan (including the tube in the middle), line the bottom with a round (with a hole in the middle) of baking pan liner paper or brown wrapping paper (in the absence of baking pan liner paper, brown wrapping paper is better than wax paper for this cake), butter the paper, and dust the pan all over with fine, dry bread crumbs (including the tube—sprinkle the crumbs on the tube with your fingertips). Be especially careful not to miss even a small spot; check the center tube carefully. Then, turn the pan upside down over a piece of paper, and tap to shake out excess crumbs.

Place the citron, pineapple, cherries, and orange rind in a large, wide mixing bowl (use one larger than you think you will need, or you will not be able to flour the fruit well—and it should be large enough to add all the remaining ingredients). Add ½ cup of the sifted flour (reserve 3½ cups). With your fingers, toss the fruit and flour so each piece of the fruit is thoroughly separated and floured. Then add the nuts and toss again. Set aside.

In the large bowl of an electric mixer, cream the butter until it is soft and smooth. Beat in the vanilla and 1⅔ cups (reserve the remaining ⅓ cup) of sugar. Add the yolks two or three at a time, scraping the bowl with a rubber spatula and beating until thoroughly incorporated after each addition.

Sift the reserved 3½ cups of the sifted flour with the mace and salt. Then, on low speed, add one-third of the sifted dry ingredients to the butter mixture, and mix only to blend. Beat in the milk, then another third of the dry

12 ounces (3 sticks)
unsalted butter

1 teaspoon vanilla extract

2 cups granulated sugar

6 eggs, separated

½ teaspoon mace

¼ teaspoon salt

½ cup milk

Finely grated rind of
2 to 3 lemons (some
of the juice will be
used for Icing)

1 teaspoon cream
of tartar

Additional cognac or
brandy (for brushing
on the baked cake)

ingredients, then the cognac-soaked raisins along with any cognac the raisins did not absorb, and finally beat in the remaining dry ingredients.

Remove from the mixer and stir in the lemon rind.

In the small bowl of an electric mixer, with clean beaters, beat the whites until they are barely foamy. Add the cream of tartar and continue to beat until the whites hold a soft shape. Reduce the speed to moderate and gradually add the reserved ⅓ cup of sugar. Then, on high speed again, beat until the whites hold a definite shape but are not stiff or dry.

Add the butter-sugar-flour mixture and the beaten whites to the floured fruits and, with a large wooden spoon (rubber is too soft for this thick mixture), fold the three mixtures together only until thoroughly incorporated.

Spoon into the prepared pan and smooth the top.

Bake for 3⅓ hours, until a cake tester gently inserted all the way to the bottom comes out clean and dry. During baking, if the top of the cake begins to darken too much, cover it loosely with foil.

As soon as you remove the cake from the oven, brush the top with a few tablespoons of the additional cognac or brandy. (It will soften the crust caused by the long baking.)

Then remove the cake from the oven and let it stand in the pan on a rack for at least an hour or a bit longer until it is tepid.

Cover with a rack, turn over the pan and the rack, remove the pan (do not remove the paper lining yet), cover with another rack and turn over again, leaving the cake right side up to finish cooling. When it is completely cool, turn the cake carefully over again just for a moment and peel off the paper lining. Leave it right side up.

The traditional way to age this cake is to sprinkle a cheesecloth or a thin towel with cognac or brandy and wrap the cake with it, then place it in a large plastic bag or wrap it in foil. About once every week or two, moisten the cheesecloth or towel with more cognac or brandy. Or, untraditionally, omit the cheesecloth and just brush the cognac onto the cake (an easier procedure, I think); keep the cake wrapped in wide plastic wrap or in a large plastic bag.

They say that fruitcakes can be kept at room temperature for a year or more; however, I store mine in the refrigerator or freezer.

The icing is optional. If you do use it, it may be applied either a few hours before serving or the day before.

FRUITCAKE ICING

1 cup plus 2 tablespoons sifted confectioners' sugar

2 tablespoons unsalted butter, melted

1 tablespoon milk

2 teaspoons lemon juice

NOTE: *Although I love the old-fashioned simplicity of this cake without any decoration on the icing, you can, if you wish, make a design (plain or fancy) with cut-up candied fruits or whole candied cherries or large pecan halves, or any combination of fruits and nuts.*

In a small bowl, stir together all the ingredients until smooth. The icing should be a thick but flowing mixture, and may be adjusted as necessary with additional sugar, milk, or lemon juice. It will be a very smooth icing with a pale yellow color (from the butter), and it should be used immediately.

Place the cake on a serving plate and spoon or pour the icing over the top of the cake. With a long, narrow metal spatula spread it to make a thin and even layer over the top only. If the consistency is exactly right, it may run down the sides slightly in a few spots. Just leave it—do not spread the icing on the sides.

After several hours the icing will dry, and although it will not become hard, it will not be sticky.

Transfer the cake to a serving plate.

If possible, refrigerate the iced cake before serving; all such cakes slice best when they are cold. Serve in thin slices, two or three slices to a portion. (Use a very sharp, strong knife.)

THE ORIGINAL KENTUCKY WHISKEY CAKE

24 OR MORE PORTIONS

This is an heirloom recipe for an extravagant and marvelous raisin/nut/bourbon fruitcake. It is a cake traditionally served for Thanksgiving and Christmas, but it is wonderful any time. It lasts well and makes a magnificent gift. It is 5½ pounds of deliciousness. Make it at least several days before serving, or make it whenever and freeze it. Prepare the raisins at least a day before baking.

You will need an extra-large mixing bowl for folding in the beaten egg whites.

1½ pounds (4½ cups) dark and light (or all dark) raisins

1 cup bourbon

2 cups sifted all-purpose flour

1 teaspoon baking powder

½ teaspoon salt

8 ounces (2 sticks) unsalted butter

1 nutmeg, freshly grated, or 2 teaspoons powdered nutmeg

2 cups granulated sugar

6 eggs, separated

1 pound (5 cups) pecan halves or large pieces

At least a day before baking (or a week before) place the raisins in a jar with a tight-fitting top. Add the bourbon. Turn occasionally from top to bottom. (If the jar might leak when it is upside down, place it in a bowl.)

Prepare the oven to 300° and adjust a rack one-third up from the bottom of the oven. You will need a 10 x 4-inch tube pan, which may have a separate bottom or may be all in one piece, and it may have a nonstick lining or not. Butter the pan (even if it is nonstick), line the bottom with baking pan liner paper or brown wrapping paper cut to fit, butter the paper, and dust with fine, dry bread crumbs (with your fingertips, sprinkle the crumbs on the tube). Then, over a piece of paper, tap to shake out excess crumbs.

Sift together the flour, baking powder, and ¼ teaspoon of the salt (reserve ¼ teaspoon of salt). Set aside.

In the large bowl of an electric mixer, beat the butter until it is softened. Add the nutmeg and 1¾ cups of the sugar (reserve the remaining ¼ cup) and beat for 5 minutes until the mixture is very creamy. Add the egg yolks (it is okay to add them all at once) and beat for a few minutes, scraping the bowl as necessary with a rubber spatula. On low speed add about one-third of the sifted dry ingredients and beat only to mix. Then mix in about half of the raisins, along with any bourbon that was not absorbed. Then add another third of the dry ingredients, the remaining raisins and bourbon, and finally the remaining dry ingredients, scraping the bowl as necessary with a large rubber spatula and beating only until incorporated after each addition.

Remove from the mixer and stir in the nuts. Now transfer the mixture to a larger bowl in order to have room to fold in the beaten whites. Set aside.

In the small bowl of an electric mixer, with clean beaters, beat the whites and the reserved ¼ teaspoon of salt until the whites hold a soft shape. Reduce the speed to moderate and gradually add the remaining ¼ cup

NOTE: *If you wish, you can wrap the cake in a napkin that has been soaked with bourbon or you can just stuff the center hole with a piece of cheesecloth that has been soaked with bourbon, and then wrap the cake with plastic wrap or foil and let it age that way at room temperature for at least a few days. It is a fine cake either way, with or without the additional bourbon—but it is possibly a little more fine with it.*

of sugar. Then increase the speed to high and beat briefly, only until the whites hold a definite shape but are not stiff or dry.

With a large rubber spatula stir one-quarter of the whites into the cake batter. Then fold in the remaining whites.

Turn the mixture into the prepared pan. Smooth the top.

Bake for about 2½ hours, until a cake tester inserted into the middle of the cake comes out clean and dry. If the top of the cake begins to darken too much during baking, cover it loosely with foil.

Remove from the oven and let stand for 30 minutes. (The top of the cake will be 1 inch below the top of the pan.)

Cover the pan with a rack, carefully turn over the pan and the rack, remove the pan, peel off the paper lining, cover with another rack and turn over again, leaving the cake right side up.

When the cake has cooled, wrap it airtight and refrigerate it for a few days before serving, or freeze it.

The cake should be cold when it is cut. Use a very sharp, firm knife and make the slices thin.

IRISH WHISKEY CAKE

ONE 9-INCH LOAF CAKE

This is an old recipe for a deliciously flavored small fruitcake with less fruit than the usual. The caraway seeds do something wonderful. It is marvelous with tea or coffee, or with wine. It keeps well and is great to give as a gift.

Adjust a rack one-third up from the bottom of the oven and preheat the oven to 350°. Butter a loaf pan that measures 8½ x 4½ x 2¾ inches and has a 6-cup capacity. Dust it with fine, dry bread crumbs, then, over a piece of paper, tap to shake out excess crumbs.

Sift together the flour, baking powder, mace, and salt, and set aside.

Mix the lemon rind and juice and set aside.

In the large bowl of an electric mixer, cream the butter. Add the vanilla and then the sugar and beat to mix well. Add the yolks and beat well.

2 cups sifted
all-purpose flour

1 teaspoon baking powder

¼ teaspoon mace

¼ teaspoon salt

Finely grated rind
of 2 lemons

1 tablespoon plus
1 teaspoon lemon juice

5 ounces (1¼ sticks)
unsalted butter

1 teaspoon vanilla extract

1 cup light brown
sugar, firmly packed

2 eggs, separated

½ cup Irish whiskey (or
any Scotch, whiskey,
bourbon, or blend)

½ cup diced candied
orange peel

½ cup light raisins

1 tablespoon
caraway seeds

¾ cup pecans, cut into
medium-size pieces

About 1 tablespoon
additional butter, at room
temperature (to be used
after the cake is baked)

On low speed add the sifted dry ingredients in three additions, alternating with the whiskey in two additions, scraping the bowl as necessary with a rubber spatula and beating only until incorporated after each addition.

Remove from the mixer. Stir in the lemon rind and juice, candied orange peel, raisins, caraway seeds, and pecans.

In a small bowl beat the egg whites until they hold a definite shape but are not stiff or dry, and fold them into the batter.

Turn into the prepared pan and smooth the top. Then, with the spatula or with a spoon, form a shallow trench lengthwise down the middle of the cake. (That makes a more level top, less of a mound, when baked.)

Bake for 1¼ hours (or longer), until a cake tester inserted into the middle comes out clean and dry. While the cake is baking, if it begins to darken too much, cover it loosely with foil. Test this carefully and be sure that you do not underbake. As you remove the cake from the oven, spread the softened butter over the top. The top of the cake will have formed a deep crack—it is okay.

Let the cake stand in the pan on a rack for about 20 minutes. Then cover it with another rack, turn over the pan and the rack, remove the pan, and carefully turn the cake right side up to cool on the rack.

It is best to wrap and refrigerate this for at least a few hours—preferably overnight or longer—or freeze it before slicing. It slices best when it is cold.

If the top has a crisp crust (delicious), slice it with a serrated bread knife.

FLORIDA RUM CAKE

16 PORTIONS

This is made in a fancy-shaped tube pan; it is a buttermilk walnut cake with a generous amount of lemon, orange, and rum glaze—the combination is divine. It is a pretty cake and may be made for a party dessert, or it may be served as a coffee cake. It should be made at least a day before serving; it may be frozen.

You will need a one-piece tube pan that has a design and an 8- to 10-cup capacity.

2½ cups sifted all-purpose flour

2 teaspoons baking powder

1 teaspoon baking soda

½ teaspoon salt

8 ounces (2 sticks) unsalted butter

1 cup granulated sugar

2 eggs

1 cup buttermilk

Finely grated rind of 1 large fresh lemon

Finely grated rind of 2 large, deep-colored oranges (juices of lemon and oranges will be used for the Glaze)

4 ounces (generous 1 cup) walnuts, chopped into small pieces (⅛- to ¼-inch pieces)

Adjust a rack one-third up from the bottom of the oven and preheat the oven to 350°. Butter a one-piece kugelhopf or Bundt-type tube pan that has an 8- to 10-cup capacity; it is best to use soft (not melted) butter and a pastry brush. Dust the pan all over with fine, dry bread crumbs, then, over a piece of paper, tap to shake out excess crumbs. Set aside.

Sift together the flour, baking powder, baking soda, and salt, and set aside.

Beat the butter in the large bowl of an electric mixer until it is soft. Add the sugar and beat to mix well. Add the eggs one at a time, and beat to mix after each addition. Then, on low speed, add the sifted dry ingredients in three additions alternately with the buttermilk in two additions, scraping the bowl as necessary with a rubber spatula and beating only until smooth after each addition.

Remove from the mixer. Stir in the grated rinds and then the nuts.

Turn into the prepared pan and smooth the top.

Bake for 55 to 60 minutes, until the top springs back sharply when it is lightly pressed with a fingertip.

Meanwhile, prepare the glaze.

GLAZE

3 tablespoons fresh
lemon juice

½ cup fresh orange juice

1 cup granulated sugar

5 tablespoons dark rum

NOTE: *When you cut the cake you will see that it has absorbed the glaze on the outer edges, not all the way through to the middle.*

Place both juices and the sugar in a small saucepan and set aside.

When the cake is done, remove it from the oven and set it on a rack; immediately place the saucepan over moderate or high heat and stir with a small wooden spoon until the sugar is dissolved and the mixture just comes to a low boil. Remove it from the heat and stir in the rum.

Pierce all over the top of the cake with a cake tester. Then, gradually spoon the hot glaze over the hot cake (still in the pan), spooning only about a tablespoonful at a time (or a little more at the beginning). When about half of the glaze has been added, and some of it remains around the rim of the cake pan (instead of being absorbed immediately), use a small, narrow metal spatula or a table knife and gently ease the edges of the cake (around the tube also) just a bit away from the pan, allowing the glaze to run down the sides. Continue adding the glaze (and releasing the sides occasionally) until it is all absorbed. (Toward the end you will wonder, but the cake will absorb it all.)

Let stand for about 10 minutes, until the bottom of the pan is not too hot to touch. Then cover the pan with a cake plate, hold the pan and plate firmly together, and turn them over. Remove the pan. If it does not come away easily, bang both the pan and the plate against the work surface; once should be enough. Remove the pan. Brush away any loose crumbs on the plate.

Let stand for a few hours and then cover airtight with plastic wrap. Let stand overnight (if possible).

Serve this in thick slices.

MRS. O'SHAUGHNESSY'S CAKE

1 8½- OR 9-INCH LOAF CAKE

This is an Irish loaf cake with a generous amount of currants that don't sink. It bakes with a richly browned crust, a nicely rounded top, and a mild lemon-orange flavor. It is delicious, easy to make, keeps well, and is lovely to wrap as a gift.

5 ounces (1 cup) currants

Boiling water

1¾ cups sifted
all-purpose flour

1 teaspoon baking
powder

¼ teaspoon salt

½ teaspoon mace

4 ounces (1 stick)
unsalted butter

1 teaspoon vanilla extract

1 cup minus
2 tablespoons
granulated sugar

2 eggs

½ cup milk

Finely grated rind
of 2 lemons

Finely grated rind
of 1 large, deep-
colored orange

½ teaspoon
caraway seeds

Adjust a rack one-third up from the bottom of the oven and preheat the oven to 350°. You can use either an 8½ x 4½ x 2½-inch loaf pan or a 9 x 5 x 3-inch loaf pan (the batter will not fill a 9 x 5 x 3-inch pan, but it will be an attractive loaf anyhow). Butter the pan and dust it with fine, dry bread crumbs, then, over a piece of paper, tap to shake out excess crumbs.

Cover the currants with boiling water and let stand for 5 minutes. Drain in a strainer and turn out onto several thicknesses of paper towels. Fold the paper over the currants and press to absorb excess water. Let stand.

Sift together the flour, baking powder, salt, and mace, and set aside.

In the large bowl of an electric mixer, beat the butter until it is soft. Add the vanilla and then the sugar and beat to mix well. Add the eggs one at a time, beating until thoroughly mixed after each addition. On low speed add about one-third of the dry ingredients, scraping the bowl as necessary with a rubber spatula and beating only until incorporated. Gradually add the milk and beat until smooth. Then add the remaining dry ingredients and beat only until smooth.

Remove from the mixer and stir in the grated rinds. Turn into the prepared pan, smooth the top, and then, with a rubber spatula or with the bottom of a spoon, form a slight trench (about ½ inch deep) down the length of the loaf. That will keep it from rising too high in the middle.

Sprinkle the caraway seeds all over the top.

Bake for about 1 hour, until a cake tester gently inserted into the middle comes out clean and dry.

Let the cake stand in the pan on a rack for about 10 minutes, then cover it with a rack, turn over the pan and the rack, remove the pan, and gently turn the loaf right side up to cool on the rack.

If you can wait, wrap this and refrigerate it overnight or freeze it for about an hour before serving. It is best to cut this with a serrated bread knife.

Cuban Coconut Pound Cake
16 portions

This cake has a fine-grained, compact texture. It keeps well, slices well, freezes well, and is quick and easy to make. It has a generous amount of coconut and some sliced almonds. The original Cuban version uses freshly grated coconut, which is wonderful. If you buy the coconut already shredded, you may use either sweetened or unsweetened—the cake is super-special with either. Everyone who has tasted this raves about it and I recommend it mucho!

8 ounces (2 sticks) unsalted butter

1 teaspoon vanilla extract

½ teaspoon almond extract

½ teaspoon salt

2 cups granulated sugar

5 eggs

3 cups sifted all-purpose flour

1 cup milk

7 ounces (2⅔ loosely packed cups) shredded coconut

3 ounces (1 cup) unblanched almonds, thinly sliced (see Note)

Note: *Although the original Cuban version of this cake was made with unblanched almonds, if you cannot get them, use the blanched ones.*

Adjust a rack one-third up from the bottom of the oven and preheat the oven to 325°. You will need a 10-inch tube pan (a plain pan with no design). The baked cake will be 2½ inches high, but if the pan is deeper it is all right. I have used a 10 x 4-inch tube pan and the cake was beautiful. The pan can be in one piece or two (the sides being a separate piece from the bottom and tube); it can be nonstick or not. If it is nonstick it does not have to be buttered, but it does have to be lined with a round of baking-pan liner paper or buttered wax paper (buttered side up) cut to fit. If the pan is not nonstick, butter the bottom and sides, line it with a round of baking-pan liner paper or wax paper cut to fit, butter the paper, and dust the pan all over with fine, dry bread crumbs; then, over a piece of paper, tap to shake out excess crumbs.

In the large bowl of an electric mixer, cream the butter until it is soft and smooth. Add the vanilla and almond extracts, the salt, and the sugar, and beat to mix. Add the eggs one at a time, beating until incorporated after each addition (the mixture will appear curdled—it is okay). On low speed alternately add the flour in three additions with the milk in two additions, scraping the bowl with a rubber spatula and beating only until incorporated. Remove from the mixer and fold in the coconut and the nuts.

Turn into the prepared pan and smooth the top.

Bake for 1½ hours until the top is golden brown and a cake tester inserted into the cake, all the way to the bottom, comes out clean.

Let stand on a rack for 15 minutes. Then cover with a rack, turn the rack and the cake pan over, remove the pan (do not remove the paper yet), cover with another rack and invert again, leaving the cake right side up. Let stand until cool.

When the cake is cool, carefully peel off the paper lining.

Wrap the cool cake in plastic wrap. If possible, refrigerate it overnight before serving. Or place it in the freezer for about 45 minutes. It must be cold when it is sliced or it will crumble. Serve two or three thin slices to a portion.

SURVIVAL CAKE

16 LARGE SLICES

This recipe is from friends in Colorado who always make it to take on river-rafting or mountain-climbing and camping trips. Make it for a picnic, or for lunch boxes, or just for surviving whatever. It is wonderfully satisfying, not too sweet, and it keeps well and travels well. It is made in a shallow, square pan and is cut into slices for serving.

4 ounces (1 stick) unsalted butter

½ cup dark or light brown sugar, firmly packed

½ cup dark or light molasses

¾ cup prepared black coffee, water, or apple juice

5 ounces (1 cup) raisins

12 ounces (1½ cups) pitted dates, cut into large pieces

2 cups strained or sifted all-purpose whole wheat flour (see Note)

½ teaspoon salt

1 teaspoon baking soda

1 teaspoon baking powder

2 teaspoons cinnamon

½ teaspoon mace

½ teaspoon cloves

¼ teaspoon ginger

Ingredients continued on next page.

Adjust a rack to the center of the oven and preheat the oven to 350°. Prepare a 9-inch square cake pan (1¾ to 2 inches deep) as follows: Center a 12-inch square of aluminum foil shiny side down over an overturned pan, fold down the sides and the corners to shape the foil, then remove the foil, turn the pan right side up, lay the foil in the pan, and press carefully into place. To butter the foil, put the pan in the oven with a piece of butter in it to melt as the oven heats. Then spread the melted butter with a brush or with crumpled wax paper.

Place the 4 ounces of butter in a heavy 2-quart saucepan over moderate heat to melt. Add the brown sugar, molasses, coffee (or water or apple juice), raisins, and dates. Stir occasionally until the mixture comes to a boil. Remove from the heat, pour into a large mixing bowl, and stir occasionally until the mixture cools to room temperature.

Meanwhile, sift together the flour, salt, baking soda, baking powder, cinnamon, mace, cloves, ginger, and black pepper.

When the hot mixture has cooled, add the eggs and stir with a wooden spoon to mix. Then stir in the wheat germ, then the sifted dry ingredients and finally the nuts.

Turn into the prepared pan and smooth the top.

Bake for about 40 minutes, until the cake feels firm when lightly pressed with a fingertip.

Cool in the pan for 10 to 15 minutes. Then cover with a rack, turn over the pan and the rack, remove the pan, peel off the foil, cover with another rack, and turn over again, leaving the cake right side up to cool.

When completely cool and firm enough to slice (placing it in the freezer for about half an hour or so will make the slicing easier), transfer the cake to a board. With a long, thin, sharp knife cut the cake in half. Then cut each half into 8 slices.

¼ teaspoon finely
ground black pepper

3 eggs

½ cup wheat germ,
toasted or untoasted

5½ ounces (1½ cups)
walnuts, cut or broken
into medium-size pieces

To preserve the freshness and make it generally stronger for packing and for surviving, wrap each slice individually in clear cellophane, wax paper, or foil.

NOTE: *Any whole wheat flour that did not go through the strainer or sifter should be stirred back into the part that did go through.*

SOUR CREAM COFFEE CAKE

12 SQUARES

Extra scrumptious! This is an easy-to-make, deliciously moist sour cream raisin cake with a crunchy, nutty topping that sinks into the cake in places and is too good! It is baked in an oblong shallow pan and is great for a picnic or whenever you want to carry the cake with you right in the pan. Or make it for a fancy coffee or tea party, or Sunday brunch, or for any other time. But make it.

TOPPING

1 tablespoon sifted
all-purpose flour

1¼ teaspoons cinnamon

¾ cup dark or light brown
sugar, firmly packed

2 tablespoons firm
unsalted butter, cut
into ½-inch squares

3½ ounces (1 cup)
pecans, cut into medium-
small pieces, about ¼
inch in diameter (walnuts
may be substituted)

Adjust a rack to the center of the oven and preheat the oven to 350°. Generously butter a 13 x 9 x 2-inch meal baking pan. Or use an oven-proof glass pan and a 325° temperature (see Note).

Stir the flour, cinnamon, and sugar together in a bowl. Add the butter and with a pastry blender cut it into the dry ingredients until the mixture resembles coarse meal. Do not overmix; a few slightly larger pieces of butter will not hurt. Stir in the nuts. Set aside at room temperature unless the room is very warm, in which case, refrigerate.

CAKE

2 cups sifted all-purpose flour	Sift together the flour, baking powder, baking soda, and the salt, and set aside.

2 cups sifted all-purpose flour

Sift together the flour, baking powder, baking soda, and the salt, and set aside.

1 teaspoon baking powder

1 teaspoon baking soda

Scant ¼ teaspoon salt

4 ounces (1 stick) unsalted butter

In the large bowl of an electric mixer, cream the butter until it is soft. Add the sugar and beat to mix well. Add the eggs one at a time, scraping the bowl with a rubber spatula and beating until thoroughly incorporated after each addition. On low speed add the sifted dry ingredients in three additions alternating with the sour cream in two additions, beating only until incorporated after each addition.

Remove from the mixer and fold in the raisins.

1 cup granulated sugar

3 eggs

1 cup sour cream

Turn into the prepared pan and smooth the top. Sprinkle the prepared topping loosely and evenly all over the cake.

Bake for 30 to 35 minutes, until a toothpick or a cake tester gently inserted in the middle comes out clean and dry. The cake might take a little longer to bake in a glass pan.

2½ ounces (½ cup) light raisins

This may be served warm or after it has cooled to room temperature.

NOTE: *The pan may be buttered as directed and then the cake may be cut into squares directly in the pan and removed with a wide metal spatula. If you plan to carry the cake in the pan to a picnic—or if you simply like a cake that you can leave in the pan until you cut portions—that is definitely the way to handle it.*

But I prefer to remove the cake from the pan in one piece, and cut the portions with a long knife (which can be done only if the cake has been removed from the pan). If you want to do it this way, here's how. First line the pan with foil as follows: Turn the pan over and cover the bottom with a 16- or 17-inch length of foil, fold down the sides and the corners of the foil to shape it, remove the foil, turn the pan right side up, lay the foil in the pan, and press it into place. To butter the foil, place a piece of butter in the pan and put the pan in the oven so the butter melts. Then brush it with a pastry brush or spread it with crumpled wax paper.

To remove the baked cake from the foil-lined pan, let the cake cool for 10 or 15 minutes in the pan. Then, to keep the crumb topping from falling off, cover the cake securely with foil, cover that with a cookie sheet, turn over the cake pan and the cookie sheet (pressing them firmly together), remove the pan, peel off the foil lining, cover the cake with a serving platter, a board, or another cookie sheet, and turn over again, leaving the cake right side up.

WHOLE WHEAT WALNUT CAKE

16 TO 18 PORTIONS

This is a large, compact cake, somewhat like a pound cake full of nuts, somewhat like a fruitcake with nuts only. It is beautiful and delicious, every bite full of large chunks of walnuts. It is 5 pounds of cake, an impressive gift. Serve it as a coffee cake or with wine. Or serve it with ice cream. It calls for both whole wheat and white flour, and long, slow baking.

Adjust a rack one-third up from the bottom of the oven and preheat the oven to 275°. You will need a 10 x 4-inch tube pan (a plain pan with no design); it can be either a one-piece pan, or the sides can be separate from the bottom and tube; it can be plain metal or it can have a nonstick finish. Butter the pan (even if it is nonstick), line the bottom with a round of wax paper or baking-pan liner paper cut to fit, butter the paper, and dust all over with fine, dry bread crumbs; then, over a piece of paper, tap out excess.

Place the butter, salt, and pepper in the large bowl of an electric mixer and beat until soft. Add the vanilla and almond extracts, the ginger, powdered instant coffee, and allspice, and then 1½ cups of the sugar (reserve the remaining ½ cup of sugar). Beat well for about 3 minutes, scraping the bowl as necessary with a large rubber spatula. Add the egg yolks all at once and continue to beat for about 5 minutes more.

On low speed, add about half the white flour and beat only to mix. Then add half the milk, beat only to mix, then the second half of the white flour, and then the balance of the milk. Next, add half the whole wheat flour, then the cognac, and finally the balance of the whole wheat flour, continuously scraping the bowl with the rubber spatula and beating only until incorporated.

Transfer the mixture to a mixing bowl larger than the large bowl of the mixer. Stir in the nuts.

If you do not have an additional large bowl and an additional set of beaters for the mixer, wash the ones you have just used. Place the egg whites in the large bowl, add the cream of tartar, and beat until the whites hold a soft shape. On moderate speed gradually add the reserved ½ cup of sugar. Increase the speed to high and beat until the whites have a thick, marshmallowlike consistency.

12 ounces (3 sticks)
unsalted butter

½ teaspoon salt

½ teaspoon finely
ground black pepper

1 teaspoon vanilla extract

½ teaspoon
almond extract

1 teaspoon
powdered ginger

1 teaspoon powdered
(not granular)
instant coffee

½ teaspoon allspice

2 cups granulated sugar

6 eggs, separated

2 cups sifted
all-purpose white flour

⅔ cup milk

1½ cups sifted
all-purpose whole
wheat flour

⅓ cup cognac,
brandy, or whiskey

1 pound (generous 4
cups) walnut halves
or large pieces

1 teaspoon cream
of tartar

Add about one-third of the whites to the walnut mixture (which will be quite thick) and fold or stir until incorporated. Then add all of the remaining whites and fold together until incorporated. Be patient; it will seem to take a long time.

Turn the mixture into the pan and smooth the top.

Bake for 2¾ to 3 hours, until a cake tester gently inserted into the cake, all the way to the bottom, comes out clean. Remove from the oven. Let the cake stand in the pan for about half an hour. The top of the cake will be about 1 inch below the top of the pan.

Cover with a rack, turn over the pan and the rack, remove the pan (but not the paper lining), cover with another rack and turn over again, leaving the cake right side up to cool. Do not remove the paper lining until the cake has cooled completely.

Wrap the cooled cake in plastic wrap or in a plastic bag and refrigerate overnight or longer, or freeze.

Cut into very thin slices, and serve two or three slices to a portion.

NOTE: *If some of the whole wheat flour did not go through the sifter, it should be stirred into the part that did go through.*

BLUEBERRY-NUT LOAF CAKE

ABOUT 10 PORTIONS

This is a delicate orange-flavored loaf, loaded with fresh blueberries and walnuts. It is delicious as a dessert or as a coffee cake. When you cut into it you will see the darker purple and magenta berries against a lighter, glowing orange background of cake. Gorgeous! Remember this cake in blueberry season.

1¼ cups fresh blueberries

2 cups sifted
all-purpose flour

½ teaspoon salt

⅔ cup granulated sugar

1½ teaspoons
baking powder

½ teaspoon baking soda

1 egg

2 tablespoons unsalted
butter, melted

¾ cup orange juice
(grate the rinds of
2 oranges before
squeezing the juice)

Finely grated rind
of 2 large, deep-
colored oranges

5 ounces (1¼ cups)
walnut or pecan halves
or large pieces

Adjust a rack one-third up from the bottom of the oven and preheat the oven to 350°. Butter a 10½ x 4 x 3-inch or 9 x 5 x 3-inch loaf pan. Dust it all with fine, dry bread crumbs, then, over a piece of paper, tap to shake out excess crumbs. Set the pan aside.

Wash the berries in a large bowl of cold water. Then spread them out in a single layer on a towel. Pat the tops lightly with paper towels and let stand until dry—the berries must be completely dry.

Place the dry berries in a bowl. Measure out the flour, then remove 1 teaspoon and toss the teaspoon of flour very gently with the berries. Set aside.

Sift together the remaining flour, salt, sugar, baking powder, and baking soda. Set aside.

In the large bowl of an electric mixer, beat the egg just to mix. Mix in the butter and orange juice. Then, on low speed, add the sifted dry ingredients and beat only to mix. Remove from the mixer.

Stir in the grated rind and then the nuts.

Spread about one-quarter of the mixture in the prepared pan—it will be a very thin layer.

Gently and carefully (without squashing) fold the floured berries into the remaining batter. Place over the thin layer of batter in the pan. Smooth the top.

Bake for about 70 minutes, until a cake tester gently inserted into the middle comes out clean and dry. (The cake will form a crack on the top during baking—it is supposed to. It looks beautiful.)

Let the cake cool in the pan on a rack for about 10 minutes—but no longer, or it will steam and the bottom crust will be wet.

This is a tender and fragile cake—be extremely careful when you remove it from the pan. If any of the berries run out to the sides of the cake they might stick and it could be necessary to cut around the sides with a small, sharp knife or with a small, narrow metal spatula to release the cake.

Cover the cake with a rack. Gently turn the cake pan and the rack over. Remove the pan, cover with another rack, and very carefully turn over again, leaving the cake right side up to cool.

Oatmeal Cake

16 SQUARES

This cake is extremely popular all around the country, and it has been for a long, long time. It is made in a shallow oblong pan and is cut into squares; it may be left in the pan for picnics or occasions when it is important to carry a cake in the pan. It is unusually and wonderfully moist, mild, spiced, and has a butterscotch-candylike crunchy topping. It keeps well; it can be frozen. Serve plain as a coffee cake, or with ice cream as a dessert.

1 cup quick (not instant) rolled oats

1¼ cups boiling water

1½ cups sifted all-purpose flour

1 teaspoon baking soda

1 teaspoon cinnamon

¼ teaspoon nutmeg

½ teaspoon salt

4 ounces (1 stick) unsalted butter

1 teaspoon vanilla extract

1 cup granulated sugar

1 cup dark or light brown sugar, firmly packed

2 eggs

Adjust a rack to the center of the oven. Preheat the oven to 350°. Butter a 9 x 13 x 2-inch metal cake pan. Dust it all over with rolled oats (in addition to those called for in the recipe), then, over a piece of paper, tap out excess. Set aside.

Place the cup of oats in a bowl, stir in the boiling water to mix, and let stand for 20 minutes.

Sift together the flour, baking soda, cinnamon, nutmeg, and salt, and set aside.

In the large bowl of an electric mixer, cream the butter. Beat in the vanilla. Add both sugars and beat well. Then add the eggs and beat well. Beat in the rolled oats. On low speed add the sifted dry ingredients, scraping the bowl with a rubber spatula and beating only until incorporated.

Turn into the pan and smooth the top.

Bake for about 40 minutes, until the cake begins to come away from the sides of the pan and until it springs back when lightly pressed with a fingertip.

While the cake is baking, prepare the following topping.

NUT-COCONUT TOPPING

5 ounces (1¼ sticks) unsalted butter

⅔ cup dark or light brown sugar, firmly packed

¼ cup light cream

⅔ cup walnuts or pecans, cut into medium-size pieces

3 ounces (1 packed cup) shredded coconut

Cream the butter. Add the sugar and then the cream, mixing well. Stir in the nuts and coconut.

Use two teaspoons, one for picking up and one for pushing off, and place the topping all over the top of the hot cake, covering the cake as thoroughly as you can.

This should then be placed about 12 inches below a preheated broiler until it bubbles well all over. Watch carefully—it takes only a few minutes. (If the topping is not level, it is easy to spread with the back of a spoon as soon as it is removed from the broiler.)

Cool in the pan.

This is such a moist cake that it will not cut evenly or neatly, but it really doesn't matter. But if you put it in the freezer for about an hour it will cut beautifully.

Cakes with Fruits or Vegetables

Sauerkraut Chocolate Cake

10 to 12 portions

America is a young country, and Americans are not steeped in the traditions of centuries. We are bold and creative and we have the daring of youth. I tip my hat to whoever dared to try putting sauerkraut into a cake and discovered that they had made a delicious, moist, and fudgy cake. They must have had a bumper crop of cabbage, and they must have made more sauerkraut than they could eat.

No one will ever know about the sauerkraut unless you tell them, and even then they will think you are kidding.

⅔ cup drained
sauerkraut, firmly packed

2¼ cups sifted
all-purpose flour

¼ teaspoon salt

1 teaspoon baking
powder

1 teaspoon baking soda

½ cup unsweetened
cocoa powder (preferably
Dutch-process)

5⅓ ounces
(10⅔ tablespoons)
unsalted butter

1 teaspoon vanilla extract

1½ cups granulated sugar

3 eggs

1 cup cold tap water or
prepared strong coffee,
cooled (see Note)

Adjust a rack to the middle of the oven and preheat the oven to 350°. Butter two 9-inch round layer-cake pans, line the bottoms with parchment paper or wax paper cut to fit, then butter the paper, dust all over with fine, dry bread crumbs; invert over paper and tap out excess crumbs. Set aside.

Place the sauerkraut in a large bowl, add cold water to cover, and with your hands work the water all through the sauerkraut to rinse it lightly, drain in a strainer, and then squeeze the sauerkraut a bit in your hands to remove most of the water that remains (but don't overdo it or you will make the cake dry). It is okay if the sauerkraut still smells like sauerkraut—the cake will not taste, or smell, like it.

Now, to chop the sauerkraut: If you have a round, wooden chopping bowl with a chopping knife that has a curved blade, use it now. (There are many times when I find this old-fashioned kitchen tool the only thing that seems right.) Or, in a food processor fitted with the metal chopping blade, chop for only 10 to 15 seconds. Or place the sauerkraut on a large chopping board and chop it with a large chef's knife. It should be rather fine. Set the sauerkraut aside.

Sift together the flour, salt, baking powder, baking soda, and cocoa, and set aside.

In the large bowl of an electric mixer beat the butter until soft. Beat in the vanilla and sugar, then the eggs one at a time. On low speed add the sifted dry ingredients in three additions alternating with the water or coffee in two additions. Beat until smooth. Remove the bowl from the mixer and stir in the sauerkraut.

Place half of the mixture in each of the prepared pans and smooth the tops.

Bake for about 30 minutes, until the tops of the cakes just barely spring back when pressed lightly with a fingertip. Do not overbake.

Let the layers stand in the pan for a few minutes. Then cover each pan with a rack, turn the pan and rack over, remove the pan and the paper lining, cover with another rack, and turn over again, leaving the layer right side up.

The cake might stick to the rack. Therefore, after about 5 minutes, cover each layer with a rack and turn over again only briefly to loosen the bottom and make sure it is not sticking, then replace it right side up to finish cooling.

To ice the cake, place four 10 x 3-inch strips of parchment paper or wax paper in a square around the sides of a large cake plate. Place one cake layer on the plate upside down and check to be sure that it is touching the papers all around. If you have a cake-decorating turntable, place the cake plate on it.

ICING

16 ounces (1 pound) milk chocolate

1 cup sour cream

NOTE: *Dissolve 1 tablespoon of instant coffee in a few spoons of hot water in a 1-cup glass measuring cup; then fill the cup with cold water to the 1-cup line.*

Break up the chocolate and place it in the top of a large double boiler over warm water on low heat. Cover and let cook slowly only until partly melted. Then uncover and stir until completely melted. Transfer the chocolate to the small bowl of an electric mixer.

Add the sour cream and beat until smooth. Use immediately.

Spread about one-third of the icing over the layer on the plate. Cover the frosted layer with the other layer right side up (bottoms together in the middle). Pour the remaining icing over the cake. With a long, narrow metal spatula smooth the icing over the top, allowing a bit to run down on the sides. Then, with a small, narrow metal spatula, smooth the icing over the sides.

Remove the paper strips under the cake by pulling each one gently toward a narrow end.

Refrigerate and serve cold.

To serve, be prepared with a pitcher of very hot water to dip the knife into; the hot, wet blade will prevent sticking.

Red Beet Cake

About 12 portions

This chocolate cake made with beets is a county fair prizewinner from Twin Falls, Idaho. Fairs have been showcases of Americana and a part of our heritage since the early 1800s. Farmers see the latest equipment, animals are paraded and bought and sold, incredible examples of farm produce (such as 100-pound pumpkins) are displayed, kids eat cotton candy and ride Ferris wheels, and farm wives from coast to coast have a chance to swap recipes and to show off their cooking and baking skills. Recipes that win blue ribbons at fairs are sought after as rare treasures. Many of the recipes, such as this one, were created especially to use up some of the plentiful farm crops.

This is made with beets, but if you do not tell, no one will ever suspect. It is a coal-black cake—moist, tender, delicious—somewhat like a wonderful devil's food cake. The chocolate icing is a thick, fluffy mixture the color of coffee with cream; it stays soft and fluffy and does not form a crust.

1¼ to 1½ cups puréed cooked beets (see Notes)

1¾ cups sifted all-purpose flour

1½ teaspoons baking soda

¼ teaspoon salt

3 ounces unsweetened chocolate

3 eggs

1½ cups granulated sugar

1 cup vegetable oil

1 teaspoon vanilla extract

Adjust a rack to the middle of the oven and preheat the oven to 350°. Butter the bottom and sides of a 13 x 9 x 2-inch cake pan. Dust the bottom of the pan well with fine, dry bread crumbs. Set aside.

Prepare the beets and set them aside.

Sift together the flour, baking soda, and salt, and set aside.

Place the chocolate in the top of a small double boiler over warm water on moderate heat, cover the pot with a folded paper towel (to absorb steam) and then with the pot cover, and let stand until almost melted. Then uncover and stir until completely melted. Remove the top of the double boiler and set aside to cool slightly.

In the large bowl of an electric mixer beat the eggs just to mix. Then beat in the sugar, oil, vanilla, melted chocolate (which may still be warm), the beets, and the sifted dry ingredients, beating only until incorporated after each addition.

Turn into the prepared pan, smooth the top, and bake for 35 minutes, until the top springs back when pressed gently with a fingertip, a toothpick inserted in the middle comes out clean, and the cake just begins to come away from the sides of the pan.

Either let the cake cool completely in the pan (if you are going to ice it in the pan—see Notes) or let it cool for 20 minutes, then cover with a large oblong board or tray, hold the board or tray and the pan firmly together, and turn them both over. Remove the pan and let the cake cool.

FLUFFY CHOCOLATE ICING

2 ounces unsweetened
chocolate

6 ounces (1½ sticks)
unsalted butter

1 cup granulated sugar

1 teaspoon vanilla extract

Pinch of salt

¼ cup sifted
all-purpose flour

1 cup milk

Place the chocolate in the top of a small double boiler over warm water on moderate heat. Cover the pot with a folded paper towel (to absorb steam) and with the pot cover. Let stand for a few minutes until the chocolate is partly melted, then uncover and stir until completely melted and smooth. Set aside to cool.

Place the butter in the small bowl of an electric mixer and beat until soft. Add the sugar and beat at high speed for about 5 minutes. Beat in the vanilla and the salt.

Meanwhile, in a small, heavy saucepan, beat the flour and about ¼ cup of the milk with a small wire whisk until smooth. Gradually beat in the remaining milk. Place over moderate heat and stir constantly with a rubber spatula until the mixture comes to a low boil. Reduce the heat a bit and let simmer, still stirring and scraping the bottom and sides of the pan, for 2 minutes. Remove from the heat, place the bottom of the saucepan briefly in a bowl of ice and water, and continue to stir gently and scrape the pan until the mixture cools. (Do not stop the gentle stirring or the mixture might form lumps; if so, beat it briskly with a small wire whisk.)

Add the melted chocolate to the sugar-and-butter mixture, beat a bit to incorporate, and then gradually add the thickened milk mixture, beating only as necessary to incorporate.

Pour the icing over the cake and spread it smoothly over the top (do not cover the sides) and either leave it smooth or, with the back of a teaspoon, form swirls and peaks.

Refrigerate the cake either just long enough for the icing to set, or longer. It may be served cold or at room temperature (however, if it is practical to serve it cold, do).

NOTES: *You can use fresh beets, either boiled or baked to order, or leftovers, or canned beets. They should be well drained and then processed in a food processor fitted with the metal chopping blade until they look like baby food (turn the processor on/off a few times and scrape down the sides of the bowl once or twice—do not overprocess), or they can be sliced and mashed with a fork on a large plate and then worked through a food mill. A 1-pound can of cooked beets, when drained and puréed, will measure about 1¼ cups.*

There are many times when it is more practical to bake a cake in a square or oblong pan and ice it right in the pan, especially if you are taking it somewhere. This cake can be left in the pan, iced in the pan, and served directly from the pan.

CARROT CAKE

12 TO 20 PORTIONS

Carrot cakes seem to be popular in every part of our country. With all the traveling we do, I am constantly made aware of them. They are served not only at tearooms, coffee shops, and luncheonettes, but on airplanes, at a Long Island chicken farm (where the farmer's daughter makes them), at a chili joint in New Mexico (where Pedro makes them), and also at a swanky place with chandeliers and thick carpets and caviar on the menu (The Four Seasons Clift Hotel in San Francisco). Some carrot cakes are better than others, but as Will Rogers said (he was talking about men—not cakes), "I have never met one I didn't like."

This is a three-layer beauty, a humdinger, it's "the bee's knees." This has more carrots than most, and the smooth and buttery cream cheese icing has less sugar than most.

Make this for a big occasion, for many people, for a happy party. And make it ahead of time. Serve the cake cold. This is foolproof and easy, but not quick.

5 ounces (1 cup) dark raisins

1 pound carrots (to make 4 cups shredded, firmly packed)

2 cups minus 2 tablespoons sifted all-purpose flour

2 teaspoons baking powder

1 teaspoon baking soda

1 teaspoon salt

2 teaspoons cinnamon

1 tablespoon unsweetened cocoa powder

4 eggs

Adjust two racks to divide the oven into thirds, and preheat the oven to 350°. Butter three round 9-inch layer-cake pans, line them with parchment paper or wax paper cut to fit, butter the paper, dust all over with fine, dry bread crumbs, invert over paper and tap out excess crumbs, then set aside.

To steam the raisins, place them in a vegetable steamer or a metal strainer over shallow water in a saucepan. Cover the pan, place on high heat, and let the water boil for about 10 minutes. Then uncover and set aside.

It is not necessary to peel the carrots; just cut off the ends, wash them well with a vegetable brush, and drain or dry them. They may be grated on a standing metal grater or in a food processor. Or they may be grated on a fine, medium, or coarse grater; I have used all these methods and found very little difference in the cakes—no one was better than the others. Measure and set aside.

Sift together the flour, baking powder, baking soda, salt, cinnamon, and cocoa, and set aside.

In the large bowl of an electric mixer (or in any other large bowl, with an eggbeater or a wire whisk), beat the eggs to mix. Beat in the vanilla, both sugars, and the oil. Then, on low speed, add the dry ingredients and mix only until incorporated. Stir in the carrots, the raisins, and the nuts.

Divide among the prepared pans. The solid ingredients have a tendency to mound in the center of the pans; use the back of a teaspoon to distribute them evenly in the pans.

2 teaspoons
vanilla extract

1 cup granulated sugar

1 cup dark brown
sugar, firmly packed

1¼ cups corn oil

5½ ounces (generous
1½ cups) walnuts, cut
into medium-size pieces

Place two layers on one rack and one layer in the center of the other rack—no pan should be directly above another. Bake for 35 to 40 minutes, until the tops just spring back when gently pressed with a fingertip and the cakes begin to come away from the sides of the pans. If the cakes are not baking evenly, you may reverse the pans, front to back and top to bottom, after about 20 minutes, but I don't find it necessary with this recipe.

Remove from the oven. Let stand for 2 or 3 minutes, cover each pan with a rack, turn pan and rack over, remove the pan (do not remove the paper linings—they keep the cake moist—but if they come off by themselves it is okay), cover with another rack and turn over again, leaving the cakes right side up to cool.

When cool, brush loose crumbs off the sides of the cakes.

Before you fill and ice the layers they should be frozen for at least an hour or so until they are firm enough to handle (or they might crack from handling), or freeze for as much longer as you wish. I like to freeze them overnight or longer and ice them a day or two before serving. If you do freeze them for an extended time, wrap them after they become firm. (If the layers have been frozen for a long time do not thaw them before icing.)

CREAM CHEESE ICING

16 ounces Philadelphia
brand cream cheese (at
room temperature)

4 ounces unsalted butter
(at room temperature)

1 teaspoon vanilla extract

2 cups sifted or strained
confectioners' sugar

In the large bowl of an electric mixer beat the cheese and butter until soft and smooth. On low speed beat in the vanilla and sugar, and then on high speed beat for a few moments until smooth.

Prepare a large flat cake plate by lining it with four strips of wax paper. If you have a cake-decorating turntable place the cake plate on it.

If the paper linings are still on the bottoms of the cakes, they should be removed now.

Place one cold and firm cake layer upside down on the plate, checking to be sure that the paper strips touch the cake all around.

Spread a thin layer (⅔ cup) of the icing evenly over the cake. Cover with the second layer, also upside down. Spread another thin layer (⅔ cup) of the icing over the second layer. Cover with the third layer, also upside down (all three layers should be upside down). Now use as much of the icing as you need to cover the sides of the cake, and then the top. You can work over this icing again and again. If you are using a turntable, take your time, work carefully, and with a long, narrow metal spatula smooth the icing around the sides and then on the top. Without a turntable, you will probably be better off swirling the icing a bit, but it is a thin layer of icing and cannot be swirled deeply.

Remove the paper strips by slowly pulling each one out toward a narrow end.

If you decorate the cake with the following optional decoration, do it immediately, before the icing dries.

OPTIONAL DECORATION

12 to 20 walnut or pecan halves or 12 to 20 marzipan carrots (see right)

The cake can be left plain, or it can be decorated with a circle of nut halves or marzipan carrots around the top rim. If you use the carrots, place them pointed end in, green end out. The carrots or the nuts should be pressed slightly into the icing to keep them in place. (Or you can place a few fresh flowers either right on top or alongside just before serving.)

Refrigerate the cake for a few hours, or for a day or two. Serve it very cold, right from the refrigerator. Cut small portions; it is rich.

Marzipan Carrots

Twenty-four 1¾-inch carrots

Marzipan fruits and vegetables are generally eaten as candy; they make gorgeous cake decorations. If you plan to use these to decorate the Carrot Cake, make them before you ice the cake—they can be made days, weeks (or more), ahead of time if you wish. The icing must not dry out or form a crust before you place the carrots on the cake, or they will not stay in place when you serve the cake.

This is such fun that once you make them, you might become addicted and never quit.

12 unsalted green
pistachio nuts
(see Notes)

3½ ounces (⅓ cup)
almond paste or
marzipan (see Notes)

Orange paste or liquid
food coloring for red and
yellow—see instructions)

Let's start with the stems. In a small saucepan of boiling water boil the pistachio nuts for 45 seconds. Quickly remove one, hold under running water, and peel the skin. If the skin comes off easily, drain the others immediately (extra boiling bleaches them), but if necessary boil a few seconds longer. Drain and peel them all. While the nuts are soft from the boiling, with a small sharp knife cut them the long way into quarters (unless they are very large, in which case you can cut them into sixths). They will not all be green, and they will not be green inside; use the greenest. Set aside.

Now, the carrots. Place the almond paste or marzipan on a smooth work surface (not wood, because the food coloring will stain it) and flatten it a bit with your hand. If you have orange food coloring place a dab of it on the almond paste or marzipan (use as much as you need to make the paste a rich carrot color). If you are using red and yellow liquid coloring (they make orange), mix 4 drops of each in a small saucer. Pour it on top of the almond paste or marzipan (use a bit of the almond paste to wipe out the saucer). With the heel of your hand, knead the color into the almond paste or marzipan. If necessary, use a dough scraper to remove the mixture from the work surface. Knead until the color is smooth.

Wash and dry your hands. If the mixture is a bit sticky, powder your hands lightly with confectioners' sugar. Form the mixture into a ball and then, with your hands, roll it into a 12-inch sausage shape.

Cut into ½-inch lengths. Roll the pieces between your hands into carrot shapes, about 1¾ inches long.

Then, to score them with uneven lines that go around (like real carrots), place one on the work surface. Use the dull side of a small paring knife, or a not-too-sharp table knife. Rest the edge of the knife across the carrot and roll the carrot back and forth, with the knife pressing very gently, to make a line around the carrot. (Actually, the line should not go all the way around—it should stop a little short of being a complete circle. The lines should not all be the same length and they should not all start/stop at the same place around the carrot.) Score lines about ⅛ inch apart from each other all over the carrots.

Now, with a toothpick, make one or two small holes in the wide end of the carrot and insert one or two strips (they may look more like wedges) of the pistachio nuts.

Is that not adorable? So cute you could eat it.

If you do not plan to use these soon (within a few hours), cover them on a dish or tray with plastic wrap. They can wait at room temperature for many weeks.

NOTES: *In place of pistachios you may use slivered (julienned) almonds. Using a brush, paint them with green food coloring before inserting them into the carrots.*

Although this recipe uses very few pistachios, they seem to last for years in the freezer. And if you have them you will find many other uses for them. (A few, chopped fine, sprinkled on whipped cream or chocolate icing, add an elegant touch. And mixed with other nuts in brownies they are gorgeous.)

Almond paste or marzipan is generally available at better food stores across the country. (The ingredients listed on the almond paste are almonds, sugar, and liquid glucose. On marzipan they are almonds, sugar, liquid glucose, and sorbitol. So they are very similar.)

Store leftover almond paste or marzipan tightly wrapped in plastic wrap and aluminum foil, or it might dry out and form a crust.

CALIFORNIA CARROT CAKE

16 PORTIONS

Dense, moist, rich, solid, tantalizing, loaded with goodies, and as pretty as a picture (made in a fancy tube pan). You will love this. Make it as a dessert, a coffee cake, or as a wonderful gift.

1½ cups *unsifted* all-purpose whole wheat flour

½ cup *unsifted* all-purpose white flour

2 **teaspoons** baking soda

2 teaspoons cinnamon

¾ teaspoon nutmeg

½ teaspoon allspice

½ teaspoon ground cloves

½ teaspoon salt

¾ pound carrots (to make 2 cups shredded)

3 eggs

¾ cup vegetable oil

¾ buttermilk

1½ cups honey

One 8-ounce can (1 cup) crushed pineapple (packed in natural juice)

5 ounces (1 cup) raisins

4 ounces (generous 1 cup) walnuts, cut or broken into medium-size pieces

Optional: Confectioners' sugar

Adjust a rack one-third up in the oven and preheat the oven to 375°. Butter a fancy-shaped tube pan with 12-cup capacity (I use the 10-inch Bundt pan)—butter it even if it has a nonstick finish—and dust it all over with fine, dry bread crumbs. Invert over a piece of paper and tap to shake out excess crumbs. Set aside.

Sift together the whole wheat and white flours, the baking soda, cinnamon, nutmeg, allspice, cloves, and salt. Set aside.

Wash the carrots (do not peel them) and cut off the ends. Shred the carrots with a fine shredder—you can use a manual grater (on a 4-sided metal grater use the small round openings) or a food processor (use the fine shredding disk). You should have 2 cups, firmly packed. Set aside.

In a really large mixing bowl, beat or whisk the eggs just to mix. Gradually beat in the oil, buttermilk, and honey. Then stir in the carrots, pineapple (with its juice), raisins, and nuts.

Add the sifted dry ingredients all at once and stir/mix only until the dry ingredients are moistened. (Do not overmix; if the bowl is large enough and if you stir with a large rubber spatula, you will not overmix.) It will be a very liquid (thin) mixture.

Turn into the prepared pan and rotate the pan a bit to smooth the top.

Bake for 50 to 60 minutes, until a cake tester inserted in the middle comes out clean.

Let the cake cool in the pan for about 15 minutes. Then cover it with a rack, hold the pan and rack firmly together, and invert. Remove the pan and let the cake stand until it is completely cool.

Carefully, with two wide metal spatulas, transfer the cake to a plate.

Before serving, sprinkle the top generously with the optional confectioners' sugar, shaking it through a fine strainer held over the top of the cake.

Ginger Carrot Cake

12 to 16 portions

This cake is similar to a pound cake, with more body and chewiness supplied by the whole wheat flour and grated carrots. It is a marvelous coffee or tea cake, a new and unusual recipe.

2¼ ounces (⅔ cup) walnuts (for coating the pan)

2 ounces (¼ cup) preserved ginger in syrup

2 ounces (a piece about 3 inches long and 1 to 1½ inches wide) fresh ginger (see Fresh Ginger, page 7)

¾ pound carrots (to make 3 cups shredded, firmly packed)

2 cups sifted all-purpose flour

1 cup sifted all-purpose whole wheat flour

2 teaspoons baking powder

¼ teaspoon salt

5 eggs

1 teaspoon vanilla extract

2 cups granulated sugar

1 cup vegetable oil

1 cup milk

Adjust a rack one-third up from the bottom of the oven and preheat the oven to 350°. Generously butter a tube pan with at least a 12-cup capacity (butter the pan whether it is nonstick or not). I especially like this in the 12-cup "swirl-design" tube pan (see page 10), which does not have a nonstick finish.

Chop the walnuts finely in a food processor fitted with the metal chopping blade; process on/off quickly 10 to 12 times (10 to 12 seconds). Or chop the nuts finely any other way. Turn them into the buttered pan. Over paper, tap and turn the pan to coat it all with the nuts (use your fingers to sprinkle the nuts on the tube), then invert the pan over the paper to allow loose nuts to fall out (but do not tap the pan or you will tap out too many nuts). Reserve the loose nuts that fall onto the paper, and set the pan aside.

With a small, sharp paring knife slice the preserved ginger very thin. You should have ¼ cup of sliced ginger, firmly packed, along with any syrup that clings to the ginger. Set aside.

Grate the fresh ginger fine and set it aside.

It's not necessary to peel the carrots; wash them well and trim both ends. Grate them fine, medium, or coarse, either in a food processor or on a standing metal grater. Set aside.

Sift together both the flours, baking powder, and salt, and set aside.

Place the eggs in the large bowl of an electric mixer and beat well at high speed for a few minutes. Add the vanilla and sugar and beat until well mixed. Then, add the oil and the milk and beat well. On low speed, gradually add the sifted dry ingredients, beating only until mixed.

Remove the bowl from the mixer and stir in the reserved chopped nuts, the sliced preserved ginger, the grated fresh ginger, and the grated fresh carrots. (If you add the carrots while you are still using the mixer, they will form lumps on the blades and it will be difficult to smooth them out.)

The batter will be thin; turn it into the prepared pan.

Bake for 1 hour and 5 to 10 minutes, until a cake tester inserted gently into the middle of the cake comes out clean and the top of the cake springs back when it is pressed lightly with a fingertip.

Cool in the pan for 15 minutes. Then cover with a rack, hold the rack and the pan together, and turn them over. Remove the pan. If you have used a pan with a fancy design, leave the cake upside down. If you have used a pan with a flat bottom you might prefer to serve the cake right side up; if so, cover it with another rack and gently turn the rack and the cake over again.

Cool completely. I like to chill this for an hour or so in the freezer, or longer in the refrigerator, before slicing. Cut into thin slices.

SWEET POTATO POUND CAKE
ABOUT 16 PORTIONS

This can be made with fresh or canned sweet potatoes or yams. It is a big, beautiful cake; plain, rich, dense, fine-textured, moist, delicious, with a fascinating coating of ground salted peanuts. This is wonderful any time but seems especially at home on a Thanksgiving table. Or at Halloween. But don't wait.

⅔ cup salted peanuts

2½ cups mashed, cooked sweet potatoes (see Note)

3 cups sifted all-purpose flour

2 teaspoons baking powder

1 teaspoon baking soda

1 teaspoon cinnamon

¾ teaspoon nutmeg

Ingredients continued on next page.

Adjust a rack one-third up from the bottom of the oven and preheat the oven to 350°. Butter a 10-inch Bundt pan (or any other tube pan with a design and a 14-cup capacity), even if it has a nonstick finish. Place the peanuts in the bowl of a food processor fitted with the metal chopping blade and process them for about 5 seconds until they are fine but uneven, or chop/grind them any other way. Place the peanuts in the buttered pan (use your fingertips to sprinkle them on the center tube), rotate and tilt the pan to coat all parts of it, then invert the pan over paper to tip out excess nuts. About half of the nuts that fall onto the paper should be sprinkled back over the bottom of the pan to make a heavy layer; the remaining nuts should be set aside to be sprinkled over the top of the cake.

If you are using canned sweet potatoes or yams, pour them into a strainer to drain off all the syrup. In a food processor fitted with the metal chopping blade, process half of the sweet potatoes at a time; it will be necessary to stop the machine frequently and scrape the sides of the bowl with a

193

¼ teaspoon salt

8 ounces (2 sticks)
unsalted butter

1 teaspoon vanilla extract

1 cup granulated sugar

1 cup light brown
sugar, firmly packed

4 eggs

NOTE: *If you use canned sweet*
potatoes or yams, you will need
two 17-ounce cans (which will
just make a scant 2½ cups
when mashed but it is enough),
or one 40-ounce (2 pounds, 8
ounces) can (which will be a
little bit more than you need—
measure and use only 2½ cups).

To use fresh sweet potatoes
either bake or steam them in a
vegetable steamer; do not boil
them in water (they should be dry).

rubber spatula. Do not add any liquid; the sweet potatoes should be dry. Or they can be mashed in a large bowl with a potato masher. They must be perfectly smooth. Set aside.

Sift together the flour, baking powder, baking soda, cinnamon, nutmeg, and salt, and set aside.

In a large bowl of an electric mixer, beat the butter until soft. Add the vanilla and both sugars and beat until mixed. Beat in the eggs one at a time (the mixture will appear curdled but it will be okay). Add the mashed sweet potatoes and beat to mix. Then, on low speed, add the sifted dry ingredients and beat until incorporated, scraping the bowl, as necessary, with a rubber spatula.

Turn the batter into the prepared pan. Smooth the top. Sprinkle with the reserved chopped nuts.

Bake for 1 hour and 15 minutes, until a cake tester comes out dry and clean.

Let the cake stand in the pan for 15 minutes. Then remove it to the serving plate or to a rack as follows. To remove it to the serving plate just cover the pan with the plate, hold them together and turn them both over, and remove the pan. But to transfer the cake to a rack first, cover the top of the cake pan with a 12-inch square of aluminum foil, fold down the sides, cover with a rack, hold them together and turn everything over, and remove the pan (this keeps the loose nuts from flying around). Let stand until cool and then transfer to a serving plate or board.

LONG ISLAND POTATO CAKE

2 SMALL LOAVES

This has mashed potatoes, which add to its moistness without affecting the flavor. It is coal-black, semisweet dense choco-
late—with a generous amount of prunes and nuts.

You can cut the recipe in half and make only one loaf, if you wish.

¾ pound raw potatoes
(to make 1 cup,
mashed—see Note)

Adjust a rack one-third up from the bottom of the oven and preheat the oven to 300°. Butter two 8 x 4 x 2½-inch loaf pans (each with a scant 5-cup capacity), dust them with fine, dry bread crumbs, invert them over a piece of paper, and tap lightly to shake out excess. Set aside.

8 ounces dried pitted prunes, soft and moist (to make 1 cup, firmly packed)

2 cups sifted all-purpose flour

1 tablespoon baking powder

1 teaspoon cinnamon

1 teaspoon powdered (not granular) instant coffee or espresso

¾ teaspoon salt

½ teaspoon nutmeg

¾ cup unsweetened cocoa powder (preferably Dutch-process)

4 ounces (1 stick) unsalted butter

1 teaspoon vanilla extract

1½ cups granulated sugar

4 eggs

½ cup milk

6 ounces (1½ cups) walnuts, broken into large pieces

NOTE: *If you prefer, you can use dry instant mashed potatoes prepared with only water or water and milk (no salt or butter). Use a metal cup made for measuring dry ingredients.*

Peel the potatoes, cut into quarters or eighths, place in a saucepan with about an inch of water over moderate heat, and cook, partially covered, until tender when tested with a toothpick. Drain and mash in a food mill or processor or potato ricer to make 1 cup mashed potatoes. Set aside.

Meanwhile, with scissors, cut the prunes into pieces the size of large raisins (or small olives) and set aside.

Sift together the flour, baking powder, cinnamon, powdered coffee, salt, nutmeg, and cocoa. Set aside.

In the large bowl of an electric mixer beat the butter until it is soft. Beat in the vanilla and sugar, then add the eggs one at a time, beating until incorporated after each addition.

Add the potatoes (which may be warm or cool) and beat until smooth. Then, on low speed, add half of the sifted dry ingredients, then the milk, and then the remaining dry ingredients, beating until smooth after each addition.

Remove the bowl from the mixer, stir in the prunes (be sure to stir them well enough to separate all the pieces), and finally stir in the nuts.

Place half of the mixture in each pan, smooth the tops, and then with the back of a teaspoon form a trench down the length of each loaf; the trench should be about 1 inch deep and about 1 inch wide, and it should stop about 1 inch from each narrow end of the pan. (The trench prevents the cake from rising too high in the middle; it will make a beautifully shaped loaf with a nicely rounded top.)

Bake for 1 hour and about 25 minutes, until a cake tester inserted gently in the middle comes out clean—do not overbake.

Cool in the pans for 10 minutes. Then place a pot holder or a folded towel over the top of a loaf and, with a pot holder under the pan, turn the loaf out into the palm of your right hand, remove the pan, cover the loaf with a rack, and turn the loaf and the rack over, leaving the loaf right side up to cool. Remove the other loaf from its pan.

Wrap the cooled loaves in plastic wrap or foil and refrigerate overnight, or for a few days, or place in the freezer for about an hour before serving.

TOMATO SOUP CAKE

16 SQUARES

A can of Campbell's Tomato Soup is such a symbolic bit of Americana that prints of it hang in the country's best museums. But who ever thought of putting it into a cake?

This is a date-and-nut spice cake baked in a square pan, covered with a sensational new bittersweet chocolate icing. If you don't tell what's in the cake no one will guess. They will think it is gingerbread even though it has no ginger or molasses. You could call it a soup-to-nuts cake.

2 cups sifted
all-purpose flour

¼ teaspoon salt

1 teaspoon baking soda

2 teaspoons baking powder

1½ teaspoons cinnamon

¾ teaspoon nutmeg

¼ teaspoon ground cloves

1 tablespoon unsweetened
cocoa powder (preferably
Dutch-process)

4 ounces (1 stick)
unsalted butter

1 teaspoon vanilla extract

1 cup granulated sugar

2 eggs

One 10¾-ounce can
tomato soup (undiluted)

4 ounces (½ cup, packed)
pitted dates, cut into
medium-size pieces (easiest
to cut with scissors)

4 ounces (1 cup) walnut
halves or pieces

Adjust a rack one-third up from the bottom of the oven and preheat the oven to 375°. Butter a 9-inch square cake pan. Dust it over with fine, dry bread crumbs, then invert the pan over paper, and tap lightly to shake out excess crumbs; set aside.

Sift together the flour, salt, baking soda, baking powder, cinnamon, nutmeg, cloves, and cocoa, and set aside.

In the large bowl of an electric mixer, beat the butter until it is soft. Add the vanilla and sugar and beat to mix. Add the eggs one at a time and beat until incorporated after each addition. On low speed, add half of the sifted dry ingredients, scraping the bowl and beating until incorporated. Then beat in the tomato soup. Finally add the remaining dry ingredients and beat until smooth.

Remove the bowl from the mixer and stir in the dates and nuts.

Turn into the prepared pan and smooth the top.

Bake for about 40 minutes, until a toothpick inserted in the middle comes out clean.

Remove from the oven. Either let the cake cool completely in the pan (if you are going to ice it in the pan, see Note), or let stand for about 20 minutes, then cover with a rack, turn the pan and rack over, remove the pan, cover with a serving plate or a board, and turn again, leaving the cake right side up to cool completely. Then prepare the icing.

BITTERSWEET CHOCOLATE ICING

If you prefer a sweeter flavor you can substitute semisweet chocolate for all or part of the unsweetened chocolate.

½ cup whipping cream

3 ounces unsweetened chocolate, chopped coarsely

5 ounces milk chocolate, chopped or broken coarsely

NOTE: *Like the Red Beet Cake (see page 184), this can be baked and iced in the pan and served directly from the pan.*

Place the cream in a small saucepan over moderate heat and let it cook, uncovered, until there is a slightly wrinkled skin on the top or small bubbles around the edge.

Add the unsweetened chocolate and stir until it is almost all melted. Then add the milk chocolate, reduce the heat to low, and stir until completely melted.

Transfer the mixture to the small bowl of an electric mixer. Beat at medium-high speed for a minute or two until the mixture becomes beautifully smooth/shiny/thick. Then, without waiting, pour it onto the cake and quickly spread it over only the top with a long, narrow metal spatula. If you wish, form wide ridges in the icing, using the tip of the spatula.

Savannah Fig Cake
10 to 12 portions

This is an old and famous Southern recipe for a wonderful cake that is light, tender, delicate, almost as moist as a pudding, and easy to make. It is baked in a fancy tube pan and is topped with a divine butterscotch icing. It keeps well, and can be made a day ahead.

One 17-ounce can Kadota figs in syrup

7 ounces (2 cups) walnuts

2 cups sifted all-purpose flour

1 teaspoon baking soda

½ teaspoon salt

1 teaspoon cinnamon

1 teaspoon allspice

3 eggs

1 teaspoon vanilla extract

1 cup buttermilk

1 cup vegetable oil

1 cup granulated sugar

½ cup light brown sugar, firmly packed

Before you do anything else, place the figs in a wide strainer set over a wide bowl and let stand to drain (you will not use the drained syrup for this recipe).

Adjust a rack one-third up from the bottom of the oven and preheat the oven to 350°. You will need a tube pan with a design and about an 11-cup capacity, about 9 inches in diameter, preferably (but not necessarily) with a nonstick finish. Butter the pan (even if it has a nonstick finish). Place ¾ cup of the nuts (reserve the remaining 1¼ cups nuts) in the bowl of a food processor fitted with the metal chopping blade and process for 7 seconds, or chop very fine any other way. Place the finely chopped nuts in the buttered pan and tilt the pan from side to side to coat it all with the nuts; any loose nuts that remain in the pan may be left there to form a nice nutty coating on the top of the cake. Set the pan aside.

Process the remaining 1¼ cups of nuts for 5 seconds; they should be a bit coarser than those for coating the pan. Or chop them into medium-size pieces any other way. Set them aside.

Sift together the flour, baking soda, salt, cinnamon, and allspice. Set aside.

In the large bowl of an electric mixer, beat the eggs to mix, then add the vanilla, buttermilk, oil, and both sugars, and beat to mix. On low speed, add the sifted dry ingredients, scraping the bowl as necessary with a rubber spatula and beating only until mixed. Remove the bowl from the mixer.

With a small knife, cut the drained figs roughly into quarters. With a rubber spatula, fold the reserved nuts and the figs into the batter. Turn the mixture into the prepared pan and smooth the top.

Bake for 50 to 60 minutes, until a cake tester inserted gently into the middle of the cake comes out clean and the top of the cake springs back when it is pressed lightly with a fingertip.

Let cool in the pan for 10 to 15 minutes. Then cover with a cake plate and, holding the pan and the plate firmly together, turn them both over. Remove the pan. Let the cake stand until cool.

BUTTERSCOTCH CARAMEL ICING

This Early American icing is remarkable. It has a caramel and butterscotch flavor, is as smooth and creamy as honey, and although it is poured onto the cake, it sets quickly so it stops running but remains deliciously soft—it will not become hard or granular. I find this foolproof, even though it will remind you a bit of classic fudge, which it is definitely not.

You will need a candy thermometer and a heavy saucepan with a 2-quart capacity. Butter the sides of the pan; it discourages sugar granules from clinging to the sides.

½ cup buttermilk

1 cup granulated sugar

6 ounces (1½ sticks) unsalted butter

½ teaspoon baking soda

1 tablespoon light corn syrup

1 teaspoon vanilla extract

Place the buttermilk, sugar, butter, baking soda, and corn syrup in a heavy 2-quart saucepan over medium-low heat. As the butter and sugar begin to melt, stir occasionally with a wooden spoon and if necessary wash down the sides a few times with a pastry brush dipped in water to remove any undissolved sugar granules.

When the mixture boils, reduce the heat to low, stir occasionally to be sure that it does not burn on the bottom (which it wants to do if you leave it alone too long or if the heat is too high). Do not raise the heat. The mixture will foam up high to the top of the pan when it starts to boil, but after a while it will settle down to a lower level. Insert a candy thermometer. Continue to scrape the bottom occasionally. The temperature will reach 220° rather quickly, but then it will take a long time to go higher. As the mixture boils, it will gradually turn golden. And when the temperature goes over 220°, the color will darken to a rich caramel. Continue to cook until the temperature reaches 238°. Be patient. Or, if you must, raise the heat to medium-high, scraping the bottom and stirring constantly.

When the icing reaches 238° remove it from the heat. Pour it into the small bowl of an electric mixer and add the vanilla. Place the bowl into the large bowl of the mixer. Fill the space in the large bowl about halfway up with ice and cold water. Adjust the mixer stand to the setting for the small bowl, and beat at high speed for several minutes until the mixture lightens slightly in color (it should become about the color of coffee with cream) and thickens slightly. It should be a consistency so that when you pour it over the cake it will run down the sides a bit, but not so thin that it runs off the cake onto the plate.

Very gradually, pour the icing in a ribbonlike stream onto the top of the cake. Pour it slowly, around and around, pouring it over itself several times. Do not pour very much onto one spot at one time or it will run down onto the plate. It should not be necessary to smooth or spread this. When it is perfect, the sides of the cake should be only partly covered with the icing. Very little, if any, should actually run down onto the plate.

PRUNE AND APRICOT POUND CAKE

2 SMALL LOAVES

A brown sugar buttery cake with a crunchy toasted almond coating, it is made with both cream cheese and butter, prunes and apricots, both walnuts and almonds. Delicious and beautiful, it may be served for almost any occasion. Or make it for a friend; since this is such a very unusual recipe (yet easy to make), a loaf of the cake—and the recipe—make a special gift. You can cut the recipe in half and make only one cake, if you wish.

2 ounces (½ cup) blanched almonds (for coating the pans)

8 ounces (1 cup, tightly packed) dried pitted prunes, soft and moist

6 ounces (⅔ cup, tightly packed) dried apricots, soft and moist

2 cups sifted all-purpose flour

2 teaspoons baking powder

½ teaspoon salt

8 ounces Philadelphia brand cream cheese

8 ounces (2 sticks) unsalted butter

1¼ cups light brown sugar, firmly packed

4 eggs

Finely grated rind of 1 large lemon

Adjust a rack one-third up from the bottom of the oven and preheat the oven to 350°. Butter two 8½ x 4½ x 2¾-inch loaf pans, each with a 6-cup capacity (see Note). Crisp the almonds by placing them in a shallow pan in the preheated oven for about 10 minutes only until they are hot but have not begun to color. To chop the almonds, place them in the bowl of a food processor fitted with the metal chopping blade and process for 20 to 25 seconds, turning the processor on/off a few times, until the almonds are chopped finely but unevenly (do not overprocess); or chop them any other way.

Place all of the chopped almonds in one of the buttered pans. Over a piece of wax paper tilt the pan from side to side to coat all of the surfaces. Then invert the pan over the wax paper; do not tap the pan, just allow loose almonds to fall out onto the paper. Pour all of the almonds from the wax paper into the second pan and repeat the directions to coat all its surfaces, and then allow the loose almonds to fall out onto the wax paper. With your fingers sprinkle just a few of the remaining chopped almonds over the bottoms of the pans to make a generous coating. (Reserve the remaining chopped almonds to sprinkle over the tops of the loaves.) Set aside.

With scissors, cut the prunes and apricots into uneven slices or pieces ¼ or ½ inch wide and set them aside.

Sift together the flour, baking powder, and salt, and set aside.

In the large bowl of an electric mixer, beat the cream cheese with the butter until soft and smooth. Beat in the brown sugar. Then add the eggs one at a time, beating until incorporated after each addition. On low speed, gradually add the sifted dry ingredients, scraping the bowl with a rubber spatula as necessary and beating only until the mixture is smooth. Beat in the prunes and apricots. Remove the bowl from the mixer.

With a heavy wooden spoon, stir in the grated rinds, and then the walnuts.

Finely grated rind of
1 deep-colored orange

3½ ounces (1 cup) walnut
halves or large pieces

NOTE: *I have also made this in slightly smaller pans; they measured 8 x 4 x 2½ inches, and they had a scant 5-cup capacity. They worked fine and the loaves were lovely. In these smaller pans the batter will fill the pans almost to the top, but it will not run over during baking—don't worry. In the smaller pans the loaves should be loosely covered with aluminum foil after only about 30 minutes of baking but the total baking time remains about the same.*

Place half of the mixture in each of the pans. Smooth the tops.

Sprinkle the reserved chopped almonds all over the tops.

Bake for 1 hour, then cover the top loosely with foil to prevent over-browning and continue to bake for an additional 20 to 30 minutes until a cake tester gently inserted in the middle comes out dry (total baking time is 1 hour and 20 to 30 minutes).

Cool the loaves in the pans for 20 minutes.

Then cover the top of one of the pans with foil and fold it down around the sides (to prevent any loose nuts from flying around), cover the foil with a pot holder, turn the pan over into the palm of your right hand, remove the pan, cover the loaf with a cake rack and turn the loaf and the rack over again, leaving the loaf right side up on the rack. Remove the foil. Repeat with the other loaf. Let stand until cool.

Wrap the loaves in plastic wrap and let stand for several hours or overnight, or refrigerate for an hour or so. All pound cakes should rest a bit before they are served.

VARIATION: *Raisin Pound Cake: Follow the above recipe, using 5 ounces (1 cup) dark raisins and 5 ounces (1 cup) light raisins in place of the prunes and apricots.*

APRICOT STRIP
12 TO 18 GENEROUS PORTIONS

It occurred to me one day to use apricots instead of figs for a new version of Fig Newtons. The filling developed into a wonderful preserve that remains slightly more gooey than the original fig filling. Therefore, serve these on a plate with a fork. They are wunderbar! They can be made weeks ahead; they freeze perfectly.

The preserve and the dough should both be refrigerated overnight or longer, if you wish. Shaping these is a bit tricky—it takes patience—but they are well worth the effort.

You will need a large cookie sheet with three flat sides to use as a spatula for transferring the roll of filled pastry, both before it is baked, and then again after (unless you have something else that will serve the same purpose). I also use that kind of cookie sheet for baking these, although rims would not be in the way for baking.

APRICOT PRESERVE

5 CUPS

The apricots should be soaked overnight, so plan accordingly.

12 ounces dried apricots

1½ cups water

1 large navel orange

3 ounces (⅔ cup, packed) light raisins

1 cup granulated sugar

One 15- or 16-ounce can (2 cups) crushed pineapple, packed in its own juice (no sugar)

3½ ounces (1 cup) walnuts, cut into medium-size pieces

Place the apricots in a wide, heavy saucepan (or you can soak them in a bowl and transfer them to the saucepan for cooking). Add the water. Cover and let stand overnight, stirring once or twice when the apricots on the bottom have absorbed water and those on top are above the water. After the fruit has softened, press down on it occasionally with a fork or spoon to keep all of it wet.

The next day, grate the orange-colored rind of the orange (see page 15) and add it to the apricots. Then peel the orange—cut away every bit of white, and, working over a bowl to catch the juice, with a small, sharp knife cut down against the membrane of each section, releasing the sections. Squeeze the remaining membrane in the palm of your hand to squeeze out any remaining juice. Add the orange sections and the juice to the apricots. Then add the raisins, sugar, and pineapple (including its juice).

Place the saucepan over moderate heat. Bring to a boil, stirring once or twice to avoid burning. Reduce the heat and simmer, covered, for 10 minutes—again stirring once or twice.

Then uncover, stir frequently with a wooden spoon, and cook until all the moisture has evaporated. As the mixture thickens, lower the heat to prevent burning. The preserve should be as thick as you can get it without letting it burn. (If the mixture is dry but the apricots seem to need more cooking, cover the saucepan briefly.) Total cooking time is 1 to 1¼ hours.

Cooking and stirring will break up the apricots and the orange sections and turn the mixture into a divine jam. While the fruit is cooking, cut it with the edge of the spoon, pressing it against the sides of the saucepan. After all the cooking and stirring the fruit should remain slightly chunky; the consistency will be about like cooked oatmeal, although it will thicken a bit more when refrigerated.

When the preserve is done, remove from the heat to cool. Then stir in the nuts. Transfer to a covered container and refrigerate.

(Incidentally, this is a great spread for toast.)

DOUGH

1 cup sifted
all-purpose flour

2 cups *unsifted*
all-purpose whole
wheat flour

1 teaspoon baking
powder

½ teaspoon baking soda

½ teaspoon salt

4 ounces (1 stick)
unsalted butter

½ cup light brown
sugar, firmly packed

½ cup honey

1 egg

Sift together the sifted all-purpose flour, the unsifted whole wheat flour, the baking powder, baking soda, and the salt. Set aside.

In the large bowl of an electric mixer, beat the butter until soft. Beat in the sugar, honey, and the egg. On low speed, gradually add the sifted dry ingredients, scraping the bowl as necessary with a rubber spatula and beating until they are incorporated and the dough is smooth.

Turn the mixture out onto a work surface. With your hands form the dough into about a 6-inch square 1½ or 2 inches thick. (If the dough is too sticky to handle, place it on a long piece of plastic wrap, fold the four sides of the plastic over the dough and, with your hands, press against the plastic wrap to shape the dough into a square.)

Wrap in plastic wrap and refrigerate.

The next day (or a few days later), when you are ready to bake, adjust a rack to the top position in the oven and preheat the oven to 400°. Line a 12 x 15½-inch cookie sheet with aluminum foil, shiny side up. Set aside.

Remove the block of dough from the refrigerator and cut it in half, forming two oblongs about 3 x 6 inches. Return one piece to the refrigerator until you are ready for it.

Flour a pastry cloth and a rolling pin. If the dough is too firm to roll, place it on the cloth and pound it lightly with the pin to soften it a bit; keep the shape oblong.

Roll out the dough slowly and carefully until it is 15 inches long and 6 inches wide, keeping the shape as neat as possible.

Now, picture the finished product: the filling will be placed in a strip down the middle and the two long sides will be folded over the filling, overlapping one another. In order not to have that overlapping section too thick, roll the edges of the two long sides a little thinner, making the oblong 7 to 7½ inches wide (slightly thinner along the long edges).

Use 2 cups of the filling for each strip of dough. Measure carefully. Do not use more than 2 cups because the dough will not cover more. (You will not use the remaining preserve for this recipe.) Using two teaspoons, one for picking up with, and one for pushing off with, spoon 2 cups of the filling neatly down the middle of the dough, lengthwise, forming a band of filling that is a generous 1 inch deep and a generous 2 inches wide; stop the filling ½ inch from the narrow ends. With the back of a spoon, smooth the filling lightly to level it, but do not flatten it and do not make it any wider.

If the long sides are not exactly straight and even, just push a ruler against them to straighten them. (However, if they are very uneven they should be cut straight and patched if necessary.)

Use the pastry cloth to help fold one long side up over the filling. With a pastry brush, brush water in a ½-inch border along the edge. Then, using the other half of the pastry cloth, fold the other half of the dough up and over the wet edge. Press lightly to seal. The edges should overlap by about ½ inch.

Use the pastry cloth again to help roll the whole thing over so the seam is on the bottom. Use a flat-sided cookie sheet as a spatula and transfer the roll gently and carefully to the foil-lined cookie sheet, placing the roll either lengthwise down the middle or on an angle, seam down.

With your hands, perfect the shape of the roll, making it straight, smooth, and even. Press down gently on the two narrow ends to seal them. There will be small surface cracks in the pastry—it is all right.

Bake for 15 to 18 minutes until the pastry is golden brown all over, reversing the sheet front to back as necessary to ensure even browning.

Remove from the oven and let stand on the cookie sheet for about 15 minutes. Then use a flat-sided cookie sheet as a spatula to transfer the roll to a rack to cool. . . . HANDLE WITH CARE!!!

Shape and bake the second roll.

Place the cooled rolls in the refrigerator, or freeze until cold and firm before slicing. (I find that the strips cut more neatly with a serrated knife than they do with a straight-edged knife. Try both.)

Cut straight across or on an angle. Cut into 12 to 18 dessert-size bars (6 to 9 from each strip), or they can be cut narrower, if you wish.

The strips can be served either cold or at room temperature, either plain or with ice cream.

DATE-NUT EXTRA

A 10-INCH LOAF

This is a most unusual loaf. It is a date-nut bread cake, an applesauce cake, and a banana cake, all in one. You have a treat in store. Moist, not too sweet, wonderful with tea or coffee.

This makes a large loaf (slightly over 3 pounds). You need a pan with a 10-cup capacity. I use a heavyweight metal loaf pan that measures 10 x 5 x 3 inches. However, in place of a large loaf pan, you can use two smaller loaf pans, or a tube or Bundt pan with a 10-cup capacity. (In two smaller loaf pans, or even in a tube pan, it might take a little less baking time; test carefully and do not underbake.)

7 ounces (2 cups) walnuts

8 ounces (1 cup, firmly packed) pitted dates

1 cup sifted all-purpose flour

1 cup sifted all-purpose whole wheat flour

1 teaspoon baking powder

¾ teaspoon baking soda

1 teaspoon cinnamon

½ teaspoon nutmeg

½ teaspoon ground ginger

¼ teaspoon salt

¼ teaspoon allspice

¼ teaspoon ground cloves

¼ teaspoon mace

4 ounces (1 stick) unsalted butter

Ingredients continued on next page.

Adjust a rack one-third up from the bottom of the oven and preheat the oven to 350°. Butter a 10-cup loaf pan (see above) and set it aside. Chop ½ cup of the walnuts very finely (reserve the remaining 1½ cups) either on a board with a long, heavy chef's knife or in a food processor fitted with the metal chopping blade (turning the processor on/off 7 times to chop the nuts finely enough, but not too finely).

Place the chopped nuts in the buttered loaf pan. Hold the pan over a piece of paper and tilt and turn the pan in all directions to coat it heavily with the nuts. Allow excess nuts to fall out onto the paper.

Now break the reserved 1½ cups of walnuts into large pieces, add the excess chopped nuts, and set aside.

With scissors cut the dates into medium-size pieces, cutting each date into 4 or 5 pieces, and set aside.

Sift together the white flour, the whole wheat flour, the baking powder, baking soda, cinnamon, nutmeg, ginger, salt, allspice, cloves, and mace, and set aside.

In the large bowl of an electric mixer, beat the butter until soft. Beat in the sugar, and then the eggs one at a time. Add the applesauce and beat to mix. (It will cause the mixture to look curdled—it is okay.) On a flat plate with a fork, mash the bananas coarsely (they should not be liquefied in a food processor). Measure ¾ cup and add to the batter; mix well.

On low speed, gradually add the sifted dry ingredients, scraping the bowl with a rubber spatula and beating only until mixed.

Remove the bowl from the mixer and stir in the reserved walnuts and the dates.

1 cup light brown
sugar, firmly packed

2 eggs

1 cup unsweetened
applesauce (I use
Mott's Natural Style)

2 medium-small fully
ripened bananas (to
make ¾ cup, mashed)

Turn into the prepared pan and smooth the top. Then, if you have used a loaf pan, form a slight trench with the back of a teaspoon down the length of the top surface (it will prevent the cake from rising too high).

Bake for 1¼ hours, until a cake tester inserted gently in the middle of the cake comes out clean and dry. Remove from the oven. Let stand for 10 to 15 minutes. (During baking the cake will form a crack on top—it is okay.)

If you have used a loaf pan, place a folded towel or a large pot holder on the palm of your right hand. With your left hand, turn the pan gently over onto the folded towel or pot holder and lift off the loaf pan. Cover the loaf with a rack and turn the rack and the loaf over, leaving the cake right side up to cool. To remove the cake from a tube or Bundt pan, cover it with a rack, turn both over, remove the pan, and leave the cake upside down.

Let stand until cool. Or, if you want it sooner, use a serrated bread knife to cut with. It is delicious still warm.

BANANA BLACK CAKE
25 PORTIONS

There are many old Southern recipes called Black Cake. Usually it is a dark and heavy cake made with candied fruit. This one is different: a date-nut, jam, and banana cake, huge (almost 7 pounds—over 3½ inches high); it keeps well and can be made several days ahead. It is dense, chewy, moist, mildly spiced, and not too sweet.

10 ounces (3
cups) walnuts

10 ounces (1½ cups,
firmly packed) pitted
dates, soft and moist

2¼ cups sifted
all-purpose flour

1 cup *unsifted*
all-purpose whole
wheat flour

Adjust two racks, one (for the cake) one-third up from the bottom of the oven; another (for a shallow pan of water) at the lowest position. Preheat the oven to 300°. Butter a plain (no design) 10 x 4-inch tube pan (with an 18- to 20-cup capacity), preferably (but not necessarily) with a nonstick finish; butter the pan even if it has a nonstick finish. Line the bottom with a round of parchment paper cut to fit. Butter the paper. Set aside briefly.

To coat the pan with nuts, chop ⅔ cup of the walnuts finely (reserve the remaining 2⅓ cups), either in a food processor fitted with the metal chopping blade (process for 7 seconds) or any other way (they must be fine). Turn the nuts into the buttered and lined pan and tilt the pan in all directions to coat it all over (use your fingers to sprinkle the nuts on the tube). Loose nuts should be distributed evenly on the bottom of the pan to make a heavy layer on what will be the top of the cake. Set the pan aside.

¼ cup unsweetened cocoa powder (preferably Dutch-process)

1 teaspoon nutmeg

1 teaspoon allspice

½ teaspoon salt

½ teaspoon ground cloves

½ teaspoon ground ginger

1 teaspoon cinnamon

8 ounces (2 sticks) unsalted butter

2 teaspoons vanilla extract

1 cup granulated sugar

1 cup light brown sugar, firmly packed

4 eggs

One 1-pound (1½ cups) seedless blackberry jam

5 medium-size fully ripened bananas

2 teaspoons baking soda

⅓ cup buttermilk

5 ounces (1 cup) dark raisins

Optional: Confectioners' sugar

Chop the remaining 2⅓ cups of nuts less fine; they should be cut into medium-size pieces. Either process them on/off 5 times (5 seconds) or cut them any other way. Set the nuts aside.

Cut the dates into medium-size pieces, cutting each date into 4 or 5 pieces. (If the pieces stick together, place them in a bowl and toss with about a tablespoon of the granulated sugar to coat and separate them.) Set the dates aside.

Sift together the white flour, whole wheat flour, cocoa, nutmeg, allspice, salt, cloves, ginger, and cinnamon, and set aside.

In the large bowl of an electric mixer beat the butter until soft. Beat in the vanilla and both sugars. Then add the eggs one at a time, beating after each addition until it is incorporated. (The mixture will probably appear curdled—it is okay.) Beat in the blackberry jam.

Peel the bananas and place them on a wide, flat plate. Mash them coarsely with a fork. Measure 2 cups and beat this into the batter.

In a 1-cup measuring cup stir the baking soda into the buttermilk until the baking soda dissolves. Add to the batter and beat well, scraping the sides of the bowl, as necessary, with a rubber spatula.

On low speed, gradually add the sifted dry ingredients, beating until incorporated. Remove the bowl from the mixer.

With a heavy wooden spoon, stir in the prepared dates, the nuts, and the raisins.

Turn the mixture into the prepared pan and smooth the top. Cover the top of the pan with a piece of aluminum foil large enough to fold the sides down (heavy-duty foil is best for this).

Place the covered pan in the oven.

Place a shallow pan of hot water on the lowest rack (to keep steam in the oven).

Bake for 1 hour, then remove the aluminum foil and continue to bake for another 1½ hours (total baking time is 2½ hours), until a cake tester inserted gently in the cake, all the way to the bottom, comes out clean. (During baking, the top will crack; it is okay.)

Let the cake stand in the pan for about 20 minutes.

Now, be careful! This cake is so heavy that turning it out of the pan is tricky. First—again—cover the pan with foil large enough to fold down the sides (to keep any loose chopped nuts from flying around) or work over the sink. Cover the cake pan with a rack. Hold the pan and the rack firmly together and—here goes—turn them both over. The cake will immediately fall out of the pan onto the rack; don't be surprised when it does.

Let stand until cool. Chill the cake until cold and firm, then wrap it airtight in a large plastic bag. Refrigerate overnight or for a few days, if you wish.

If you wish, sprinkle the top of the cold cake with confectioners' sugar.

Cut the cake while it is cold into thin, thin slices.

Serve plain or with vanilla ice cream.

EAST BLUE HILL BLUEBERRY COFFEE CAKE
8 OR 9 PORTIONS

This simple cake is made in an 8-inch square cake pan, then cut into squares and served from the pan, preferably while it is still warm. It is quick and easy, a Down East, state of Maine cake. You will love to serve it for breakfast or brunch or any time you would serve a coffee cake. Or serve it with ice cream for a dinner dessert—wonderful.

6 ounces (1½ cups)
fresh blueberries

1½ cups sifted
all-purpose flour

2 teaspoons
baking powder

½ teaspoon cinnamon

¼ teaspoon nutmeg

¼ teaspoon salt

Adjust a rack one-third up from the bottom of the oven and preheat the oven to 350°. Butter an 8-inch square cake pan and dust it all over with fine, dry bread crumbs or with toasted or untoasted wheat germ, invert the pan over paper, and tap lightly to shake out excess. Set aside.

Wash the berries and let drain.

Sift together the flour, baking powder, cinnamon, nutmeg, and salt, and set aside. In the small bowl of an electric mixer, beat the butter until it is soft. Beat in the vanilla and ¾ cup of the granulated sugar (reserve the remaining 3 tablespoons). Beat in the egg. Then, on low speed, add half of the sifted dry ingredients, then the milk, and then the remaining dry ingredients, beating only until incorporated. Remove the bowl from the mixer and stir in the grated rind. Turn into the prepared pan and smooth the top.

2 ounces (½ stick) unsalted butter

1 teaspoon vanilla extract

¾ cup plus 3 tablespoons granulated sugar

1 egg

⅔ cup milk

Finely grated rind of 1 large lemon

Optional: Crystal sugar (see page 3) or additional granulated sugar

In a bowl toss the berries gently with the remaining 3 tablespoons of granulated sugar. Spoon the berries and sugar evenly over the top of the cake.

Bake for 45 or 50 minutes, until the top is lightly browned and the cake barely begins to come away from the sides of the pan.

If you wish, after the cake is baked sprinkle it lightly with crystal sugar or granulated sugar and place under a preheated broiler for only a minute or so (watch it carefully) to darken and glaze the top a bit more.

Cool slightly in the pan. Then cut into squares and serve warm.

Blueberry Surprise Cake
8 to 10 portions

Light, tender, delicate, moist, delicious, quick, and easy—a one-layer sour cream cake with fresh blueberries hidden inside. This is a lovely coffee cake for breakfast or brunch, either while it is still warm or after it has cooled.

Blueberry Surprise

1 cup fresh blueberries

3 tablespoons granulated sugar

1 teaspoon cinnamon

¼ teaspoon nutmeg

1 teaspoon lemon juice (before squeezing the juice, grate the rind and reserve to use in the cake)

Wash and dry the berries. Then, in a bowl, combine the sugar, cinnamon, and nutmeg. Stir in the berries gently. Drizzle in the lemon juice. Let stand.

Cake

2 cups sifted all-purpose flour

2 teaspoons baking powder

¼ teaspoon salt

8 ounces (2 sticks) unsalted butter

1 teaspoon vanilla extract

1⅓ cups granulated sugar

2 eggs

Adjust a rack one-third up from the bottom of the oven and preheat the oven to 350°. Butter a 9 x 3-inch springform pan and dust all over with fine, dry bread crumbs. Invert the pan over paper and tap lightly to shake out excess crumbs. Set aside.

Sift together the flour, baking powder, and salt, and set aside. In the large bowl of an electric mixer, beat the butter until it is soft. Beat in the vanilla and sugar. Then add the eggs and beat until incorporated. Add the sour cream and, scraping the bowl as necessary with a rubber spatula, beat only until incorporated. On low speed add the sifted dry ingredients and beat only until smooth.

Remove the bowl from the mixer and stir in the grated rind.

Turn half of the mixture into the prepared pan, smooth the top, and then spoon on the blueberry mixture, keeping it ½ to 1 inch away from the sides of the pan.

1 cup sour cream

Finely grated rind of
1 small lemon (reserve
from Blueberry Surprise)

⅓ cup toasted pecans
(see To Toast Pecans,
page 6), cut into
medium-small pieces

Stir the pecans into the remaining batter and spoon it over the batter in
the pan. Spread it smooth.

Bake for 1 hour and 20 to 30 minutes, until the top of the cake springs
back when it is pressed lightly with a fingertip.

Let the cake stand in the pan for about 15 minutes. Meanwhile, prepare
the glaze.

GLAZE

1 cup confectioners' sugar

1 tablespoon lemon juice

A few drops of
boiling water

In a bowl, beat the sugar and lemon juice with just a few drops of boiling
water as necessary to make it semi-liquid; the mixture should be thick—
just barely thin enough to pour (if necessary, adjust with more sugar or
drops of water).

Release and remove the sides of the springform pan. Cover the cake with
a rack, turn the cake and the rack over, remove the bottom of the cake
pan, cover the cake with a cake plate, and very carefully turn the cake and
the plate over again, leaving the cake right side up.

Stir the glaze and drizzle it over the warm cake, letting some of it run
down the sides.

When you cut the cake you will see that the weight of the berries has not
allowed the bottom half of the cake to rise—you will barely see the bottom half—but the top half more than makes up for it; it is wonderfully
light and all in all, a joy.

RAISIN CAKE WITH APPLES

10 PORTIONS

This is an old, traditional Swedish coffee cake. Or if you serve it with ice cream, it becomes a dessert cake. It is an easy cake made with sliced raw apples that are rolled in cinnamon-sugar and placed into the top of the cake before it is baked. It is delicious and best the day it is made.

You will need a springform pan 9 inches in diameter; it may be either 2 or 3 inches deep (if you have both sizes, use the 2-inch).

1¾ cups sifted
all-purpose flour

1 teaspoon baking
powder

½ teaspoon salt

5 ounces (1¼ sticks)
unsalted butter

1 teaspoon vanilla extract

1¼ cups granulated sugar

3 eggs

Finely grated rind
of 1 large lemon

2½ ounces (½ cup) light
raisins (dark raisins
may be substituted
but the light are
traditional in this cake)

Adjust a rack to the center of the oven and preheat the oven to 350°. Butter a 9-inch springform pan (see introduction to recipe) and set it aside. Sift together the flour, baking powder, and salt, and set aside.

In the large bowl of an electric mixer, beat the butter until it is soft and smooth. Add the vanilla and then the sugar and beat to mix very well. Add the eggs one at a time and beat until thoroughly incorporated after each addition. Beat for 1 minute after the last addition. On low speed gradually add the sifted dry ingredients, scraping the bowl with a rubber spatula as necessary and beating only until incorporated. Remove from the mixer.

Stir in the lemon rind and then the raisins.

Turn into the prepared pan and smooth the top. Let stand while you prepare the topping.

TOPPING

2 large firm and tart apples (about 1 pound; Granny Smith or Red or Golden Delicious are good for this)

2 teaspoons cinnamon

1 tablespoon plus 2 teaspoons granulated sugar

Confectioners' sugar (to be sprinkled on top before serving)

Peel, quarter, and core the apples. Cut each section into lengthwise slices about ⅓ inch wide at the outside edge.

In a small bowl stir the cinnamon and granulated sugar together.

One at a time, turn an apple slice in the cinnamon-sugar and then place it into the cake, placing it at an angle, pointed edge down, deep into the dough (just the outside of the apple should remain above). The slices should be placed at a right angle to the rim to form a ring around the edge of the pan. They should be as close to each other as possible. The remaining slices should be cut into smaller pieces to fill in the middle and empty spaces around the edge.

Bake for 1 to 1¼ hours, until a toothpick gently inserted in the middle comes out dry.

Let the cake cool in the pan for 15 minutes. Remove the sides of the pan. Cover the cake with a rack, turn over the cake and the rack, remove the bottom of the pan, cover the cake with another rack, and turn over again, leaving the cake right side up.

This may be served while it is still slightly warm. Or let it stand to cool completely.

Just before serving, cover the top generously with confectioners' sugar, sprinkling it through a fine strainer; sprinkle it heavily in the center but not around the rim.

CRANBERRY UPSIDE-DOWN CAKE

8 PORTIONS

If you like the tart flavor of cranberries, you will be wild about this; I do and I am. It is a single layer of lovely, moist white cake covered with a generous topping of fresh cranberries that is brushed with red currant jelly after baking. It is shiny cranberry-red gorgeous. This is traditionally served with a generous ladleful of whipped cream. Although this is all quick and easy, I would be happy to serve it at a Thanksgiving dinner. This can be a luncheon or dinner dessert, or a brunch coffee cake, or a treat to serve with tea or coffee in the afternoon.

You need fresh cranberries for this.

12 ounces (4 cups)
fresh cranberries

5 ounces (1¼ sticks)
unsalted butter, at
room temperature

1 cup plus 2 tablespoons
granulated sugar

1¼ cups sifted
all-purpose flour

1½ teaspoons
baking powder

¼ teaspoon salt

1 egg

1 teaspoon vanilla extract

⅔ cup milk

Finely grated rind of 1
large deep-colored orange

⅓ cup red currant
jelly (to be used after
the cake is baked)

Adjust a rack one-quarter up from the bottom of the oven and preheat the oven to 350°. You will need a 9 x 1½-inch round layer-cake pan (it should not be shallower).

Wash the cranberries briefly in cold water, discard loose stems, drain, and then spread the berries on a towel to dry a bit.

Use 4 tablespoons (½ stick) of the butter (reserve the remaining ¾ stick of butter)—it must be soft but not melted. Spread a bit of it on the sides of the pan and then, with the back of a spoon, spread the remainder (of the 4 tablespoons) over the bottom of the pan. Sprinkle ½ cup plus 2 tablespoons of the sugar (reserve the remaining ½ cup) over the butter. Sprinkle the berries over the sugar. They will almost fill the pan—it is okay. Set the pan aside.

Sift the flour, baking powder, and salt together with the remaining ½ cup of sugar and set aside.

In the small bowl of an electric mixer, beat the remaining ¾ stick of butter until soft. Beat in the egg and vanilla. Then, on the lowest speed, add the sifted dry ingredients in three additions alternately with the milk in two additions, mixing only until just combined (the mixture might appear slightly curdled—it is okay). Remove the bowl from the mixer, stir in the grated rind, and pour over the berries.

Smooth the top. The pan will be full—it is okay.

Bake for 1 hour; the top will become quite brown during baking.

Cool the cake in the pan on a rack for 20 minutes. After 10 minutes cut around the sides with a small, sharp knife to release the cake.

Meanwhile, place the jelly in a small pan over moderate heat; stir occasionally until the jelly melts and comes to a boil. Set aside briefly.

After the 20 minutes are up, cut around the sides of the cake again. Then cover with a flat cake plate, hold the pan and the plate firmly together, and turn them both over. Remove the pan.

Pour the melted jelly onto the cake and with the back of a spoon spread it to cover the top completely (right up to the edges—if a bit runs over the sides it is okay, but not too much).

Let stand until completely cool. Serve the cake at room temperature. If you serve this by itself it is really quite tart, but with something bland and creamy and icy cold it is divine. You could serve vanilla ice cream or whipped cream (with a bit of sugar and vanilla), or if you have my book *Maida Heatter's Pies & Tarts*, make and serve Ricotta Cream. To serve 6 to 8 portions of the cake, use two 5-ounce containers of ricotta cheese. Be sure that the Ricotta Cream is very, very cold (even place it in the freezer for 15 to 20 minutes before serving), and place a mound of it on each plate next to the cake.

KATHY'S CRANBERRY LOAF
12 TO 16 PORTIONS

My friend Kathy Fleegler of Cleveland, Ohio, is a caterer and cooking teacher. This is one of her favorite recipes to cater, to teach, and to make for her family and friends. It is a moist loaf with a texture somewhat like a moist fruitcake. Loaded with nuts and whole cranberries, the combination is gorgeous—crunchy and cranberry-sour. And the loaf is brushed with a generous amount of orange glaze that soaks into the cake. It should be made at least a day ahead, but it freezes wonderfully and may be made way ahead.

The loaf is made with either fresh cranberries or frozen whole cranberries. Kathy says to buy extra cranberries when they are in season and freeze them. (To freeze: Do not wash before freezing [because if they are not thoroughly dry before freezing, they become mushy); in a plastic bag, they will keep for a year. To use: Just pour out as many as you need, rinse quickly, drain well, and use them frozen. Do not thaw.)

Serve this as a dessert, or as a tea or coffee cake.

2 cups whole cranberries

2½ cups sifted all-purpose flour

¼ teaspoon salt

1 teaspoon baking powder

1 cup granulated sugar

7 ounces (2 cups) walnut halves or large pieces

Ingredients continued on next page.

Adjust a rack to the center of the oven (if it is lower the loaves will be too pale on top) and preheat the oven to 350°. You will need two loaf pans measuring 8½ x 4½ x 2½ inches or slightly smaller (they should each have a 5- or 6-cup capacity). Butter the pans, dust them with fine, dry bread crumbs, then, over a piece of paper, tap out excess crumbs. Set aside.

If you are using fresh cranberries, pick over them, rinse, drain, and spread out on a towel to dry. If you are using frozen berries, they should wait in the freezer until you are ready for them, then rinse and drain quickly and use them frozen.

Sift together in a large bowl the flour, salt, baking powder, and sugar. Then stir in the nuts and the cranberries.

2 eggs

1 cup buttermilk

¾ cup vegetable oil

Finely grated rind of
1 or 2 deep-colored
oranges (juice will be
used for the Glaze)

In a bowl beat the eggs to mix; beat in the buttermilk and vegetable oil, and then stir in the orange rind.

Pour the liquids over the dry ingredients and stir to mix. Spoon half of the mixture into each of the prepared pans and smooth the tops; the pans should be half or three-quarters filled.

Bake for about 1 hour, or until a cake tester gently inserted into the middle comes out clean and dry.

About 15 minutes before the baking time is finished, if the tops look too pale, raise the racks to a higher position. (A crack will form down the length of each loaf while it is baking—it is okay.) The loaves will not reach the tops of the pans, they will be only about 2 inches high. Remove from the oven and let stand for 10 minutes. Meanwhile, prepare the glaze.

Orange Glaze

1 cup granulated sugar

1 cup orange juice

Stir the sugar and the orange juice in a small saucepan over moderate heat until the sugar is dissolved.

(The loaves will be transferred to two plates or platters or trays, or one large enough to hold both, or to anything with a rim to keep the glaze from running over.)

Cover each loaf with a rack, turn over the pan and the rack, remove the pan, cover with another rack, and turn over again, leaving the loaf right side up. Now, with your hands, gently transfer each loaf to the rimmed plate, platter, tray, or what-have-you. Pierce the tops gently in many places with a cake tester.

With a pastry brush, brush the hot glaze generously over the tops and sides of the loaves. When much of the glaze has run down off the loaves, use a wide metal spatula and gently raise one end of the loaf, at the same time tilting the plate, to let the glaze run under the bottom of the loaf. Continue to brush on the glaze from the plate. After a while you will think that there is too much glaze and that the loaves simply will not absorb all of it. You are about right—there will probably be a little left on the plate. The remaining syrup will become thicker and syrupy as it chills; spread it over the loaves with a spoon or spatula.

NOTE: *You might like to try this with vanilla ice cream—the combination of the sour berries with the sweet ice cream is wonderful.*

Refrigerate the loaves, uncovered, for several hours or overnight before serving. Or if you are going to freeze them, first place each loaf on wax paper or foil on a tray and freeze uncovered. Then transfer to a large piece of plastic wrap and wrap airtight. The outsides of the loaves will be sticky (yummy), but when you unwrap them only a very little will cling to the wrapping, and the loaves will look shiny/gorgeous.

To serve after freezing, the loaves should be unwrapped while they are frozen (so the glaze does not stick too much to the wrapping), transferred to a plate, and refrigerated uncovered for a few hours or left at room temperature to thaw.

Cut with a very sharp knife. Serve two slices (about ½ inch thick) to a portion. Each loaf should serve 6 to 8.

PINEAPPLE UPSIDE-DOWN CAKE
6 TO 8 PORTIONS

This pretty cake is quick and easy, light and delicious, and although it is very old-fashioned, it never goes out of style. It makes a lovely dessert cake but is also wonderful as a coffee cake to serve at breakfast, brunch, or a kaffeeklatsch. Serve it while it is fresh; it is extra good while it is still hot and for several hours after it is baked.

TOPPING

You will need a frying pan with a heatproof handle or a pie plate with an 8-cup capacity. (The average deep 10-inch frying pan or 12-inch pie plate should be the right size, but measure the capacity to be sure.)

Adjust a rack to the center of the oven and preheat the oven to 350°. Spray the pan or plate with Pam—this recipe works better with a nonstick spray than it does with a buttered pan.

Place the butter in a small pan over moderate heat to melt.

Pour the melted butter evenly over the bottom of the sprayed pan or plate. Sprinkle the sugar evenly all over the butter, then, with your fingers, pat the sugar to press it into an even layer, making sure it is all moistened with the melted butter.

2⅓ ounces
(5⅓ tablespoons)
unsalted butter

½ cup light brown
sugar, firmly packed

One 20-ounce can or
two 8¼-ounce cans
sliced pineapple (packed
in natural juice)

Optional: Pecan halves,
canned black Bing
cherries, stewed prunes,
candied cherries, or
maraschino cherries

Drain the pineapple, reserve the juice for the cake batter, and place the slices on paper towels to dry.

Now, with the pineapple rings, make a pretty design around the outside of the plate on top of the sugar. And if there is room, place one ring in the middle. If there is not room for a whole ring in the middle, you can use one half of a ring. Cut it into quarters and form a design with the pieces.

You will probably not use all of the pineapple slices.

Traditionally, pecan halves are arranged flat side up in a pattern in the spaces between the pineapple rings. And a black Bing cherry, a piece of stewed prune, or a pitted fresh cherry or a candied cherry is put in the middle of each ring.

Either arrange the fruit as described or make up your own pattern. My favorite design is as follows: Place one pineapple ring directly in the center. Cut the other rings in half, making two half circles from each ring. Place the half circles, touching each other (and touching the ring in the center) and fitting one against the other, all facing the same way—the cut sides of one against the round side of another, all around the pan.

Set the pan aside and prepare the batter.

Cake Batter

1 cup sifted
all-purpose flour

⅓ teaspoon baking
powder (measure 1
level teaspoon, mark
it into thirds, return
⅔ to the box and use
the remaining ⅓)

¼ teaspoon salt

2 eggs

Sift together the flour, baking powder, and salt, and set aside. In the small bowl of an electric mixer, beat the eggs at high speed for about a minute. Gradually add the sugar while beating and continue to beat (total beating time about 5 minutes) until the mixture is thick and pale. Add the vanilla and the pineapple juice and beat on low speed, scraping the bowl with a rubber spatula, beating only until smooth. Still on low speed, add the sifted dry ingredients, scraping the bowl and beating only until smooth.

Pour the batter evenly over the fruit.

Bake for 45 to 50 minutes, until the top just barely springs back when it is lightly pressed with a fingertip and a toothpick gently inserted into the middle comes out clean and dry. (The cake might begin to come away from the sides of the pan—another sign that it is done.)

⅔ cup sugar

1 teaspoon vanilla extract

6 tablespoons drained pineapple juice from the canned rings

While it is baking, prepare the glaze (see below).

The very second that the cake comes out of the oven it must be removed from the pan. Cover the cake with a serving plate or board. If you have baked the cake in a frying pan, the handle might be in the way; use good pot holders and be careful. Center the plate carefully, and immediately turn over the plate and the frying pan or pie plate—hold it all firmly to prevent the cake plate from slipping. Having turned everything over, do not remove the frying pan or pie plate immediately; wait a minute or so to allow all of the butter/sugar topping to settle onto the cake. Remove the pan or pie plate carefully. If any nuts have slipped out of place on the cake, rearrange them.

Apricot Glaze

½ cup apricot preserves

The preserves should be bubbling hot and ready to be used as soon as the frying pan or pie plate is removed. Therefore, 5 or 10 minutes before the cake is done, melt the preserves in a small pan over moderate heat. Force them through a strainer. Return to the pan and bring to a boil.

With a pastry brush, brush the hot preserves generously over the top and sides of the hot cake.

Serve the cake hot or cooled.

Use a serrated knife for slicing, preferably the small one called a tomato knife.

Yeast
Cakes

About Yeast Cakes

USING YEAST

All of these recipes are written for active dry yeast that comes in little envelopes, packaged three together. The expiration date is printed on the back; be sure to check it.

DISSOLVING

The liquid that the yeast is dissolved in should be from 105° to 115° when tested with a thermometer—I use a candy thermometer. To test it without a thermometer, sprinkle a bit of it on the inside of your wrist; it should feel comfortably warm.

RISING

Yeast doughs rise best at a temperature of about 85° to 90°. If the outdoor temperature or room temperature is close to that, simply cover the bowl or pan as directed and pick a draft-free spot. Or if you have to create the right temperature, here's how: Place a large shallow pan of hot water on the bottom rack of the oven. And if your oven has one, turn on the light (this adds heat). Place a room thermometer in the middle of the oven (mine does not stand so I hang it from an oven rack adjusted to the top position). Watch the thermometer; you will be able to maintain a steady temperature by adding additional hot water, or by opening the oven a bit when necessary.

In many gas ovens, the pilot light gives off enough heat to maintain the correct temperature. And then once the yeast has started to grow and the dough has started to rise, the dough itself gives

off heat. Therefore it is not always necessary to use the pan of hot water.

If you want to delay the rising process at any stage, place the dough in the refrigerator. The cold will slow down the rising. Then, when it is placed in a warm temperature again, it will resume rising.

If a yeast dough has been shaped or poured into the pan, and has been rising in an 85° oven, it may be removed from the oven and may stand at room temperature while the oven is heating to the temperature specified for baking. But before you turn the oven on, don't forget to remove the room thermometer.

KNEADING

Flour the dough lightly and shape it into a ball. Place it on a large board or roomy work surface. Push the heel of your right hand down into the dough and push hard, pushing away from you. Then, with your left hand, fold the far edge of the dough toward you and over the center, and at the same time give the dough a quarter turn to the right. Repeat pushing, folding, and turning the dough with a smooth rhythm. Keep extra flour handy as you knead; if the dough becomes sticky, flour the dough and the work surface as necessary. And keep a dough scraper handy to use if the dough sticks to the work surface.

THE EMBASSY'S NUT CRESCENTS

48 CRESCENTS

These are from the Austrian Embassy in Washington, D.C., where they are the talk of the town. They are one of the very best pastries I ever ate; the lightest, tenderest, most delicate, most delicious, and most irresistible. This recipe can make your reputation as a pastry chef. And they are easy and fun to make, although they do take time.

There is a theory that crescents (croissants) of various doughs were first made in Vienna around 1683, at the time when the Turks were besieging Vienna. The crescent moon was the Turkish symbol. In a gesture of defiance the Viennese pastry chefs made bread and pastry in the crescent shape, implying "we can break you up and crumble you and eat you and there won't be anything left of you."

Serve these with afternoon tea or coffee, with breakfast, brunch, or a light luncheon, or, since they are so good, serve them anytime at all with or without anything at all.

The dough must be frozen for 1½ hours or refrigerated overnight before the pastries are shaped. Then they must rise for 2 hours before they are baked. Then you will be in heaven.

3 eggs

½ cup sour cream

8 ounces (2 sticks) unsalted butter, cold and firm

½ cup granulated sugar

5 cups plus 2 tablespoons sifted all-purpose flour

¾ teaspoon salt

¼ cup warm water (105° to 115°; see Dissolving, page 222)

2 envelopes active dry yeast

Finely grated rind of 1 large or 2 small lemons

1 egg white (to be used just before baking for brushing on top)

In a small bowl, with a beater or whisk, beat the eggs to mix. Add the sour cream and beat to blend. Set aside. On a board or flat plate, cut the butter into small pieces: Cut each stick lengthwise into quarters and then cut across into small dice. Set aside.

Remove and reserve about ½ teaspoon of the sugar. Into a large mixing bowl sift the remaining sugar with the flour and salt (see Notes). Add the butter. With a pastry blender cut the butter into the sifted dry ingredients until the mixture resembles coarse meal. Set aside.

Warm a 1-cup glass measuring cup by filling it with warm water. Let stand for a few minutes. Empty, and then pour in the ¼ cup warm water. Add the reserved ½ teaspoon sugar. Sprinkle the yeast on top. Stir with a table knife to mix. Let stand for a few minutes until the mixture rises to near the top of the cup.

Then stir the yeast mixture, the egg mixture, and the grated lemon rind into the butter-and-flour mixture. Mix thoroughly with a heavy wooden spoon.

Spread out a long piece of wax paper (about 20 inches long). You will use it after the dough is kneaded.

Turn the dough out onto a large board or work surface. It will be sticky. To knead it, hold a dough scraper or a wide metal spatula in your left hand and, with the scraper or spatula, lift the mass of dough, turn it over, and with the palm of your right hand push off the dough and then spread it away from you, pushing it against the work surface. Continue for 5 minutes. The dough will be sticky. (But kneading it is not a bad experience; actually, you can really just handle it roughly—any way that is comfortable for you.)

Then, with the scraper or spatula, transfer the dough to the spread-out wax paper. Fold the paper over the top and, with your hands, form the dough into a flat, round shape about 8 inches in diameter.

Without spoiling the shape, slide the dough in the wax paper into a plastic bag.

Freeze for 1½ hours (or longer) or refrigerate overnight. (If the dough is frozen much longer, or for a few days, it must be refrigerated overnight or it will be too stiff to handle.)

FILLING

5 ounces (1¼ cups) walnuts

2½ ounces (½ cup) currants

1 cup granulated sugar

3 ounces (¾ stick) unsalted butter, melted

¼ cup heavy cream

1 teaspoon vanilla extract

Chop the walnuts very fine. In a bowl, mix the nuts with the currants and sugar. Then stir in the butter. Mix the cream and vanilla, and add to the mixture. Refrigerate.

Before shaping the crescents, lightly butter cookie sheets, or have ready nonstick sheets or jelly-roll pans.

To shape the crescents, cut the cold dough into 8 equal pie-shaped wedges. Work with one piece at a time, keep the others refrigerated or frozen.

Flour your hands and press the piece of dough into a ball. Flatten it a bit. Then, on a lightly floured board, with a floured rolling pin, roll the dough out to form a 9-inch round. The shape does not have to be perfectly even.

With a pastry cutter or a pizza wheel, or with a long, sharp knife, cut the dough into 6 pie-shaped wedges.

Place a slightly rounded teaspoon of the filling close to the wider base of each wedge; do not spread it out. Starting at the base, roll the wedge toward the point, enclosing the filling. (It is not necessary to fuss with the ends, or to pinch any seams together, because when the dough rises and bakes it will meld together and form one mass of dough with the filling in the middle.)

NOTES: *To use a food processor for cutting the butter
into the dry ingredients, fit
the processor with the metal
blade. Then, unless you have
an extra-large processor, do it
in two batches, placing half of
the dry ingredients in the bowl
and adding half of the cut-up
butter in each batch. Process for
about 10 seconds with quick
on/off pulses until the mixture
resembles coarse meal. Transfer
both batches to a large mixing
bowl and stir in the remaining
ingredients.*

*It is not necessary to bake
these all at once. The dough
may be stored for a few days in
the freezer or refrigerator, and
the crescents may be baked only
6 at a time.*

*The baked crescents may
be frozen. Place them in a
single layer on a tray and cover
airtight with plastic wrap. Or,
package them two together,
bottoms together, in plastic
sandwich bags, and place
all the bags in a strong box.
Handle them as carefully as you
possibly can.*

Place each roll, as you roll it up, on the prepared sheet, with the point underneath. Turn the ends down to shape into short, fat crescents. Place the crescents 2 inches apart.

Cover loosely with a thin, lightweight linen or cotton towel or napkin or with loose plastic wrap or wax paper, and let rise (see Rising, page 222) for 2 hours until double in size.

About 15 or 20 minutes before the crescents have finished rising, adjust two racks to divide the oven into thirds (if you bake only one sheet at a time bake it in the center of the oven) and preheat the oven to 350°.

Beat the egg white only until it is fairly foamy. With a soft brush, gently brush the white over the top of the crescents.

Bake for 15 minutes until nicely browned. If you bake two sheets at once, reverse them top to bottom and front to back after 10 minutes to ensure even browning. If you bake only one sheet at a time and if the crescents in the back are browning sooner than those in front, turn the sheet front to back.

A little bit of the filling might run out of a few of these—it will not be too much—don't worry about it.

With a wide metal spatula (or a plastic spatula if you are using a nonstick pan) transfer the crescents to racks to cool.

After only a few minutes, eat a crescent while it is still quite warm. These are sensational warm or cold, but please do taste one warm.

Two or three crescents should be an adequate portion, but I saw an entire batch disappear when a few friends stopped in unexpectedly while I was baking.

Miniature Schnecken

ABOUT 36 MINIATURE SCHNECKEN

This has to be one of the most exciting and most gratifying of all my kitchen activities. If you have never used yeast before, don't be afraid to make these. They are easy, but they do take time. And they must be started a day ahead, as the dough must be refrigerated overnight. But if they had to be started a month ahead, I would make arrangements; they are that good.

Schnecken is the German word for snails. They are made of a rich dough rolled around a filling of sugar, cinnamon, nuts, and currants and baked in pans lined with sugar, butter, and pecans. When the Schnecken are turned out of the pans, the sugar, butter, and pecans become a scrumptious topping. They are incredibly delicious, light, tender, delicate, gorgeous, and extremely popular.

The recipe is written for pans that make small muffins. I especially like using one of my pans that came from a wholesale restaurant supply store. It has 24 muffin forms, each one is 2 inches in diameter at the top and 1¼ inches in depth. That size is slightly larger than the forms for small muffins that are sold in hardware stores. Either size works well. And I bake them in two ovens. But you can bake part of the recipe at a time. The dough can wait in the refrigerator for as long as 3 days if you wish. Or the shaped and risen dough can wait in the kitchen for about 20 minutes until you have room in the oven. To be sure that the bottoms get dark enough, it is best to bake these on only one rack at a time.

Dough

1 envelope active
dry yeast

2 tablespoons warm
water (see Dissolving,
page 222)

¼ cup granulated sugar

3 ounces (¾ stick)
unsalted butter, cut
into small pieces, at
room temperature

2 tablespoons milk, scalded

1 egg, at room temperature

½ cup sour cream, at
room temperature

Sprinkle the yeast over the warm water in a small bowl, stir with a fork or a table knife to mix, and set aside.

Place the sugar and butter in a large mixing bowl (this may be mixed in an electric mixer or by hand with a wooden spoon or rubber spatula). Add the hot milk and mix until the butter is melted. Add the egg and stir or beat to mix; mix in the sour cream, and then the yeast. Add the salt and 1¾ cups of the flour (reserve the remaining 1 cup of flour until the following day), and beat until the mixture is very smooth. (It will be thick and sticky.)

Lightly butter a 6-cup bowl (if you double the recipe, the bowl must be twice as large). Place the dough in the buttered bowl, cover airtight with plastic wrap or foil, and refrigerate overnight, or for as long as 3 days. The refrigerated dough should rise to double in bulk, or to the top of the bowl. Use a wooden spoon and stir the dough briefly to deflate it.

When you are going to bake the Schnecken, prepare the pan as follows:

½ teaspoon salt

About 2¾ cups *unsifted*
all-purpose or bread flour

Mixture #1: Topping

8 ounces (2 sticks)
unsalted butter

Remove and set aside 5½ ounces (1 stick plus 3 tablespoons) of the butter.

Use the part of the melted butter to prepare the muffin pans; brush it on generously with a pastry brush. Reserve the remaining melted butter to brush on the rolled-out dough.

1 tablespoon plus 1
teaspoon light corn syrup

1 cup plus 3 tablespoons
light brown sugar,
firmly packed

3½ ounces (1 cup)
pecan halves

Beat the reserved 5½ ounces of unmelted butter with the corn syrup to mix, add the sugar, and beat until thoroughly mixed. Divide this mixture among the buttered muffin forms, placing a generous teaspoonful in the bottom of each form (it is not necessary to spread it around). Then place 2 or 3 of the pecan halves (depending on their size) in each form, placing them touching each other, flat side up, and pressing them deeply into the butter-and-sugar mixture. Set aside the prepared pans.

To Shape the Schnecken

Place the 1 cup of flour reserved from the dough on a large board or work surface and spread it out slightly. Turn the chilled dough onto the board. Knead (see Kneading, page 222) for about 8 minutes, incorporating all of the flour. (At first it will look as though you have too much flour, but after a few minutes of kneading you will see that the dough will absorb all of it.) Form the dough into a ball, flour it lightly, cover it loosely with a kitchen towel, and let stand for 10 to 15 minutes.

Then form the dough into a cylinder about 15 inches long and 2½ inches in diameter (the shape must be even). With your fingers, flatten it slightly. With additional flour, lightly flour a large board or work surface and a rolling pin. Roll the dough in both directions until it is about 25 inches long and 9 to 10 inches wide. While you are rolling, do try to keep the shape oblong and the edges even—at least as even as you can. If the dough seems rubbery and shrinks back after you roll it (and it probably will), let it stand for about 10 minutes and then roll again. It might be necessary to let it stand more than once during the process.

Brush the rolled-out dough with the remaining melted butter.

MIXTURE #2: FILLING

Boiling water

½ cup currants

½ cup granulated sugar

2½ teaspoons cinnamon

2½ ounces (generous
¾ cup) pecans, finely
chopped (they should
not be ground but
they must be fine)

Finely grated rind of
2 large lemons

Pour boiling water over the currants to cover them and let stand for 1 minute (no longer—they lose their taste and texture if they soak too long), drain them in a strainer, and then turn them out onto several thicknesses of paper towel, fold the paper over the top, and press on it to remove excess water. Set aside.

Mix the sugar and cinnamon, and with a large spoon sprinkle it over the buttered dough (sprinkle all the way to both narrow ends or the end Schnecken won't have any). Then with your fingers sprinkle with the currants, pecans, and grated rind (again all the way to both narrow ends but stop a bit short of one long side).

Now carefully roll like a jelly roll, rolling tightly from the long side where the filling reaches the edge. As you roll, watch the ends of the roll; pull out the dough a bit or push it in as necessary to keep the ends about the same thickness as the rest of the roll. Pinch the seam to seal it.

With your hands, stretch the rolled-up dough gently until it is 36 inches in length. (If your work area is not wide enough, the roll of dough may be cut in half, and each half handled separately.)

With a sharp knife carefully cut the roll into slices. (It is a good idea to mark the slices with a ruler in order to have them all the same size.) If the muffin forms measure 2 inches in width and 1¼ inches in depth, the slices should be a scant 1 inch in width. But if the forms are smaller, the slices should be only about ½ inch in width. (See Note.)

Place the slices, one cut side down, in the prepared pans.

With your fingers, press each slice firmly down into the pan. (The tops of the slices will come just about to the tops of the pans, but they may be a bit higher or lower.)

Cover each pan loosely with plastic wrap or with a lightweight kitchen towel or cloth napkin; it must not be tight—the dough needs room to rise. Place the pans in a warm spot (see Rising, page 222) and let stand for 1½ to 1¾ hours until the dough is puffy and slightly risen. (It will feel light and airy if you touch it very gently, although it might not look actually doubled.) The Schnecken will rise a bit more while they are baking.

Note: If the muffin forms are very small, and if you cut slices that are less than 1 inch thick, you will make more than 36 miniature Schnecken. If you have only a few extra, they may be baked in any small pans. I have used individual brioche pans and baba pans. Or you could use custard cups. Or you could place them close to each other in a small round or square pan that they fit. If you do not have any of the butter-sugar-corn syrup mixture left over, it is enough if you just butter the extra pan. Small pans or cups should be placed on a cake pan or on any small sheet to keep them from toppling over in the oven. They can wait at room temperature until you have room for them in the oven. Or before you let them rise, they can be covered and refrigerated to rise and bake some other time. (The rising time will naturally be longer if they are taken directly from the refrigerator.)

About 20 minutes before the Schnecken have finished rising, adjust a rack one-third up from the bottom of the oven. Preheat the oven to 375°.

Bake the Schnecken for 20 to 25 minutes, until they are richly colored. They should not be pale. If you have used one large pan, when the baking time is slightly more than half finished, reverse it front to back if necessary to ensure even browning.

You will need a flat cookie sheet or a jelly-roll pan to turn the baked Schnecken onto; the sheet or pan must be slightly larger than the pan of Schnecken.

As soon as they are removed from the oven, DON'T WAIT, immediately cover with a flat sheet, hold firmly with pot holders at both sides, and turn both the sheet and the pan over. Let stand for only 10 or 15 seconds, then lift the pan an inch or so from the sheet and wait briefly for all the Schnecken to slip out.

Any caramelized sugar-butter mixture that runs off the Schnecken may be scooped up (with a table knife) and replaced on top of the Schnecken while they are still hot.

Now, if you can, wait about a minute (at least) before you gobble these up. Serve them warm. Or let them stand and serve them cool. Or freeze them; thaw before serving.

SAVARIN

10 PORTIONS

According to culinary history, in the year 1609, Sigismund III, the king of Poland, was eating a piece of dry kugelhopf. He was inspired to pour some rum over the cake. It was genius; the rum-soaked cake was so delicious it became his favorite, and, incidentally, one of Sigismund's main claims to fame. The king named the cake Ali Baba, the name of the hero in his favorite story from A Thousand and One Nights. It became the rage in Paris at the beginning of the 19th century, and the name was then abbreviated to Baba. In the year 1840, a French pastry chef made the recipe without the raisins and he named it after his hero, Brillat-Savarin. This too became famous, and the name was later shortened to Savarino. It is a light and airy Baba au Rhum without raisins.

It is an easy yeast dough (no kneading and only one rising), made in a fancy pan, soaked, after baking, with a mild rum syrup and coated with a shiny apricot glaze. It is a dessert cake either just as it is or with whipped cream and brandied fruit.

Since this is such a deluxe dessert, and quite easy, consider it for your next party. Or, if you are like I am, make it immediately for yourself.

You will need a one-piece fancy tube pan or a deep ring mold with a 10-cup capacity.

The method for using yeast in this recipe is called the "sponge method." It was a more popular method in the days when yeast might have been stale when it was sold; this method assured that the yeast was alive and well before it was used.

SPONGE

½ cup warm milk
(100° to 115°; see
Dissolving, page 222)

1 envelope active
dry yeast

2 tablespoons
granulated sugar

½ cup sifted
all-purpose flour

To warm the large bowl of an electric mixer, place the bowl in the sink and run hot tap water into it for a minute, and then pour the water out. Pour the warm milk into the warm bowl. Sprinkle the yeast over the milk, let stand for 5 minutes, and then stir briefly with a fork. Add the sugar and stir. Add the flour and stir (or beat with the mixer) just to mix well. Cover with plastic wrap and let stand at a temperature of 80° to 90° (see Rising, page 222) for about 30 minutes, or just until the mixture is bubbly. (Sugar and flour are the two foods that yeast needs in order to grow. It will bubble as it grows. And a warm temperature will make it grow quickly.)

While the yeast is proofing (or proving, as in "proving that it is okay"), butter a 9-inch (10-cup) fancy tube pan or a plain ring mold and dust it all over lightly with fine, dry bread crumbs (butter and crumb the pan even if it has a nonstick finish), and tap to shake out excess crumbs over a piece of paper. Set aside.

Dough

2½ ounces (½ cup) blanched almonds

4 ounces (1 stick) unsalted butter

4 eggs, at room temperature

1½ cups sifted all-purpose flour

¼ teaspoon salt

The almonds may be prepared way ahead of time if you wish. First, they should be toasted. Place them in a shallow pan in a 350° oven and shake or stir occasionally until they become a pale, light gold color. Then they must be ground into a fine powder; this may be done in a food processor (see To Grind Nuts in a Food Processor, page 13) or a nut grinder. Set the toasted, ground nuts aside.

The butter should be melted very slowly. Cut it into pieces and melt it over low heat; it should become only lukewarm. Set it aside briefly.

Now, beat the sponge mixture with the mixer only to deflate it. Add the almonds and beat only to mix. Then, on low speed, add the eggs alternately with the flour and salt, scraping the bowl with a rubber spatula and beating until smooth after each addition. Beat in the butter before the last addition of flour.

Then beat at medium-high speed for 10 minutes until the dough becomes elastic. (If it starts to crawl up on the beaters, reduce the speed as necessary.)

Pour into the prepared pan, smooth the top, and cover with plastic wrap. Let rise (see Rising, page 222). It will take about 50 minutes for the dough to double in bulk; at that time it will be about ½ inch below the side of the pan, slightly higher in the middle. Fifteen or 20 minutes before the dough has finished rising, adjust a rack one-quarter or one-third up from the bottom of the oven and preheat the oven to 375°. Bake the cake for 20 minutes until it's light brown; the top will have risen almost another inch.

Cover the hot cake with a rack, turn over the cake pan and the rack, remove the pan (don't wash it—you are going to use it again), and let the cake stand fancy side up for about 15 minutes.

Meanwhile, prepare the syrup.

Rum Syrup

1 cup granulated sugar

2 cups water

½ cup dark rum

Mix the sugar and water in a saucepan over moderately high heat, stirring until the sugar is dissolved and the mixture comes to a boil. Simmer without stirring for 15 minutes. Remove from the heat and stir in the rum.

Carefully replace the pan that the cake was baked in over the cake. Turn the cake pan and the rack over, leaving the cake in the pan again. With a small, sharp knife cut many shallow slits in the crust on top of the cake (in order to make it easy for the cake to absorb the syrup).

Slowly pour the hot syrup over the cake. It will absorb it all and it will remain miraculously light. Let stand for 1 to 1½ hours in the pan.

Cover the cake with a flat cake plate. Turn the cake pan and the plate over and remove the pan again, leaving the cake flat side down on the plate.

Prepare the glaze.

Apricot Glaze

½ cup apricot preserves

2 tablespoons granulated sugar

2 tablespoons dark rum

Note: *The Savarin may be frozen, but it will look best if you freeze it without the syrup and glaze; apply the syrup and glaze the day it is served. The cake does not have to be hot when the syrup is applied, but it must be completely thawed.*

In a small saucepan over moderate heat cook the preserves and sugar, stirring constantly, until the mixture comes to a boil. Boil slowly, stirring, for 5 minutes, or until the mixture registers 225° on a candy thermometer.

Press the hot glaze through a strainer and stir in the rum.

With a pastry brush, brush the hot glaze all over the cake.

This can be served (deliciously) with sweetened and vanilla-flavored whipped cream (which may be served separately or heaped in the center of the cake) and brandied fruit (i.e., black Bing cherries, apricots, pears, peaches, or pineapple), or with any simple stewed fruit without the brandy. Or with fresh raspberries or strawberries.

BABKA

1 LARGE 9-INCH CAKE

This Polish cake is traditionally served at Easter time, but it is so popular that many bakeries in many countries make it all year. It is one of the most elegant coffee cakes; plain but rich and buttery, generously studded with raisins, and golden colored from the many egg yolks. It is easily made without kneading, and has only one rising. This keeps well and is even better a day after it is baked. You will need a one-piece 9-inch kugelhopf pan or other fancy tube pan with a 10-cup capacity. But there is one hitch. If the cake is baked in a shiny metal pan, it will be too pale. It will be gorgeous if it is baked in a 10-cup, nonstick Bundt pan (if you have one this size, treasure it—it seems that the manufacturer has stopped making it), or in a black iron kugelhopf pan made by Le Creuset under the name "Cousances."

¼ cup very warm water
(105° to 115°; see
Dissolving, page 222)

1 envelope active
dry yeast

½ cup plus 1 teaspoon
granulated sugar

6 ounces (1½ sticks)
unsalted butter

6 egg yolks

3 cups *unsifted*
all-purpose flour

½ teaspoon salt

¾ cup milk

Finely grated rind of
2 medium-size lemons

5 ounces (1 cup) raisins
(you may use half
dark and half light or
all of either color)

Optional:
Confectioners' sugar

Fill a small bowl with hot water to warm it; shake out the water but do not dry the bowl. Place the ¼ cup of warm water in the bowl, sprinkle the yeast over it, add 1 teaspoon of the sugar (reserve the remaining ½ cup of sugar), and stir with a fork or knife to mix. Let stand at room temperature for about 10 minutes; the mixture will start to increase in bulk.

Meanwhile, in the large bowl of an electric mixer, beat the butter until it is soft. Add the reserved ½ cup of granulated sugar and mix well. Add the yolks, two or three at a time, and beat until the mixture lightens a bit in color. Add the yeast mixture, about half of the flour (reserve the remaining half), and the salt. Beat to mix.

Meanwhile, in a small saucepan on low heat, warm the milk until it registers 105° to 115° on a candy thermometer.

Gradually add the warm milk to the yeast mixture, and then add the reserved flour and beat on low speed until smooth.

Continue to beat on low speed for 3 minutes, and then remove from the mixer.

Sprinkle the lemon rind over the batter (do not drop it on in one lump or it will stay that way) and stir with a heavy wooden spoon or a large rubber spatula to mix well. Then mix in the raisins.

Butter a 10-cup, fancy-shaped tube pan (see above—butter the pan even if it is nonstick); it is best to do this with a pastry brush and soft (not melted) butter.

Pour the dough evenly into the pan. With the back of a spoon, smooth the top.

NOTE: *You can keep this in the freezer and, for an unplanned occasion, you can slice it frozen—it will slice nicely. Then the slices will thaw quickly. Or, for a special treat, toast them.*

Cover with buttered plastic wrap (buttered side down). Let rise (see Rising, page 222) for about 2 hours or a little longer until the dough reaches the top of the pan; in the center, the dough should be just slightly above the top of the pan—on the edges, slightly below. However, before it is quite that high, remove the plastic wrap (the dough might stick to it even though it is buttered).

Before baking, adjust a rack one-third up from the bottom of the oven and preheat the oven to 400°.

Bake the cake at 400° for 5 minutes, then reduce the temperature to 350° and bake for 30 minutes more (total baking time is 35 minutes). The top should be well browned, but if it seems to be getting too dark, cover it loosely with foil.

Remove from the oven and let the cake stand in the pan for 10 minutes. Then cover with a rack, carefully turn over the pan and rack, and remove the pan. Let stand until completely cool.

Wrap the cooled cake and let it stand overnight, or for at least several hours. If you are in a hurry for it, refrigerate or freeze it briefly.

If you wish, sprinkle the top with confectioners' sugar before serving.

KUGELHOPF

1 LARGE CAKE THAT MAKES ABOUT 16 PORTIONS

This is a plain but rich and buttery, slightly dry, not-too-sweet raisin-nut coffee cake made with an easy yeast dough. There is no kneading and only one rising. The traditional kugelhopf mold is a tube pan with a fluted design. The shape was said to have been inspired by the sultan's turban (the pan is also called a Turk's head). When the Turks were defeated at the gates of Vienna in 1683, the Viennese bakers who helped defend their city during the siege created this as a victory cake (although some history books say it was created in the year 1609 at Lemberg, Poland; see Savarin, page 230).

You will need a one-piece fancy tube pan with a 12-cup capacity. Generally, a fancy tube pan with a 10-inch diameter across the top has a 12-cup capacity. Start this ahead of time. It is best to marinate the raisins overnight, and I think the cake is best the day after it is baked, although many people like it fresh from the oven.

2½ ounces (½ cup) dark raisins and 5 ounces (1 cup) light raisins (or use 1½ cups dark raisins)

⅓ cup kirsch or light rum

About 15 whole blanched almonds (to prepare the cake pan)

1 cup milk

2 envelopes active dry yeast

¾ cup granulated sugar

8 ounces (2 sticks) unsalted butter

1 tablespoon vanilla extract

¼ teaspoon ginger

¼ teaspoon nutmeg

5 eggs, at room temperature

4 cups *unsifted* all-purpose flour

1 teaspoon salt

Finely grated rind of 2 large lemons

2½ ounces (½ cup) blanched or unblanched almonds, thinly sliced

Ingredients continued on next page.

Place both the raisins and the kirsch or rum in a jar with a tight cover. Let them stand for a few hours or overnight, turning the jar from side to side occasionally.

Prepare a 12-cup fancy tube pan by brushing soft (not melted) butter all over the pan. The 10-inch Bundt pan makes a gorgeous kugelhopf; butter and crumb the pan even if it has a nonstick lining. Dust it with fine, dry bread crumbs and then tap to shake out excess crumbs over a piece of paper. Place a whole blanched almond in the bottom of each flute in the design. Set the prepared pan aside.

Heat the milk until it reaches 105° to 115° on a candy thermometer; when it is right it will feel comfortably warm if it is sprinkled on the inside of your wrist. Transfer to a small bowl to stop the cooking. Sprinkle the yeast over the milk. Add 1 teaspoon of the sugar (reserve the remaining sugar) and stir with a fork or a table knife until all the yeast is moistened. Set aside.

Place the butter in the large bowl of an electric mixer and beat until it is soft. Add the vanilla, ginger, nutmeg, and the reserved sugar, and beat until very well mixed. Add the eggs one at a time, beating well after each addition. On low speed mix in about half (2 cups) of the flour and beat until smooth, gradually add the yeast mixture and beat until smooth, then add about 1 more cup of the flour. Beat at moderate speed for about 5 minutes. Add the remaining 1 cup of flour and the salt and beat for 2 or 3 minutes more. (If the batter climbs up on the beaters, use the lowest speed or beat with a wooden spoon.)

Remove from the mixer. Stir in the lemon rind, sliced almonds, optional citron or orange peel, and the marinated raisins (along with any unabsorbed kirsch or rum). Stir well to be sure that the nuts and fruits are evenly distributed.

Pour gently (in order not to disturb the almonds) into the prepared pan, smooth the top with the back of a spoon, and cover with buttered plastic wrap (buttered side down). Let rise at 80° to 90° (see Rising, page 222) for about 1 hour until doubled in size; it will probably be 1¼ inches below the top of the pan on the rim and even with the top, or slightly above, in the middle. (Don't worry if it rises a little higher. Traditionally, kugelhopf rises so high it looks as though the pan is too small.) It will be necessary to

Optional: ½ cup diced candied citron or orange peel

Confectioners' sugar (to be sprinkled over the baked cake)

remove the plastic wrap before the dough rises into it; it might stick even though the plastic is buttered. Then let it finish rising uncovered.

To prepare the oven for baking, adjust a rack to the lowest position. (Remove any other racks—they will be in the way when you reach in to cover the pan with foil.) Preheat the oven to 400°.

Bake the cake for 10 minutes (it will rise about another inch above the top of the pan during those 10 minutes, but during baking it will settle down a bit). Reduce the temperature to 350° and continue to bake for another 20 minutes, then cover it loosely with foil to prevent the top from becoming too dark and continue to bake another 20 minutes (total baking time is about 50 minutes).

When the cake is done, a cake tester inserted into the middle will come out clean and dry and the cake will begin to come away slightly from the sides of the pan.

Cool in the pan for 10 minutes, then cover with a rack, turn over the pan and rack, remove the pan, and let the kugelhopf cool for several hours or overnight before serving. Sprinkle it with confectioners' sugar (either plain or vanilla sugar; see page 3), straining the sugar through a fine strainer held over the cake.

ELECTION DAY CAKE
FOUR 8-INCH LOAVES

This is more than a recipe, it is a lesson in American history. More than a century ago this cake was a payoff that was given by politicians to men who voted a straight party ticket. I can't find out which political party it was; it might have been both parties. The custom started in Hartford, Connecticut, and spread through much of New England.

It is light and airy, brandied and spiced, not-too-sweet raisin bread with white icing—plain and old-fashioned. Hosts and hostesses make it today to serve as a coffee cake at election parties while waiting for the returns to come in, or as a sweet bread for breakfast or brunch. Apart from its original payola purpose, it is marvelous any time and I cast my vote for it any day.

The fruit should be marinated overnight or for at least 6 hours before you mix the dough.

This recipe makes 4 loaves in 8 x 4 x 20-inch pans. That size has a 5-cup capacity. If you must use slightly larger pans it will be okay, but if the pans are much larger the loaves will not be as high and pretty.

5 ounces (1 cup)
light raisins

5 ounces (1 cup)
dark raisins

½ cup diced citron
(candied pineapple
could be substituted)

4 ounces (generous
1 cup) walnuts,
cut or broken into
medium-size pieces

½ cup brandy

¾ cup warm water
(105° to 115°; see
Dissolving, page 222)

1 cup granulated sugar

4 envelopes active
dry yeast

¾ cup milk

1¼ teaspoons salt

8 ounces (2 sticks)
unsalted butter, cut
into small pieces, at
room temperature

2 eggs, beaten

8 cups sifted
all-purpose flour
(you might need a bit
more for kneading)

Ingredients continued on next page.

Place both kinds of raisins, the citron, walnuts, and brandy in a jar with a tight cover (1-quart size is okay if you push the fruit down tightly). Cover the jar securely, place it in a bowl (in case it leaks), and turn it from side to side and from top to bottom occasionally and let stand overnight.

When the fruit is ready, proceed with the recipe.

Warm a bowl with about a 4-cup capacity by letting warm water run into it. Dry it quickly. Place the ¾ cup warm water in the warm bowl. Add 2 tablespoons of the sugar (reserve the remaining sugar) and sprinkle the yeast over the top. Stir with a table knife to mix. Set aside uncovered at room temperature to rise for about 10 minutes.

Meanwhile, place the milk, the reserved sugar, the salt, and the butter in a saucepan over moderate heat and stir until the mixture is warm (105° to 115°). The butter will not all be melted, but it should be soft.

Transfer the warm milk-and-butter mixture to a very large mixing bowl. Add the eggs and the yeast mixture. Stir to mix well. (If the butter is still in lumps, stir briefly with a strong wire whisk.)

Resift 1 cup of the flour with the cinnamon, nutmeg, allspice, and cloves, and stir into the yeast mixture. Then, with a heavy wooden spoon, stir in 5 or 6 more cups of the flour, or as much as you can stir in.

Spread out the remaining flour on a large board or work surface. Turn the dough out on top of it. Knead to incorporate all of the flour. Then (see Kneading, page 222) knead the dough (if it is too sticky to knead, add additional flour—but only as necessary) for 5 minutes until it is beautifully smooth and elastic. (It is a wonderful dough to handle.)

You will need a large bowl for the dough to rise in. Mine has a 7-quart capacity. Butter the bowl. Place the dough in the bowl, turn it over to butter all sides, cover with plastic wrap, and let rise (see Rising, page 222) for 1 hour, in which time it will more than double in bulk (in a 7-quart bowl it will rise to about 1 inch from the top of the bowl).

Meanwhile, drain the marinated fruit in a strainer. If there is any brandy that has not been absorbed, do not use it for this recipe. Spread out several long thicknesses of paper towel, spread the fruit on the paper, and pat the top with more paper to dry the fruit a bit.

½ teaspoon cinnamon

½ teaspoon nutmeg

½ teaspoon allspice

¼ teaspoon ground cloves

When the dough has risen, make a fist and punch down the middle of the dough to deflate it. Then turn the sides in toward the middle.

Turn the dough out onto a lightly floured board or work surface. With a floured rolling pin, roll it out until it is about ¼ inch thick and about 20 inches in diameter (any shape is okay).

Spread the drained fruit all over the rolled-out dough. Roll it up like a jelly roll. Then fold both ends in toward the center. Press down firmly and knead all together for a few moments to distribute the fruit evenly. Form the dough into a ball. With a long, heavy knife, cut it carefully into quarters.

Then form each quarter into a ball by holding it in your hands and pulling the sides around to the bottom and pushing them into the center. Let the balls stand for a few moments.

Butter 4 loaf pans that measure 8 x 4 x 2½ inches. On the floured board with the floured rolling pin, roll one ball of dough into an oblong or oval about 7 x 12 inches. Roll up from a narrow end like a jelly roll. (It should be a nice, even shape, but if not, shape it a bit with your hands. Or, if necessary, reroll it.)

Place the rolled-up dough, seam down, in a buttered pan. Do not press down or flatten the loaf; there will be a little empty space in the pan on both long sides. Prepare all 4 loaves.

Cover the loaves loosely with a lightweight towel and let rise (see Rising, page 222) for 1¼ to 1½ hours; the loaves should rise a generous 1 inch above the tops of the 8 x 4 x 2½-inch pans.

About 20 minutes before the loaves have finished rising, adjust a rack one-third up from the bottom of the oven and preheat the oven to 350°. Remove the towel and place the loaves in the oven. They will start to brown rather quickly; when the tops are dark enough, cover them loosely with foil. If the loaves in the back of the oven brown faster than those in the front, reverse the pans from front to back after about 25 minutes. Bake for a total of 50 minutes until done.

As soon as the loaves are removed from the oven they should be turned out onto racks to cool. (A few raisins will probably have popped out on top and become burnt; pick them off.)

Place the loaves on racks over foil or wax paper.

After about 10 minutes, while the loaves are still warm, prepare the glaze.

Glaze

¼ cup heavy cream

1 teaspoon vanilla extract

2 cups strained confectioners' sugar

In a small pan over moderate heat, heat the cream until it is hot but not boiling. Remove from the heat. Stir in the vanilla.

In a bowl, mix the hot cream with the sugar until smooth. It should be a thick but pourable mixture.

Brush the glaze heavily over the tops of the warm loaves, letting it drip down the sides.

Let stand until completely dry.

This makes absolutely marvelous toast, but watch it carefully; it browns (burns) unusually fast.

These loaves freeze perfectly.

Swedish Leaf Cakes

2 large, long, narrow cakes

This recipe will make two sensational-looking, long, narrow, hand-formed coffee cakes that should be planned for a special occasion. They not only look fantastic but they have a delicious raisin-nut filling and everyone raves about them.

Serve them when they are very fresh, or freeze them.

Do not make these when you are in a hurry; there are two risings, and mixing, kneading, shaping, cutting, twisting, icing, etc. It is all fun to do anyhow, but especially gratifying when you see the beautiful results.

Dough

To heat the large bowl of an electric mixer, place it in the sink and let hot water run into it for about a minute. Pour out the water and shake the bowl, then pour in the 1 cup of warm water, 1 teaspoon of the sugar, and the yeast. Twirl the bowl gently to mix the ingredients a bit and then let stand for 5 or 6 minutes.

1 cup warm water
(105° to 115°; see
Dissolving, page 222)

½ cup granulated sugar

2 envelopes active
dry yeast

⅓ cup instant
nonfat dry milk

1 teaspoon salt

2 eggs, at room
temperature

4 ounces (1 stick) unsalted
butter, cut into pieces,
at room temperature

5 to 5¼ cups *unsifted*
all-purpose flour

Add the remaining sugar, the dry milk, salt, eggs, butter, and 2½ cups of the flour (reserve the remaining flour). Beat at high speed for 2 minutes. Then gradually, on low speed, add about another cup of the flour and beat only to mix. Remove from the mixer.

Add another 1¼ cups of the flour (you will still have another ¼ to ½ cup of flour in reserve). With a heavy wooden spoon or spatula, stir to mix.

Lightly flour a large board or work surface. Turn the dough out onto the floured surface. Knead (see Kneading, page 222) the dough briefly until it is smooth. If it is sticky, add some of the reserved flour—you might not need all of it. Then continue to knead the dough for 6 or 7 minutes until it is very smooth and elastic.

Lightly butter a deep mixing bowl. Form the dough into a ball, place it in the bowl, turn it around in the bowl to butter all the sides, and then cover the bowl with plastic wrap. Let rise (see Rising, page 222) for about 1½ hours or until it doubles in volume.

Meanwhile, prepare the ingredients for the filling.

FILLING

2 ounces (½ stick)
unsalted butter

½ cup granulated sugar

4 teaspoons cinnamon

½ teaspoon nutmeg

4 ounces (1 cup) walnuts
or pecans, finely chopped

5 ounces (1 cup) raisins
(you may use dark
or light, or currants,
or a combination
of any of these)

The ingredients listed are to fill two cakes; use half for each cake.

Melt the butter and set it aside.

In a small bowl mix the sugar, cinnamon, and nutmeg and set aside. Have the nuts and raisins ready; do not stir them into the sugar mixture.

You will need two large cookie sheets or jelly-roll pans (one for each cake). It is best to use nonstick pans, but if you don't have them, butter the pans lightly and set them aside.

When the dough has risen, punch it down with your fist, turning the edges in toward the center. Form the dough into a ball and cut it in half. Return one-half to the buttered bowl, cover, and set aside.

Form the other half into a ball. On the floured surface, with a floured, heavy rolling pin, roll the dough out into a 10 x 15-inch rectangle. If the

240

dough is too elastic and shrinks back each time you roll it, simply cover it lightly with a towel and allow it to stand for 5 to 10 minutes. Then it will be easier to work with. But this is one of those things where you have to remember that you are the boss; be firm, get tough with it if you must.

Brush the rolled-out dough with the melted butter. Sprinkle with the sugar mixture. Then sprinkle on the nuts and raisins, keeping them about an inch away from the far long side.

Roll up like a jelly roll, starting at the long side where the nuts and raisins go all the way to the end.

Pinch the seam to seal. Then, with your hands, stretch the roll a bit until it is as long as the measurement from one corner of the baking sheet to the diagonally opposite corner.

Place the roll diagonally on the sheet. Now to form the roll into "leaves": Hold a pair of scissors over and at one end of the roll, with the blades pointing toward the roll; the blades should be at about a 45° angle. You are going to make slanting cuts about ½ inch apart, without cutting through to the bottom. Here's how:

Open the scissors to straddle the roll and lower the blades until the points are a scant ½ inch from the pan. Make the first cut, bringing the blades together and cutting through all but the lower ¼ to ½ inch of the roll. Continue to cut these slices about ½ inch apart (the narrower the slices are—within reason—the fancier the cake will be).

Next step: Start at one end and, with your fingers, gently move one "leaf" to the right of center and the next one to the left. It is not necessary to move each "leaf" all the way onto its side; just alternate them away from the center. Do not handle too much or the filling might fall out.

Cover lightly with a smooth, lightweight towel or cloth napkin, and set aside to rise (see Rising, page 222) for 1 hour.

Meanwhile, prepare the second cake the same way, place it on another sheet, cover, and let rise.

About 20 minutes before baking, adjust a rack one-third up from the bottom of the oven and preheat the oven to 350°.

Bake the cake that was shaped first (let the second cake wait). Bake for 25 to 30 minutes, until golden brown. Do not underbake.

ICING

½ cup strained
confectioners' sugar

1 tablespoon milk

¼ teaspoon vanilla extract

These amounts are for one cake. Do not mix enough for both cakes at once; the icing should be used shortly after it is prepared.

Simply mix the ingredients until smooth.

When the cake is removed from the oven, bake the second cake.

Let the baked cake stand on the sheet for about 3 minutes. Then, with a firm metal spatula, cut under the cake to be sure it is not stuck to the pan. Carefully (I always appreciate another person's help at this stage), using a flat-sided cookie sheet as a spatula, or two long and strong metal spatulas, or the bottoms of two loose-bottomed quiche pans, transfer the cake to a large rack. Place the rack over a long piece of foil or wax paper.

With a pastry brush, brush the icing all over the hot cake, including the exposed filling.

Let cool completely.

Meanwhile, bake, ice, and cool the second cake.

Place each cake on a long, narrow board (a chocolate-roll board is perfect) or on any long, narrow, flat tray.

STOLLEN
1 LARGE STOLLEN (2½ POUNDS)

A Stollen is a free-form, long, oval, rich-and-buttery yeast cake generously studded with a variety of rum-soaked candied fruits and nuts. It comes from Germany; the best ones, I have heard, are from Dresden. Although Stollen are generally made at Christmas and are a popular Christmas gift, they're wonderful any time as coffee cake with breakfast, or with tea, coffee, wine, milk, etc. It is a firm and compact (not light and airy) cake that lasts extremely well (for weeks in the refrigerator or a year in the freezer)—it should be refrigerated for at least a few days before it is served. It makes marvelously crisp and crunchy toast.

For a brunch buffet party, I sliced the loaf a bit thinner than bread slices, placed the slices overlapping on a long, narrow board, and placed the board next to a toaster on a side table near the rest of the food. Everyone toasted his or her own (I should have had three or four toasters).

½ cup diced candied orange rind (I use a combination of lemon, orange, and citron)

¼ cup currants

¼ cup light raisins

¼ cup candied cherries, halved

⅓ cup dark rum

2 tablespoons warm water (105° to 115°; see Dissolving, page 222)

1 envelope active dry yeast

½ cup milk

¼ cup plus 2 tablespoons granulated sugar

1 teaspoon salt

3 ounces (¾ stick) unsalted butter, at room temperature

½ teaspoon almond extract

3 cups *unsifted* all-purpose flour

1 egg, at room temperature

Finely grated rind of 1 or 2 fresh lemons

Ingredients continued on next page.

The candied citrus fruits, currants, raisins, and cherries should be marinated in the rum for an hour or two, or overnight. It is best to do it in a jar with a tight cover so that you can turn it upside down and from side to side occasionally to soak all the fruits thoroughly (do it on a tray or dish in case the jar leaks).

Before preparing the dough, pour the fruits and rum into a large strainer set over a bowl to drain. Reserve the drained rum. Let stand.

Rinse a small bowl with hot water to warm it. Do not dry. Pour the 2 tablespoons of warm water into the bowl, sprinkle the yeast over the water, and add a pinch of the sugar. Stir with a fork or a table knife to mix and set aside at room temperature. (After about 10 to 15 minutes it will begin to rise.)

Pour the milk into a small, preferably narrow saucepan. Add the ¼ cup plus 2 tablespoons of sugar, the salt, and the 3 ounces of butter. Stir frequently over low heat until the mixture reaches 105° to 115° on a candy thermometer. Remove from the heat and add the almond extract.

Meanwhile, place 1¾ cups (reserve the remaining 1¼ cups) of the flour in the large bowl of an electric mixer. Add the warm milk, butter mixture, the egg, lemon rind, yeast, and the drained-off rum (reserve the fruits). Beat on moderate speed, scraping the bowl occasionally, for 8 to 10 minutes. Remove from the mixer.

Add the reserved 1¼ cups of flour and stir with a heavy wooden spoon to mix. (Or, if your mixer has a dough hook, you can add the full 3 cups of flour at once and beat with the dough hook for 8 to 10 minutes.)

Flour a large board or smooth work surface, turn the dough out, and knead it (see Kneading, page 222) for a few minutes until smooth. It will be necessary to add a bit more flour so you can handle it; add only enough to keep the dough from sticking.

Now, to incorporate the fruits and nuts: Add about ⅓ cup of them at a time and knead them in. Add more flour as necessary while you are kneading in the fruits and nuts, but not so much more that the dough becomes dry.

Form the dough into a ball, flour it lightly, place it in a large bowl, cover airtight with plastic wrap, and let rise (see Rising, page 222) for about 2 hours until almost double in bulk.

½ cup whole
blanched almonds

Additional flour

2 tablespoons additional
butter, at room
temperature (to be
used after baking)

Confectioners' sugar

Traditionally, a Stollen is shaped like an elongated monster Parker House roll, but this one is like a fat French bread loaf.

Flour a large board or work surface and a rolling pin. Make a fist and punch down the dough, folding the sides in toward the middle. Then turn it out onto the floured surface. With the rolling pin, roll it onto an oval shape measuring 15 x 9 inches. From one long side, roll it up like a jelly roll. Pinch the seam securely to hold it in place; be sure it is tightly sealed. (If it does not want to hold, dampen the edge with a bit of water.) Then, with your hands, roll the Stollen to taper the ends a bit, and then push the long sides together to mound it high in the middle. It should measure 16 inches in length and should be 3 inches across the middle.

If you have a nonstick cookie sheet or jelly-roll pan, place the Stollen on it diagonally. Otherwise, place it on a lightly floured buttered sheet or pan.

No matter which sheet or pan you have used, now place it on another sheet or pan to prevent the bottom from becoming too dark.

Push the long sides of the cake together again to shape it fat and high.

Cover the Stollen loosely with plastic wrap and let it rise again for 1½ hours (see Rising, page 222) until almost double in bulk.

Shortly before it has finished rising, adjust a rack to the center of the oven and preheat the oven to 350°.

Bake the Stollen for 45 minutes. If it starts to become too dark, cover it loosely with foil.

As soon as the Stollen is done, use a flat-sided cookie sheet to transfer it to a large rack placed over aluminum foil. Brush the additional 2 tablespoons of butter generously all over the hot cake and, without waiting, coat the top generously with confectioners' sugar, sprinkling it through a fine strainer; it should be a solid coating of sugar, not just a sprinkling.

Let the cake cool. Wrap it in plastic wrap and refrigerate for at least a few days before serving, or freeze it.

Just before serving, you may want to sugar the top again.

This should be cut into rather thin slices (about ⅜ inch thick). It is best to use a serrated bread knife.

Aunt Leah's Raspberry Squares

32 SQUARES

These are from Leah Snider, a wonderful cook and baker, in Detroit. They are made with a dough that must be refrigerated overnight. But there is no kneading and no rising. They are especially attractive and delicious and equally quick and easy. They are not too sweet and are wonderful as a coffee cake with breakfast or brunch, with a fruit salad at lunch, or at a tea party.

¼ cup warm water
(105° to 115°; see
Dissolving, page 222)

1 envelope active
dry yeast

3 cups sifted
all-purpose flour

¾ teaspoon salt

3 tablespoons
granulated sugar

8 ounces (2 sticks)
unsalted butter

1 egg

½ cup evaporated milk

Confectioners' sugar
(to be sprinkled over
the baked cakes)

Rinse a small cup in hot water to warm it. Dry it quickly, or just shake it out well. Pour in the warm water and sprinkle the yeast on top. Stir with a fork to mix and set aside.

Mix the flour, salt, and sugar in a large bowl. With a pastry blender cut in the butter until the particles are fine and the mixture resembles coarse meal.

Beat the egg and the milk just to mix, and add, along with the yeast, to the dry ingredients. Stir thoroughly to mix.

(The above steps—mixing the dry ingredients, cutting in the butter, and then mixing in the liquids and yeast—may all be done in a food processor if you wish.)

Transfer the mixture to a bowl, cover airtight, and refrigerate overnight.

Filling

Adjust a rack to the center of the oven and preheat the oven to 350°. Lightly butter a 10½ x 15½ x 1-inch jelly-roll pan. It should not be a non-stick pan.

Flour a pastry cloth and a rolling pin. Turn the dough out onto the cloth, form it into a ball, and cut it in half. Set aside and reserve one piece. Shape the other piece into a rectangle, flouring the dough and your hands as

1 pound (1½ cups) thick raspberry preserves

Finely grated rind of 1 large lemon

2½ ounces (½ cup) blanched almonds, chopped into medium-size pieces

necessary. Then, with the rolling pin, roll the dough out to measure 12 x 17 inches, keeping the corners as square as you can, and the sides as straight as you can. Loosely drape it over the rolling pin and transfer it to the buttered pan. With a small, sharp knife, trim the sides of the dough even with the top of the pan.

Mix the filling ingredients and spread over the dough. Go all the way to all edges. Set aside.

Flour the remaining dough, form it into a rectangle, and roll it out to measure about 10½ x 15½ inches. (This time don't worry about the corners or edges.) With a zigzag or a plain pastry wheel or with a pizza cutter, slice the rolled-out dough into lengthwise strips ½ inch wide. Place half of the strips on a diagonal ½ inch apart over the filling, pinching them off level with the rim of the pan. Place the remaining strips crisscrossing in the opposite directions, forming a lattice (or diamond) design. Pinch off these ends also.

With your fingers, fold over the dough around the edges. Fold it in toward the center to form a border about ½ inch wide all around. With a fork, press down on it lightly to seal.

Without waiting for the dough to rise, place the pan in the oven and bake for 25 to 30 minutes, until nicely colored.

Cool in the pan.

With a small, sharp knife cut the cake into squares and with a wide metal spatula transfer them to wax paper. Generously sprinkle confectioners' sugar over them, sprinkling it through a fine strainer held over the top.

Transfer to a serving plate.

These may be frozen.

SALLY LUNN

1 LARGE ROUND BREAD OR 2 SMALL LOAVES

There was a young lady from England who sold round, flat buns on the streets in the town of Bath toward the end of the eighteenth century. Some say that her name was Sally Lunn and the buns were named after her. Another story is that the round buns looked like the sun and the moon—soleil et lune in French. When she cried it out with her cockney accent, it sounded like sally lunn.

Enough history. Now, about this recipe. It is not for buns. It is for a large, light and airy, sweet bread, only slightly sweeter than plain bread—it is rich and delicious.

This is not really a dessert; it is a very plain coffee cake. Or serve it toasted at the table (to toast this, cut it in thick slices and toast in the oven) with room-temperature butter and marmalade or a thick honey spread. Serve it at a brunch, or luncheon, or a tea or coffee party.

This is extremely easy to make.

This can be baked in a 9-inch (10-cup) tube pan with or without (see Note) a fancy design, or in two 9 x 5 x 3-inch loaf pans.

4 cups *unsifted* all-purpose flour

⅓ cup plus 1 tablespoon granulated sugar

2 teaspoons salt

2 envelopes active dry yeast

1 cup milk

½ cup water

4 ounces (1 stick) unsalted butter, cut into pieces, at room temperature

3 eggs, at room temperature

In the large bowl of an electric mixer (or a larger bowl if you want to mix it by hand), place 1½ cups of the flour (reserve the remaining 2½ cups to add later). Add the sugar, salt, and dry yeast to the 1½ cups flour. Stir to mix.

In a saucepan, combine the milk, water, and butter. Stir over low heat until the mixture is warm (105° to 115° on a candy thermometer). Don't worry if the butter is not completely melted—it is okay.

Gradually pour the warm liquids into the dry ingredients, beating on low speed in a mixer, or stirring with a large wooden spoon. When it is incorporated, beat for 2 minutes in a mixer, or stir briskly by hand for 3 minutes.

Add the eggs and 1 more cup of the flour and beat or stir to mix. Then, in a mixer, beat for 2 minutes more, or stir by hand for 3 minutes more. Add the remaining 1½ cups flour and beat or stir to mix until smooth.

Scrape down the sides of the bowl with a rubber spatula. Cover the top of the bowl airtight with plastic wrap and set aside to rise (see Rising, page 222) for about 1 hour, or until the dough has doubled in volume.

Meanwhile, prepare a 9-inch (10-cup capacity) tube pan or two 9 x 5 x 3-inch loaf pans as follows: Butter the pan or pans—if the pan is a tube pan with a fancy design, the best way to butter it is with soft, not melted, butter, brushing it on with a pastry brush—then coat the pan or pans all

247

over with fine, dry bread crumbs. Tap to shake out excess crumbs over a piece of paper. Set aside.

When the dough has doubled, with a heavy wooden spoon stir it to deflate it completely; then stir for about half a minute. Pour the dough into the prepared pan or pans. Smooth the top or tops.

Now, to let this rise again: Butter a piece of plastic wrap and place it buttered side down over the top of the pan or pans. Set the dough to rise again (see Rising, page 222) for 30 to 40 minutes, or until double in volume. Even though the plastic wrap is buttered, when the dough rises it might stick, therefore, remove the plastic just before the dough reaches it and let the dough finish rising uncovered. (If you are now asking, "Then why butter it?" the answer is that if it does stick, it will stick less if the plastic is buttered. If the dough rises to touch the plastic, and if it is not buttered, peeling the plastic away might disturb the dough too much and cause it to deflate.) It should rise a scant 1 inch above the top of the pan, but watch it—this is a very lively mixture and it should not rise higher or it might run over the sides during baking.

About 20 minutes before the Sally Lunn is ready to be baked, adjust an oven rack one-third up from the bottom of the oven and preheat the oven to 375°. Bake for 35 to 40 minutes; after about 20 minutes of baking cover the top loosely with foil. When the bread is done, a cake tester inserted in the middle will come out clean and dry, the top of the bread will be richly browned, and if you tap it with your fingertips or knuckles it will make a hollow sound.

(If the bread is baked in a tube pan, during baking it will rise to about 3 inches above the top of the pan; however, when it is done, it will settle down to about 1 inch above the top.)

Cool in the pan or pans for about 3 minutes. Then cover with a rack, turn over the pan and rack, remove the pan, and leave the bread upside down to finish cooling.

This freezes perfectly.

VARIATION: *Sally Lunn with walnuts is unusual and delicious and I like it even better than the plain version. Cut or break 1 cup of walnuts into large pieces. Follow the above recipe, and add the nuts when you stir down the dough after the first rising.*

CREAM CHEESE COFFEE CAKE
10 TO 12 PORTIONS

This delicious, delicious cake is made from a rich and tender, slightly sweetened yeast dough, filled with a generous amount of cream cheese filling similar to a cheesecake, and topped with dark, shiny strips of dough, arranged to resemble a braid. It looks spectacular, it tastes sensational, it is a challenge—exciting, fun, gratifying—you will love it.

Actual preparation and baking time are little, but the dough is a slow riser; it takes 2 to 2½ hours to rise in a bowl before it is shaped and 1 hour to rise after it is shaped before it is baked.

The dough can be mixed in a food processor or it can be stirred by hand.

3 ounces (¾ stick) unsalted butter

⅔ cup warm water (105° to 115°; see Dissolving, page 222)

1 tablespoon plus ½ cup granulated sugar

2 envelopes active dry yeast

About 3 cups *unsifted* bread flour or *unsifted*, unbleached all-purpose flour

½ teaspoon salt

1 egg

Butter a 10- to 12-cup bowl for the dough to rise in; set aside. To mix the dough in a food processor, cut the butter into small pieces, melt it slowly in a small pan over very low heat, and then set it aside to cool but not to harden.

Meanwhile, measure the warm water in a 2-cup glass measuring cup, stir in 1 tablespoon of the sugar (reserve the remaining ½ cup of sugar), sprinkle on the yeast, stir with a knife to mix, and set aside for 5 to 10 minutes until the yeast rises to about the 1-cup line.

Place 3 cups of the flour, the salt, and the remaining ½ cup of sugar in the processor bowl fitted with a metal chopping blade. Process on/off once or twice to mix. In a 1-cup glass or plastic measuring cup (or anything small that has a spout), stir the egg into the melted butter to mix. Then start the processor again, and while it is going, add the egg-and-butter mixture and the yeast mixture (which may be stirred a bit to deflate—to make it easier to pour—if you wish). Process until the ingredients form a ball and then continue to process for 1 minute. (I have made this recipe many times with different flours, and 3 cups of flour was always the right amount. However, if the mixture is too sticky to handle, add a bit more flour, 1 teaspoon at a time; if it is too dry, add a bit more water, 1 teaspoon at a time.)

Flour a large work area lightly and knead the dough for 1 minute. Then place it in the buttered bowl, cover with plastic wrap, and place the bowl in a draft-free spot to rise (see Rising, page 222).

To mix the dough by hand, read the above directions and adapt them as follows. Melt and cool the butter, mix the yeast with the warm water and 1 tablespoon of the sugar, and let rise. Then in a large bowl mix the egg, melted butter, and the yeast mixture and gradually stir in as much of the remaining flour as you can. Place the balance of the flour on a large work surface, turn the dough out onto the flour, and knead until incorporated. Then knead for about 5 minutes until smooth and elastic. Place in the buttered bowl, cover, and let rise.

The dough should rise until more than doubled in volume. In my kitchen, 2 hours is the time it takes when I have used unbleached all-purpose flour; and 2½ hours when I have used bread flour.

CREAM CHEESE FILLING

1 tablespoon water

1 tablespoon granulated sugar

½ cup light raisins

1 tablespoon dark rum

16 ounces Philadelphia brand cream cheese, at room temperature

½ cup confectioners' sugar

1 egg yolk

½ teaspoon vanilla extract

Finely grated rind of 1 deep-colored orange or 1 very large lemon

⅓ cup apricot preserves (to be used later)

Stir the water and granulated sugar in a very small saucepan or frying pan over moderate heat. Bring to a boil, add the raisins, stir for 15 seconds, add the rum, and stir for 15 seconds more. Remove from the heat and set aside, stirring occasionally until cool. (There will be no liquid remaining, or almost none.)

In the small bowl of an electric mixer, beat the cheese until it is soft and smooth. Add the confectioners' sugar, yolk, and vanilla, and continue to beat until completely mixed. Remove the bowl from the mixer and stir in the grated rind and the prepared raisins (along with any remaining rum syrup even if it is a minute amount). Set aside.

When the dough has risen, punch it down, fold in the sides, and press on them to deflate. Turn the dough out onto a large, lightly floured work surface, knead it once or twice, form it into a square or oblong, cover loosely with plastic wrap, and let stand for 15 minutes.

This cake will be shaped and baked on a 15½ x 12½-inch cookie sheet. You will now line part of the cookie sheet with foil, which will line the section the cake is on and will also form little retainers at the two narrow ends of the cake, which is where the cheese filling might run out. Tear off a piece of aluminum foil about 4 inches longer than the cookie sheet. Fold the foil in half lengthwise, shiny side out. Butter the full length of one side of the folded foil and place the foil, buttered side up, in the middle of the sheet, lengthwise, with about 2 inches of overhang at each end. Set aside.

With a lightly floured rolling pin, roll the dough out until it is the size of the cookie sheet. This dough is elastic and it will resist you; just let it rest occasionally for a few minutes and then roll it again. Gently pull out the corners of the dough from time to time to keep it oblong, but if the shape turns out uneven you will be able to fix it (push the sides in or pull them out) with your fingers after it is on the cookie sheet.

Place the rolling pin along the narrow end of the dough and loosely roll the dough up around the pin to transfer it to the cookie sheet. Then unroll it onto the sheet (on top of the foil). Adjust the shape with your fingers to make it even and rather squared off on the corners.

In a small bowl, stir the preserves to soften and spread them over the dough, staying about 2 inches away from the edges (it will be a very thin layer of preserves).

With a spoon, place the cheese filling in a strip 4 inches away from the two narrow ends. Smooth the strip a bit but do not make it any wider than 4 inches.

With a ruler and the point of a small knife, mark 1-inch lengths along the long sides of the dough, then with a sharp knife cut through the dough at the marks, making cuts at right angles to the filling. Start the cuts a scant 1 inch away from the filling and cut through the outside border of the dough.

Now, to form an interwoven braid design on the top: Place the sheet in front of you with a short side of the sheet nearest to you. Start at the far end and bring each one of the strips up and over the filling, placing it at a slight downward angle. Cross first one side and then the other. Each strip seals and holds down the one before it. When you get to the last two strips, stretch them out gently to make them long enough to tuck under the sides of the cake. Wet their undersides with water to hold them in place, and with your fingers or a pastry brush, also dab a little water between the top and bottom of the dough at the end of the cake and press them together to seal. Finally, at each end of the cake, fold the overhanging foil in half to strengthen it. This will make the overhang about 1 inch. Then lift up the end of the foil and press it against the cake, pinching it together at both sides to keep it in place.

Cover the cake loosely with plastic wrap and set aside to rise (see Rising, page 222) for 1 hour. (The cake will rise more in the oven.)

About 20 minutes before baking, adjust a rack one-third up from the bottom of the oven and preheat the oven to 350°. Prepare the egg wash.

EGG WASH

1 egg yolk

Scant 1 tablespoon milk

Stir the yolk and milk to mix and pour through a fine strainer into a small cup.

Shortly before baking, brush the wash all over the top and sides of the cake, using a soft brush. Repeat, making two layers of the wash. Try not to allow the wash to run down onto the pan; use a paper napkin to soak up any that might run down.

Bake the cake for 28 to 30 minutes, until the top is beautifully browned, reversing the sheet front to back once after about 20 minutes if the cake is not browning evenly.

Cool the cake on the pan for about 10 minutes. Then, using a flat-sided cookie sheet as a large spatula, transfer the cake to a rack to cool.

If there are leftovers this can be refrigerated for a day or two and it will still be just as delicious. Or it can be frozen. The cake can be served cold or at room temperature.

DOUGHNUTS

24 TO 48 DOUGHNUTS, DEPENDING ON THE SIZE OF THE CUTTER

These doughnuts are light, moist, delicate, with a mahogany-colored crust and a shiny, almost transparent glaze all over.

This is a yeast dough made with mashed potatoes (a.k.a. spudnuts). After the dough rises, it is refrigerated for 2 to 24 hours. Then it is rolled out and cut into doughnut shapes.

At that point you have a choice: Either let the doughnuts rise for about 1½ hours and fry them, or refrigerate the doughnuts to be fried later in the day or the following day, or freeze the doughnuts for up to a week before frying. With all these options it is easy to serve doughnuts while they are still hot, when they are at their best. You can serve them fresh for breakfast (if you get up enough ahead of time).

Doughnuts are an American institution; making them in your own kitchen is a real thrill.

My large doughnut cutter measures 3½ inches in diameter and the hole in the middle is ¾ inch. It is available at Bridge Kitchenware.

You will need a deep-frying thermometer and, if possible, a household thermometer to take the room temperature.

¾ pound fresh white
potatoes (to make
1 cup, mashed)

About 1½ cups tap water

¼ cup warm water
(105° to 115°; see
Dissolving, page 222)

¾ cup granulated sugar

1 envelope active
dry yeast

1 teaspoon salt

About 6½ cups *unsifted*
all-purpose flour
or bread flour

4 ounces (1 stick)
unsalted butter, at
room temperature,
cut into small pieces

2 eggs

¾ teaspoon nutmeg

1 teaspoon vanilla extract

Fat for deep frying
(I use a 3-pound can
of solid Crisco)

Generously butter a 4- to 6-quart bowl for the dough to rise in; set it aside. Peel the potatoes, cut them into quarters or eighths, place them in a saucepan, add about 1½ cups tap water, cover, place over high heat until the water comes to a boil, and then reduce the heat and let simmer, partially covered, until the potatoes are tender when tested with a toothpick. Remove from the heat.

Meanwhile, place the ¼ cup warm water in a 1-cup glass measuring cup. Add 1 teaspoon of the sugar (reserve the remaining sugar) and the yeast. Stir a bit with a knife and let stand for about 10 minutes to rise.

Measure 1 cup of the warm potato water, pour it into the large bowl of an electric mixer, add the remaining sugar, the salt, and 1 cup of the flour (reserve the remaining flour). Beat well.

After the yeast mixture has risen an inch or two, beat it into the dough.

Drain the potatoes and mash them smoothly in a food processor or in the small bowl of an electric mixer or in the food mill. Measure 1 cup of the mashed potatoes (which should still be warm) and add it to the yeast mixture along with the butter, eggs, nutmeg, and vanilla. Beat until the butter is smoothly incorporated and the ingredients are thoroughly mixed. Then, gradually, on low speed, add the remaining flour—½ cupful at a time.

When the mixture begins to thicken so much that it crawls up on the beaters, remove the bowl from the mixer and, with a heavy wooden spoon, stir in more of the flour, adding only as much as can be stirred in.

Any remaining flour should be set aside on the far corner of a large board or work surface. Smooth a bit of it onto the middle of the work space. Turn the dough out onto the floured space. Start to knead the dough, adding the remaining flour (or more) as necessary to make a dough that you can knead. But do not add any more than you really must have. Knead for about 5 minutes until the dough is smooth, rubbery, and feels alive.

Form the dough into a ball, place it in the buttered bowl, turn the dough around to butter all sides of it, cover the bowl with plastic wrap, and place it in a warm, draft-free spot to rise until it is double in volume (see Rising, page 222).

Make a fist and punch down the risen dough, then fold in the sides and press down to deflate. Replace the dough in the bowl, cover airtight, and refrigerate for 2 to 24 hours.

Turn the dough out onto a floured pastry cloth, cut it in half, and work with one-half at a time, reserving the other half in the bowl in the refrigerator.

With a floured rolling pin, roll the dough out on a lightly floured pastry cloth until it is about ⅓ inch thick. (If the dough is rubbery and resists being rolled out, just let it rest for 5 to 10 minutes and then roll it again; repeat as necessary.)

With a floured doughnut cutter or with two floured round cookie cutters (one for the doughnut and one for the hole) cut out the doughnuts, start-ing at the outside edge of the dough and cutting right next to each other, in order not to have any more leftover scraps than necessary. (See Note.)

Roll and cut the remaining half of the dough.

Reserve the little rounds that made the holes in the doughnuts; fry those just as they are when you fry the doughnuts. Reserve all the other scraps, knead them together a bit, let rest briefly, then roll and cut.

Now, to fry the doughnuts without refrigerating or freezing (for frying at a future time), place them on cookie sheets lined with lightly oiled aluminum foil in a warm, draft-free spot to rise, uncovered, for about 1½ hours (see Rising, page 222). To refrigerate the doughnuts to be fried several hours later, or the following day, place them on cookie sheets lined with lightly oiled aluminum foil, cover them with plastic wrap, and refrigerate. To freeze them before frying, place them on the lightly oiled foil-lined sheets in the freezer until firm. Then wrap them airtight—indi-vidually, in plastic wrap—and return to the freezer.

Before frying either refrigerated or frozen doughnuts, bring them to room temperature, wrapped, then unwrap and place them on lightly oiled foil-lined sheets in a warm, draft-free spot for 1 to 1½ hours until double in size.

To fry the doughnuts, you will need a wide, rather shallow pan (about 10 by 3 inches is a good size). About 30 minutes before frying, place the fat (or oil, if you wish) in the pan (it should be about 1½ inches deep) and heat slowly to 365°.

Have ready two long forks or flat wire whisks for turning the doughnuts and for removing them from the fat. And have a wide metal spatula (pancake turner) ready to transfer the doughnuts to the fat. Have large brown paper bags ready for draining the doughnuts.

While the fat is heating, prepare the glaze.

GLAZE

1 pound (3¼ cups packed) confectioners' sugar

1 teaspoon vanilla extract

¼ teaspoon almond extract

About ¾ cup milk

NOTE: *Many experts say that you should press the cutter down firmly and then lift it up without wiggling it (the theory being that if you wiggle it, it squashes the sides together and the doughnuts will not rise properly). My cutter does not cut completely through without a wiggle or two—so I wiggle. But try it without wiggling.*

Place the sugar and flavorings in the small bowl of an electric mixer and gradually add the milk while beating. Add enough milk to make a thick but pourable mixture that forms a wide ribbon when poured. Cover and let stand.

Place a large rack over aluminum foil to glaze the doughnuts.

When everything is ready, dip the wide metal spatula into the hot fat to coat it and then gently slide it under a doughnut, pressing down against the foil (and away from the doughnut). Transfer to the hot fat and hold it briefly until the doughnut slides off.

Immediately add another doughnut to the fat. (After you have made a few you can try three or four at a time, but do just two at a time at first.)

Keep the thermometer in the fat and adjust the heat as necessary to maintain a 365° temperature. Fry the doughnuts for 2 minutes on one side, then turn them over gently with the two flat whisks or forks (without piercing the doughnuts) and fry on the other side for 2 minutes. They will become beautifully dark brown and extravagantly high and gorgeous, and they will probably have a pale streak around their middles.

With the flat whisks or a wide fork, lift a fried doughnut from the fat and place it on a brown paper bag to drain a bit (for less than a minute).

Quickly transfer it to the large rack set over foil and with a wide pastry brush generously brush the glaze all over the top and sides of the hot doughnut, then turn it over and glaze the other side. Repeat with the remaining doughnuts. Let them stand on the rack briefly until the glaze dries.

Serve immediately or let stand and serve later, but the fresher the better. "Get 'em while they're hot," if possible.

CINNAMON BUNS

12 VERY LARGE BUNS

Arlene Train of Albany, Oregon, sent this sensational recipe to me with a note saying, "They are wonderfully light and delicious and they disappear quickly." I don't think she would believe just how quickly. My husband lost all control with these. He ate more than I will tell. I hadn't planned it that way, but it was his dinner. Then he had to go to bed. A few hours later, he asked for more.

These are the largest, lightest, old-fashioned, country-style, sweet yeast rolls. Yeast loves potatoes. When yeast dough is made with potatoes, as this is, it becomes especially alive and fat and happy.

These are not really an after-dinner dessert; serve them as coffee cake, or a sweet bread.

1 cup mashed potatoes (see Notes)

1 cup milk

½ cup plus 1 tablespoon granulated sugar

½ teaspoon salt

2 ounces (½ stick) unsalted butter, cut up

¼ cup warm water (105° to 115°; see Dissolving, page 222)

1 envelope active dry yeast

1 egg

1 teaspoon vanilla extract

About 4¼ cups *unsifted* all-purpose flour or bread flour

Additional flour

Generously butter a 4- to 6-quart bowl for the dough to rise in; set it aside. Place the mashed potatoes (which may be warm or cool) in a saucepan and, stirring constantly, add the milk very gradually. Stir in ½ cup of the sugar (reserve the remaining 1 tablespoon of sugar), and the salt and butter. Place over low heat and stir occasionally until the mixture is warm (105° to 115°). It is not necessary for the butter to have melted completely.

Meanwhile, in a 1-cup glass measuring cup, stir the warm water with the remaining tablespoon of sugar, sprinkle on the yeast, stir briefly with a knife, and set aside for about 10 minutes until the mixture rises to about the ¾-cup line.

In a small bowl, beat the egg to mix and add the vanilla.

When the potato-and-milk mixture is warm enough, transfer it to the large bowl of an electric mixer. Beat in the yeast mixture and the egg. On low speed, gradually add about 3 cups of the flour. Beat on low speed for a minute or two. Remove the bowl from the mixer. The dough will be wet and sticky now. With a heavy wooden spoon, gradually stir in the remaining 1¼ cups of flour.

Flour a large work surface. Turn the dough out onto the floured surface. The dough will probably still be too sticky to knead. If it is, add a bit of additional flour and, with a dough scraper or a wide metal spatula, turn the dough over and over with the additional flour—adding still a bit more if necessary—until you can handle the dough. Then knead it for 5 minutes, again adding additional flour if necessary. (You might have to add a total of ½ to ¾ cup additional flour. But potato flour has a tendency to remain a bit sticky even when it has enough flour so do not use more than you must.) After about 5 minutes of active kneading, the dough should be smooth and feel alive.

Notes: *The mashed potatoes can be made with instant dry mashed potatoes or fresh potatoes. It takes about ¾ pound fresh potatoes to make 1 cup mashed. Peel, cut into chunks, place in a small saucepan with water, boil, partially covered, until tender, drain, and then mash the potatoes. If you are using fresh potatoes save the water they boiled in and use some of it for dissolving the yeast (first heat it as necessary); since yeast loves potatoes so much, this will make it extra happy.*

Place the dough in the buttered bowl, turn it around in the bowl to butter all sides, cover the bowl with plastic wrap, and place it in a warm, draft-free spot to rise for 1 to 1½ hours (see Rising, page 222), until the dough is at least double in volume.

Then make a fist, punch down the middle of the dough, and fold in and press down the sides of the dough to deflate it all. Turn the dough out onto a lightly floured surface, cover it loosely with plastic wrap, and let stand for about 10 minutes.

Meanwhile, butter a 15½ x 10½ x 1-inch jelly-roll pan.

With a long, heavily floured rolling pin, roll out the dough into about an 18-inch square. The dough will be rubbery and will resist you. Just let it stand occasionally for a few minutes and then roll it again. After a few tries it will do what you want.

Filling

2 tablespoons granulated sugar

1½ teaspoons cinnamon

¼ teaspoon nutmeg

1 ounce (¼ stick) unsalted butter, melted

5 ounces (1 cup) dark raisins, steamed (see Notes)

In a small bowl, mix the sugar with the cinnamon and nutmeg. With a wide pastry brush, or with the palm of your hand, spread the butter all over the surface of the rolled-out dough. With a large spoon, sprinkle the cinnamon-sugar on the dough, then sprinkle on the raisins.

With your hands, roll the dough up like a jelly roll. The roll of dough should be the same thickness all over; shape it as necessary.

Place the roll, seam down, in front of you. With a ruler and toothpicks mark the dough into 12 even pieces. With a sharp, heavy knife cut the pieces, using a sawing motion.

Place the pieces cut side down (and up) in the prepared pan, making 3 rows with 4 buns in each row.

Cover loosely with a lightweight towel and set to rise again for about 1 hour. During rising, the buns will rise and grow into each other.

(If the dough is rising in the oven, remove it about 20 minutes before the baking time and let stand, covered, at room temperature in a draft-free spot.)

NOTES: To steam the raisins, place them in a vegetable steamer or a strainer over shallow water in a saucepan. Cover, place over moderate heat, and let the water boil for about 5 minutes until the raisins are soft and moist. Then uncover and set the raisins aside until you are ready for them.

Adjust a rack one-third up from the bottom of the oven and preheat the oven to 375°.

Bake for about 12 minutes, then reverse the pan front to back and continue to bake for about 8 minutes more (total baking time, about 20 minutes), until the buns are nicely, but lightly, browned. (Do not overbake or the buns will dry out.)

Remove from the oven and let stand for about 5 minutes. Meanwhile, prepare the glaze.

GLAZE

1 tablespoon unsalted butter, at room temperature

¾ to 1 cup confectioners' sugar

Pinch of salt

½ teaspoon vanilla extract

A few drops almond extract

About 2 tablespoons light cream

In the small bowl of an electric mixer, beat all of the ingredients together until the mixture is smooth. It should be thick, barely thin enough to pour—adjust the cream and/or sugar as necessary.

Drip the glaze in a rather narrow stream every which way all over the warm buns.

Let stand until completely cool. (I think they are even better a few hours later.)

Just before serving, cut the rolls apart with a small, sharp knife and with a wide metal spatula remove them from the pan.

CINNAMON BUN FRENCH TOAST

If any of the above Cinnamon Buns have lasted long enough to become stale, they make divine French toast.

Cut each bun straight down into 3 wide slices. For each 2 portions use 2 buns, 1 egg, and ¼ cup of milk. Beat together the egg and milk, transfer to a shallow baking dish, add the slices, and let stand for about 30 minutes, turning the slices very carefully to keep them from falling apart. Then fry them in a wide frying pan in clarified butter. Turn them over gently, using a wide metal spatula in one hand and a fork in the other hand. Fry over moderate heat until golden brown (do not try to fry the top sides of the slices). Serve with warm maple syrup, or with marmalade.

Old Granddad Sticky Buns

24 buns

Light and airy, sticky and gooey, shiny, nutty, divine—they are great fun to make and they look sensational. When you make these you might decide to open a bakery, and if you carry these, the bakery will be a huge success.

It is best to use nonstick muffin pans—hardware stores and supermarkets have them. You need two pans, each for 12 standard-size muffins (buns).

½ cup warm water
(105° to 115°; see
Dissolving, page 222)

2 tablespoons
granulated sugar

1 envelope active
dry yeast

1 cup milk

About 4 cups *unsifted*
all-purpose flour
or bread flour

½ teaspoon salt

1 egg yolk

2 cups light brown
sugar, firmly packed

½ cup plus a few
teaspoons of
additional bourbon

4 ounces (generous 1
cup) large pecan halves,
toasted (see To Toast
Pecans, page 6)

2 ounces (½ stick) unsalted
butter, at room tempera-
ture (it must be soft)

2 teaspoons cinnamon

Butter a large bowl for the dough to rise in; set it aside. Stir the water and granulated sugar together in a 1-cup glass measuring cup, add the yeast, stir briefly with a knife, and set aside for about 10 minutes until foamy.

Place the milk in a small pan, over low heat, and warm it to 105° to 115°.

This dough can be made in a food processor or by hand.

To make it in a processor, fit the bowl with the metal chopping blade. Place about 3 cups of the flour in the processor bowl. Add the salt. Turn the motor on and, through the feed tube, add the egg yolk, gradually add the warm milk, and then the yeast mixture (which will have risen up near the top of the cup—incidentally, you can stir and deflate it before you add it to the flour mixture or you can pour it in just as it is). Process until the mixture forms a ball and comes away from the sides of the bowl, then continue to process for about 45 seconds more.

To mix this by hand, place about 3 cups of the flour in a large mixing bowl, add the salt, egg yolk, warm milk, and the yeast mixture, and beat well with a heavy wooden spoon (or electric mixer).

Whichever way you have mixed the ingredients, now place the remaining flour on a large work surface. Turn the dough out near the flour and knead, adding only as much of the flour as you need to be able to handle the dough. You probably will not use all of it.

If you prepare the dough in a processor, it needs only about 1 minute of kneading; otherwise, it needs about 5 minutes of kneading.

When the dough becomes smooth and feels alive, form it into a ball and place it in the buttered bowl, turn the dough around in the bowl to butter all sides of it, cover the bowl with plastic wrap, and set it to rise in a draft-free spot where the temperature is about 80° to 85° (see Rising, page 222). The dough should rise until it doubles in volume; it will take 45 to 60 minutes.

Meanwhile, prepare the muffin pans. Butter the pans generously (use additional butter to the ½ stick called for). Place a rounded tablespoonful of the light brown sugar in each pan (that should use up about half of the sugar—reserve the balance). Place a teaspoon of bourbon in each pan to wet the sugar. Place 3 pecan halves in each pan, rounded sides down. Set the pans aside.

When the dough has risen, make a fist, punch down the middle of the dough, fold over the sides and press them in, and then turn the dough out onto a lightly floured surface. Knead it just two or three times, cover it loosely with plastic wrap, and let stand for about 10 minutes.

Cut the dough in half, set aside and cover one piece, and place the other piece on the lightly floured surface. Flour a rolling pin and roll the dough out into a rectangle 10 x 12 inches. As you roll the dough, occasionally use your fingers and gently pull out the corners of the dough to make a rectangle with squared corners.

With a narrow metal spatula or the back of a spoon, spread 1 ounce of the soft butter over the dough. With your fingers, sprinkle half of the remaining brown sugar over the butter. Then sprinkle lightly with a few teaspoons of the additional bourbon. Then, through a fine strainer, sprinkle 1 teaspoon of the cinnamon (reserve the remaining teaspoon of cinnamon for the other pan) all over the surface.

Roll the dough up tightly like a jelly roll, starting at a 12-inch side. With a ruler and the tip of a small, sharp knife mark the roll into 12 equal pieces.

When you cut this roll into pieces, the dough will want to stick to the knife, causing the slices to squash (which really will not matter a bit). But to avoid some of the sticking and squashing, spray the knife blade with Pam before making the first cut (and possibly one more time after making several additional cuts). Cut into 12 pieces.

Flatten each piece slightly, cut side up (and down), either by pressing it between your hands or by pressing it against the work surface with your fingertips.

Place the pieces cut side up (and down) in the prepared muffin pan. Cover the pan loosely with plastic wrap and place in a draft-free spot, preferably where the temperature is about 80°, and let stand to double in volume.

Prepare the second panful, and let it rise too. It will take about 35 minutes, more or less, for the buns to rise.

Before baking, adjust a rack one-third up from the bottom of the oven and place a large piece of aluminum foil on the rack below to catch any syrup that might bubble over. Or, if your oven does not have another rack below, place the foil on the floor of the oven. Preheat the oven to 375°.

Bake these only one pan at a time; first bake the ones you shaped first—the others can wait. Bake for about 25 minutes until the buns are beautifully browned (they will rise magically during baking).

As soon as you remove a pan from the oven, immediately cover it with a cookie sheet and turn the pan and the sheet over; hold the pan upside down for a moment, to allow the syrup to run out onto the sheet, then with two wide metal spatulas (or what have you) pick up any nuts that fell off, place them on the buns, and scrape up any syrup that runs onto the cookie sheet and replace it on top of the buns.

When the syrup stops running, use the spatulas to transfer the buns to a dish or tray.

Let the buns cool for about 20 minutes, or completely, before serving.

Aren't they gorgeous? And delicious?

Leftovers may be frozen. Place them on a foil-covered tray, freeze the buns, and then cover airtight with plastic wrap. Thaw before uncovering.

CAROL'S CRESCENTS
80 CRESCENTS

Carol Whiteside is a charming young lady who loves to bake so much that she fulfilled a popular American dream; she went into a dessert business from her home, in Lawrenceville, New Jersey. She specializes in a variety of popular chocolate chip cookies (Carol's are thick and chewy—very different from the usual because they contain ground nuts), lemon cake (East 62nd Street Lemon Cake, to be exact, on page 20), and these crescents.

Traditionally these are also called nut horns, or rugelach. Variations of these (with yeast, without yeast, with cream cheese, without cream cheese) came to America from Europe generations ago with many of our ancestors. They are popular now with home cooks and with bakery cooks and at classy takeout food stores all over the country.

They are delicate, crisp, flaky, cinnamon-nutty, bite-size pastries; wonderful with tea or coffee, or along with a fruit or ice cream dessert. Or to wrap as a gift. They take time and patience and are a creative pastime.

The dough must be refrigerated overnight before it is shaped and baked.

DOUGH

8 ounces (2 sticks) unsalted butter

1 tablespoon granulated sugar

1 envelope active dry yeast

3 egg yolks

1 teaspoon vanilla extract

¼ teaspoon almond extract

1 teaspoon salt

1 cup sour cream

3 cups *unsifted* all-purpose flour

In a 10- or 12-cup heavy saucepan, over low heat, melt the butter. Remove from the heat. Stir in the sugar. Cool to lukewarm (105° to 115°). Then sprinkle on the yeast and stir briefly with a knife. Let stand for 5 minutes. Add the yolks, vanilla and almond extracts, salt, and sour cream, and stir with a wire whisk until smooth. Add the flour and stir with a wooden spoon until incorporated.

Now, process half of the dough at a time in a food processor with the metal chopping blade (or process it all at once in the large-size processor) for 45 seconds, or just stir and beat it well by hand for a few minutes.

Place the dough in a buttered bowl (the dough will rise only very little, therefore it is necessary for the bowl to be only slightly larger than the volume of dough), cover with plastic wrap, and refrigerate overnight.

Any time before shaping the dough, prepare the filling.

FILLING

4 ounces (generous 1 cup) walnuts

1 cup granulated sugar

3½ teaspoons cinnamon

6 ounces (1¼ cups) currants

The walnuts must be chopped until very fine; they should not be ground. It is best to chop them on a large board using a long, heavy chef's knife. Some of the pieces will be larger than others; the large pieces should not be larger than grains of rice.

In a bowl, stir the chopped nuts with the sugar and cinnamon. Set aside.

To plump the currants, cover them with boiling water, let stand for 3 to 4 minutes, strain, and then spread them out on paper towels to dry. Pat the tops a bit with paper towels and set aside. (Do not add the currants to the nut mixture.)

When you are ready to bake, adjust one rack to the middle of the oven (for one sheet) or adjust two racks to divide the oven into thirds (for two sheets). Preheat the oven to 350°. Line cookie sheets with parchment paper or with aluminum foil shiny side up (the paper is better but the foil will do).

With a strong, heavy metal spoon, or with a wooden spoon, remove the dough from the bowl and place it on a countertop or work surface (it will be sticky and stiff and difficult to transfer). With your hands, press it together, knead it for a few moments, and form it into a fat sausage. Mark and then cut the sausage shape into 5 equal pieces. Wrap them individually in plastic wrap or wax paper and refrigerate.

Place about one-fifth of the sugar-cinnamon-nut mixture on an unfloured pastry cloth. Unwrap 1 piece of the dough and place it on the sugar mixture. Press down on the dough with the palm of your hand to flatten the dough, turn it over and press with your hand again to coat both the top and the bottom of the round of dough thoroughly with the sugar mixture.

Then, with a rolling pin, roll out the dough until it is a very thin round, 11 or 12 inches diameter. The dough may be turned over a few times to keep both sides well sugared. While rolling, if a crack forms at the edge, pinch it together before it becomes too large.

Sprinkle one-fifth of the currants on the round of dough, placing them more heavily around the outside of the dough than at the center.

With a very long, sharp, heavy knife cut the dough into 16 pie-shaped wedges. (Use the full length of the blade and cut straight down; first cut into quarters and then cut each quarter into 4 wedges—cutting all the way across the round each time.)

With your fingers, roll each wedge from the outside toward the point. Place the rolls 1 inch apart, point down, on the lined sheets. (Some of the currants should peep out at the edges.)

Cover the sheet loosely with plastic wrap and let stand at room temperature for 10 to 15 minutes before baking. Do not look for these to rise.

You can bake either one or two sheets at a time. If you have only one sheet in the oven, reverse it front to back once during baking to ensure even browning. If you have two sheets in the oven, reverse them top to bottom and front to back, as necessary, to ensure even browning. Bake for 20 to 25 minutes until the crescents are lightly colored all over; they should not be too pale. (They will rise only slightly during baking.)

If you have used parchment paper, the crescents can be lifted off as soon as they come out of the oven; if you have used foil, the crescents should stand on the foil for a few minutes until they can be lifted off easily. Cool the crescents on racks.

Repeat the directions to shape and bake the remaining dough.

These are best when they are very fresh, but they can be frozen.

ZWIEBACK

The name is German for "twice baked." It originated as a way of using up stale rolls. But in Miami Beach it is so popular that bakeries make fresh rolls specifically for Zwieback, and they can't make it fast enough. It is indeed twice baked to make very hard, dry, brittle, crisp, crunchy, only slightly sweetened crackers. Wonderful with tea or coffee or just to have around for a nibble any time.

¼ cup warm water
(105° to 115°)

½ cup granulated sugar

1 envelope active dry yeast

1 cup milk

2 ounces (½ stick) unsalted butter, at room temperature, cut into small pieces

About 4 cups *unsifted* all-purpose flour or bread flour

1 teaspoon salt

¾ teaspoon nutmeg

1 egg

Butter a bowl with about a 3-quart capacity and set it aside to have ready for the dough to rise in. Place the water in a 1-cup glass measuring cup. Add 1 teaspoon of the sugar (reserve the remaining sugar) and the yeast, stir with a knife, and set aside at room temperature to rise about an inch or two.

Place the milk and butter in a small saucepan over moderate heat to warm to 105° to 115°. It is not necessary for the butter to melt completely.

To make this in a food processor, fit the machine with the metal chopping blade. Place about 3½ cups of the flour in the processor bowl (reserve the remaining ½ cup of flour), add the salt, the nutmeg, and the remaining sugar, and process on/off once or twice to mix; then, through the feed tube, add the warm milk and butter, the egg, and the yeast mixture (which may be stirred down before it is added or not). Process until the mixture forms a ball. If it is sticky, add all or part of the remaining ½ cup of flour (as necessary) through the feed tube to make a mixture that can be kneaded. Process for about 45 seconds.

To make this without a processor, in a large bowl beat the egg to mix, mix in the warm milk and butter, the yeast mixture, and then about 3½ cups of the flour, the salt, nutmeg, and the remaining sugar. If the mixture is too sticky to knead, add all or part of the remaining flour (as necessary).

Whichever way you have reached this stage, now flour a work surface and turn the dough out onto the floured surface. If the dough was made in a processor, knead it for about 5 minutes, adding additional flour if necessary.

Form the dough into a ball, place it in the buttered bowl, turn it around and around to butter all sides of it, cover with plastic wrap, and set aside to rise (see Rising, page 222) for about 1 hour until doubled in volume.

Then make a fist, punch down the dough, fold in the sides and press down to deflate, turn out onto a lightly floured surface, and form into an even oblong. With a large knife cut the dough into 12 even pieces.

Line two large cookie sheets with parchment paper or with foil shiny side up.

Pick up 1 piece of the dough. Flatten it between your hands. Then, to shape it into a round ball, fold the sides in—tuck them under—toward the bottom and pinch them together (on what will be the bottom of the ball shape).

Shape all of the pieces and place them, pinched sides down, on the two sheets, 6 on each sheet.

Lightly oil or butter two pieces of plastic wrap large enough to cover the balls of dough and place them oiled side down. (Or, if you prefer, sift a little flour over the balls of dough to prevent sticking, and then cover with plastic wrap.)

Set aside to rise in a warm, draft-free spot, for 1 to 1½ hours until double in volume.

Adjust two racks to divide the oven into thirds. (If you are using the oven as a place for the rolls to rise, it is all right to remove the rolls from the oven about 20 minutes before baking and let the sheets stand at room temperature in a draft-free spot.) Preheat the oven to 400°.

Bake the two sheets of rolls at 400° for 10 minutes. (If the rolls on one sheet brown more than the other, reverse the sheets top to bottom during this phase of baking.) Then reduce the temperature to 350°, open the oven door a crack to allow it to cool a bit, and bake for 15 minutes more (total baking time is 25 minutes).

Remove from the oven and transfer the rolls to racks to cool completely.

The rolls will slice better if they are chilled first, either in the refrigerator or freezer.

Meanwhile, heat the oven to 300°.

With a very sharp knife, or a serrated knife, slice the rolls, cutting straight down. Traditionally Zwieback is cut into slices ½ inch wide; I usually cut it a little bit thinner.

Place the slices cut side down (and up) on cookie sheets and bake, 30 to 45 minutes, reversing the sheets top to bottom and front to back occasionally, and turning the slices over as necessary for the Zwieback to become lightly golden on both sides by the time they feel completely hard to the touch.

Let stand to cool. Store airtight.

Chocolate Bread

1 LARGE LOAF

I am so in love with making yeast breads and cakes that for about a year when I started this book, I thought it was going to be a yeast book. But then one day, a new ice cream was born in our kitchen, and several other things came along, as they do, and I saw that it was not to be a yeast book. But this recipe, which is a bread and not a dessert, refuses to be left out of this book of desserts.

It is a huge loaf that makes giant-size slices, light and airy in texture, dark as pumpernickel in color. It has a few raisins and nuts. Serve it lightly buttered, or use it for cream cheese or peanut butter and bacon sandwiches, or serve it at the table with honey butter (mix ½ cup of honey into ¼ pound of unsalted butter).

Generously butter a large bowl to have ready for the dough to rise in. And butter an 8-cup loaf pan (mine is 9¼ x 5¼ x 2⅓ inches). Set the bowl and the pan aside.

Stir the water and 1 tablespoon of the sugar (reserve the remaining ½ cup of sugar) in a 1-cup glass measuring cup, add the yeast, stir briefly with a knife, and set aside for about 10 minutes, until foamy.

Meanwhile, place the milk and butter in a small saucepan over moderate heat until warm (105° to 115°). It is not necessary for the butter to melt.

¼ cup warm water
(105° to 115°)

1 tablespoon plus ½
cup granulated sugar

1 envelope active
dry yeast

1 cup milk

2 tablespoons *unsalted*
butter, cut into pieces

About 4 cups *unsifted*
all-purpose flour
or bread flour

1 teaspoon salt

⅔ cup unsweetened
cocoa powder (preferably
Dutch-process)

2 teaspoons powdered
(not granular) instant
coffee or espresso

2 eggs

1 teaspoon vanilla extract

4 ounces (generous 1
cup) walnuts, cut into
¼- to ⅓-inch pieces

2½ ounces (½ cup)
dark raisins

Place the scant 4 cups of flour, the salt, cocoa, coffee, and the remaining ½ cup of sugar in a large mixing bowl. Stir to mix.

Beat the eggs just to mix, and add them to the flour mixture along with the vanilla, warm milk and butter, and the foamy yeast mixture. Add the walnuts and the raisins. Stir as well as you can with a long, heavy wooden spatula. (Or mix these ingredients in a large-size food processor, or in a mixer with a dough hook.)

Turn out onto a lightly floured board and knead for 5 or 6 minutes until smooth and elastic. (If you have used a food processor or an electric mixer, a minute or two of kneading will probably be enough.) Add additional flour (very little at a time), if necessary, to make the dough manageable.

Place the dough in the large, well-buttered bowl, turn the dough to butter it on all sides; cover with plastic wrap, and let rise at a temperature of 80° to 85° (see Rising, page 222) until the dough has doubled in volume—it will take 1¼ to 2 hours.

Make a fist, punch it into the dough, knead the dough three or four times, and turn the dough out onto a lightly floured board. Cover with plastic wrap and let stand for about 5 minutes.

To shape the dough, form it roughly into an oval and, with a rolling pin, roll it out into a large oval 8 or 9 inches across the narrow width. Then roll it up the way you would a jelly roll, rolling from one narrow end to the other narrow end, and place the loaf, seam side down, in the buttered pan.

Loosely cover the pan with a piece of buttered plastic wrap, buttered side down. Let rise again until doubled in size—it will take 1¼ to 1½ hours.

Before the dough has finished rising, adjust a rack one-third up from the bottom of the oven and preheat the oven to 350°.

Bake the loaf for 20 to 30 minutes, then cover the top loosely with foil to prevent overbrowning. Continue to bake for 30 to 40 minutes (total baking time is about 60 minutes).

Let the loaf cool in the pan for 5 to 10 minutes and then lift it gently with pot holders to remove it from the pan and place it on a rack to cool.

Sweet
Breads

ZUCCHINI LOAF FROM SEATTLE

14 TO 16 SLICES

When we stopped at a restaurant named E.A.T., in Seattle, I spotted several large, dark loaves that looked homemade. After two thick slices that turned out to be my lunch, I started asking questions. They told me it was zucchini (I never would have guessed), they gave me the recipe (which I have since divided by six), and they said that they are not connected with any other business by the same name (they never heard of the one in New York). This is sweet enough to be a plain cake or a coffee cake; it can also be served as a sweet bread. It is deliciously moist, is wonderful for a gift, and has gotten top ratings from the friends I have served it to.

3 cups sifted
all-purpose flour

Scant 1 teaspoon salt

1 teaspoon baking soda

½ teaspoon
baking powder

3 teaspoons cinnamon

Scant 1 pound zucchini
(to make 2 packed cups,
shredded; see Note)

2 eggs

2 cups granulated sugar

1 cup vegetable oil

1 teaspoon vanilla extract

4 ounces (generous
1 cup) walnuts,
cut or broken into
medium-size pieces

Adjust an oven rack one-third up from the bottom of the oven and preheat the oven to 350°. Butter a 10 x 5 x 3-inch loaf pan, or any other bread-loaf pan that has a 10-cup capacity (measured to the very top of the pan). Or, if you wish, use two smaller pans. Dust the pan or pans with fine, dry bread crumbs and tap to shake out excess crumbs over paper. Sift together the flour, salt, baking soda, baking powder, and cinnamon, and set aside.

Wash the zucchini well under running water, scrubbing with a vegetable brush, and cut off both ends. Now to grate it, either use the coarse grater attachment of a food processor, or use the large round openings of a metal grater. Either way, the zucchini should be grated into julienne-shaped slivers; it should not be puréed. Do not drain. Press it firmly into a 2-cup measuring cup; you should have 2 firmly packed cups. Set aside. It is not necessary to use an electric mixer for this, but if you would like to you can. In a large bowl, beat the eggs just to mix. Mix in the sugar, oil, and vanilla. Add the sifted dry ingredients and beat/stir to mix. It will be thick. Then add the zucchini along with any juice that has collected and mix thoroughly with a wooden spoon—the zucchini will thin the batter. Stir in the nuts.

Turn into the prepared pan or pans, smooth the top or tops, and bake. In the one large pan it will take 1 hour and 45 to 50 minutes or a few minutes longer; in two smaller pans it will take slightly less time. Either way, bake until a cake tester gently inserted into the middle comes out clean and dry. (It will rise high and form a crack in the top.)

Cool in the pan for 15 minutes. Then cover with a rack, turn over the rack and the cake pan, remove the pan, and turn over again, leaving the cake right side up.

Note: You can use any zuc-chini for this, either young and small or old and large. It is a delicious way to use up zuc-chini from your garden that has grown to a monster size.

Let stand until cool. It will probably be best to cut this with a serrated bread knife.

Joan's Pumpkin Loaf
14 to 16 slices

The first time I ate this there was also a huge tray piled high with California crabs and a marvelous string bean salad, and although the whole meal was memorable, I especially remember getting up for more and more slices of this pumpkin loaf that made me an addict with the first bite. It is so good, there ought to be a law . . .

2½ cups sifted
all-purpose flour

2 teaspoons baking soda

½ teaspoon salt

1½ teaspoons cinnamon

½ teaspoon ground cloves

2 eggs

2 cups granulated
sugar, or light brown
sugar, firmly packed

½ cup vegetable oil
(Mazola, peanut oil,
corn oil, or any one of
the health-food oils
that has no flavor)

Ingredients continued on next page.

Adjust an oven rack one-third up from the bottom of the oven and preheat the oven to 350°. Butter a 10 x 5 x 3-inch loaf pan, or any other loaf pan that has a 10-cup capacity, measured to the very top of the pan. Or use two or more smaller pans if you wish. Dust the pan (or pans) with fine, dry bread crumbs, and tap over a piece of paper to shake out excess crumbs.

Sift together the flour, baking soda, salt, cinnamon, and cloves, and set aside.

It is not necessary to use an electric mixer for this, although you can if you wish (I do). In any large bowl, beat the eggs just to mix. Add the sugar and oil and beat lightly just to mix. Mix in the pumpkin and then the dates. Now add the sifted dry ingredients and stir, mix, or beat only until they are smoothly incorporated. Stir in the nuts.

Turn into the prepared pan (or pans) and smooth the top (tops).

Bake for 1½ hours in the large pan, less time in smaller pans (in two 8½ x 4½ x 2¾-inch [6-cup capacity] pans, bake for 65 to 70 minutes), until a cake tester gently inserted into the middle comes out just barely clean.

Cool in the pan (pans) for 15 minutes. Cover with a rack, turn over the rack and the pan, remove the pan, and then turn the loaf right side up again on a rack. Let stand until cool.

1 pound (2 cups) canned pumpkin (solid pack, not pumpkin-pie filling)

8 ounces (1 cup) pitted dates, each date cut into 2 or 3 pieces—no smaller (see Note)

4 ounces (generous 1 cup) walnuts, cut or broken into medium-size pieces

NOTE: *It will be a more delicious loaf if you use whole dates and cut them yourself rather then using the diced dates— they are too sweet and the pieces too small.*

Now, if you can wait, wrap the loaf (loaves) in plastic wrap and refrigerate for a day or two, or freeze.

To serve, cut into slices a generous ½ inch thick. If you do not wait for the loaf to age a day or two, it is best to cut it with a serrated bread knife.

DATE-NUT LOAF

ONE 9-INCH LOAF

This is an all-American classic—very popular, very delicious, and a wonderful loaf to make as a gift. Although this is sweet enough to be a cake, it is often served as a sweet bread.

8 ounces (1 packed cup) pitted dates

5 ounces (1 cup) raisins (they may be half dark and half light, or all dark)

1 teaspoon baking soda

1 cup boiling water

Adjust a rack one-third up from the bottom of the oven and preheat the oven to 350°. Butter an 8 or 9 x 4½-inch or 5 x 3-inch loaf pan or any loaf pan with at least a 6-cup capacity. Dust all over with fine, dry bread crumbs, then, over a piece of paper, tap to shake out excess crumbs.

Cut the dates into medium-size pieces (each date should be cut into 4 or 5 pieces); if you wish, cut with scissors frequently dipped into cold water to keep them from sticking. Place the dates and raisins in a mixing bowl.

Dissolve the baking soda in the boiling water and pour it over the dates. Stir to mix, then let stand until tepid.

4 ounces (1 stick)
unsalted butter

1 teaspoon vanilla extract

1 cup granulated sugar

¼ teaspoon salt

Optional: ½ teaspoon
powdered instant
espresso or other
powdered instant
coffee (see Note)

1 egg

1⅓ cups sifted
all-purpose flour

7 ounces (1¾ cups)
walnut or pecan halves
or large pieces

NOTE: *If you use granular
instead of powdered coffee,
dissolve it in the boiling water
with the baking soda to pour
over the dates, instead of adding it to the butter mixture.*

In the large bowl of an electric mixer, cream the butter. Add the vanilla, sugar, salt, and optional coffee, and beat well. Add the egg and beat well. On low speed add the flour, scraping the bowl with a rubber spatula and beating only until incorporated. Remove from the mixer.

Add some of the liquid from the dates and raisins and stir it in well; add most of the remaining liquid and stir it in. Then add all of the dates and raisins and stir well. Stir in the nuts.

Pour into the prepared pan and smooth the top. The batter might fill the pan to about ½ inch from the top.

Bake for about 1½ hours. About 30 minutes before the baking time is over, check to see if the top is becoming too dark; if so, cover loosely with foil. To test for doneness, insert a small, sharp paring knife into the center of the loaf almost all the way to the bottom; when the knife comes out clean, the loaf is done.

Cool in the pan for 20 to 30 minutes. Cover with a rack, turn over the pan and rack, remove the pan, and carefully turn the loaf right side up to cool. When it is completely cool, wrap in plastic wrap or foil and refrigerate at least overnight, or freeze it for about an hour. (This can be sliced, and even served, while it is frozen.)

APPLESAUCE LOAF
ONE 9- OR 10-INCH LOAF

Long ago when I started teaching, this is one of the first recipes I taught. A friend just told me that she has been making it all those years—I had forgotten it. It is one of the best-looking loaves and one of the most delicious. Dark, firm, solid, compact, loaded with nuts and raisins, it is a delicious plain tea or coffee cake, and may also be served at the table with butter, or used for sandwiches. It is a lovely loaf to make for a gift. (It is made with both white and whole wheat flour.) You will need a pan with an 8-cup capacity; I especially like one that measures 10¼ x 3¾ (width at top) x 3⅜ inches (in depth), but you can use any other loaf pan with the same capacity.

5 ounces (1 cup) raisins

1 cup *unsifted* all-purpose white flour (stir to aerate before measuring)

6 ounces (1½ cups) walnuts, cut or broken into halves or large pieces

½ teaspoon salt

1½ teaspoons cinnamon

1 teaspoon baking powder

1 teaspoon baking soda

1 teaspoon powdered instant espresso or other powdered (not granular) instant coffee

4 ounces (1 stick) unsalted butter

¾ cup light or dark brown sugar, firmly packed

2 eggs

1¼ cups sweetened or unsweetened applesauce

1 cup *unsifted* all-purpose whole wheat flour

Adjust an oven rack to the center of the oven and preheat the oven to 350°. Butter a 9 x 5 x 3-inch or 10¼ x 3¾ x 3⅜-inch loaf pan with an 8-cup capacity, dust it with fine, dry bread crumbs, and tap to shake out excess over a piece of paper. Set aside.

Place the raisins in a large mixing bowl. Add 2 or 3 tablespoons of the white flour to the raisins (reserve the remaining flour) and, with your hands, toss to coat the raisins with flour. Add the nuts and toss again. Set aside.

Sift the reserved white flour together with the salt, cinnamon, baking powder, baking soda, and powdered instant coffee. Set aside.

In the large bowl of an electric mixer, beat the butter until it is soft. Add the sugar and beat to mix. Mix in the eggs and then add the applesauce and beat to mix. On low speed, add the whole wheat flour and the sifted ingredients and, scraping the bowl with a rubber spatula, beat only until smoothly incorporated. Remove from the mixer and stir in the floured raisins and nuts, and any flour remaining in the bowl.

Turn into the prepared pan, smooth the top, and then, with the back of a spoon, form a shallow trench down the length (it keeps the loaf from rising too high in the middle).

Bake for about 1 hour and 5 minutes, until a cake tester gently inserted into the middle comes out clean and dry. (The loaf will form a shallow crack on top—okay.)

Cool in the pan for 10 minutes, cover with a rack, turn over the pan and the rack, remove the pan, and then very carefully turn the loaf right side up to cool on the rack.

Wrap the cooled loaf and refrigerate it for a few hours or overnight (it slices better if it has been chilled).

Whole Wheat Banana Bread
One 9-inch loaf

Of the many sweet breads, banana bread seems to be the most popular. There is one secret to any banana bread: The bananas must be fully ripened or the bread will not have enough, if any, banana flavor. This one is quick and easy and deliciously moist.

1 cup sifted all-purpose whole wheat flour (see Note)

½ cup sifted all-purpose white flour

1 teaspoon baking soda

¾ teaspoon salt

½ teaspoon mace

About 3 ripe bananas (to make 1⅓ cups, mashed)

¼ cup buttermilk

4 ounces (1 stick) unsalted butter

½ teaspoon vanilla extract

¾ cup dark or light brown sugar, firmly packed

1 egg

Finely grated rind of 1 large lemon

4 ounces (1 cup) pecans or walnuts, cut or broken into medium-size pieces

Adjust a rack to the center of the oven and preheat the oven to 350°. Butter a 9 x 5 x 3-inch loaf pan and dust it all with wheat germ or with fine, dry bread crumbs. Tap to shake out excess crumbs over a piece of paper. Set aside.

Sift together both flours, the baking soda, salt, and mace, and set aside.

Mash the bananas either on a plate with a fork, in a food processor, in a blender (in a processor or blender be careful not to liquefy the bananas), or in the small bowl of an electric mixer. You need 1⅓ cups. Stir the bananas and buttermilk to mix and set aside.

In the large bowl of an electric mixer (if you used the mixer for mashing the bananas it is not necessary to wash the beaters), cream the butter. Beat in the vanilla and the sugar. Add the egg and beat well. On low speed, add the sifted dry ingredients in three additions alternately with the banana mixture in two additions, scraping the bowl as necessary and beating only until incorporated after each addition.

Remove the bowl from the mixer and stir in the grated rind and the nuts.

Turn into the prepared pan and smooth the top.

Bake for 50 to 55 minutes, until a cake tester inserted into the middle comes out clean and dry.

Let cool in the pan for about 20 minutes.

Cover with a rack, turn the pan and the rack over, remove the pan and very gently (the loaf is delicate—do not squash it) turn the loaf over again, leaving it right side up to cool.

If there is time, wrap the loaf in plastic wrap and refrigerate overnight before serving. This is especially good sliced rather thick and well toasted—it becomes very crisp and crunchy; it is best to toast it on a cookie sheet under the broiler.

Note: *When you sift whole wheat flour, some of the flour may be too coarse to go through the sifter. That part should be stirred into the part that did go through.*

Cuban Banana Bread
One 10-inch Loaf

Hundreds of loaves of this were sold at a street festival in Little Havana in Miami (they could have sold many more if they had them), and thick slices of it were served along with small cups of strong black coffee, and everyone loved it. It is moist, dark, chewy, coarse (it has bran in it), crunchy, dense, and not too sweet. Serve it as a coffee cake or a sweet bread, or make cream cheese sandwiches with it, or peanut butter, or peanut butter and bacon. Or make it to give as a gift; it is beautifully shaped, richly colored, and mucho delicious.

1½ cups sifted
all-purpose flour

1 teaspoon salt

2 teaspoons
baking powder

½ teaspoon baking soda

2 ounces (½ stick)
unsalted butter

1 teaspoon vanilla extract

½ cup dark brown sugar

1 egg

1 cup bran cereal
(not flakes—I use
Kellogg's All-Bran)

3 to 4 medium-size,
thoroughly ripe bananas
(to make 1½ cups
mashed—see directions in
the recipe for mashing)

2 tablespoons water

½ cup raisins

4 ounces (generous 1 cup)
walnuts, cut or broken
into medium-size pieces

Adjust a rack one-third up from the bottom of the oven and preheat the oven to 350°. Butter a 10¼ x 3¾ x 3⅜-inch loaf pan (see page 10) or any other with at least a 7½-cup capacity. Dust it all with fine, dry bread crumbs, and tap to shake out excess crumbs over a piece of paper. Set the pan aside.

Sift together the flour, salt, baking powder, and baking soda, and set aside.

In the large bowl of an electric mixer, beat the butter until soft. Add the vanilla and then the sugar and beat until well mixed. Add the egg and beat until pale in color. Add the bran cereal and beat just to mix. Set aside.

The bananas should be mashed on a large, flat plate with a fork (a processor or blender liquefies them too much); they may be slightly uneven with a few coarse pieces.

Add the water to the bananas and stir to mix. Then add the bananas to the bran mixture, beating only to mix. (The mixture might appear curdled—that is okay.)

Add the raisins and nuts and beat only to mix. Then, on low speed, add the sifted dry ingredients, scraping the bowl with a rubber spatula, and beating only until incorporated—do not overbeat.

Turn into the prepared pan and smooth the top.

Bake for 1 hour, until a cake tester gently inserted in the middle comes out clean and dry.

Cool in the pan for 10 to 15 minutes.

Turn over onto a rack, remove the pan, and then turn the loaf right side up to finish cooling.

Let stand for several hours or overnight, or refrigerate for at least 1 or 2 hours before slicing.

French Spice Bread

I could become so completely hooked on this that I would totally lose all control. The flavor and the texture leave me limp and helpless with pleasure. When I see that I have just polished off almost half a loaf, I try to reason with myself. And then I answer, "But it has no butter, or oil, or eggs; no cream, or nuts, or chocolate." I win!

1 tablespoon whole
anise seeds

5 ounces candied orange
peel (to make ⅔ cup diced)

2 ounces candied ginger
(to make ½ cup diced)

3 cups *unsifted*
all-purpose flour (stir to
aerate before measuring)

1 cup *unsifted* rye
flour—available at
health-food stores)

1 teaspoon ground ginger

½ teaspoon cinnamon

½ teaspoon powdered
mustard

¼ teaspoon salt

1 cup honey

1 cup granulated sugar

2 teaspoons baking soda

1 cup hot tap water or coffee

½ teaspoon finely
ground black pepper

2 ounces (⅓ cup)
light raisins

Crush the anise seeds in a mortar with a pestle just to bruise them. Set aside. The candied orange peel and ginger should be cut into pieces about ¼ inch in diameter, no smaller. Set aside. Sift together both flours, the ground ginger, cinnamon, mustard, and salt, and set aside.

Place the honey, sugar, baking soda, and hot water or coffee in the large bowl of an electric mixer, and beat to mix. On low speed add the sifted dry ingredients and the pepper and beat only until smooth. Remove from the mixer and stir in the anise seeds, orange peel, candied ginger, and raisins.

Transfer to a smaller bowl if you wish, cover, and refrigerate at least overnight or up to a week. Or, if you wish, bake now without waiting.

Before baking, adjust a rack one-third up from the bottom of the oven and preheat the oven to 350°. Butter two loaf pans measuring 8 x 4 x 2½ inches (5-cup capacity). Dust the pans with fine, dry bread crumbs, and tap to shake out excess crumbs over a piece of paper.

The batter will be quite sticky. Spoon it into the pans, smooth the tops, and bake for 1 hour and 15 to 20 minutes, until the tops just barely spring back when gently pressed with a fingertip.

Cool in the pans for 15 minutes. Then cover with a rack, turn over the pan and rack, remove the pan, and carefully turn the loaf right side up to cool. Then wrap airtight and let stand for a few days if you wish, or serve without waiting.

The crust will be very hard and crisp right after the loaf has cooled. But you can slice it with a serrated knife and great care. If you wrap the loaf and let it stand overnight, the crust will soften quite a bit and will be easier to slice. Then it can be sliced very thin.

Dutch Honey Bread

1 LARGE LOAF

This is a beautiful, mildly spiced, interesting, sweet loaf, like the ones that come from Holland. It keeps very well, travels well, and makes a nice gift. Soft, tender, fine-grained—it slices beautifully.

2 cups sifted
all-purpose flour

½ teaspoon ginger

½ teaspoon cinnamon

½ teaspoon ground cloves

¼ teaspoon salt

½ cup light raisins

8 ounces (1 cup) diced
candied orange peel

¼ pound (1 stick)
unsalted butter

1 teaspoon powdered
instant espresso or
other powdered (not
granular) instant coffee

1 cup dark or light brown
sugar, firmly packed

2 eggs

½ cup honey

1 teaspoon baking soda

½ cup buttermilk

Adjust a rack to the center of the oven and preheat the oven to 350°. Butter a 10 x 5 x 3-inch loaf pan, or any other loaf pan with a 10-cup capacity. Dust it all over with fine, dry bread crumbs, and tap to shake out excess crumbs over a piece of paper. Set aside.

Sift together the flour, ginger, cinnamon, cloves, and salt. In a small bowl stir and toss the raisins and orange peel with about 2 tablespoons of the sifted dry ingredients. Set aside the fruit and the remaining sifted dry ingredients.

In the large bowl of an electric mixer, beat the butter until it softens slightly. Mix in the powdered espresso and then the sugar and beat to mix. Add the eggs one at a time, beating until incorporated after each addition.

Place the honey in a bowl. Add the baking soda through a fine strainer, stir to mix, then add the buttermilk, and stir to mix. (The mixture will foam slightly.)

To the butter mixture, add the sifted dry ingredients in three additions, alternating with the liquid in two additions, scraping the bowl with a rubber spatula and beating on low speed only until incorporated after each addition.

Remove from the mixer and stir in the floured raisins and orange peel.

Turn into the prepared pan and smooth the top.

Bake for about 1 hour and 10 minutes, until the top feels semifirm to the touch. If the top begins to brown too much during baking, cover it loosely with foil. (The top will be flat, not rounded.)

Let the loaf stand in the pan for 15 to 20 minutes. Then cover it with a rack, turn the pan and the rack over, and remove the pan, leaving the loaf upside down. Let the loaf stand until completely cool. Then wrap it in plastic wrap and refrigerate for a few hours or overnight, or freeze it for about an hour.

Cut into thin slices.

PORTUGUESE SWEET WALNUT BREAD

1 LARGE LOAF

This beautiful, old-fashioned, moist loaf—packed with walnuts—is like a not-too-sweet pound cake. It is a coffee cake to serve between meals with tea or coffee. It is best to let this stand overnight before serving.

8 ounces (2 sticks)
unsalted butter

1½ teaspoons
vanilla extract

¾ cup granulated sugar

6 eggs

Finely grated rind
of 1 large lemon

8 ounces (2 cups) walnut
halves or large pieces

NOTE: *I especially like a pan I recently bought that measures 10¼ x 3¾ inches across the top, and 3⅜ inches in depth. It makes a higher and more narrow loaf than usual. A 9 x 5 x 3-inch pan is all right, but 9 x 5 x 2¾ is too small.*

Adjust a rack one-third up from the bottom of the oven and preheat the oven to 350°. Butter a loaf pan that has an 8-cup capacity (see Note). Dust it all over with fine, dry bread crumbs, and tap to shake out excess crumbs over a piece of paper. Set aside.

Beat the butter in the large bowl of an electric mixer just to soften it slightly. Add the vanilla and sugar and beat to mix. Add the eggs one or two at a time, scraping the bowl with a rubber spatula and beating until incorporated after each addition. On low speed gradually add the sifted dry ingredients, scraping the bowl and beating only until incorporated.

Remove from the mixer and stir in the lemon rind and walnuts.

Turn the mixture into the prepared pan and smooth the top. Then, with a spatula or a spoon, form a trench about ½ inch deep down the length of the loaf. (This keeps the loaf from mounding too high, but it will mound somewhat anyhow and will form a crack on the top. It will be gorgeous.)

Bake for 1 hour and 25 to 30 minutes. You will be able to tell when it is done by pressing gently with a fingertip on the top of the cake; when it is done it will resist the pressure.

Cool in the pan for about 15 minutes. Then cover with a rack, turn over the pan and the rack, remove the pan, and carefully turn the loaf right side up. Let the loaf stand for 8 hours, or wrap the cooled loaf and let it stand overnight. Or freeze it for an hour or two.

Use a very sharp knife for slicing—this slices beautifully—the large pieces of walnut look wonderful.

GEORGIA PECAN BREAD

ONE 8-INCH LOAF

A luscious little loaf loaded with pecans; gorgeous and delicious.

2 cups sifted
all-purpose flour

2 teaspoons
baking powder

½ teaspoon baking soda

½ teaspoon salt

1 teaspoon cinnamon

¼ teaspoon nutmeg

1 egg

1 cup buttermilk

3½ tablespoons unsalted
butter, melted

¾ cup light brown
sugar, firmly packed

6 ounces (1½ cups)
pecans, cut or broken
into large pieces

Adjust a rack one-third up from the bottom of the oven and preheat the oven to 350°. Butter an 8-inch loaf pan, or any pan with at least a 4-cup capacity (the pan should not be much larger or the loaf will be too shallow). Dust the pan all over with fine, dry bread crumbs, and tap to shake out excess crumbs over a piece of paper. Set aside.

Sift together the flour, baking powder, baking soda, salt, cinnamon, and nutmeg, and set aside.

This can be mixed with an electric mixer or by hand. In a large bowl, beat the egg to mix. Mix in the buttermilk, the butter, and the sugar. Add the dry ingredients and stir or beat only to mix. Stir in the nuts.

Turn into the prepared pan and smooth the top. (In an 8-inch pan, the pan might seem too full, but if it has a 4-cup capacity it will be okay.)

Bake for 1 hour and 5 to 10 minutes, until the top feels semifirm to the touch and a cake tester comes out clean. Do not overbake.

Cool in the pan for 10 to 15 minutes. Cover with a rack and turn the pan and the rack over, remove the pan, and then very carefully turn the loaf right side up to cool.

Wrap the cooled loaf and refrigerate it overnight. (Sometimes I cannot follow that last direction. If you slice it immediately, as soon as it has cooled, use a serrated bread knife.)

FRESH APPLE BREAD
ONE 9-INCH LOAF

This is a plain loaf, not quite as sweet as cake. It has a rather light texture, a mildly spiced flavor, and a beautifully golden-brown crust.

2 cups sifted
all-purpose flour

2 teaspoons
baking powder

1 teaspoon baking soda

½ teaspoon salt

1 teaspoon cinnamon

½ teaspoon nutmeg

¼ teaspoon ginger

¼ teaspoon allspice

1 large firm and tart
apple, or 2 smaller ones

4 ounces (1 stick)
unsalted butter

¾ cup plus 2 tablespoons
light brown sugar,
firmly packed

2 eggs

2 tablespoons buttermilk
or sour cream

Finely grated rind
of 1 large lemon

4 ounces (1 cup) walnuts,
cut or broken into
medium-size pieces

Adjust a rack one-third up in the oven and preheat the oven to 350°. Butter a 9 x 5 x 3-inch loaf pan (8-cup capacity), dust it all with fine, dry bread crumbs, and tap to shake out excess over a piece of paper. Set the pan aside.

Sift together the flour, baking powder, baking soda, salt, cinnamon, nutmeg, ginger, and allspice, and set aside.

You will need 1¼ to 1⅓ cups of finely diced apple. Peel, quarter, and core the apple or apples. Dice each piece into ¼- to ⅓-inch squares. Set aside.

In the large bowl of an electric mixer, beat the butter until it is soft. Add the sugar and beat to mix. Add the eggs one at a time, beating until incorporated after each addition. Beat in the buttermilk or sour cream, then the diced apple. Then, on low speed, gradually add the sifted dry ingredients, scraping the bowl with a rubber spatula and beating only until thoroughly incorporated.

Remove from the mixer. Stir in the lemon rind and then the nuts.

The mixture will be very thick. Turn it into the prepared pan, smooth the top, and let stand for 10 minutes before baking.

Bake for about 1 hour, until a cake tester gently inserted into the middle comes out clean and dry.

Let the loaf cool in the pan for 10 to 15 minutes. Cover with a rack, turn the pan and the rack over, remove the pan, cover with another rack and turn over again, leaving the loaf right side up to finish cooling.

When completely cool, wrap in plastic wrap and refrigerate overnight or at least for a few hours.

Cut with a very sharp knife into slices about ½ inch thick.

Fig Bread

One 9- or 10-inch loaf

This is a wonderfully chewy and coarse, old-fashioned and kind-of-healthy-tasting, not-too-sweet loaf. Serve it plain or toasted (super), just by itself or with butter, cheese, thick honey, or marmalade. This is wonderful as a coffee cake—or make a grilled cheese sandwich with it.

12 ounces (1½ packed cups) dried brown figs (soft and moist)

1 cup sifted all-purpose white flour

1 teaspoon salt

1 teaspoon baking powder

1 teaspoon baking soda

1 cup *unsifted* all-purpose whole wheat flour (stir to aerate before measuring)

½ cup honey

1½ cups buttermilk

2 ounces (½ stick) unsalted butter, melted

4 ounces (1 cup) walnut halves or pieces

Adjust a rack one-third up in the oven and preheat the oven to 375°. Butter a 10¼ x 3¾ x 3⅜-inch or a 9 x 5 x 3-inch loaf pan or any loaf pan with at least an 8-cup capacity; dust it all with toasted wheat germ (toasted wheat germ makes a beautiful brown crust), oatmeal (that makes a nice chewy crust), or with fine, dry bread crumbs; and tap over a piece of paper to shake out any excess. Set aside.

With a knife or with scissors, cut off and discard the stems of the figs and cut the figs into slices about ¼ inch thick or into pieces—the slices or pieces should not be too thin or small; noticeable chunks are delicious. Set aside.

Sift together into a large mixing bowl the white flour, salt, baking powder, and baking soda. Add the whole wheat flour and stir to mix thoroughly. Add the figs and toss with your fingers thoroughly to separate and coat the pieces.

In another bowl mix the honey, buttermilk, and melted butter (a small wire whisk will blend them easily). Stir in the nuts. Add the liquid to the dry ingredients and stir lightly only until the dry ingredients are moistened—it will be a thick mixture.

Turn into the prepared pan and smooth the top. The batter will almost fill the pan. Bake for 50 to 60 minutes until the top is a rich golden brown, semifirm to the touch, and until a cake tester inserted into the middle comes out clean (test it carefully). The top will be quite flat.

Cool in the pan for 15 minutes, then cover with a rack, turn over the pan and the rack, remove the pan, cover with another rack, and turn over again, leaving the cake right side up to cool. It is best to chill the loaf before you slice it.

HEALTH-FOOD RAISIN BREAD
ONE 8- OR 9-INCH LOAF

This is firm, solid, chewy, beautiful, and deliciously satisfying. Serve it plain, or with butter, cream cheese, cottage cheese, jelly, or marmalade. It is too easy to make.

2 cups *unsifted*
all-purpose whole
wheat flour

¼ cup *unsifted*
all-purpose white flour

¾ teaspoon salt

1 teaspoon baking soda

6 ounces (1¼ cups)
raisins (they may be a
combination of dark
and light, or all dark)

¼ cup wheat germ,
untoasted or toasted

½ cup milk

1 cup buttermilk

¼ cup honey

¼ cup dark or
light molasses

Adjust a rack one-third up from the bottom of the oven and preheat the oven to 350°. You will need a loaf pan with a 6-cup capacity. It can be either an 8- or 9-inch pan, about 4½ inches across and 3 inches deep. Or it can be longer and narrower. Butter the pan and dust it all over with wheat germ (additional to what is called for in the ingredients list—toasted wheat germ makes a very nice crust).

Place both flours and the salt in the large mixing bowl. Add the baking soda through a fine strainer. Stir well to mix. Stir in the raisins, making sure that they are all separated and floured. Stir in the wheat germ. Mix the milk, buttermilk, honey, and molasses. Add the milk mixture to the batter and, with a wooden spoon, stir only until mixed.

Turn into the prepared pan. Smooth the top, and then, with the back of a spoon, form a slight trench down the length of the loaf.

Bake for about 50 minutes, until the top feels semifirm to the touch and a cake tester inserted into the middle comes out clean. Cool in the pan for about 15 minutes.

Cover with a rack, turn the pan and the rack over, and remove the pan. Let the loaf cool either side up.

Delicious Bran Loaf
1 MEDIUM-SIZE LOAF

This is ridiculously easy and so good I can't stop. It is full of raisins, dates, and nuts and the wonderful taste and chewy quality of bran and whole-wheat. It is not too sweet—serve it as bread with a meal—or serve it between meals with tea or coffee. Wrap it as a gift—it keeps well and travels well.

1 cup 100% bran cereal
(I use Kellogg's All-Bran)

⅔ cup raisins

½ cup dark or
light molasses

2 tablespoons unsalted
butter, cut into small pieces

¾ cup boiling water

1 egg

4 ounces (generous 1
cup) walnut or pecan
halves or large pieces

½ cup dates, cut into pieces

Optional: ¼ cup unsalted
sunflower or pumpkin seeds

½ cup *unsifted*
all-purpose whole
wheat flour

½ cup *unsifted*
all-purpose white flour

½ teaspoon baking soda

½ teaspoon salt

½ teaspoon ginger

½ teaspoon cinnamon

Adjust a rack to the center of the oven and preheat the oven to 350°. Butter an 8½ x 4½ x 2¾-inch loaf pan with a 6-cup capacity (see Note). Dust the pan all over with wheat germ, quick-cooking oatmeal, or fine, dry bread crumbs. Tap to shake out excess over a piece of paper. Set aside.

Place the bran, raisins, molasses, and butter in a large mixing bowl. Add the boiling water and stir to mix and to melt the butter. Beat the egg lightly just to mix and stir it in. Stir in the nuts, dates, and optional seeds.

Sift over the bran mixture both flours and the baking soda, salt, ginger, and cinnamon. Stir to mix but do not handle any more than necessary.

Turn into the prepared pan and smooth the top.

Bake for about 40 minutes, until the top is barely firm to the touch.

Cool in the pan for 10 to 15 minutes. Then cover with a rack and turn over the pan and rack. Remove the pan and very carefully turn the loaf right side up. (The top of the loaf will be quite flat; this can be served either side up.) Let stand until cool.

NOTE: *If you use a large pan (9 x 5 x 3 inches) the loaf will not fill the pan but it will bake well and will look fine.*

BANANA CARROT LOAF
ONE 9-INCH LOAF

Banana cakes and carrot cakes are two American favorites; this combines both in one delicious, slightly spicy loaf that perfumes the house while baking and drives everyone crazy with desire. This is homey and old-fashioned, and yet it is brand new.

5 ounces (1 cup) light raisins

About 3 medium-size carrots (to make 1 packed cup, grated)

2 cups sifted all-purpose flour

1 tablespoon unsweetened cocoa powder (preferably Dutch-process)

1 teaspoon baking soda

1 teaspoon cinnamon

¼ teaspoon nutmeg

½ teaspoon salt

2 eggs

1 cup dark brown sugar, firmly packed

¾ cup vegetable oil

About 2 large fully ripened bananas (to make 1 cup, mashed)

Adjust a rack one-third up from the bottom of the oven and preheat the oven to 350°. Butter a 9 x 5 x 3-inch loaf pan (8-cup capacity) and dust it with fine, dry bread crumbs or with toasted wheat germ; invert the pan over paper and tap lightly to shake out excess crumbs. Set aside.

Steam the raisins as follows: Place them in a strainer or colander over shallow hot water in a saucepan over moderate heat, cover, and let the water boil for about 5 minutes. Then remove the strainer or colander and set aside.

Wash the carrots with a brush or vegetable sponge (it is not necessary to peel them) and grate them on a fine, medium, or coarse grater. On a four-sided standing metal grater use the side that has small round—not diamond-shaped—openings (look at the shape of the openings from the inside or underside of the grater). You need 1 cup, packed. Set aside.

Sift together the flour, cocoa, baking soda, cinnamon, nutmeg, and salt, and set aside.

In the large bowl of an electric mixer, beat the eggs just to mix. Beat in the sugar and oil.

Peel the bananas and mash them on a wide, flat plate with a fork; they should be coarsely mashed and slightly lumpy. (Do not use a processor or blender, which might mash them too much.)

Beat the bananas, raisins, and carrots into the egg mixture. Then on low speed add the sifted dry ingredients and beat, scraping the bowl with a rubber spatula, until thoroughly mixed.

Turn the mixture into the prepared pan and smooth the top. Bake for about 1 hour and 10 minutes, until a cake tester inserted gently into the middle of the loaf, all the way to the bottom, comes out clean. Toward the end of the baking time, if the top of the loaf becomes too dark, cover it loosely with foil. During baking the top of the loaf will form a wide crack—that is okay.

Cool the loaf in the pan for 10 or 15 minutes. Then cover the pan with a rack, hold the pan and rack together and turn them over, remove the pan, cover with another rack, and gently and carefully turn both racks over again, leaving the loaf right side up to cool on the rack.

PECAN-PEANUT BUTTER-BANANA BREAD

2 SMALL LOAVES

Dark, moist, sweet, wheaty, nutty, even adorable. This very old recipe is said to have been used by George Washington's family. There was a lady named Corrie M. Hill, from Montgomery, Alabama, who was one of the most famous hostesses in her day, and Mrs. Hill's great-great-grandfather was George Washington's uncle. This banana bread was one of Corrie Hill's specialties.

1 cup sifted
all-purpose flour

1 cup sifted
all-purpose whole
wheat flour

1 teaspoon baking soda

½ teaspoon salt

¼ teaspoon nutmeg

3 ounces (¾ stick)
unsalted butter

½ cup smooth
peanut butter

1 cup dark brown
sugar, firmly packed

2 eggs

2 to 3 large fully ripened
bananas (to make
1 cup, mashed)

Adjust a rack one-third up from the bottom of the oven and preheat the oven to 375°. Butter two small loaf pans, each with a 4- to 5-cup capacity (the pans may measure about 8 x 4 x 2½ inches). Dust them all over with toasted wheat germ or fine, dry bread crumbs or uncooked oatmeal, invert over paper, and tap to shake out excess. Set aside.

Sift together both the flours, the baking soda, salt, and nutmeg, and set aside. In the large bowl of an electric mixer, beat the butter until softened. Add the peanut butter and beat to mix. Beat in the sugar, and then the eggs one at a time.

Peel the bananas and mash with a fork on a large plate (do not use a blender or processor, because the bananas should not be liquefied); they may remain coarse and uneven with a few slightly larger pieces.

Beat the bananas into the mixture. Then, on low speed, add the sifted dry ingredients and beat only until incorporated. Remove the bowl from the mixer and stir in the pecans.

Pour half of the batter into each of the prepared pans and smooth the tops.

Bake at 375° for 15 minutes and then reduce the temperature to 350° and bake for 35 to 40 minutes more (total baking time is about 50 to 55 minutes). Test by inserting a cake tester to the bottom of each loaf; bake until the tester comes out dry. The loaves will not fill the pans to the top; it is okay—they are not supposed to. During baking

6 ounces (1½ cups) pecan halves or large pieces, toasted (see To Toast Pecans, page 6)

the tops of the loaves will crack, and the cracks will remain paler than the rest.

Let the loaves cool in the pans for 5 to 10 minutes, then turn each loaf out onto a folded towel in your hand and place the loaves on a rack to cool.

Peanut Banana Bread
One 9-inch loaf

Years ago my husband owned a restaurant in Miami Beach. During that time the Republican party held their convention in Miami Beach to nominate a candidate for the presidency. I thought it would be a good idea, in order to get some publicity for the restaurant, to serve elephant meat omelets (the symbol of the Republican party being an elephant). We found that we could buy canned elephant meat at Bloomingdale's. To get some ideas about how to serve the omelet, I called the Explorers Club in Washington, D.C., and Treetop, William Holden's restaurant in Kenya. I spoke to the chef at each restaurant; they loved the idea. After much discussion and consideration we decided that the omelet would be rolled around the elephant meat (which resembled beef stew), on each side there would be half a sautéed banana, and over the top a generous handful of coarsely chopped peanuts. (It was a huge success; the publicity was tremendous.)

Since then I never see bananas without thinking of peanuts and elephant meat, and I never see peanuts without thinking of bananas and elephant meat.

This delicious banana bread has peanuts (but no elephant meat)—and is gorgeous.

1¾ cups sifted all-purpose flour

1 teaspoon baking powder

1 teaspoon baking soda

4 ounces (1 stick) unsalted butter

1 cup dark brown sugar, firmly packed

3 eggs

Ingredients continued on next page.

Adjust a rack one-third up from the bottom of the oven and preheat the oven to 325°. Butter a 9 x 5 x 3-inch loaf pan (with an 8-cup capacity) and dust it with fine, dry bread crumbs; invert it over paper, and tap to shake out excess crumbs. Set aside.

Sift together the flour, baking powder, and baking soda, and set aside.

In the large bowl of an electric mixer, beat the butter until it is soft, then beat in the sugar, then the eggs one at a time.

Peel the bananas and mash them coarsely on a large, flat plate with a fork; do not mash them smooth. Add the mashed bananas and the sour cream to the batter and beat to mix.

On low speed, gradually beat in the sifted dry ingredients, beating only until just incorporated.

To chop the peanuts coarsely, place in the bowl of a food processor fitted with the metal chopping blade and process on/off 2 or 3 times (for 2 to

3 large fully ripened bananas (to make 1½ cups, mashed)

⅓ cup sour cream

4 ounces (1 cup) salted peanuts

½ cup light raisins

3 seconds)—or chop them on a board with a long, heavy knife. Mix the peanuts and raisins into the batter.

Turn into the prepared pan and smooth the top.

Bake for about 1 hour and 15 minutes, until a cake tester inserted gently in the middle comes out clean.

Cool in the pan for 10 to 15 minutes. Then cover with a rack. Hold the pan and the rack firmly together and turn both over. Remove the pan. With your hands, carefully and gently turn the loaf right side up and let stand to cool. Then wrap and refrigerate until serving time.

This makes divine toast, but it is better toasted under the broiler than in the toaster. Toasted or not, eat it plain, or with cream cheese and jelly.

HOLLYWOOD HONEY CAKE
ONE 9-INCH LOAF

No butter, no eggs, no sugar; a delicious and nutritious loaf with whole wheat flour, raisins, and nuts. Not too sweet. Serve it as a plain cake, or use it for cheese sandwiches, or toast it and serve with butter or cream cheese (toasted, plain and dry, is my favorite way). Toasted, it becomes very chewy and crunchy. This takes long and slow baking. It keeps wonderfully—it even seems to get better. Easy to make.

3½ ounces (¾ cup) dark raisins

3½ ounces (1 cup) walnuts

1 cup sifted all-purpose flour

2 cups sifted all-purpose whole wheat flour

Scant 1 teaspoon salt

¾ teaspoon baking soda

Adjust a rack one-third up from the bottom of the oven and preheat the oven to 275°. Butter a 9 x 5 x 3-inch pan (butter the pan even if it has a nonstick finish). Even though it is a larger pan than necessary, I especially like this in a 9¼ x 5¼ x 2⅓-inch pan with a nonstick finish. Set the pan aside.

Steam the raisins by placing them in a vegetable steamer or in a strainer over shallow water on moderate heat; cover and let the water boil for about 5 minutes. Then uncover and let stand, off the heat.

Break the walnuts into medium-size pieces and set aside.

Into the large bowl of an electric mixer sift together both the flours and the salt, baking soda, and baking powder. Add the milk and honey and beat on low speed until smooth. Remove from the mixer.

Stir in the raisins and nuts.

2½ teaspoons
baking powder

1½ cups milk

½ cup honey

Turn into the prepared pan, smooth the top, and bake for 1 hour and 20 minutes, until the top springs back when pressed lightly with a fingertip, the loaf begins to come away from the sides, and a cake tester inserted gently in the center of the loaf comes out clean and dry.

Cool in the pan for about 10 minutes. Then cover the pan with a pot holder or a folded towel and turn it over into the palm of your hand. Remove the pan, cover the cake with a rack and turn over again, leaving the cake right side up to cool completely.

BLUEBERRY APPLESAUCE LOAF
TWO 8-INCH LOAVES

Cake? Coffee cake? Sweet bread? All three. Two golden-brown loaves with crisp, nutty crusts and soft, moist slices loaded with juicy, purple blueberries and pecan halves that do not sink. Make this in the summer during blueberry season and plan to serve it while it is very fresh.

6 ounces (1½ cups)
pecan halves or large
pieces, toasted (see To
Toast Pecans, page 6)

2 cups fresh blueberries

2 cups sifted
all-purpose flour

1 cup sifted
all-purpose whole
wheat flour

1 tablespoon
baking powder

½ teaspoon baking soda

½ teaspoon salt

½ teaspoon mace

Ingredients continued on next page.

Adjust a rack to the middle of the oven and preheat the oven to 350°. Generously butter two loaf pans that measure about 8 x 4 x 2¼ inches (each with a 4- to 5-cup capacity). To coat the pan with chopped nuts, grind ¾ cup of the pecans (reserve the remaining ¾ cup of pecans) in a food processor or a nut grinder until they are quite fine (but not until they become buttery). Sprinkle the ground or chopped nuts in the buttered pans. Tilt the pans from side to side, then invert them over paper, but do not tap to shake out excess nuts. The pans should be heavily coated. Any loose nuts that fall out should be reserved to sprinkle on top of the loaves before baking. Set the pans and the reserved ground nuts aside.

Wash the berries and let them drain.

Remove and reserve 1 tablespoon of the all-purpose flour. Sift together the remaining all-purpose flour, the whole wheat flour, baking powder, baking soda, salt, and mace, and set aside.

In the large bowl of an electric mixer, beat the eggs just to mix. Beat in the oil and 1 cup of the sugar (reserve the remaining 2 tablespoons of sugar). Mix in the applesauce and lemon juice. On low speed, add the sifted dry ingredients and beat only until smoothly mixed. Remove the bowl from the mixer.

2 eggs

¼ cup vegetable oil

1 cup plus 2 tablespoons granulated sugar

1 cup unsweetened applesauce (Mott's Natural Style has no sugar and no preservatives)

2 teaspoons lemon juice

Stir in the remaining ¾ cup of pecan halves or pieces.

Place the washed-and-dried blueberries in a wide bowl. Add the reserved tablespoon of all-purpose flour and toss gently with a rubber spatula to flour the berries without squashing them.

Gently fold the floured berries into the batter with a rubber spatula. Barely mix and be careful not to squash the berries.

Place half of the mixture in each pan and gently smooth the tops. Sprinkle the tops with any reserved ground nuts. Then sprinkle the tops with the remaining 2 tablespoons of sugar.

Bake for 50 to 55 minutes, until a cake tester inserted gently into the loaves comes out clean and the loaves begin to come away slightly from the sides of the pans. During baking the tops of the loaves will crack—it is okay.

Cool the loaves in the pans for 10 to 15 minutes. Then carefully cut around the sides to release. Place a folded towel or a pot holder on the palm of your hand. Turn a pan over onto the towel or pot holder, carefully lift off the pan, and then carefully place the loaf right side up on a rack to cool. Repeat with the other loaf.

Let the loaves stand until they reach room temperature before serving. You can speed up the process by putting them in the freezer, if you wish. A serrated tomato-slicing knife cuts these loaves beautifully.

If you do not plan to serve a loaf while it is really very fresh, it is best to freeze it; if it stands at room temperature or even in the refrigerator, the moisture from the berries makes the loaf soggy.

SCONES

12 SCONES

Scones, lightly sweetened biscuits, came to America with the first settlers from England. Recently, in bakeries and in tearooms, in South Carolina, in New England, and in California, we ate scones. I was surprised to see them, because the main thing about scones is to eat them immediately as they come out of the oven—difficult to do in a bakery or tearoom. But no one seemed to mind, and I was told that they are extremely popular now. If you have had scones hours after they were baked and you like them, wait until you taste these right out of the oven.

The only secret for making scones is that the mixing should be as quick as possible; there should be a minimum of handling. They are divine for breakfast. Or tea. Or with a fruit salad luncheon. They are elegant and homey at the same time.

Although these can literally be put together in a few minutes, much of the recipe can be done ahead of time. The eggs and milk can be mixed and refrigerated overnight; the butter can be cut into the sifted dry ingredients and that mixture can be refrigerated overnight. Then, before baking, the two mixtures can be quickly stirred together even before the oven has time to heat (give the oven a head start).

These scones are dropped, not rolled; they are more tender than scones that have enough flour to be rolled out.

1 egg plus 1 egg yolk

½ cup milk

2 cups sifted all-purpose flour

2 teaspoons baking powder

½ teaspoon salt

¼ cup granulated sugar

3 ounces (¾ stick) unsalted butter, cold and firm, cut into ½-inch squares (it is best to cut the butter ahead of time and refrigerate it)

¼ cup currants

Additional granulated sugar (to sprinkle over the tops)

Adjust a rack to the middle of the oven and preheat the oven to 450°. Line a cookie sheet or a jelly-roll pan with parchment paper, or use it unlined and unbuttered (scones stick to foil).

In a small bowl, beat the egg and the yolk just to mix. Mix in the milk and set aside.

Sift together into a wide bowl the flour, baking powder, salt, and sugar. Add the butter and, with a pastry blender, cut until the mixture resembles coarse meal; some of the butter particles may be the size of dried split peas (or thereabouts). Stir in the currants. Form a well in the middle.

Add the egg mixture all at once to the well and with a fork stir quickly only until the dry ingredients are barely moistened. Do not stir one bit more than necessary. The mixture will be quite moist.

Using a rounded tablespoon of the batter for each scone, drop the mounds of batter at least 1 inch apart (12 scones will fit on one 15½ x 12-inch sheet), and sprinkle the tops lightly with a bit of additional sugar.

Bake for 15 minutes, reversing the sheet front to back once during baking to ensure even browning. Bake only until the scones are lightly (and unevenly) golden.

Serve immediately. Delicious plain, but traditionally served with butter and preserves or marmalade.

If you have some left over, even from the day before, split and toast them under the broiler, then butter them, return them to the broiler for a few seconds to melt the butter (watch them carefully), and serve. (Actually, these are so good toasted that you might plan to make them a day ahead for that purpose.)

VARIATION: *A few spoonfuls of chopped walnuts and/or candied ginger may be stirred in along with, or instead of, the currants. You can use ¾ cup of whole wheat flour in place of ¾ cup of the white flour—then they're called Brown Tea Scones.*

Muffins, Cupcakes, and Tassies

BRAN MUFFINS
18 MUFFINS

These are moist, dark, chewy-crunchy, sweet, and very good for you. They can become a delicious habit. My mother made them almost every day, dozens at a time; we ate them for breakfast and lunch and between meals, we took them on picnics and fishing trips and in lunch boxes and to Ebbets Field and Yankee Stadium and to the movies. I can't remember ever being without them for long.

Once, in beautiful Rancho Santa Fe, California, my husband and I spotted a little sign saying SONRISA BAKERY OPENING SOON. *We quickly made friends with Linn Hadden and Bruce Munter, the wonderful young couple who built Sonrisa (which is Spanish for "smile"). Although they both bake and have many of their own recipes, I gave them this bran muffin recipe. The day their convection oven was installed this was the first thing they baked. They were ecstatic. They said these were the best bran muffins they ever ate and they planned to make them a daily specialty.*

They are quick and easy to make. But if you want them fresh for breakfast, you can prepare everything the night before; mix the liquids in a bowl and refrigerate, sift the dry ingredients and set aside, then put them together in a jiffy in the morning. (See Note.)

2 ounces (½ stick) unsalted butter

½ cup dark brown sugar, firmly packed

¼ cup dark or light molasses or honey

2 eggs

1 cup milk

1½ cups bran cereal (not bran flakes—I use Kellogg's All-Bran)

5 ounces (1 cup) raisins

4 ounces (generous 1 cup) walnuts, cut or broken into large pieces

Adjust a rack to the center of the oven. (If your oven is not wide enough for the two muffin pans described below to fit on the same rack, adjust two racks to divide the oven into thirds.) Preheat the oven to 400°. Butter eighteen 2¾-inch muffin forms (I use one pan with 12 forms and another with 6 forms). Butter them even if you are using a nonstick pan. Or line the forms with paper liners for muffin pans. It is a toss-up as to whether lining the pans or buttering them is best. Buttered pans make a nice crust; lined pans make no crust but the muffins probably keep fresher longer.

Place the butter in a small pan over low heat to melt, and then pour it into a large mixing bowl. Add the sugar and then the molasses or honey, stirring to mix well.

In a small bowl, beat the eggs only to mix. Gradually add the milk and beat to mix.

Slowly add the egg mixture to the butter mixture, stirring with a wire whisk to blend. Mix in the bran and the raisins and let stand for a few minutes (or cover and refrigerate overnight).

Then stir in the walnuts.

Sift together the whole wheat flour, white flour, salt, and baking soda. Add to the bran mixture. Stir with a rubber spatula very little and very quickly, only until the dry ingredients are moistened.

½ cup *unsifted* all-purpose whole wheat flour (stir lightly to aerate before measuring)

½ cup *unsifted* all-purpose white flour (stir lightly to aerate before measuring)

¾ teaspoon salt

1½ teaspoons baking soda

With a large spoon, spoon the mixture into the prepared cups, filling them about two-thirds of the way.

Bake for 15 minutes, just until the tops spring back when they are lightly pressed with a fingertip. (If you are baking on two racks, reverse the pans top to bottom and front to back once during baking to ensure even baking.) If the wet ingredients were mixed ahead of time and refrigerated overnight, the muffins will take about 4 minutes longer to bake.

Immediately cover each pan with a rack and turn over the pan and the rack, then remove the pan. If you have used paper liners, turn the muffins right side up, if not, leave them upside down.

NOTE: It takes only a few minutes to prepare bran muffins from scratch—doing part ahead of time does not actually save very many minutes—but it is a nice feeling and a pleasant experience early in the morning to have both the wet and the dry mixtures, as well as the muffin pans, prepared and ready.

VARIATIONS: You can vary these by adding about 12 coarsely cut dates or 6 coarsely cut dried prunes along with the raisins. Or, if you wish, add a few spoonfuls of pumpkin or sunflower seeds (unsalted) along with the nuts. Or sprinkle the tops with sesame seeds before baking.

BLUEBERRY MUFFINS

12 MUFFINS

Especially light, tender, and delicate, these pale golden muffins are generously spotted with deep purple berries. Quick, easy, delicious, and they freeze well. Serve these either hot or cooled, either as a sweet bread with a meal or between meals with tea or coffee.

Adjust a rack to the center of the oven and preheat the oven to 400°. These can be baked in any muffin forms lined with paper liners. However, without the liners, buttered pans give the muffins a nicer crust. I use a buttered, nonstick muffin pan.

The berries must be washed and thoroughly dried; rinse them in cold water, drain, and spread them out in a single layer on paper towels. Pat the tops with paper towels, and let stand until the berries are thoroughly dry.

1 cup fresh blueberries

1½ cups sifted
all-purpose flour

2 teaspoons
baking powder

½ teaspoon salt

½ cup granulated sugar

1 egg

2 tablespoons unsalted
butter, melted

½ cup milk

Finely grated rind
of 1 lemon

Into a very large mixing bowl, sift together the flour, baking powder, salt, and sugar. Add the berries (when thoroughly dried) and stir to mix without breaking the berries.

In a mixing bowl, beat the egg lightly with a whisk or a beater just to mix. Mix in the melted butter and then the milk. Stir in the grated rind.

The secret of muffins is not to overmix. Add the liquid ingredients all at once to the dry ingredients and, with a large rubber spatula, stir/fold very little—only until the dry ingredients are barely moistened. It should take only a few seconds. If you do not handle it too much the batter will be lumpy, which is the way it should be.

Spoon into the muffin forms, filling them two-thirds full.

Bake for 20 to 25 minutes, until golden. Cool in the pan for 2 or 3 minutes. Then cover with a rack, turn over the pan and the rack, and remove the pan. Turn the muffins right side up.

Gingerbread Muffins

16 muffins

It is hard to believe that anything so quick and easy can be so light and delicious; as a matter of fact it is hard to believe that anything can be so light and delicious—quick and easy or not.

Serve as a plain coffee cake or cupcakes or as a dessert with vanilla ice cream and Bittersweet Glaze (page 310). Or pass them with baked apples.

You need two pans, each for 12 standard-size muffins, although you will use only 16 of the forms.

1¾ cups sifted
all-purpose flour

1 teaspoon baking soda

¼ teaspoon salt

¼ teaspoon finely
ground black pepper,
preferably freshly ground

Adjust two racks to divide the oven into thirds and preheat the oven to 400°. Butter 16 standard-size cupcake forms and dust them with fine, dry bread crumbs (butter and crumb them even if they are nonstick), tap and turn the pans over a large piece of paper to crumb them thoroughly, and then invert them over the paper to tap out excess crumbs. Set the pans aside.

Sift together the flour, baking soda, salt, pepper, ginger, cloves, cinnamon, and mustard, and set aside. In the large bowl of an electric mixer, beat the egg and yolk just to mix. Beat in the sugar, molasses, and oil. Then on low speed, add the sifted dry ingredients and beat until incorporated.

1 teaspoon ground ginger

½ teaspoon ground cloves

½ teaspoon cinnamon

¼ teaspoon dry
powdered mustard

1 egg and 1 egg yolk

½ cup granulated sugar

½ cup molasses
(preferably dark)

½ cup vegetable oil

1 tablespoon granular or
powdered instant coffee

½ cup boiling water

Dissolve the coffee in the boiling water and, on low speed, gradually add it to the batter, scraping the bowl with a rubber spatula and beating only until smooth. It will be a thin mixture.

Transfer to a pitcher that is easy to pour from, and pour into the 16 prepared forms, filling them about two-thirds full.

Bake for 18 to 20 minutes, reversing the pans top to bottom and front to back once during baking to ensure even browning, until the muffins spring back when they are pressed gently with a fingertip. Do not overbake even by a minute.

Remove from the oven, cover each pan with a rack, and turn the pan and rack over, remove the pan, and with your fingers turn the muffins right side up.

Serve hot or cold.

Raisin Date Cupcakes
12 cupcakes

These are quite sweet and cakelike even though they have very little sugar; the generous amount of dates supplies a natural sweetening and a wonderful flavor.

It is more efficient to line the forms for these with paper liners than it is to butter them, because when they are lined the paper makes them slightly deeper and you need all the room you can get for these.

10 ounces (1¼
cups, firmly packed)
pitted dates

2½ ounces (½ cup)
light raisins

¾ cup plus 2 tablespoons
boiling water

Ingredients continued on next page.

Adjust a rack one-third down from the top of the oven and preheat the oven to 350°. Line a standard-size muffin pan (twelve 2¾-inch muffins) with paper liners and set aside.

Cut each date into three or four pieces and place them in a small mixing bowl. Add the raisins, the boiling water, and the baking soda, and stir to mix. Let stand to cool (either completely or partly).

In the large bowl of an electric mixer beat the butter until soft. Add the salt, vanilla, and sugar, and beat to mix. Beat in the eggs one at a time and then on low speed add the flour and beat until incorporated. The mixture

1 teaspoon baking soda

4 ounces (1 stick) unsalted butter

¼ teaspoon salt

1 teaspoon vanilla extract

⅓ cup dark brown sugar, firmly packed

2 eggs

1⅓ cups sifted all-purpose flour

Finely grated rind of 1 deep-colored orange (see Note)

will be thick. On low speed, very gradually add the raisin-and-date mixture, scraping the bowl with a rubber spatula as necessary and beating until smoothly incorporated. (The dates remain in chunks.)

Remove the bowl from the mixer and stir in the grated orange rind. Spoon the mixture into the lined cups (the cups will be three-quarters full). It is not necessary to smooth the tops.

Bake for about 30 minutes, until the tops of the cupcakes spring back when pressed gently with a fingertip; check carefully right in the middle of the cupcakes.

Remove from the pan and cool on a rack.

NOTE: *If you wish, you can substitute ¼ teaspoon of almond extract for the grated orange rind. If so, stir it in along with the vanilla.*

RAISIN BANANA CUPCAKES

20 CUPCAKES

These are from the Florida Keys, where I think the people know more about banana breads than anyone else. At least they make the best I've had. The most important thing to remember about any banana bread is that the bananas must be thoroughly ripe with brown/black spots on the skins or the bread will not have any flavor.

These are moist, juicy, flavorful—wonderful.

Adjust a rack to the middle of the oven and preheat the oven to 375°. Line a standard-size muffin pan (twelve 2¾-inch muffins) with paper liners, or butter the forms; set aside.

Steam the raisins by placing them in a vegetable steamer or in a strainer over shallow water in a saucepan on high heat. Cover the pan, bring the

3½ ounces (¾ cup)
light raisins

1 cup sifted
all-purpose flour

¾ teaspoon
baking powder

¾ teaspoon baking soda

¼ teaspoon salt

¼ teaspoon nutmeg

¼ teaspoon cinnamon

3 large (a generous 1¼
pounds) fully ripened
bananas (to make
1½ cups, mashed)

1 egg

⅓ cup dark brown
sugar, firmly packed

¼ cup safflower oil
(or other vegetable oil)

water to a boil, and let it boil for only a minute or two, until the raisins are barely moist. Remove the steamer or strainer from the pan and set aside.

Sift together the flour, baking powder, baking soda, salt, nutmeg, and cinnamon, and set aside.

To mash the bananas (the way it is done in the Florida Keys), peel them and place them all in the large bowl of an electric mixer. Beat on moderate speed, scraping the sides occasionally with a rubber spatula, until the bananas are mashed coarsely. They should not be beaten until they completely liquefy; they should be uneven—some small chunks should remain. Set aside.

Without washing the bowl or beaters, beat the egg, sugar, and oil to mix, add the bananas and beat to mix, then, on low speed, gradually add the sifted dry ingredients and beat only until incorporated.

Remove the bowl from the mixer and stir in the raisins.

Divide the batter among the prepared forms. (They should be filled two-thirds to three-quarters of the way.)

Bake for about 25 minutes, until the tops spring back when they are pressed gently with a fingertip.

Remove from the pan and cool on a rack.

Vermont Maple Syrup Cupcakes

12 cupcakes

This wonderful old recipe has lasted through many generations; one taste and you will see why. Quick and easy.

1¾ cups *unsifted*
all-purpose flour

2½ teaspoons
baking powder

¼ teaspoon salt

Ingredients continued on next page.

Adjust two racks to divide the oven into thirds (these will bake first on the lower rack and then on the upper) and preheat the oven to 350°. Line standard-size cupcake forms with cupcake paper liners, or butter the forms (even if they are nonstick). Set the pan aside.

Sift together the flour, baking powder, and salt, and set aside. In the small bowl of an electric mixer, beat the egg just to mix, then beat in the milk and almond extract. On low speed, gradually add the sifted dry ingredients in three additions alternately with the maple syrup in two additions,

1 egg

¼ cup milk

¼ teaspoon almond extract

1 cup maple syrup

2 ounces (½ stick) unsalted butter, melted and just barely cooled

2½ ounces (¾ cup) toasted pecans (see To Toast Pecans, page 6), broken into large pieces

A bit of untoasted wheat germ, a few thinly sliced almonds, or a bit of chopped pecans (to be used as a topping)

scraping the sides of the bowl as necessary with a rubber spatula. Add the butter and beat briefly, only until partly incorporated.

Remove the bowl from the mixer. Stir/fold a bit to finish mixing in the butter, then fold in the nuts only until they are distributed.

The mixture will be rather thin. It is best to ladle it into the prepared pan, distributing the nuts evenly.

Sprinkle lightly with whichever topping you wish.

Bake on the lower rack for about 15 minutes. Then reverse the pan front to back and transfer it to the higher rack and bake for 15 minutes more, until the tops spring back when they are pressed gently with a fingertip. (Total baking time is about 30 minutes.)

Remove these from the pan as soon as they are done or they will steam and become soggy. These are especially tender—handle with care as you transfer them to a rack to cool.

Please taste one soon, even before it has cooled.

APPLE CRANBERRY MUFFINS

12 MUFFINS

These are loaded with goodies; they have the tart flavor of cranberries and apples, the spiciness of nutmeg and ginger, the chewiness of raisins and nuts, and the body of whole wheat flour.

I have made these only with fresh cranberries (as opposed to frozen); remember these when you see fresh cranberries.

1¼ cups fresh cranberries

1 egg

Finely grated rind of 1 large deep-colored orange

2½ ounces (½ cup) raisins

Adjust a rack to the top position in the oven and preheat the oven to 350°. Line twelve 2¾-inch standard muffin forms with cupcake paper liners, or butter the forms (even if the pans are nonstick), and set aside.

Wash the berries briefly in a bowl of cold water, drain, and let dry on paper towels.

In a small bowl, beat the egg just to mix. Stir in the grated rind, raisins, orange juice, and vanilla and set aside.

⅓ cup orange juice

1 teaspoon vanilla extract

1 or 2 tart apples (to make 1 cup, diced)

½ cup sifted all-purpose whole wheat flour

½ cup sifted all-purpose flour

1 teaspoon baking powder

¼ teaspoon baking soda

¾ teaspoon cinnamon

¾ teaspoon nutmeg

¼ teaspoon ground ginger

¼ teaspoon allspice

¼ teaspoon salt

½ cup granulated sugar

2 ounces (½ stick) unsalted butter, cold and firm, cut into small pieces

4 ounces (generous 1 cup) walnuts, broken into medium-size pieces

Additional granulated sugar

Peel, quarter, and core the apples and cut them into ¼-inch dice. Measure 1 cup of the diced apples and set aside.

Sift into a large mixing bowl both the flours, the baking powder, baking soda, cinnamon, nutmeg, ginger, allspice, salt, and sugar. Add the butter and with a pastry blender cut it into the dry ingredients, until the mixture resembles coarse crumbs (some particles may be the size of small peas).

Add the egg-and-orange juice mixture and with a rubber spatula fold together only until the dry ingredients are barely moistened. Then briefly mix in the apples, cranberries, and walnuts; again, do not handle any more than necessary.

Spoon the mixture into the prepared muffin forms. They will be mounded high above the tops; it is all right. Do not smooth the tops.

Sprinkle the tops generously with additional sugar (it gives the tops a light glaze).

Bake for 25 to 28 minutes, until the muffins are just barely firm to the touch.

Remove the muffins from the pan and place them on a rack.

Serve warm or at room temperature; the fresher the better.

Pecan Sour Cream Muffins

12 large muffins

Mr. Stanley Marcus, chairman emeritus of Neiman-Marcus, is a charming and remarkable gentleman. One of his many talents is his recognition of quality in almost every field—and his good taste. When he hired Helen Corbitt to be in charge of all the food served in the Neiman-Marcus stores in Texas, it was because she was "the best." Her reputation as a cook/caterer/hostess soon become national.

This is a simple little sweet muffin that Helen Corbitt served at breakfast, brunch, or lunch. These muffins and a cup of tea or coffee were a frequent treat during the day for many Texans. Plain, moist, rich, very easy, and beautiful.

1⅓ cups sifted all-purpose flour

1 teaspoon baking powder

½ teaspoon baking soda

⅛ teaspoon salt

Generous pinch of nutmeg, preferably freshly grated

2 ounces (½ stick) unsalted butter

⅔ cup granulated sugar

2 eggs

¾ cup sour cream

5½ ounces (1⅓ cups) toasted pecans broken into large pieces, plus 12 large toasted pecan halves (see To Toast Pecans, page 6)

Adjust an oven rack to the middle of the oven and preheat the oven to 450°. Either butter twelve 2¾-inch muffin forms or line them with cupcake paper liners. (There will be a difference in the muffins if you butter the forms or line them. The muffins in lined forms come out taller, but they have pale sides and bottoms when the papers are removed. If you butter the forms, the muffins will not rise quite so high, but they will have browned sides and bottoms. Frankly, I can't decide which is better; I think they taste equally good.)

Sift together the flour, baking powder, baking soda, salt, and nutmeg, and set aside.

In the small bowl of an electric mixer, beat the butter until soft. Beat in the sugar to mix, then add the eggs one at a time, beating until incorporated after each addition. On low speed, add half of the sifted dry ingredients, then all of the sour cream, and then the remaining sifted dry ingredients. Beat only until smoothly incorporated. Remove the bowl from the mixer and stir in the 5½ ounces of pecan pieces.

Spoon into the prepared muffin forms. It is not necessary to smooth the tops; the muffins will do it themselves during baking.

Place a pecan half, flat side down, on each muffin; press them only slightly into the muffins.

Bake for 15 to 20 minutes, until the muffins spring back when pressed lightly with a fingertip. During baking the muffins will rise with high, nicely rounded, golden-brown tops.

Remove from the pans immediately and place on a rack.

These may be served warm or cooled.

TASSIES

48 "LITTLE CUPS"

These are miniature pastry tarts with a pecan filling. They are buttery, crisp, caramelized, crunchy; they remind me of pecan pie and buttercrunch and caramel and sugar and everything nice all in one. Serve tassies as a dessert or with tea or coffee.

It takes time to prepare these, but they are worth it.

Many years ago I attended a drawing class at which the students were mostly chic ladies. It was a quick-sketch class at which we were all told to draw with charcoal. The teacher explained how to hold the piece of charcoal flush with the paper in order to draw with the sides of it rather than the point. A lady in the class said she couldn't do it. The teacher said it was because her fingernails were too long. To which the student replied, "Miss so-and-so, if you told me that I could draw like Picasso if I cut my fingernails, I would not do it."

No connection with this recipe except that if you have long fingernails I don't think you will be able to make these.

Tassies are regional food in many different parts of this country. I was told that they originated in Texas. And Georgia. And Virginia. This recipe is based on one that was given to me in San Francisco by Jane Benet and Fran Irwin, food writers for the San Francisco Chronicle.

You need muffin forms with a nonstick finish that measure 1¾ inches in width and ¾ inch in depth. I have four such pans, each with 12 forms. If you have fewer, the tassies do not have to be baked all at once. The remaining dough can be refrigerated and the filling can wait at room temperature, or it can be refrigerated as well. The pans are generally available in any kitchen supply store.

PASTRY

8 ounces Philadelphia brand cream cheese, preferably at room temperature	In the large bowl of an electric mixer, beat the cream cheese and butter until they are soft. On low speed, gradually add the flour and the salt, and beat until smoothly incorporated.
8 ounces (2 sticks) unsalted butter	Turn the mixture out onto a length of wax paper or foil and refrigerate or freeze it briefly, until the mixture is not too sticky and can be shaped lightly.
2 cups sifted all-purpose flour	Transfer the dough to a work surface and with your hands form it into an even oblong. Wrap and return to the refrigerator or freezer for about 10 minutes (or much longer, if you wish) until it is firm enough to be cut and handled.
Pinch of salt	Cut into 4 equal pieces. Cut each piece into 12 equal pieces. Roll each piece between your hands into a ball and place the balls in the (unbuttered) miniature muffin forms.

Keep some flour for flouring your fingers next to your work space. With floured fingertips, press each ball of dough into a cup, pressing down in the middle and then working the dough up on the sides. The shaped pastry shells should be flush with the tops of the forms, but it does not matter if they are slightly uneven (it will all bake together more or less and the filling will run over the edges in spots anyhow).

FILLING

8 ounces (1 cup, packed) pitted dates

5½ ounces (1½ cups) pecans, toasted (see To Toast Pecans, page 6), plus 48 perfect pecan halves, untoasted (to be used on the tops)

4 ounces (1 stick) unsalted butter

1 tablespoon vanilla extract

Pinch of salt

2 cups light brown sugar, firmly packed

1 egg

Adjust a rack one-third up from the bottom of the oven. Do not bake these any higher or the tops will become too brown. Preheat the oven to 350°. Since these are very rich, some of the butter might bubble and ooze out of the pans; therefore place a cookie sheet or aluminum foil on a rack below. (If your oven does not have a rack below, place aluminum foil on the bottom of the oven.)

With scissors cut the dates into ¼-inch pieces and set aside. Break up or cut the 5½ ounces of pecans (reserve the remaining 48 halves) into medium-small pieces (it will be difficult to place the filling in the pastry cups if the pieces of nuts are too large) and set aside. In the small bowl of an electric mixer, beat the butter until it is soft. Beat in the vanilla, salt, sugar, and the egg. Remove the bowl from the mixer. Stir in the dates and the 5½ ounces of the pecans.

With a small spoon (a demitasse spoon works well), spoon the filling into the unbaked pastry shells. If you have four pans and are making these all at one time, you will see that when you have used up all of the filling, the cups will be filled to the tops; that is right.

Then place a pecan half, flat side down, on each tassie, pressing the nut gently into the filling just a bit.

Bake two pans at a time, on the same rack, for about 35 minutes, until the pastry that shows around the edges is lightly browned. During baking, if the tassies are not browning evenly, reverse the pans front to back and left to right.

When the tassies are done, let them stand in the pans until completely cool.

Now, to remove the tassies from the pans. Since some of the filling will have bubbled up and run over the edges of the forms, it will tend to stick them to the pans and will not allow them to slip out (nonstick or not); therefore, use the dull side of a table knife and gently and carefully (without cutting into the finish on the pan) cut away any edge that ran over. Then the tassies should lift out easily. If necessary, turn the pan upside down. Or, if necessary, stick the tip of a small, sharp knife into the pastry on an angle and gently pry the tassie up and out of the pan. Whatever, be gentle, because these will break if you are rough with them.

When I make these, if I don't plan to serve them soon, I wrap them individually in plastic wrap and place them in a freezer bag. They can wait at room temperature or in the refrigerator for a day or two or they can be frozen. But when they are very fresh—well, taste one when it is almost, but not completely, cool.

SURPRISE CAKES

24 SMALL CUPCAKES

Fancy, dainty, buttery—delicious. These are tiny cupcakes with a crisp butter-cookie base, a jelly-and-nut surprise filling, and a light, cakelike topping. Make them for a tea party, a shower, a children's party, a bake sale, or just any time you feel like playing in the kitchen.

You will need two miniature muffin pans each with twelve 1¾ x ¾-inch forms and a nonstick finish. These pans are generally available at hardware stores and supermarkets. And you will need a round cookie cutter about 1½ inches in diameter.

The dough for the bottom layer should be refrigerated for an hour or two, or overnight, before it is rolled out and cut.

BOTTOM LAYER

Sift into a large mixing bowl the flour, salt, baking powder, and sugar. With a pastry blender cut in the butter until the mixture resembles coarse crumbs; there may be some pieces of butter about the size of grains of rice, or even a bit larger—it is okay.

In a small bowl, beat the egg, vanilla, and milk to mix. Add it all at once to the flour mixture and stir briskly with a fork, until the dry ingredients are all moistened and the mixture just holds together.

1½ cups *unsifted* all-purpose flour

Pinch of salt

1 teaspoon baking powder

½ cup granulated sugar

4 ounces (1 stick) unsalted butter, cold and firm, cut into ½-inch dice (it is best to cut the butter ahead of time and refrigerate it)

1 egg

½ teaspoon vanilla extract

¼ cup milk

Turn the mixture out onto a length of plastic wrap, bring up the sides of the plastic tightly against the dough to form it into a ball, press it together, wrap, and refrigerate for an hour or two or overnight. When you are ready to bake, adjust a rack to the middle of the oven and preheat the oven to 425°. Butter 24 miniature muffin forms, even though they are nonstick, and set aside.

Cut the chilled dough in half and work with one piece at a time; refrigerate the other piece. On a lightly floured pastry cloth, with a lightly floured rolling pin, roll out the dough until it is ⅓ inch thick.

You need a round cookie cutter about 1½ inches in diameter (it should be slightly wider than the base of the muffin forms). Cut out 12 rounds of the dough. Repeat with the remaining half of the dough. Reserve scraps of the dough (see Note).

Place a round of dough into each buttered form, pressing down gently in the middle to make it cup-shaped (it is not necessary to fuss with the shapes—they will take care of themselves during baking).

Filling

About ⅓ cup red currant jelly, orange marmalade, or any other jam, jelly, or preserves

A few spoonfuls of rather finely chopped walnuts or 24 walnut halves

Place a rounded ½ teaspoon of the jelly in the middle of each muffin form on top of the dough (it does not have to be exactly in the middle), and either sprinkle a bit of the chopped walnuts over the jelly, or place 1 walnut half on each.

Set aside while you prepare the top layer.

TOP LAYER

2 ounces (½ stick)
unsalted butter, at
room temperature

¼ cup granulated sugar

1 egg

Scant ¼ teaspoon
almond extract

2 tablespoons *unsifted*
all-purpose flour

½ teaspoon
baking powder

NOTE: *You will most probably have some leftover dough from the bottom layer. It makes delicious crisp sugar cookies. Roll it out to a scant ¼-inch thickness, cut with a round cutter or cut into squares with a knife. Place on unbuttered cookie sheets, sprinkle with a bit of sugar or cinnamon-sugar, and bake on a high rack in a 425° oven until the cookies are sandy colored with darker rims. Cool on a rack.*

Adjust a rack to the middle of the oven and preheat the oven to 425°.

In the small bowl of an electric mixer, beat the butter until it is soft. Beat in the sugar and then the egg and almond extract. Then add the flour and baking powder and beat until smooth.

Place a teaspoonful of this mixture over the filling in each form; there will be just enough for the 24 cakes.

Bake the two pans, side by side, on the same rack for 13 to 15 minutes, reversing the pans front to back once after about 10 minutes. When done, the little cakes will be golden with darker rims and the tops will spring back when they are pressed gently with a fingertip.

Let the cakes stand in the pans for about 5 minutes. Then cover each pan with a rack, turn the pan and the rack over, and remove the pans (the cakes will slip out easily). Then, with your fingers, turn the cakes right side up to cool.

VARIATION: *I don't see any reason you could not play with this recipe and substitute other fillings. I think about peanut butter or dates or a piece of chocolate . . .*

Texas Chocolate Muffins

12 MUFFINS

These are not muffins; they are my idea of brownies baked like cupcakes. But in Texas for some reason they call them muffins. They have two kinds of chocolate and cocoa. They are dense, rich, and very chocolaty. Especially beautiful—totally plain. They are quickly and easily mixed in a saucepan.

1 cup sifted
all-purpose flour

Pinch of salt

3 tablespoons
unsweetened
cocoa powder

8 ounces (2 sticks)
unsalted butter

2 ounces unsweetened
chocolate

2 ounces semisweet
chocolate

1½ cups granulated sugar

4 eggs

1 teaspoon vanilla extract

¼ teaspoon
almond extract

7 ounces (2 cups)
toasted pecans (see To
Toast Pecans, page 6),
broken into large pieces

Adjust a rack one-third up from the bottom of the oven and preheat the oven to 350°. Line 12 standard-size muffin forms (line them or butter them even if they are nonstick). Set aside.

Sift together the flour, salt, and cocoa, and set aside.

Place the butter and both of the chocolates in a heavy 2½- to 3-quart saucepan over moderately low heat, and stir frequently with a wooden spoon until melted and smooth.

Remove the pan from the heat. Stir in the sugar, the eggs one at a time, the vanilla and almond extracts, and then the sifted dry ingredients. After the dry ingredients are moistened, stir briskly until smooth. If necessary, whisk with a firm wire whisk. Then stir in the nuts.

This is a thick and gooey mixture and I find it clumsy to spoon into the prepared muffin forms. Instead, I pour it, part at a time, into a 2-cup plastic measuring cup with a spout (which is wide and easy to pour from). Then, with the help of a teaspoon, I pour it into the forms. This is a large amount of batter for 12 muffins; the forms will be filled to the tops. It is okay. The muffins will mound high during baking but they will not run over. They might run into one another a bit on the sides, but they will not stick to each other.

Bake for 33 to 35 minutes, reversing the pan front to back once during baking. To test for doneness, insert a toothpick into the middle of a muffin; it should come out just barely or almost dry and clean. A bit of moist batter may cling to the toothpick. Do not overbake. During baking, these will rise with inch-high, perfectly rounded tops that have a gorgeous crackly texture.

Remove the muffins from the pan and cool them on a rack. When cool, these will develop a hard and crunchy crust that is delicious.

MINIATURE GINGER CAKES
FORTY-EIGHT 1¾-INCH CAKES

Ginger and chocolate are a great combination. These are adorable little honey cakes, as light as a breeze, with an irresistible, spicy, orange and ginger flavor and a thin, dark, bittersweet, mocha chocolate glaze.

Miniature cakes were a popular conceit during the Victorian period, when they were usually very fancy and elaborate. These, which were adapted from an old recipe, are totally simple. If you have tea parties for dolls in your family, they will love these. People love them too, at tea parties, or at a buffet, or along with ice cream or fruit after dinner. Or make them for a bake sale.

By the way, the combination of cream of tartar and baking soda takes the place of baking powder. It was commonly used before baking powders were manufactured.

You will need four pans, each with twelve 1¾ x ¾-inch miniature muffin forms with nonstick finish. They are generally available at hardware stores and supermarkets.

3 ounces candied ginger
(to make ½ cup, diced)

1½ cups sifted
all-purpose flour

3 teaspoons
ground ginger

½ teaspoon coriander

½ teaspoon mace

½ teaspoon cinnamon

½ teaspoon cream
of tartar

½ teaspoon baking soda

¼ teaspoon salt

Finely grated rind
of 1 orange

2 tablespoons
orange juice

Ingredients continued on next page.

Adjust two racks to divide the oven into thirds and preheat the oven to 325°. Butter the miniature muffin forms, even though they are nonstick, and set aside.

Cut the ginger into ⅛- to ¼-inch dice and place it in a small bowl. Add about 2 teaspoons of the flour and toss with your fingers to separate and coat the pieces thoroughly. Set aside.

Sift together the remaining flour with the ground ginger, coriander, mace, cinnamon, cream of tartar, baking soda, and salt, and set aside.

Combine the rind and juice and set aside.

In the small bowl of an electric mixer, beat the butter until soft. Beat in the sugar, then add the honey and beat until smooth. Add the eggs one at a time, beating until incorporated after each addition. On low speed, gradually add about half the sifted dry ingredients, then the milk, and then the remaining dry ingredients. Beat until smooth.

Remove the bowl from the mixer and stir in the orange rind-and-juice mixture and then the diced candied ginger.

Spoon the mixture into the buttered muffin forms; they will be about three-quarters full.

Place two pans side by side on each oven rack and bake for 20 to 23 minutes, reversing the pans top to bottom once during baking (after about 15 minutes) to ensure even browning. Bake only until the tops spring back when they are pressed lightly with a fingertip.

2 ounces (½ stick) unsalted butter

3 tablespoons granulated sugar

½ cup honey

2 eggs

¼ cup milk

When done, let the cakes stand in the pans for about a minute. Then cover each pan with a rack and turn the pan and the rack upside down. If the cakes do not fall out of the pan easily, tap the pan against the rack to knock them out. Then, with your fingers, turn the cakes right side up to cool.

The glaze can be made while the cakes are baking or after they have baked.

BITTERSWEET GLAZE

This glaze makes a fantastic sauce on vanilla ice cream. If you plan it for ice cream, double the amounts to serve about 6 portions. Serve it slightly warm or at room temperature. If it is made ahead of time, it can be reheated before serving.

¼ cup boiling water

1 teaspoon granular instant coffee

3 ounces semisweet chocolate

1 ounce unsweetened chocolate

1 teaspoon vegetable shortening (e.g., Crisco)

Stir the water and coffee in a very small saucepan over moderate heat, add the chocolates and shortening, and then stir occasionally until the chocolates are melted.

Transfer to the small bowl of an electric mixer and beat briskly until the glaze is as smooth as honey. The glaze can be warm or cooled when you use it. Transfer it to a small, shallow custard cup.

One at a time, pick up a ginger cake, hold it upside down, and dip the top of the cake into the glaze to coat it. Then turn the cake right side up and place it on the rack again for the glaze to set a bit.

These can be served in about an hour or they can stand for several hours. (The glaze will become dull as it dries. Sorry about that.)

Gingerbreads

Gyngerbrede

16 SQUARES OR 32 SLICES

This is a recipe that was used by Mary Ball Washington, George's mother. It is very spicy. And equally delicious. Serve it as a coffee cake or a tea cake, or serve it with ice-cold buttermilk (a great combination). Or with vanilla ice cream as a dessert.

3 cups sifted
all-purpose flour

2 tablespoons ginger

1½ teaspoons cinnamon

1½ teaspoons nutmeg

1½ teaspoons mace

1 teaspoon cream
of tartar

½ teaspoon salt

5 ounces (1 cup) raisins

Boiling water

4 ounces (1 stick)
unsalted butter

¼ cup dark or light brown
sugar, firmly packed

½ cup light molasses
and ½ cup dark
molasses—or 1 cup of
either dark or light

½ cup honey

¼ cup bourbon, dark
rum, brandy, or sherry

½ cup milk

Adjust a rack one-third up from the bottom of the oven and preheat the oven to 350°. Line a 13 x 9 x 2-inch pan as follows: Turn the pan over, and cover it with a piece of foil (shiny side down), 17 or 18 inches long. Fold down the sides and the corners of the foil to shape it, remove the foil, turn the pan right side up, put the foil in the pan, and carefully press it into place. To butter the foil, place a piece of butter in the pan, place the pan in the oven until the butter melts, then, with a pastry brush or wax paper, spread the butter all over the foil. Set the pan aside.

Sift together the flour, ginger, cinnamon, nutmeg, mace, cream of tartar, and salt. Set aside.

Cover the raisins with boiling water, let stand for about 5 minutes, drain in a strainer, and then spread on paper towels to dry.

In the large bowl of an electric mixer, cream the butter until soft, add the sugar, and beat to mix. Add the molasses and honey and beat well. Then add the sifted dry ingredients in three additions, alternating with the bourbon and milk in one addition, and the eggs and orange juice in another addition.

Dissolve the baking soda in the warm water and mix into the batter. (This is a very old-fashioned method that still works well.)

Remove the bowl from the mixer and stir in the grated orange rind and the raisins.

Turn into the prepared pan and smooth the top.

Bake for 45 to 50 minutes, until the top springs back when lightly pressed with a fingertip.

Let the cake cool in the pan for about 10 minutes. Then cover it with a cookie sheet or a large rack, turn over the pan and the sheet or rack, remove the pan, peel off the foil, cover with a large rack, and turn to finish cooling right side up.

312

3 eggs, beaten to mix

¼ cup orange juice (grate
the rind before squeezing)

1 teaspoon baking soda

2 tablespoons
warm water

Finely grated rind
of 1 orange

When the cake is cool, carefully slide it onto a board. Use a long, thin, sharp knife to cut it into squares or slices.

West Indies Ginger Cake
One 9-inch loaf cake

Gingerbread is said to be the oldest sweet cake in the world; The Dictionary of Gastronomy (McGraw-Hill) puts its creation at about 2800 B.C., in Greece. Although it has remained rather popular ever since, it seems to be a craze now.

This Jamaican cake is not the usual ginger cake; this is made with chunks of preserved ginger (delicious), walnuts, honey, and sour cream. Serve it as a tea or coffee cake or as a dessert cake. It keeps well, it freezes well, it is a wonderful gift, it is a wonderful whatever.

2 cups sifted
all-purpose flour

1 teaspoon baking soda

1 teaspoon
powdered ginger

½ teaspoon salt

8½ ounces (about ⅔
cup) preserved ginger
with its syrup (see Note)

4 ounces (1 stick)
unsalted butter

Ingredients continued on next page.

Adjust a rack one-third up from the bottom of the oven and preheat the oven to 350°. Butter a 9 x 5 x 3-inch pan, or any pan of a similar shape with an 8-cup capacity. Dust it all with fine, dry bread crumbs, and tap to shake out excess over a piece of paper. Set aside.

Sift together the flour, baking soda, ginger, and salt, and set aside. Place pieces of the preserved ginger on a plate or board and, with a small, sharp knife, cut them one at a time into pieces ¼ to ⅓ inch in diameter (no smaller). Mix together the cut ginger and its syrup and set aside.

In the large bowl of an electric mixer, beat the butter until it is soft. Add the sugar and beat well for a few minutes. Add the egg yolks and beat well. On low speed mix in about a third of the dry ingredients, then all the sour cream, another third of the dry ingredients, all the honey, and then the remaining dry ingredients, mixing only until incorporated after each addition. Remove from the mixer and stir in the ginger with the syrup and the nuts.

½ cup light brown
sugar, firmly packed

2 eggs, separated

½ cup sour cream

½ cup honey

3½ ounces (1 cup)
walnuts, cut into
medium-small pieces

NOTE: *The preserved ginger
that I buy is put out by Roland
in an 8.5-ounce jar.*

In a small bowl, beat the egg whites only until they hold a point but are not stiff or dry. Fold them into the batter. Then turn the batter into the prepared pan, smooth the top, and bake for 1 hour and 15 minutes, until the top springs back when it is lightly pressed with a fingertip. Cakes made with honey have a tendency to become too dark on the top; about 20 minutes before this cake is done (or whenever it has formed a top crust and begins to look too dark) cover it loosely with foil.

Let the cake cool in the pan for 15 minutes. Then cover it with a rack. Hold the pan and rack carefully together and turn them over, remove the pan, and very carefully (the cake is fragile now) turn the cake right side up to cool on the rack.

When the cake has cooled, wrap it in plastic wrap and place it in the freezer or refrigerator until it is well chilled before slicing it.

WHOLE WHEAT YOGURT DATE-NUT GINGERBREAD
ONE 9- OR 10-INCH LOAF

The name tells it all, except that it has no eggs, no butter, no oil, no sugar. It is a hefty, dense, moist loaf from central Europe. Serve it as a coffee cake, a plain dessert, a sweet bread, or use it to make unusual and wonderful cheese sandwiches (butter the slices lightly, and add sharp Cheddar cheese and a bit of mustard).

This is best the day after it is baked.

½ cup *unsifted*
all-purpose white flour

½ teaspoon
baking powder

2 teaspoons baking soda

2 teaspoons ginger

½ teaspoon ground cloves

¾ teaspoon salt

Adjust a rack one-third up from the bottom of the oven and preheat the oven to 350°. Butter a loaf pan with an 8-cup capacity 10¼ x 3¾ x 3⅜ or 9 x 5 x 3 inches). Dust it with fine, dry bread crumbs or wheat germ; tap to shake out excess over a piece of paper. Set the pan aside.

Sift together the white flour, baking powder, baking soda, ginger, cloves, and salt, and set aside.

In a large mixing bowl, stir the yogurt and molasses with a wire whisk until smooth (the yogurt will become thin). With a rubber spatula or wooden spoon stir in the dates and then the nuts and ginger. Then add the sifted dry ingredients and stir just to mix. The mixture will foam up; do not wait for the foam to subside, but as soon as the ingredients are mixed, add the whole wheat flour and stir only until thoroughly mixed. It will be a stiff mixture.

16 ounces (2 cups)
plain yogurt

½ cup dark or
light molasses

8 ounces (1 cup) pitted
dates, each date cut
in half the long way

4 ounces (1 cup) walnut
halves or large pieces

2½ ounces (⅓ cup)
candied or preserved
ginger, cut into small
pieces (about ¼-inch size)

2 cups *unsifted*
all-purpose whole wheat
flour (stir to aerate
before measuring)

Spoon it into the prepared pan and smooth the top.

Bake for 1½ hours; do not underbake. (Testing this the usual way can be deceiving; it is best to be sure of your oven temperature and bake the specified time.)

Cool in the pan for about 15 minutes.

Then cover with a rack and turn over the pan and the rack. Remove the pan and then gently turn the loaf right side up to cool.

Wrap and let stand overnight before slicing.

Whole Wheat Gingerbread from New Orleans
12 to 16 slices

This is too delicious for words—that is, if you like sharp, spicy, chunky, wonderful gingerbread. Serve it between meals with strong, hot coffee or ice-cold milk or buttermilk. Or serve it as a dessert with vanilla ice cream or applesauce. This is baked in a shallow square pan.

Adjust a rack to the center of the oven and preheat the oven to 350°. Prepare an 8 x 8 x 2-inch metal cake pan as follows: Turn the pan upside down, center a 12-inch square of foil over the pan shiny side down, fold down the sides and corners of the foil, then remove the foil, turn the pan right side up, and place the shaped foil in the pan, pressing it carefully into place. To butter the foil, brush it with melted butter. Set aside.

¼ pound (1 stick)
unsalted butter

1½ teaspoons dry
powdered (not granular)
instant coffee

2 tablespoons
granulated sugar

¾ cup light molasses

2 eggs

½ cup milk

1 cup sifted
all-purpose white flour

1 cup strained or sifted
all-purpose whole
wheat flour (see Note)

½ teaspoon salt

¾ teaspoon baking soda

2 teaspoons
powdered ginger

½ teaspoon mace

4 ounces (1 generous
cup) walnuts, cut
or broken into
medium-size pieces

4 ounces (1 scant
cup) raisins

⅓ cup candied or
preserved ginger, cut
into ¼-inch pieces

In a 4- to 6-cup saucepan, melt the ¼ pound butter. Remove from the heat, add the coffee and sugar, and stir to dissolve. Then stir in the molasses, and set aside to cool slightly.

Place the eggs in a bowl and beat just to mix. Mix in the milk and set aside. Sift both flours, salt, baking soda, powdered ginger, and mace into a large bowl. Add the nuts, raisins, and candied ginger, and stir well. Add the melted butter and the egg-and-milk mixtures and, with a wooden spoon or rubber spatula, stir only until thoroughly mixed.

Transfer to the prepared pan and smooth the top.

Bake for 40 to 45 minutes, until the top springs back when it is lightly pressed with a fingertip.

Cool the cake in the pan for about 10 minutes. Then cover with a rack, turn over the pan and the rack, remove the pan and the foil lining, cover with another rack, and turn the cake right side up to cool. To keep the cake from drying out, slice only as much as you might need. Cut the cake in half, and then cut each half into 6 or 8 slices.

NOTE: *When you sift whole wheat flour, some of the flour may be too coarse to go through the sifter. That part should be stirred into the part that did go through.*

MARMALADE GINGERBREAD
ONE 9-INCH LOAF

This is a beautiful, fine-grained, honey-colored loaf—plain, not too sweet, moist, mildly spiced, and delicious. Serve it as a sweet bread with a meal, as a tea or coffee cake, or make thin bread-and-butter or cream-cheese sandwiches with it.

2 cups sifted
all-purpose flour

½ teaspoon salt

1 teaspoon baking soda

1 teaspoon ginger

½ teaspoon nutmeg

Finely grated rind of
2 large lemons

1 tablespoon dark or
light rum or cognac

4 ounces (1 stick)
unsalted butter

½ cup honey

1 cup sweet orange
marmalade

2 eggs

Adjust a rack to the center of the oven and preheat the oven to 350°. Butter a 9 x 5 x 3-inch loaf pan, dust it all over with fine, dry bread crumbs, and tap lightly over a piece of paper to shake out excess crumbs. Set the pan aside.

Sift together the flour, salt, baking soda, ginger, and nutmeg, and set aside.

Mix the rind and rum or cognac and let stand.

In the large bowl of an electric mixer, cream the butter. Add the honey and beat to mix. Mix in the marmalade. On low speed add half the dry ingredients, scraping the bowl and beating only to mix. Then mix in the eggs one at a time, and then the balance of the sifted dry ingredients. Remove from the mixer and stir in the rind and rum or cognac.

Turn into the prepared pan and smooth the top.

Bake for 1 hour, until the top feels semifirm to the touch and a cake tester inserted into the middle comes out clean. If the loaf begins to brown too much during baking, cover it loosely with foil.

Cool in the pan for 10 to 15 minutes. Cover with a rack, turn over the pan and the rack, remove the pan, and leave the loaf upside down to cool.

PUMPKIN GINGERBREAD
1 LOAF

This bakes into a beautiful, richly browned, perfectly shaped loaf. The combination of spices adds a mild and deliciously gingery flavor that is just right, and the pumpkin gives it a wonderfully moist texture. You will be proud of this. It makes a marvelous gift. Serve it with tea or coffee, or milk or buttermilk.

Adjust a rack to the center of the oven and preheat the oven to 350°. You will need a loaf pan that has a 7-cup capacity; that may be 9 x 5 x 3 inches (which has an 8-cup capacity), 9 x 5 x 2¾ inches, or it may be longer and

2 cups sifted
all-purpose flour

¾ teaspoon salt

1 teaspoon baking soda

¼ teaspoon
baking powder

2 teaspoons
powdered ginger

½ teaspoon nutmeg

½ teaspoon cinnamon

¼ teaspoon cloves

¼ teaspoon dry
powdered mustard

4 ounces (1 stick)
unsalted butter

1½ cups granulated sugar

2 eggs

⅓ cup strong prepared
black coffee (you
can use 1 rounded
teaspoon instant coffee
in ⅓ cup water)

1 cup mashed cooked
pumpkin (see Note)

7 ounces (2 cups)
pecans, cut or broken
into large pieces

narrower. Butter the pan; dust it all over with fine, dry bread crumbs; and tap over a piece of paper to shake out excess crumbs. Set aside.

Sift together the flour, salt, baking soda, baking powder, ginger, nutmeg, cinnamon, cloves, and mustard, and set aside.

In the large bowl of an electric mixer, cream the butter. Add the sugar and beat to mix. On low speed, add half of the dry ingredients, scraping the bowl with a rubber spatula. Beat only until barely incorporated. Mix in the coffee. Add the remaining dry ingredients and beat only until incorporated. Add the pumpkin and, scraping the bowl as necessary, beat only until incorporated. Remove the bowl from the mixer.

Stir in the pecans.

Turn into the prepared pan and smooth the top. Then, with the back of a spoon, form a trench down the middle, ½ to 1 inch deep. The trench will prevent the middle from rising too high, although it will rise some anyhow and form a crack down the length of the cake (it is supposed to). It will be as pretty as a picture.

Bake for 1 hour and 10 to 15 minutes, until the top feels slightly firm to the touch and a cake tester inserted into the middle comes out clean.

Cool the cake in the pan for 10 to 15 minutes. Cover the pan with a rack, turn over the pan and the rack, remove the pan, cover the cake with another rack, and very carefully (do not squash the cake) turn over again (or gently turn it over with your hands), leaving the cake right side up to cool.

NOTE: *If you use canned pumpkin, it should be labeled "solid-pack pumpkin," not "pumpkin-pie filling."*

Ice Cream, Sauces, and More

About Ice Cream

*I*f no one ever told you that you would love to have an ice cream maker, I am telling you now. I wish someone had told me. Now I know what it is like; I am sorry about all the years I did not have one. I thought it was too much work and too difficult. It is neither. It is great fun and exciting, and I become transported to ice cream heaven every time I use the machine.

To Soften Ice Cream

Some of these recipes may become too firm if they are frozen for a few days. Here's how to make them way ahead of time (a week or two) and still serve them at their very best.

Immediately before serving, or as long as an hour or two (or three) before serving, use a large, strong, firm kitchen spoon to cut up the too-firm ice cream or ice so it can be transferred to either an electric mixer or a food processor.

In a mixer: Chill the large bowl of the mixer and the beaters ahead of time. Place the cut-up ice cream in the chilled bowl. Beat until fluffy and creamy but not until melted. Use a rubber spatula or a wooden spoon to continually push the hard mixture into the beaters.

In a food processor: Chill the bowl and metal blade ahead of time. With the motor running, add pieces of the frozen mixture through the feed tube, adding a few pieces at a time, and processing until smoothly softened but not until melted. Do not process too much at once; refreeze each batch immediately.

After softening the too-hard mixture either in a mixer or a processor, serve it immediately in chilled cups, or replace it in the freezer in a chilled container. It will retain its wonderful texture for an hour or two or three (recipes vary).

This procedure can be repeated again days or weeks later, as often as you wish.

Fantastic Vanilla Ice Cream

1½ PINTS

Rich, luxurious, extravagant, delicious, deluxe, smo-o-oth; the best! This fabulous ice cream will not freeze too hard to serve easily—it will remain creamy and heavenly and perfect—even after days in the freezer.

2 cups heavy cream

4 egg yolks

½ cup granulated sugar

1 teaspoon vanilla extract

Place 1 cup of the cream (reserving the remaining 1 cup) in the top of a double boiler over hot water on moderate heat. Let stand, uncovered, until a slightly wrinkled skin forms on the top of the cream.

Meanwhile, in the small bowl of an electric mixer, beat the yolks for a few minutes until they are pale and thick. On low speed gradually add the sugar. Then beat on high speed again for 2 or 3 minutes more.

When the cream is scalded, on low speed, very gradually add about half of it to the beaten-yolks-and-sugar mixture. Scrape the bowl well with a rubber spatula. Then add the yolk mixture to the remaining cream. Mix well, and place over hot water again, on moderate heat.

Cook, scraping the bottom and sides frequently with a rubber spatula, until the mixture thickens to a soft custard consistency. It will register 178° to 180° on a candy thermometer. (When the mixture starts to thicken, scrape the bottom and sides constantly with the rubber spatula.)

Remove from the hot water, transfer to a larger bowl, stir occasionally until cool, and mix in the vanilla and the reserved 1 cup of heavy cream.

It is best to chill this mixture for an hour or more before freezing it. Freeze in an ice cream maker, following the manufacturer's directions.

Ginger Ice Cream

1½ QUARTS

This is a plain, old-fashioned vanilla ice cream with tiny chunks of candied or preserved ginger all through it; the flavor is only mildly gingery.

Place the milk and 1 cup of the cream (reserving the remaining 2 cups cream) in the top of a double boiler over hot water on moderate heat, or in a heavy saucepan over low heat. Cook, uncovered, until scalded, or until you see a slightly wrinkled skin on top or small bubbles around the edge.

321

1½ cups milk

3 cups heavy cream

¾ cup granulated sugar

1½ tablespoons sifted
all-purpose flour

⅜ teaspoon salt

3 egg yolks

⅜ cup chopped
candied or preserved
ginger (see Note)

1 teaspoon vanilla extract

NOTE: *Chop the ginger either on a board with a sharp knife or in a small, round chopping bowl with a knife that has a rounded blade. Either way, do not chop it all too fine; leave some chunky pieces to really bite into.*

Meanwhile, sift or strain the sugar, flour, and salt together and add them to the hot milk mixture, stirring well.

In a bowl, stir the yolks slightly, just to mix. Gradually add about 1 cup of the hot milk mixture, stirring constantly. Then gradually stir the yolks into the remaining hot milk mixture. Cook, uncovered, stirring and scraping the bottom and sides almost constantly with a rubber spatula, for about 15 minutes, until the mixture barely coats a wooden spoon; it should register 180° to 185° on a candy thermometer.

Remove from the heat. To stop the cooking, transfer the mixture to a bowl, or stir over ice and water. Let stand until completely cool.

Stir the ginger and vanilla into the cooled mixture.

In a large chilled bowl, with chilled beaters, whip the reserved 2 cups heavy cream until it holds a shape but not until it is really stiff.

Then gradually fold the milk-and-ginger mixture into the whipped cream.

Freeze in an ice cream maker following the manufacturer's directions.

This does not need a sauce, but a nice and easy one, if you wish, is sweet orange marmalade; just stir it to soften.

PALM BEACH ORANGE ICE CREAM

1¼ QUARTS

This delicate and refreshing ice cream has a beautiful pale orange color and a mild and creamy flavor. A scoop of it is delicious on a fresh fruit salad for a luncheon. Or serve it for dessert, either plain or in combination with vanilla ice cream—a small scoop of each. It was served to us after a festive dinner party in large, wide, shallow glasses on tall stems. Each portion had a few thin wedges of peeled kiwi fruit on one side, a few small strawberries on the other side, and a perfect white gardenia on the top. Pretty as a picture.

¾ cup milk

Finely grated rind
of 1 orange

Place the milk in the top of a double boiler over hot water on moderate heat. Add the grated rinds and let cook uncovered until small bubbles form around the edge.

Meanwhile, in a small mixing bowl, stir the yolks lightly with a whisk just to mix them. Then, stirring constantly, gradually mix in about half of the

Finely grated rind
of 1 lemon

3 egg yolks

⅜ cup granulated sugar

⅓ cup light corn syrup

⅛ teaspoon salt

¾ cup heavy cream

1½ cups fresh
orange juice

1 tablespoon fresh
lemon juice

scalded milk. Add the yolk mixture to the remaining milk, stirring well. Add the sugar, syrup, and salt.

Stir over hot water until the mixture thickens slightly and barely coats a metal spoon; it will register 180° on a candy thermometer.

Strain the mixture (if you leave the grated rinds in, they will collect in one lump on the edge of the dasher during the freezing) and set aside to cool.

Add the cream and both juices. Chill in the refrigerator or freezer.

Freeze the ice cream in an ice cream maker, following the manufacturer's directions.

PUMPKIN ICE CREAM
1 QUART

This is a wonderful recipe. It is most unusual, a beautiful color, and everybody is wild about it. It has no season.

3 egg yolks

½ cup mashed cooked
pumpkin (about one-
quarter of a 1-pound
can of solid-pack
pumpkin, not pie filling)

½ cup granulated sugar

⅛ teaspoon salt

¼ teaspoon cinnamon

¼ teaspoon nutmeg

¼ teaspoon ginger

2 cups heavy cream

In the small bowl of an electric mixer, beat the yolks until they are pale, thick, and creamy. Place the pumpkin in the top of a double boiler. Add the beaten yolks, sugar, salt, and through a fine strainer add the cinnamon, nutmeg, and ginger. Place over hot water on moderate heat.

Cook, stirring and scraping the bottom with a rubber spatula, for about 10 minutes or until slightly thickened.

Remove the top of the double boiler and set aside, stirring occasionally until completely cool. (If you wish, set the top of the double boiler in a bowl of ice and water and stir constantly until cool.)

In a large chilled bowl with chilled beaters, whip the cream until it holds a soft shape. (If you beat until the cream is stiff, it will make the ice cream heavy and buttery instead of light and creamy.)

In a large bowl, fold the pumpkin mixture and whipped cream together.

Freeze according to the manufacturer's directions for your ice cream maker.

BLUEBERRY ICE CREAM

1 QUART

This has one of the most beautiful red-purple colors I have ever seen in food. But even if it were colorless, it would be magnificent. Smooth, creamy, rich, deluxe, and delicious—a memorable ice cream.

One 1-pint box
fresh blueberries

½ cup granulated sugar

Pinch of salt

1½ cups heavy cream

1½ tablespoons
lemon juice

1½ tablespoons kirsch,
crème de cassis, or brandy

NOTE: *Homemakers' hint—
the blueberries will stain both
rubber spatulas and wooden
spoons; don't use anything you
will feel sad about staining.*

Wash and drain the berries. Place them in a wide and heavy saucepan or frying pan. Add the sugar and stir to mix. Cover, and place over low heat. Cook for 5 minutes to soften the berries a little and partially melt the sugar. Then raise the heat to moderate, uncover the pan, stir until the mixture comes to a boil, and let boil for 5 minutes, stirring and mashing the berries against the sides of the pan to mash them.

Set aside to cool for a few minutes, then strain through a large-mesh strainer set over a large bowl. Do not use a strainer that has fine openings; even with a coarse strainer some of the fruit will not go through. However, press through as much as you can.

Place the puréed berry mixture in the freezer or refrigerator until very cold.

Stir in the salt, cream, lemon juice, and kirsch, crème de cassis, or brandy.

If the mixture is less than very cold, chill it in the freezer or refrigerator.

Freeze in an ice cream maker following the manufacturer's instructions.

When you serve this, you may wish to pass the kirsch, crème de cassis, or brandy to be poured over each portion.

Because of the alcohol, this does not freeze too hard to serve directly from the freezer.

CRANBERRY ICE CREAM

1 QUART

This has an exquisite bright rosy-pink color, and an equally exquisite taste and texture—creamy and tart, not too sweet; extraordinary! Start this ahead of time; the mixture must chill well before it is frozen.

½ pound (about 5 cups) cranberries, fresh or frozen

½ cup water

½ cup orange juice

½ envelope unflavored gelatin

1½ tablespoons cold water

¼ cup light corn syrup

2 tablespoons water

½ cup light brown sugar, firmly packed

¼ cup honey

½ cup heavy cream

Wash and drain the berries. Place them in a large saucepan with the ½ cup of water and the orange juice. Bring to a boil over moderate heat, then reduce the heat and let simmer, uncovered, for 10 minutes. Cool a bit and then purée in a food processor or a blender. Press the mixture through a large strainer set over a large bowl. Set aside.

Sprinkle the gelatin over the 1½ tablespoons cold water in a small cup. Set aside.

Place the corn syrup and the 2 tablespoons water in a small saucepan over moderate heat. Bring to a boil; boil gently, uncovered, for 5 minutes. Add the softened gelatin and stir to dissolve. Add the brown sugar and stir to dissolve, then stir in the honey.

In a mixing bowl, combine the cranberry mixture with the honey mixture. Set aside to cool. Cover and refrigerate for several hours or overnight, or chill it quickly in the freezer.

When you are ready to freeze the ice cream, in a chilled bowl with chilled beaters whip the cream until it holds a soft shape but not until it is stiff. Gradually fold the cranberry mixture into the cream. If the berry mixture sinks to the bottom, pour it all gently from one bowl to another to incorporate.

Then freeze the mixture, following the manufacturer's directions for your ice cream maker.

This stays semifirm for several hours after it is frozen. It is best at that consistency. If it freezes longer and becomes too hard, place it in the refrigerator for about half an hour before serving; check it after 15 or 20 minutes.

LALLA ROOKH

This was named for the heroine of a series of oriental tales by Thomas More. I seem to have had this recipe forever. It is easy, fun, and everyone loves it. It is hollowed-out ice cream filled with cognac and covered with whipped cream.

Vanilla ice cream

Heavy cream

Sugar

Vanilla extract

Cognac

Optional: Grated semisweet chocolate

NOTE: This procedure and general recipe opens up a whole world of other combinations. Homemade Palm Beach Orange Ice Cream (page 322) with amaretto is delicious. Or marinate some raisins in rum and fill coffee ice cream with the raisins and rum. Et cetera.

The ice cream can be homemade or bought. It should be soft enough so you can work with it, but not softer. The best way is to cut it into chunks and beat it in the large bowl of an electric mixer or in the bowl of a food processor fitted with the metal blade. Beat or process briefly; do not let it melt.

Quickly place a large round scoop of the ice cream in parfait glasses, wineglasses, or tall champagne glasses. Form a hollow with a teaspoon in the middle of each serving. It should be rather deep (this is for the cognac). The ice cream might not hold its shape now while it is soft—the hollow might disappear—but you can fix it when the ice cream is refrozen.

Immediately place the glasses in the freezer until the ice cream is firm again.

With a teaspoon, correct the hollow. The diameter of the scooped-out space should not be too wide, but the space can be deep if you wish. Return to the freezer.

This part can and should be done way ahead of time. Cover and let stand in the freezer until you are ready for it.

Shortly before serving (an hour or two if you wish) whip the cream with a bit of sugar and vanilla, whipping until it holds a definite shape but not until it is really stiff. Refrigerate. If you do not use it very soon it will probably separate a bit while it stands; just beat it a little with a small wire whisk before you use it until it is right.

Immediately before serving, pour the cognac into the hollowed-out space in the ice cream. (It is easiest if you pour the cognac into a small pitcher and pour it from the pitcher.) You should use 1 to 2 tablespoons of cognac in each portion. Then carefully place a large spoonful of the whipped cream on the top of the cognac and ice cream. If you wish, sprinkle with the grated semisweet chocolate. If the scooped-out hollow is not too wide, the whipped cream will rest on the top.

SPAGO'S SENSATIONAL CARAMEL ICE CREAM
1½ PINTS

This is one of the most famous ice creams made by Nancy Silverton when she was the pastry chef at Spago, Wolfgang Puck's sensational restaurant in Beverly Hills. Spago is my favorite restaurant. They serve this heavenly stuff with apple pie. Well, with or without, this is an experience.

CUSTARD

1 cup milk

1 cup heavy cream

4 egg yolks

⅓ cup granulated sugar

Place the milk and cream in a saucepan over medium heat, uncovered, until scalded (or until you see small bubbles on the surface).

Meanwhile, beat the egg yolks and the sugar in the large bowl of an electric mixer at high speed for 2 minutes.

Then, on low speed, gradually add the hot milk and cream to the egg-yolk mixture, scraping the sides of the bowl with a rubber spatula as necessary.

Transfer the mixture to the top of a double boiler over hot water on moderate heat and cook, stirring, until the mixture thickens enough to coat a spoon, or registers 168 to 170° on a sugar or candy thermometer.

Remove from the heat and strain into a large bowl.

The custard should still be hot when the following caramel is added to it. Therefore, without waiting, prepare the caramel.

CARAMEL

⅓ cup heavy cream

½ cup granulated sugar

½ teaspoon vanilla extract (see Note)

You will now heat the ⅓ cup cream and caramelize the sugar at the same time.

Place the cream in a small saucepan over low heat; by the time the sugar is caramelized the cream should be almost boiling.

To caramelize the sugar: Place the sugar in a 10- to 12-inch frying pan (use a nonstick pan if possible) over moderate heat and stir occasionally with a wooden spoon until the sugar starts to melt. Then stir constantly as the sugar continues to melt and to caramelize. (If a large chunk of the melted sugar becomes stuck to the spoon use a table knife or a metal spatula to scrape it off.) When the sugar is pretty well melted but not completely

NOTE: *At Spago they use a vanilla bean instead of the extract. To use a vanilla bean, slit it the long way, scrape out most of the seeds, and add the seeds and the bean to the milk and cream while they are heating for the custard. Remove the bean when the mixture is added to the beaten egg yolks and sugar.*

smooth, lower the heat a bit and continue to stir until it becomes smooth and a rich caramel color.

Then, off the heat, with a long-handled wooden spoon, gradually stir the almost boiling cream into the hot, caramelized sugar. If adding the cream causes a few lumps of caramelized sugar to form, just place the pan over low heat and stir again until smooth.

Slowly and gradually stir the hot caramel mixture into the still warm (or hot) custard. If the mixture is not perfectly smooth, that is, if there are any lumps of caramel, it is okay. They will melt by themselves just from the heat of the custard.

Pour the mixture into a bowl, cool, and stir in the vanilla. Then cover and refrigerate for at least a few hours—or overnight. Or, to save time, chill the mixture by placing the bowl into a larger bowl of ice.

Freeze the chilled mixture in an ice cream maker following the manufacturer's directions.

LITTLE HAVANA COCONUT ICE CREAM

1 GENEROUS QUART

Many Cuban-Americans speak lovingly of a coconut ice cream they remember having eaten in Havana, where it was often served in half a coconut shell by street vendors. After much experimenting, some of my Cuban-American friends arrived at this fabulous recipe, which is adapted from one created by Roland Mesnier, President Reagan and Mrs. Reagan's White House pastry chef. As smooth as honey, as rich as Rockefeller, with an elusive but positively tantalizing coconut flavor.

I have served this weeks after making it, and it was just as good. It is best to prepare the mixture the day before freezing it.

Serve this remarkable concoction in small portions either by itself, with any chocolate sauce, or with fresh strawberries.

Place ¾ cup of the heavy cream (reserve the remaining ½ cup) in a large, heavy saucepan. Add the light cream and shredded coconut. Stir frequently with a long-handled wooden spoon over moderate heat until the mixture comes to a low boil. Reduce the heat and let the mixture barely simmer, stirring, for about 5 minutes. Remove from the heat and let stand for 30 minutes.

1¼ cups heavy cream

2 cups light cream (a.k.a. coffee cream—it is heavier than half-and-half)

6 ounces canned or packaged sweetened shredded coconut

8 egg yolks

½ cup granulated sugar

1 tablespoon canned cream of coconut (see Note)

Note: Cream of coconut is canned by a company named Lopez in Puerto Rico. It is generally available in liquor stores (because it is most frequently used in mixed drinks) and in some large food stores.

Place a large strainer over a large bowl. Place a thin linen or cotton towel in a single layer over the strainer, letting the ends drape over the outside of the bowl.

Slowly and carefully pour the scalded coconut mixture onto the towel in the strainer (if the saucepan is too heavy to pour from, ladle the mixture). Let drain. (If the drained cream reaches the bottom of the strainer, pour it into another bowl and reserve it; you will use the cream but not the coconut.)

Twist the corners of the towel together and squeeze to remove every bit of the coconut-flavored cream. (If it is too hot to handle, wait until you can.)

Discard the coconut.

In the small bowl of an electric mixer, beat the yolks for a minute or so, add the sugar and the cream of coconut, and beat for a few minutes. With a ladle gradually add a cup of the warm, drained cream mixture to the egg-yolk mixture and mix together.

Then, very gradually, add the egg-yolk mixture to the remaining warm, drained cream mixture, stirring constantly with a large wire whisk or a long-handled wooden spoon.

Transfer the mixture to a large, heavy saucepan over moderate heat and cook, stirring constantly and scraping the bottom of the pan with a large rubber spatula until the mixture thickens enough to coat a spoon, or until it registers 178° on a candy or sugar thermometer. (Do not let the mixture come to a boil or the egg yolks will scramble and the mixture will not be smooth.) Immediately, in order to stop the cooking, pour through a wide but fine strainer set over a bowl. Then stir in the remaining ½ cup of whipping cream. Stir occasionally until cool. Then cover and refrigerate overnight. Or, if you are in a hurry, place the mixture in the freezer for about 1 hour, stirring a few times. Freeze the mixture in an ice cream maker, following the manufacturer's directions.

SUGARBUSH MAPLE ICE CREAM

1 QUART

This is smooth, creamy, mellow—sensational. Incidentally, grade B maple syrup is generally recommended for cooking—it is more flavorful and darker than grade A.

2 egg yolks

½ cup maple syrup

1¼ cups heavy cream

¼ teaspoon vanilla extract

⅛ teaspoon almond extract

In the small bowl of an electric mixer, beat the yolks for 5 to 7 minutes until very pale and thick. Meanwhile, heat the maple syrup in a saucepan, uncovered, over moderately high heat until it almost comes to a boil; you will know it is ready when it forms a pale (almost white) layer on top.

To make it easier to handle, I suggest that you transfer the hot syrup to a pitcher with a spout that is easy to pour from and, without waiting (while the syrup is almost boiling hot), gradually add it to the yolks, while beating on medium speed. Scrape the sides occasionally to be sure the ingredients are well mixed.

Transfer the mixture to the top of a double boiler over hot water on moderate heat and cook, scraping the bottom and sides almost constantly with a rubber spatula, for about 5 minutes until a candy or sugar thermometer registers 178° to 180°.

Now transfer the mixture to a rather wide, large bowl. Stir frequently until completely cool and then chill the mixture in the refrigerator or freezer. Or cool it in the wide bowl by placing the bowl into a larger bowl of ice and water and stirring until chilled.

Meanwhile, chill the large bowl of the electric mixer and the beaters. In the chilled bowl, with the chilled beaters, whip the cream only until it holds a soft shape, not until it is stiff.

Stir the vanilla and almond extracts into the chilled maple-syrup mixture.

Gradually, in several additions, fold about one-third of the maple-syrup mixture into the whipped cream and then fold the whipped cream into the remaining maple syrup mixture.

Freeze in an ice cream maker according to the manufacturer's directions.

After the ice cream has been frozen, it will still be a little softer than most ice creams that have just been frozen. And then it will take a little longer than usual to become as firm as most ice creams. Actually, it takes overnight. If it is served before then, it will have an incredible texture—you will love it—like an airy mousse-ice cream; wonderful. If you freeze it longer until it becomes firmer, it will still be wonderful. Whichever.

Devil's Food Chocolate Ice Cream
1½ quarts

Sexy, dense, rich, ravishing, never too firm, always smooth and voluptuous—with a mild honey flavor. It has a light texture and could be called Chocolate Mousse Ice Cream.

11½ ounces semisweet chocolate

1 cup milk

⅜ cup honey

7 egg yolks

⅔ cup granulated sugar

2 cups heavy cream

P.S. People often ask what my favorite dessert is. Answer: chocolate ice cream.

Break up the chocolate and place it, with the milk and honey, in a heavy saucepan over moderate heat. Scrape the bottom and sides constantly with a rubber spatula until the chocolate is melted and then whisk the mixture until smooth.

Meanwhile, place the yolks in the large bowl of an electric mixer and beat to mix. Gradually add the sugar and beat until the mixture becomes slightly pale in color. Then, very slowly and on low speed, add the warm chocolate mixture and beat until smooth. It will be a thick mixture.

Transfer the mixture to a larger heavy saucepan. Cook over rather low heat; you must scrape the bottom and sides constantly with a large, wide rubber spatula, until the mixture registers 140° on a sugar or candy thermometer.

Gradually whisk in the cream. Stir occasionally until cool. Chill in the freezer or refrigerator until very cold and then freeze in an ice cream maker according to the manufacturer's directions.

East Hampton Chocolate Icebox Cake
8 to 10 portions

It had been a perfect summer day. There was a riot of hot colors in the sky and water, and everywhere we looked there were graceful seagulls and sleek sailboats. We were on the terrace of the Clubhouse Restaurant at Wings Point Yacht Club overlooking Three-Mile Harbor in East Hampton, New York.

Everything was magical, but even so, I could not believe the dessert. They call it a Chocolate Mousse Cake; it is a traditional icebox cake. I thought I had made or at least tasted every variation of chocolate mousse as well as chocolate icebox cake, but this one was different and wonderful. (The difference is a combination of both semisweet and milk chocolate, which makes a rich, creamy, dense but not heavy mousse.)

I was invited into the kitchen, where I met the pastry chef, Linda Nessel, a darling young lady who had just graduated from a cooking school in Rhode Island. In her baker's whites she looked like a kid in her father's pajamas. But when I asked her about the recipe she spoke with detailed precision and an air of experience and authority.

You will need a 9 x 3-inch springform pan. This dessert can be made a day ahead or it can be served about 6 hours after it is made.

Two 3-ounce packages
ladyfingers

7 ounces semisweet
chocolate

9 ounces milk chocolate

6 eggs, separated

½ teaspoon vanilla extract

¼ cup Grand Marnier

½ teaspoon
unflavored gelatin

1 teaspoon cold tap water

Pinch of salt

¼ cup granulated sugar

Separate the strips of ladyfingers but do not separate each individual ladyfinger. Place strips of them, top sides against the pan, around the sides of an unbuttered 9 x 3-inch springform pan. Then cover the bottom of the pan with ladyfingers, placing them any which way and cutting them as you please (the pattern on the bottom will not show). You will probably use about 40 ladyfingers; there will be some left over that you will not need.

Break up both kinds of chocolate and place them in the top of a large double boiler over warm water on low heat. Cover the top with a folded paper towel (to absorb steam) and with the pot cover. Stir occasionally. When the chocolates are almost melted, remove the top of the double boiler and stir until completely melted and smooth. Set aside.

While the chocolates are melting, beat the egg yolks in the small bowl of an electric mixer at high speed for about 5 minutes until pale and thick. Stir in the vanilla and about one-third of the Grand Marnier (reserve the remaining Grand Marnier). Let stand.

Sprinkle the gelatin over the water in a small glass custard cup and let stand for 3 to 5 minutes to soften. Then add the remaining Grand Marnier; place the custard cup in shallow hot water in a small pan over low heat; stir occasionally with a table knife until the gelatin is dissolved.

Quickly beat the warm gelatin mixture into the egg yolks, adding it all at once and beating at high speed. Then reduce the speed to moderate and beat in the melted chocolate, beating until the two mixtures are smoothly blended. Remove the bowl from the mixer.

In the large bowl of an electric mixer, with clean beaters, beat the whites with the salt until they hold a soft shape. Reduce the speed to moderate and gradually add the sugar. Increase the speed to high again and beat until the whites hold a definite point, but are not stiff or dry.

In about three additions, with a rubber spatula fold about a third of the whites into the chocolate, folding gently and not thoroughly. Then add the chocolate to the remaining whites and again fold gently—this time fold until thoroughly incorporated, but do not handle any more than necessary.

Gently pour the chocolate mixture into the ladyfinger-lined pan. The chocolate mixture will not fill the pan to the top of the ladyfingers.

If you cover the pan (even loosely) with plastic wrap, moisture will form on the bottom of the plastic, it will drip onto the mousse, and although there will not be much of it, you don't need any. Therefore, unfold a lightweight paper napkin, place it loosely over the pan, and cover the napkin loosely with plastic wrap. The paper will absorb moisture and the plastic will prevent the mousse from drying out.

Refrigerate for about 6 hours or overnight.

Whipped Cream

1 cup heavy cream

½ teaspoon vanilla extract

2 tablespoons confectioners' sugar

In a chilled bowl, with chilled beaters, whip the ingredients until they hold a definite shape. (If you whip the cream ahead of time, refrigerate it until shortly before serving. Then, if it has separated a bit, beat it briefly with a wire whisk or a beater to incorporate.)

Place the cream by spoonfuls around the outer edge of the mousse, up against the ladyfingers—or transfer it to a pastry bag fitted with a rather large star-shaped tube and form rosettes of cream in a circle around the outer edge. If you wish, sprinkle the whipped cream with coarsely grated semisweet chocolate. And cut two slices of navel orange about ⅓ inch thick. Remove the seeds but do not remove the rind. Cut each slice into 6 pie-shaped wedges. Place the wedges, point down, into the whipped cream.

Before serving, release the catch on the side of the pan and gently and slowly remove the sides of the pan. Serve directly on the bottom of the springform on a folded napkin on a serving plate. It is possible to transfer this if you prefer and if you are very careful. First release the bottom with a long, sharp knife. Then, raise one edge a bit with a wide metal spatula, and slip a flat-sided cookie sheet slowly and gently under the cake. Using the cookie sheet as a spatula, carefully transfer the cake to a large flat platter.

Peanut Butter Sauce

1¼ cups

Smooth and creamy. Kids love this served over vanilla ice cream and sliced bananas. Not only kids.

¾ cup light corn syrup

¼ cup water

Tiny pinch of salt

⅓ cup smooth peanut butter

1 tablespoon unsalted butter

1 egg

1 tablespoon vanilla extract

⅓ cup heavy cream

In a heavy saucepan with about a 1½-quart capacity, stir the corn syrup with the water and salt. Bring to a boil, uncovered, over moderate heat. Then reduce the heat slightly and let the sauce simmer for 5 minutes. Add the peanut butter and stir well with a small wire whisk (if it appears curdled, don't worry—it is okay). Remove from the heat, add the butter, and stir gently to melt.

In a small bowl, beat the egg with a whisk just to mix. Very gradually stir about half of the warm peanut-butter mixture into the egg; then stir the egg mixture into the remaining warm peanut-butter mixture.

Place over very low heat and cook, scraping the bottom and sides constantly and gently with a rubber spatula, for 1½ minutes (to cook the egg).

Remove from the heat and cool to room temperature.

Stir in the vanilla and (unwhipped) cream.

Refrigerate. (I like this best very cold, right out of the refrigerator. It will be thick and creamy.)

Goldrush Sauce

2 cups

EUREKA!!! We struck gold. And this is the mother lode. When this is served slightly warm on ice cream it is a Goldrush Sundae (a.k.a. Gold Brick Sundae—it is most popular in the Midwest, where it is traditionally served with vanilla ice cream). The sauce is the kind that turns chewy-gooey on ice cream, and it is loaded with crunchy chunks of chopped Heath Bars or any other hard toffee candy, either chocolate-coated or not, and toasted pecans. With ice cream, the dessert is both warm and cold, thick and chewy caramel-like, smooth and crunchy-chunky, dark dark chocolate, and pure 14 karat.

The sauce can be made ahead of time, if you wish.

Place the chocolate, butter, and boiling water in a 1½-quart heavy saucepan. Cook over low heat, stirring, until the chocolate is melted. Whisk the mixture with a small whisk until it is smooth. Stir in the corn syrup and sugar.

2½ ounces unsweetened chocolate

1 tablespoon unsalted butter

⅓ cup boiling water

2 tablespoons light corn syrup

1 cup granulated sugar

1 teaspoon vanilla extract

About 1 scant cup Heath Bars (five 1¹⁄₁₆-ounce bars), cut into ½- to ⅓-inch pieces

½ cup pecans, toasted (see To Toast Pecans, page 6), either halves or large pieces

Raise the heat to moderate and stir until the mixture comes to a boil. Then stop stirring, reduce the heat as necessary, and let boil moderately for exactly 8 minutes.

Remove the pan from the heat. Place the bottom of the pan briefly in a bowl of cold water in order to stop the boiling.

Stir in the vanilla. Let cool a few minutes until the sauce is only warm, not hot. Stir in the candy and the pecans.

Serve the sauce slightly warm. It may be refrigerated and then reheated over low heat. If it is too thick after it is refrigerated and then reheated, add hot water, one teaspoonful at a time.

If the sauce becomes slightly granular when it has cooled, don't worry; it will become as smooth as satin again when it is warmed.

When this is refrigerated, it becomes too firm to be spooned or cut out of its container. Therefore, it is best to store it in something with straight or flared sides. Then, to remove it, place the container in hot water until the firm sauce loosens and will slide out. It can then be reheated in the top of a double boiler over warm water on low heat.

BITTERSWEET CHOCOLATE SAUCE

1¼ CUPS

This is especially delicious over Caramel or Coconut Ice Cream, or any other. It is really bittersweet—add a bit more sugar, if you wish—but for bittersweet lovers this is just right.

½ cup milk

½ cup heavy cream

3 ounces unsweetened chocolate

2 tablespoons (or up to a total of 3 tablespoons) granulated sugar

1 tablespoon unsalted butter

Place the milk, cream, and chocolate in a heavy saucepan, uncovered, over low heat. Let cook, stirring occasionally, until the chocolate is melted. Then use a whisk, an eggbeater, or an electric mixer and whisk or beat until perfectly smooth. At first the chocolate will form tiny specks in the liquid, but as you continue to whisk or beat, it will become smooth.

Stir in 2 tablespoons of the sugar. Taste it. Now it is extra bittersweet. Add a bit more sugar, if you wish, until the sweetness/bitterness seems just right to you; remember that with cold/smooth/sweet ice cream, the bitter sauce is a great combination. Do not make the sauce too sweet. (I use 2 tablespoons but a total of 3 tablespoons is not too sweet.)

Add the butter and stir to melt.

Let stand until room temperature. The sauce will thicken slightly as it cools. It should be served at room temperature.

If you make this ahead of time and refrigerate it, reheat it slightly before serving.

DEVIL'S FOOD CHOCOLATE SAUCE

1⅔ CUPS

Elegant, rich and buttery, dark and delicious chocolate. Serve warm or at room temperature; it may be reheated. Or serve it cold (it is great refrigerated—it becomes very thick when it is cold) over coffee ice cream.

This wants desperately to burn on the bottom of the pan while you are making it; use an enameled cast-iron pan (Le Creuset or any other equally heavy one).

4 ounces (1 stick) unsalted butter

1 ounce unsweetened chocolate

⅔ cup granulated sugar

¼ cup unsweetened cocoa powder (preferably Dutch-process)

½ cup heavy cream

1 teaspoon vanilla extract

NOTE: *I like to double the recipe and have an extra jar for our guests to take home.*

In a 1- to 2-quart saucepan over low heat, melt the butter and chocolate, stirring occasionally. Add the sugar, cocoa, and cream. Stir with a wire whisk until thoroughly incorporated. Increase the heat a bit to medium-low. Stir with a wire whisk occasionally and also scrape the bottom with a rubber spatula occasionally, until the mixture comes to a low boil. (If you are impatient and if you use medium heat, scrape the bottom constantly with a rubber spatula.) Watch carefully for burning and adjust the heat as necessary.

When the mixture comes to a low boil, remove the pan from the heat and stir or whisk in the vanilla.

Serve hot or cooled. Reheat carefully to prevent burning (a double boiler is the safest way). Refrigerate up to two weeks, if you wish.

American Chocolate Pudding

4 portions (see Note)

If you think it doesn't pay to bother making your own when you can buy a box and just add some milk, then you have not tasted the real thing. This has considerably more chocolate (as well as cocoa), less sugar, and egg yolks that make it custardy and give it body. It is dense, dark, not too sweet, smooth, semifirm, rich; it is marvelous.

This recipe is adapted from two recipes I received recently that were almost identical, but considerably different from the usual. One of the recipes is in Richard Sax's wonderful cookbook, Cooking Great Meals Every Day *(Random House, 1982). And the other recipe is from Larry Forgione, for the dessert he serves at his popular restaurant, An American Place, in New York City. (Where, incidentally, it was served to us after an elegant meal that included three kinds of caviar. It would be just as appropriate after a casual meal.)*

The recipe may be doubled, if you wish

Using cornstarch correctly is a delicate art. Overcooking or overbeating—even the least little bit—can cause cornstarch to break down and make the mixture too thin. (Although I have written these words dozens of time, it recently happened to me.) Be very careful.

1 egg plus 2 additional egg yolks	Have 10- or 12-ounce stemmed wineglasses or dessert bowls ready. Cut rounds of wax paper to place on top of the pudding, actually touching it when it is poured into the glasses or bowls. Set aside.
2 ounces unsweetened chocolate	In a bowl, beat the egg and yolks to mix and set aside.
3 ounces semisweet chocolate	On a board, with a long, heavy knife, chop both chocolates (coarsely or finely—either is okay).
2¼ cups milk	Remove and reserve ¼ cup of the milk. Place the remaining 2 cups of milk in a heavy saucepan with a 2- to 3-quart capacity. Add ¼ cup of the sugar (reserve the remaining ¼ cup plus 1 tablespoon of the sugar) and the chopped chocolate. Place over moderate heat and whisk frequently with a wire whisk until the milk just comes to a boil (flecks of chocolate will disappear by the time the milk boils).
½ cup plus 1 tablespoon granulated sugar	
Scant ⅛ teaspoon salt	
2 tablespoons unsifted cornstarch	Meanwhile, sift the reserved sugar, salt, cornstarch, and cocoa into a mixing bowl. Add the reserved ¼ cup of milk and whisk with a small wire whisk until smooth.
3 tablespoons unsifted, unsweetened cocoa powder (preferably Dutch-process)	When the milk comes to a boil, pour (or ladle) part of it into the cornstarch mixture, whisking as you pour.
Ingredients continued on next page.	Then add the cornstarch mixture to the remaining hot-milk mixture. Stir to mix. Place over moderate heat.

2 tablespoons
unsalted butter, at
room temperature,
cut into small pieces

1 teaspoon vanilla extract

Optional: 1 tablespoon
dark rum

Now, use a rubber spatula and scrape the bottom and sides constantly until the mixture comes to a low boil. Reduce the heat a bit to medium-low and simmer gently, stirring and scraping the pan, for 2 minutes.

Add about 1 cup of the hot chocolate-milk mixture to the eggs and whisk or stir to mix. Then add the egg mixture to the remaining hot chocolate-milk mixture, stirring constantly.

Cook over low heat, scraping the pan with a rubber spatula, for 2 minutes. Be sure that you do not allow the mixture to come anywhere near the boiling stage after the eggs are added. Remove from the heat. Add the butter, vanilla, and the optional rum. Stir very gently until the butter is melted. Without waiting, pour into the wineglasses or dessert bowls. Cover immediately with the rounds of wax paper, placing the paper directly on the puddings (to prevent a skin from forming).

Let stand to cool to room temperature. Then refrigerate for at least a few hours.

WHIPPED CREAM

1 cup heavy cream

2 tablespoons
confectioners' sugar

½ teaspoon vanilla extract

NOTE: *This recipe is written for good old-fashioned generous portions. But actually they should be smaller, if it is to be served after a dinner.*

In a chilled bowl, with chilled beaters, whip the cream with the sugar and vanilla until it holds a soft shape, not until it is really stiff. Shortly before serving, spoon the cream on top of the puddings. (The cream may be whipped ahead of time and refrigerated; if it separates slightly, whisk it a bit before using.)

At An American Place, the pudding is served in wineglasses, with the pudding filling the glasses only halfway and the whipped cream filling the remaining space to the top.

HOT CHOCOLATE MOUSSE

8 PORTIONS

It sounds like a mousse, looks like a cake, tastes like a soufflé; it is served piping hot but without the hectic timing involved with a soufflé—it will not fall even if it waits until it cools. Delicious, exciting, very chocolate, semisweet. Make it for a dinner party.

Most of this can be prepared during the day and can wait for the beaten whites until just before baking. It takes 45 minutes to bake and about 15 minutes to cool a bit before serving; so it can be comfortably placed in the oven to bake just before you sit down to dinner.

You will need a nonstick 10-inch Bundt pan with a 14-cup capacity.

5 ounces unsweetened chocolate

4 ounces (1 stick) unsalted butter, at room temperature

1 cup boiling water

8 eggs, separated

¾ cup granulated sugar

Pinch of salt

Adjust a rack one-third up from the bottom of the oven and preheat the oven to 350°. Prepare a nonstick 10-inch, 14-cup Bundt pan as follows: With a pastry brush, brush soft, but not melted, butter (not melted because that would run down to the bottom of the pan) all over the pan (using additional butter than called for). Sprinkle sugar (additional) all over the pan—to get the sugar on the tube sprinkle it with your fingertips, then turn the pan over paper and tap out excess. When you are ready to bake, you will also need a pan wider but not deeper than the Bundt pan.

Place the chocolate, butter, and boiling water in a 2- to 3-quart heavy saucepan over low heat and stir with a wooden spoon until the chocolate and butter are melted. Remove from the heat and let cool completely. Then place in the freezer to chill for about 15 minutes and stir with a wire whisk until perfectly smooth and slightly thickened. Set aside.

Start to beat the egg yolks in the small bowl of an electric mixer. Gradually add ½ cup of the sugar (reserve the remaining ¼ cup of sugar) to the yolks. Beat at high speed for about 10 minutes until very pale and very thick.

Remove the bowl from the mixer. Gradually fold in the chocolate mixture. Then transfer to a very large mixing bowl and set aside. (You can let everything wait now for a few hours, if you wish. If you are going to wait, don't preheat the oven until 20 minutes before baking.)

Add the salt to the egg whites in the large bowl of the electric mixer and, with clean beaters, beat at high speed until the whites have increased in volume and hold a soft shape. Reduce the speed to moderate and gradually add the remaining ¼ cup of sugar; then again on high speed continue to beat briefly until the whites hold a definite point when the beaters are raised but are not stiff or dry.

Stir a large spoonful of the beaten whites into the chocolate mixture. Then fold in about half of the whites without being too thorough, and then fold in the remaining whites only until the mixtures are barely blended.

Pour the mousse into the prepared pan, pouring first into one side of the pan and then into the opposite side. If the top of the mousse mixture is not level, smooth it a bit.

Place the Bundt pan into a larger pan (not deeper) and fill the larger pan to about half the depth of the Bundt pan with hot water.

Place in the oven and bake for 45 minutes, covering the top loosely with foil for about the last 15 minutes if it is getting too dark.

When the mousse is done, remove the foil, remove the pan from the hot water, and let it stand for 5 minutes. Then cover the pan with a wide, flat platter and, holding the pan and the platter together, carefully turn them over. Do not remove the pan immediately; let stand for 15 minutes, then remove the pan.

Serve with whipped cream.

Whipped Cream

The cream can be whipped ahead of time, if you wish. Refrigerate it and then, just before serving, whip it a bit with a wire whisk to reincorporate it.

2 cups heavy cream

¼ cup confectioners' sugar

2 tablespoons cognac, Grand Marnier, or rum (or 1 teaspoon vanilla extract)

In a chilled bowl, with chilled beaters, whip the ingredients only until the cream barely holds a soft shape. Do not whip until the cream is stiff.

Do not serve the cream on top of the mousse; the heat from the mousse would melt it. Instead, place it alongside the mousse on the individual plates.

Metric Conversions and Equivalents

METRIC CONVERSION FORMULAS

TO CONVERT	MULTIPLY
Ounces to grams	Ounces by 28.35
Pounds to kilograms	Pounds by .454
Teaspoons to milliliters	Teaspoons by 4.93
Tablespoons to milliliters	Tablespoons by 14.79
Fluid ounces to milliliters	Fluid ounces by 29.57
Cups to milliliters	Cups by 236.59
Cups to liters	Cups by .236
Pints to liters	Pints by .473
Quarts to liters	Quarts by .946
Gallons to liters	Gallons by 3.785
Inches to centimeters	Inches by 2.54

APPROXIMATE METRIC EQUIVALENTS

LENGTH

⅛ inch	3 millimeters
¼ inch	6 millimeters
½ inch	1¼ centimeters
1 inch	2½ centimeters
2 inches	5 centimeters
2½ inches	6 centimeters
4 inches	10 centimeters
5 inches	13 centimeters
6 inches	15¼ centimeters
12 inches (1 foot)	30 centimeters

VOLUME

¼ teaspoon	1 milliliter
½ teaspoon	2.5 milliliters
¾ teaspoon	4 milliliters
1 teaspoon	5 milliliters
1¼ teaspoons	6 milliliters
1½ teaspoons	7.5 milliliters
1¾ teaspoons	8.5 milliliters
2 teaspoons	10 milliliters
1 tablespoon (½ fluid ounce)	15 milliliters
2 tablespoons (1 fluid ounce)	30 milliliters
¼ cup	60 milliliters
⅓ cup	80 milliliters
½ cup (4 fluid ounces)	120 milliliters
⅔ cup	160 milliliters
¾ cup	180 milliliters
1 cup (8 fluid ounces)	240 milliliters
1¼ cups	300 milliliters
1½ cups (12 fluid ounces)	360 milliliters
1⅔ cups	400 milliliters
2 cups (1 pint)	460 milliliters
3 cups	700 milliliters
4 cups (1 quart)	0.95 liter
1 quart plus ¼ cup	1 liter
4 quarts (1 gallon)	3.8 liters

WEIGHT

¼ ounce	7 grams
½ ounce	14 grams
¾ ounce	21 grams
1 ounce	28 grams
1¼ ounces	35 grams
1½ ounces	42.5 grams
1⅔ ounces	45 grams
2 ounces	57 grams
3 ounces	85 grams
4 ounces (¼ pound)	113 grams
5 ounces	142 grams

6 ounces	170 grams
7 ounces	198 grams
8 ounces (½ pound)	227 grams
16 ounces (1 pound)	454 grams
35.25 ounces (2.2 pounds)	1 kilogram

OVEN TEMPERATURES

To convert Fahrenheit to Celsius, subtract 32 from Fahrenheit, multiply the result by 5, then divide by 9.

Description	Fahrenheit	Celsius	British Gas Mark
Very cool	200°	95°	0
Very cool	225°	110°	¼
Very cool	250°	120°	½
Cool	275°	135°	1
Cool	300°	150°	2
Warm	325°	165°	3
Moderate	350°	175°	4
Moderately hot	375°	190°	5
Fairly hot	400°	200°	6
Hot	425°	220°	7
Very hot	450°	230°	8
Very hot	475°	245°	9

COMMON INGREDIENTS AND THEIR APPROXIMATE EQUIVALENTS

1 cup uncooked white rice = 185 grams

1 cup all-purpose flour = 140 grams

1 stick butter (4 ounces • ½ cup • 8 tablespoons) = 110 grams

1 cup butter (8 ounces • 2 sticks • 16 tablespoons) = 220 grams

1 cup brown sugar, firmly packed = 225 grams

1 cup granulated sugar = 200 grams

Information compiled from a variety of sources, including *Recipes into Type* by Joan Whitman and Dolores Simon (Newton, MA: Biscuit Books, 2000); *The New Food Lover's Companion* by Sharon Tyler Herbst (Hauppauge, NY: Barron's, 1995); and *Rosemary Brown's Big Kitchen Instruction Book* (Kansas City, MO: Andrews McMeel, 1998).

Index